WHICH POLICY FOR EUROPE?

Which Policy for Europe?

Power and Conflict inside the European Commission

MIRIAM HARTLAPP
JULIA METZ
CHRISTIAN RAUH

OXFORD
UNIVERSITY PRESS

OXFORD
UNIVERSITY PRESS

Great Clarendon Street, Oxford, OX2 6DP,
United Kingdom

Oxford University Press is a department of the University of Oxford.
It furthers the University's objective of excellence in research, scholarship,
and education by publishing worldwide. Oxford is a registered trade mark of
Oxford University Press in the UK and in certain other countries

First Edition published in 2014

Impression: 1

Published in the United States of America by Oxford University Press
198 Madison Avenue, New York, NY 10016, United States of America

British Library Cataloguing in Publication Data
Data available

Library of Congress Control Number: 2014935044

ISBN 978–0–19–968803–6

Printed and bound by
CPI Group (UK) Ltd, Croydon, CR0 4YY

To Maja and Simon, Pauline,
Johanna, Theresia, and Helena

Acknowledgments

This book is the result of an intensive team effort over a number of years. Thanks to generous funding by the Volkswagen Foundation, an Independent Young Research Group on 'Position Formation in the EU Commission' was set up in 2008 at the WZB Berlin Social Science Center. We are grateful to the Volkswagen Foundation for firmly supporting our endeavor and to the WZB for hosting us and at the same time providing a highly stimulating and supportive work environment. In 2013, the project moved to the University of Bremen, whom we also wish to thank for generous support.

Miriam Hartlapp, as head of the group, was joined by Julia Metz and Christian Rauh, both of whom completed their doctoral theses on specific aspects of position formation in the EU Commission. Each of us focused on a specific policy area and studied one aspect in particular depth. Julia Metz specialized on research and innovation policies and also on expert groups and expertise in the EU Commission. Christian Rauh analyzed consumer policies and in his dissertation addressed the nexus between the public politicization of European integration and Commission position formation. Miriam Hartlapp focused on the intersection of social and common market policies, concentrated on the historical database on the European Commission and on horizontal and vertical coordination issues in the Commission. This book presents the overall findings of our research and it is a truly collaborative piece of work, much more than any one of us would have been able to achieve alone.

Our work was supported furthermore by excellent research assistance from Jacob Düringer, Hannah Kannen, Yann Lorenz, and Christine Hocker, to all of whom we are indebted for helping with the collection and the management of the data and literature. Caroline Heuer, Diana Lange, and Claudia Nentwich went above and beyond their duties in assisting the team with its daily paper work. Niamh Warde was masterful in improving the style and language of the final manuscript.

Over the years, our thinking has benefitted tremendously from valuable comments by outstanding academics. While the list of people who inspired our thoughts is long, we particularly wish to thank Michael W. Bauer, Tanja Börzel, Thomas Christiansen, Morten Egeberg, Eva Heidbreder, Liesbet Hooghe, Hussein Kassim, Fritz W. Scharpf, and Michael Zürn, who were faithful companions and outstanding commentators on our journey towards the publication of this book. Åse Gornitzka, Martin Höpner, John Peterson, and Sebastiaan Princen spent time as our guests at the WZB and likewise engaged in valuable discussions that pushed the project forwards.

This project would never have been possible but for the willingness of so many Commission officials to share their scarce time and valuable memories, untiringly answering the many questions we had on position formation in the Commission. In this regard, Luc Tholoniat and Ciavarini Azzi were particularly helpful in obtaining access for us to our interviewees and to CIS-Net. Our final thanks go to our partners, who have supported our work throughout the process; and to our children, who have enriched our daily lives with so much joy.

Contents

List of Figures

List of Tables

Glossary

AE	*Agence Europe*
ANEC	European Association for the Co-ordination of Consumer Representation in Standardization
BATNA	Best Alternative To a Negotiated Agreement
BEUC	*Bureau Européen des Unions de Consommateurs* (The European Consumer Organisation)
CAP	Common Agricultural Policy
CEN	*Comité Européen de Normalisation* (European Committee for Standardization)
CIAA	*Confédération des Industries Agro-Alimentaires de l'UE* (Confederation of the Food and Drink Industries of the EU)
CIP	Competitiveness and Innovation Framework Programme
CIS-Net	Internal Commission application for inter-service consultations
COSAC	Conference of Community and European Affairs Committees of Parliaments of the European Union
DG	Directorate-General
DG ADMIN	Directorate-General 'Personnel and Administration'
DG AGRI	Directorate-General 'Agriculture and Rural Development'
DG BUDG	Directorate-General 'Financial Programming and Budget'
DG COMM	Directorate-General 'Communication'
DG COMP	Directorate-General 'Competition'
DG DEV	Directorate-General 'Development and Cooperation'
DG EAC	Directorate-General 'Education and Culture'
DG ECFIN	Directorate-General 'Economic and Financial Affairs'
DG ELARG	Directorate-General 'Enlargement'
DG EMPL	Directorate-General 'Employment, Social Affairs and Equal Opportunities'
DG ENTR	Directorate-General 'Enterprise and Industry'
DG ENV	Directorate-General 'Environment'
DG FISH	Directorate-General 'Maritime Affairs and Fisheries'
DG INFSO	Directorate-General 'Information Society and Media'
DG JLS	Directorate-General 'Justice, Freedom and Security'
DG MARE	Directorate-General 'Maritime Affairs and Fisheries'
DG MARKT	Directorate-General 'Internal Market and Services'
DG REGIO	Directorate-General 'Regional Policy'
DG RELEX	Directorate-General 'External Relations'
DG RTD	Directorate-General 'Research and Technological Development'
DG SANCO	Directorate-General 'Health and Consumer Protection'

DG TAXUD	Directorate-General 'Taxation and Customs Union'
DG TRADE	Directorate-General 'Trade'
DG TREN	Directorate-General 'Transport and Energy'
EAGGF	European Agricultural Guidance and Guarantee Fund
EAPN	European Anti-Poverty Network
ECJ	European Court of Justice
EFSA	European Food Safety Agency
EGF	European Globalisation Adjustment Fund
EIT	European Institute of Technology
EMU	Economic and Monetary Union
ENAR	European Network Against Racism
EP	European Parliament
ERA	European Research Area
ERC	European Research Council
ERI	European Research Infrastructures
ESF	European Social Fund
EU	European Union
EUR-Lex	Database of European Union law and other formal documents
EURO COOP	European Community of Consumer Co-operatives
FBO	Fall-Back Option
FSAP	Financial Services Action Plan
FT	*Financial Times*
GDA	Guideline Daily Amount
GPSD	General Product Safety Directive
Hebdo	Weekly internal meeting of the chefs de cabinet (*meeting hebdomadaire*)
ILGA	International Lesbian and Gay Association
IP	*Information presse* (Press release series of the European Commission)
ISC	Inter-Service Consultation
ITER	International Thermonuclear Experimental Reactor
JRC	Joint Research Center
KP	Key Provision
MAP	Multiannual Programme for Enterprise and Entrepreneurship
MEP	Member of the European Parliament
NGO	Non-Governmental Organization
NUTS	*Nomenclature des unités territoriales statistiques* (Nomenclature of territorial units for statistics)
OLAF	*Office Européen de Lutte Anti-Fraude* (European Anti-Fraud Office)
PreLex	Database on inter-institutional negotiations of the Commission, the Council and the European Parliament
RAPEX	European Rapid Exchange of Information System (on unsafe consumer products)

REACH	Regulation on the Registration, Evaluation, and Authorization of Chemicals
SCF	Scientific Committee on Foodstuffs
SG	Secretariat-General of the European Commission
SJ	*Service Juridique* (Legal service of the European Commission)
SMEs	small and medium sized enterprises
Special Chefs	Internal meetings of the relevant members of each Cabinet for an area (ad hoc)
TAA	Trade Adjustment Assistance
TEC	Treaty establishing the European Community
TEU	Treaty on European Union
TFEU	Treaty on the Functioning of the European Union
UEAPME	*Union Européenne de l'Artisanat et des Petites et Moyennes Entreprises* (European umbrella organization representing small and medium sized enterprises)
UNESCO	United Nations Educational, Scientific and Cultural Organization
UNICE	Union of Industrial and Employers' Confederation of Europe
UNICEF	United Nations International Children's Emergency Fund
US	United States (of America)
WHO	World Health Organization
WTO	World Trade Organization

1

Introduction

Even a very cursory overview of prominent portrayals of the European Commission yields a colorful yet tremendously inconsistent picture. Sometimes the Commission is painted as a compliant servant of powerful member states or of obscure business interests, at other times it is celebrated as the bearer of the impartial policy expertise needed to get national policy-making back on track. On some occasions, it is charged with carrying out cold-blooded, technocratic decision-making that shows little consideration for the daily lives of the 500 million citizens affected; on others, its widely accessible consultations during policy formulation are praised. At times, the Commission is blamed for promoting neo-liberal approaches that undermine historically developed welfare state arrangements, yet now and again it is appreciated as a vibrant and intransigent promoter of minority rights in Europe. How can all of this be true at the same time? Why do the policy choices of the European Commission provoke such diverse responses? This book argues that if we want to understand which policies are being proposed for Europe, we have to look at power and conflict *inside* the European Commission in a much more systematic way.

The European Commission (in the following, EU Commission, European Commission, or simply Commission) is unquestionably located at the center of the EU's political system (Nugent 2000a). It implements community policies, upholds the Union's treaties, and runs the day-to-day activities in Brussels. In these respects, the EU Commission—as a non-majoritarian institution—can be compared to national administrations (Siotis 1964; Egeberg 2006b). And yet, in contrast to "classical" bureaucracies, it holds substantial political powers. Most importantly, the Commission has a quasi-monopoly position in setting the EU's legislative agenda. More precisely, the treaties give the Commission the right of initiative on legal acts that concern most of the internal issues of the European Union. Based on this right, each Commission tables up to 2000 legally binding acts within its five-year term and thus crucially shapes the form and substance of EU policy. The Commission's legislative proposals substantially define the policy space in which the subsequent inter-institutional process takes place (Schmidt 2000; Tsebelis and Garrett 2000: 279). In more informal terms, the pre-decision-making process led by the Commission also decisively affects the definition of issues and alternatives, the actors involved, the coalitions formed, and the availability of information (Harcourt 1998; Princen 2009). The EU's fragmented policy-making context—a fluid system with unstable majorities—has been described as "the prospective agenda-setter's paradise," where the agenda-setter can choose from among a broad range of solutions (Peters 1994: 21). Analytically, this view is often linked to accounts of "supranational agency." This concept in EU studies highlights the ability of the Commission and the European Court of Justice (ECJ) to secure their own interests while advancing integration, typically by making use of informational advantages and entrepreneurship (Cram 1997; Pollack 1997a; Tömmel 1998).

However, despite the EU Commission's outstanding role in setting the agenda for European decision-making and the fact that it is a decidedly political actor, little is known about the internal dynamics of legislative drafting. While analytical accounts have portrayed the Commission as a "preference outlier" that holds more integration-friendly positions than the member states (Crombez 1997; Hug 2003), no systematic explanation exists for why the EU Commission at times proposes legislative drafts that are opposed by a majority of member states, that introduce strikingly high or low standards, or that contradict extant European laws. A prominent example is the establishment of the European Research Council, which distributes public money to individual researchers. This move was proposed without taking into consideration any *juste retour* considerations evoked by member states. In core areas of consumer policy, the Commission proposes unusually high standards for consumer credit, for example, but at the same time markedly reduces consumer protection in other areas, such as the regulation of sales promotions. The original Commission proposal for patient mobility largely followed the country-of-origin principle, clashing sharply with the country-of-destination principle prioritized in earlier legislation on the coordination of social security systems. How can we understand such puzzling proposals?

Motivated by empirical puzzles of this kind, this book takes a problem-driven research approach. Traditionally, the Commission presents itself as a unitary actor that reaches its decisions by consensus, with majority voting taking place only on rare occasions (Art. 250 TFEU). Where the Commission is interested in securing optimal negotiation outcomes in the inter-institutional process, it is entirely rational for it to speak with a single voice vis-à-vis the Council and the European Parliament (Scharpf 1997). This led to grand integration theories and many scholars of the EU to think of *the* Commission—"in theory and in fact [as] a collegiate body" (Haas 1958/1968: 452). However, the traditional "consensual-actor" assumption and the collegiality principle typically invoked do not necessarily accurately capture the process that takes place before an official proposal passes into the legislative process. On the contrary, the picture contrasts sharply with news reports about the daily struggles between the current Commission's major administrative units—the Directorates-General (DGs)—around position formation in Brussels and also contrasts with multiple studies focusing on internal strife (Cram 1994; Peters 1994; Christiansen 1997; Harcourt 1998: 375; Cini 2000; Nugent and Saurugger 2002; Mörth and Britz 2004).

The existing literature on national political systems confirms that rifts within a governmental administration are not unusual or surprising, but the fact that they have not been systematically addressed for the EU Commission is surprising indeed. Although the EU's political system is less characterized by party-political cleavages, there are good grounds for expecting crucial political dividing lines to run through the Commission and to shape position formation. The EU Commission is far more heterogeneous than most national governments. The actors within the institution are diverse, hailing from 27 different countries[1] and from a broad range of political parties and professional backgrounds. Moreover, given that sectoral responsibilities and the dynamics between portfolios shape political outcomes at the national level (Müller-Rommel and Blondel 1993; Mayntz and Scharpf 1975: esp. 121–64; Gallagher et al. 2005: 154–63), it must be noted that organizational actors within the Commission differ significantly, even in terms of such basic characteristics as administrative costs, staff figures, and legislative output. We find cross-cutting mandates with varying breadth and specificity. Actors with a more sectoral focus, such as DG AGRI (agriculture) or DG TREN (transport and energy), exist alongside others with rather general mandates, such as DG MARKT (internal market and services) and DG SANCO (health and consumers). These are reasons to expect that centrifugal forces resulting from political and departmental heterogeneity (Andeweg 1988, 2000) will be particularly intense in the Commission. Furthermore, the division of competences, compared to member states with their smaller administrative entities, creates a greater number of intersections and, consequently, more opportunities for conflict (Hartlapp 2007: 146). At the same time, we may further assume that mediation of internal conflict within the EU Commission also differs from what happens at the national level. In contrast to the national political process, a technocratic mode of problem-solving has been identified in EU policy-making (Majone 1996) and, considering the technical nature of market regulation, a comparatively high prominence of scientific expertise in the policy process is assumed (Joerges and Neyer 1997b). Thus, while conflict seems to be particularly likely inside the Commission, interaction may follow a specific logic that challenges any predictions about the logic of position formation within the Commission.

Knowledge about the power relations and internal interactions that take place inside the Commission is thus essential in order to be able to understand the nature of the policies that are finally proposed. What is more, while it might be entirely rational for the Commission to adopt a joint proposal in the College of Commissioners before feeding it into the inter-institutional process, it is important to note that the final positions presented are likely to depend on which Commissioners or DGs were actually involved in drafting the proposal. And yet we lack systematic insights into which factors drive DGs and Commissioners to form their positions and which interests the DGs represent. In addition, contending positions may often exist within the Commission, but there is at best only selective evidence of the factors that are decisive for DGs and Commissioners in pushing through their respective positions in these struggles. In short, in the interests of better understanding the policies the EU Commission sets for Europe, this book fills the research gap on conflict and power in position formation in the EU Commission.

We can substantiate the relevance of these issues by returning to the example of the 2004 Commission proposal for the liberalization of services. This proposal gained notoriety as being decidedly neo-liberal; it was widely criticized and subsequently readjusted by the Council and especially the European Parliament (Schmidt 2009). It is thus reasonable to ask: How can we explain that the European Commission proposed a policy that was so biased in favor of market liberalization that it provoked outright resistance from member states? Were no other, more interventionist or more social positions advocated inside the Commission? Or was the Commissioner for Employment and Social Affairs, Anna

Diamantopoulou, simply not able to assert her position against her colleague Frits Bolkestein, who was responsible for the Common Market dossier? In order to answer these questions, we need to analyze the position-formation processes inside the Commission itself. We divide the overarching puzzle into two analytically distinct research questions. First: What shapes the policy position of an individual DG and its Commissioner for a specific legislative proposal? Second: What shapes the power of a DG and its Commissioner when it comes to internal conflict?

Guided by these two research questions, we trace position-formation processes in the European Commission. The volume combines in-depth case studies of policy formulation with an original database on personal and structural Commission features since its foundation. The 48 policy proposals analyzed are located in the areas of research and innovation, consumer policy, and the intersection of social and common market policies adopted during the Prodi and Barroso I Commissions (1999–2009). Based on more than 130 interviews with the Commission officials involved and on a broad array of process documentation, this results in a medium-n design that enables us to analyze the relevance of factors and their causal forces with respect to specific mechanisms, while at the same time identifying typical patterns of position formation over time and across our issue areas, types of instruments, and responsible portfolios. The descriptive evidence of these patterns is thus of great importance for understanding the hitherto unstudied early phase in the EU policy cycle. In addition, we weigh up the data against theoretical expectations, allowing us to complement and advance the current scholarly debates on the EU Commission in the EU political system and European policy-making more generally.

Studies investigating the role of the Commission in the EU political system have so far either taken a bird's-eye perspective that depicts the Commission as a unitary actor, or have provided in-depth case study insights, which risk yielding biased conclusions and do not easily lead to generalizations and a systematic evaluation of the Commission. Our analytical approach deviates from the existing body of literature in two respects. First, we open the "black box" of the EU Commission and look at its internal dynamics. Demonstrating that power and conflict prevail and make a difference in the early phase of the policy cycle, we claim that our view conceptually broadens our understanding of decision-making in the EU political system. Second, we take the Commission seriously as both an administration *and* a political actor. The more recent literature on the EU Commission concentrates primarily on the administrative structure and modernization of the organization's management (Cini 2007; Bauer 2008), as well as on the beliefs and socialization of those working in the Commission (Hooghe 2001; Suvarierol 2007; Kassim et al. 2013). The approach here is to use the institutional structure and the actors' characteristics as potential independent variables for explaining actual policy choices. Extending our knowledge in these ways should further our understanding of why the Commission fulfills its role as the EU's agenda-setter in a specific way.

Because we are studying a highly complex process and do not have a dominant theoretical expectation, the book combines deductive and inductive reasoning. Although our approach is structured by existing insights from public administration, comparative political systems, and EU studies, it nonetheless remains open to what emerges from the individual case histories. This approach results in a threefold typology of position formation inside the European Commission. We discover that the Commission is motivated either by technocratic problem-solving, by ideologically driven policy-seeking, or by maximizing its own organizational competences. Each type of Commission agency plays out in specific process patterns based on particular sets of factors and mechanisms that define the policy choices of internal actors and the power resources needed to assert them against in-house opponents. The typology seeks to elucidate actor rationales in position-formation processes and it should apply to all DGs. In the concrete processes of legislative drafting, however, these logics sometimes work in parallel and sometimes in conflict with one another. More concretely, knowing which type of process is at play indicates how Commission decision-making can be influenced to attain a desired political goal. The development of a process typology is not only analytically challenging, it also has implications for three substantially relevant issues: (1) EU Commission agency, (2) decision-making in the EU political system, and (3) the politico-economic implications of the European integration process.

1.1 EU COMMISSION AGENCY: WHAT KIND OF "ANIMAL" IS IT?

This book focuses on Commission agency, that is, the institution's development and pursuance of its own preferences or, in other words, its "actorness" or possession of action capacity of its own. It is built around an analysis of the Commission's institutional features, interest aggregation and preference formation, and an assessment of its action rationale. We start from the premise that Commission agency is produced by a multi-layered process involving a multitude of internal actors who may disagree about how the European agenda should be shaped. This view is supported by our empirical data, which show internal interaction to be the norm rather than the exception—an interaction that is quite intense and often conflictual.

EU scholars today mostly view the Commission as possessing its own actor qualities, but this has not always been the case. Studies on the European Commission have long been dominated by descriptive analyses of the organization's bureaucratic structure (Coombes 1968; Michelmann 1978a, b). Building on these early conceptualizations of the Commission as a bureaucratic organization, studies carried out in the 1990s increasingly addressed the Commission's actor qualities and highlighted its character as a "multi-organisation" (Peters 1992; Cram 1994), a point of view that has been central for our understanding of the European Commission and the EU political system. Nonetheless, this inside view remained descriptive and was not suitable for capturing the struggles between the national and supranational levels that dominated EU researchers' thinking. This caveat was addressed at that time by other studies that explicitly focused on the role and functioning of the European Commission as an agent against the background of the grand integration theories (Ludlow 1991; Cini 1996; Pollack 1997b; Rometsch 1999; Nugent 2000a).

More recently, research has taken a rather static view and has focused mainly on the institutional features of the Commission. On the one hand, works on its administrative and organizational features were mainly written after the scandal and resignation of the Santer Commission, or else addressed the post-enlargement Commission. Their focus was on the body's capacity for reform and on its managerial capabilities in terms of recruitment and career paths (Levy 2006; Cini 2007; Balint et al. 2008; Bauer 2008; Kassim 2008; Tholoniat 2009). Implicitly or explicitly oriented towards New Public Management concepts, these studies analyze decision-making efficiency rather than the Commission's actor preferences on policy substance. Core political-science notions that serve to explain preference formation, such as conflict and power within the organization, are largely absent. This strand of the literature has greatly improved our understanding of decision-making within the Commission but only indirectly contributes to explaining the Commission's actual policy positions as presented in its legislative initiatives.

On the other hand, there is a rich and methodologically sophisticated literature that perceives the analysis of personal characteristics and preferences of individuals in the Commission as being crucial for explaining Commission agency. Nationality and party-political orientation (Döring 2007; Wonka 2007), personal beliefs (Hooghe 2000, 2001, 2005; Suvarierol 2007; Ellinas and Suleiman 2012; Kassim et al. 2013) and organizational roles (Egeberg 1996, 2006a; Trondal 2010) stand out as (potentially) relevant features of individuals working inside the Commission that may explain their preferences. However, these studies' main contribution lies in explaining the mechanisms of preference formation at the individual level rather than linking this to the preference formation of the Commission as an organization. Consequently, policy implications can be hypothesized but cannot be systematically assessed on the basis of the data. Our approach, by contrast, takes internal diversity as a starting point to illustrate to what extent, and how, such personal characteristics of Commission officials play a role in policy-substance outcomes. The book deviates from the above body of literature in that it conceptualizes administrative structure and management modernization, as well as the beliefs and the socialization of those working in the Commission, as independent factors which are linked to the analysis of the dynamics and processes of position formation that lead to the EU policies proposed. Nonetheless, in assessing EU Commission agency, the question still remains as to what actually drives the Commission in these processes—what is its action rationale?

Contrasting views on the Commission's agency co-exist in EU studies. The Commission has been variously characterized as a neutral clearing-house with the goal of serving a perceived "common weal" (Mitrany 1971; also Haas 1958/1968), as an agent serving mainly the economic interests of member states (Garrett 1992; Moravcsik 1993) and as a supranational actor striving for power and being well aware of the political implications of its policy decisions (Pollack 1997b). So, in one extreme view, Commission agency is supposed to follow the ideal of a classical non-majoritarian institution acting through a functionalist logic to produce public policies that are "superior" in terms of effectiveness and efficiency (e.g. Haas 1958/1968). Other views emphasize the development of the Commission's self-interests and paint it as a much more strategic actor striving to maximize its self-interests in policy-making (e.g. Pollack 1997b; Nugent 2000a: 9). Finally, in view of increasingly controversial debates about its policy choices and signs of a politicization of the EU system, the Commission might equally be seen as an actor motivated by specific normative policy goals or values (e.g. Hooghe 2000). It has been argued that conclusions about the Commission's agency depends significantly on the puzzle at stake: a contest between the supranational and the national levels or a view inside the Commission as typically provided by in-depth case studies (Hymans 1999). The process typology presented in this book substantially builds on this work. However, rather than portraying the Commission as either a unitary actor speaking with a single voice or as a technocratic bureaucracy simply carrying out member state interests, our conceptual framework brings these perspectives together and shows under which conditions we can expect the Commission to follow one or the other logic. Thus, we come closer to explaining the policies the Commission chooses for Europe.

1.2 DECISION-MAKING IN THE EU POLITICAL SYSTEM: INTEGRATING THE EARLY PHASE

This book emphasizes how vastly important the early policy-formation phase is for EU policy-making. EU decision-making has received constant attention over the last few decades, however it is typically equated with the inter-institutional process: that is what happens after the EU Commission has tabled its proposal and the EU Council and Parliament formally negotiate and adopt EU law. The early steps of the EU policy cycle, in contrast, are a blind spot. This book claims that in order to obtain a complete view on decision-making, we have to analyze processes that take place prior to the much-studied inter-institutional decision-making phase. From a policy-cycle perspective, we are therefore on common ground with the burgeoning agenda-setting literature (national politics: Baumgartner and Jones 1993; EU: Peters 1994; Baumgartner et al. 2011; Alexandrova et al. 2012). These works place the inter-play of institutional arenas that define the actors involved ("venues") and the schemes of interpretation that attach an issue to existing lines of conflict (e.g. Harcourt 1998; Daviter 2009: 1118) at the center of a variety of arguments. Using this approach, scholars have been very successful at explaining which issues actually appear on the European agenda (see esp. Princen 2009). However, this literature is less able to explain what happens with contentious issues on their way onto the agenda and which policy option is ultimately the one proposed by the EU Commission. Broadening our conceptual understanding of decision-making by including internal dynamics within the Commission can help to explain how contending interests are aggregated at the agenda-setting stage, which has three analytical advantages for the study of EU decision-making.

First, research on the formal decision-making stage typically includes the agenda-setting function of the Commission (Garrett and Tsebelis 1996; Franchino 2000; Tsebelis and Garrett 2000 279; Thomson et al. 2006; Thomson 2011). However, the Commission's ability to shape EU policy is primarily explained on the basis of characteristics of the inter-institutional process, such as the relative distances between the actors involved or the applicable decision rules (Garrett and Tsebelis 1996; Crombez 1997; Tsebelis and Garrett 2001), the "contemporary expansion and normalization of co-decision" (Crombez 2000; Ponzano et al. 2012: 41) and the increasing number of decisions taken after the first reading (Toshkov and Rasmussen 2012). On this view, the Commission is typically conceptualized as an agent of the member states (Pollack 1997b; Tallberg 2002), which leaves little room for the internal processes within the Commission to make a difference. What is more, our analyses reveal that although preference formation within the Commission is indeed influenced by the Council and the European Parliament, this relationship is far more complex than assumed by the principal–agent view. At times, the Commission's choices seem to be foreshadowed by the inter-institutional process, but on other occasions it deliberately picks and chooses from policy templates offered by the member states. However, and most importantly, the "agent view" (e.g. Tsebelis and Garrett 2000) delivers few predictions on precise points regarding the set of possible policies. Even where the inter-institutional process imposes real constraints, the agent can still choose from a number of feasible policies. Our focus on conflict and power inside the EU Commission, by contrast, provides insights into what determines the Commission's choices in this set. We therefore suggest that research on the inter-institutional process should take a more nuanced view of the internal conditions which exist for the Commission's capacity to act in the multi-level system (also see Princen 2012). By integrating our results and this existing line of research, we come closer to explaining which policy is actually chosen for Europe.

Second, a more holistic view of the policy process enables us to trace the effects of one policy stage on another. Our analysis of position formation in the Commission systematically differentiates between typical processes and shows how the defining factors of these processes determine policy substance. In some cases, position-formation processes cannot be explained by strategic considerations and pressure politics, instead policy-efficient proposals are influenced by internal and external expertise. In other cases, Commission actors enter position formation with the goal of retaining and expanding their competences and consequently monitor national interests that are likely to deliver political support as well as acceptance. In yet another group of cases, positions are the result of pre-defined ideological or normative beliefs regarding the best possible solutions to problems. Because position formation follows different patterns, which in part depend on context factors, we should also see systematic differences in the related inter-institutional decision-making. Analyses of policy-making in the EU would therefore benefit from taking into account the determinants of position formation within the Commission.

Finally, the internal dynamics of EU institutions are theorized as a general determinant of decision-making. Here, the empirical focus on internal dynamics cuts right into an emerging field of interest that analyzes intra-institutional dynamics in the EU system (Christiansen 2001; Kreppel 2010). Scholars in this field predominantly focus on the European Parliament (Hix et al. 2005; Ringe 2005; Hoyland 2006; McElroy 2006), while, more recently, the Council (Naurin and Wallace 2008; Tallberg and Johansson 2008) and the ECJ (Höpner 2010; Solanke 2011; Vauchez 2012) have attracted increased attention. A gap remains with respect to the internal dynamics of position formation in the Commission, however. Our findings on the preparatory stages of policy-making within the EU Commission reveal that internal dynamics within the Council and the Commission may mutually influence one another. Position heterogeneity within the Council may either facilitate preference formation in the Commission or provide venues for DGs to build strategic links with the corresponding policy portfolios in the Council (Kreppel 2010). This book thus complements existing research on position formation dynamics in other EU institutions, proposing a novel "disaggregate" view on EU decision-making that goes beyond the inter-institutional view.

1.3 EU INTEGRATION AND POLITICAL ECONOMY

At a more abstract level, the book contributes to questions that concern the EU's "problem-solving capacity" (Scharpf 1999). The progressive integration process has increased supranational competences and, in turn, diminished national scope for responding to societal demands for regulation and market intervention. Accordingly, the role of the EU Commission is a vital element in the debate on the EU's capacity to intervene where national markets fail. Typically, the European Commission is seen as a crucial promoter of a market-liberal bias in EU policies. Due to an inherent asymmetry in the EU's founding treaties in favor of "negative" market integration, the Commission is encouraged by primary law to propose market-liberalizing measures, as this is where the Community's powers rest and where legislative initiatives are most promising (Scharpf 1999: 50–1, 2010). More recent arguments stressing the EU's liberal bias have added to this account by identifying the Commission as borrowing from a "strategic repertoire of ideas" (Jabko 2006: 5) and benefitting from the institutional heterogeneity of welfare states and varieties of capitalism (Höpner and Schäfer 2012). To this is added path dependency in ECJ case law (Schmidt 2012), which, in sum, impedes the political construction necessary to achieve distributive goals in the EU. However, does the perception of the European Commission as a promoter of market-liberal policies also hold if we open up the black box? What room is left for non-market policies? Or is position formation in the EU Commission perhaps another systemic factor favoring market-making?

Tracing the position-formation processes of concrete policy proposals yields evidence of little intervention and markets almost everywhere in the positions proposed by the Commission. In comparison with classical national-level welfare-state policies, such positions surely further market principles. In comparison with what would be "pure" markets, however, it is noticeable that the Commission's proposals have often avoided leaving outcomes to market forces alone. We observe the EU Single Market at times pursuing social purposes, for example. However, this is not necessarily an autonomous process (Hervey and Trubek 2007; Caporaso and Tarrow 2009: 579; but critically Höpner and Schäfer 2012), instead it depends on specific conditions linked to decisive political actors such as the European Commission. This observation advances the debate on ways to understand and address the EU's bias towards market integration and the related liberalization. By shining a light on the broader picture of the systemic features of supranational decision-making, our analysis contributes to critical assessments of the EU's systemic capacity to reach distributive goals. It suggests that we can add Commission-internal coordination structures that systematically favor the lead department and the Secretariat-General to the features of the EU system that may hinder its problem-solving capacity (Hartlapp 2011; Hartlapp et al. 2013).

In line with the political-economy perspective, our study therefore supports a more critical assessment of the EU's problem-solving capacity than claimed, for example, by the agenda-setting perspective, which highlights the fluidity and openness of the process inside the Commission as leading to better problem-solving (Harcourt 1998; Hymans 1999). The political-economy perspective argues that the imbalance between market-liberal and market-intervening policies institutionalized in EU legislation and in the rulings of the ECJ limits national governments' capacity to protect a broad range of societal interests or to sustain distributional arrangements. Not least, this is expressed in increasingly critical public opinion, as was visible in the national debates surrounding the constitutional treaty, for example, and the resulting backlash on integration. By revealing those of the EU Commission's internal conditions that favor biased policy outcomes and by showing how specific internal actors adopt public demands and exploit them in internal decision-making, the book also contributes to wider debates on the responsiveness, legitimacy, and politicization of European decision-making.

1.4 OUTLINE OF THE BOOK

The remainder of the book consists of three parts that together develop the theoretical framework, provide a comparative summary of the empirical findings and aggregate them into a typology of position formation in the EU Commission.

In the first part, Chapter 2 presents a three-step analytical framework for understanding position formation inside the Commission. First, we open the black box of internal position formation by highlighting tensions between hierarchical levels—the administrative corpus and the political College of Commissioners—and between sectoral divisions along specific policy mandates. Both point to the Directorates-General (DGs) of the Commission as the most relevant actors in the internal preparation of a Commission proposal. Second, the DGs operate in institutional contexts that narrow or broaden the maneuvering room for specific policy positions. The process of position formation within the Commission is shaped, especially, by the legal status quo ante, internal coordination requirements, the inter-institutional political system, and a range of optional power resources from the context of multi-level governance. Third, bundles of factors are derived from these contexts that together delineate the pluri-theoretical approach structuring the later empirical parts. This is followed by Chapter 3, which outlines how the analytical framework is applied to 48 systematically selected legal acts from the Prodi and Barroso I Commissions. A two-step research design combines "thick" analysis from within case studies with a structured and focused cross-case comparison in order to systematically tease out commonalities and differences in position-formation processes in the Commission.

The second part presents the empirical analyses. Chapter 4 provides structured information on how the personal characteristics of Commissioners and Director-Generals working inside the Commission have developed over time and on how they are linked to the Commission's organizational structure. It draws on a newly established and comprehensive database on the European Commission (1958–2010). Chapters 5 to 7 provide thick case study insight into three policy areas, each the responsibility of two or more DGs: processes at the intersection of social and common market policies (Chapter 5), research and innovation policies (Chapter 6), and consumer policies (Chapter 7). Each of these chapters starts with a short introduction to the relevant actors and interests, as well as to the substance and regulatory approaches of each policy field. Methodologically, they flesh out the link between the DGs' ideal positions, the final position proposed, and the factors introduced in the analytical framework. Each study concludes by highlighting the factors most relevant to explaining the positions taken and asserted, as well as the mechanisms through which they made a difference. Chapters 8 to 10 focus on specific aspects of internal position formation that shed light on the type of Commission agency involved. Chapter 8 deals with the involvement of external experts and discusses how they are either used to increase knowledge or to anticipate positions in a politicized process. Chapter 9 criticizes the image of the Commission as an insulated decision-making elite and shows that the concerns of the wider European public are actually handled strategically during position formation, at times substantially influencing the policies proposed. Chapter 10 addresses structural biases in internal position formation and analyzes how internal coordination rules and specific organizational roles affect the likelihood that particular positions will reach the actual legislative agenda of the European Union.

The third and final part of the book presents the aggregate results. Chapter 11 provides a compact summary of the relative importance of the various factors that influence internal position formation and interaction. It shows that internal Commission actors draw much more on external resources and constraints—such as the legal status quo and the inter-institutional process—when forming their positions individually, while resorting more to internal resources and constraints—such as existing supranational competences and formal coordination rules—when trying to assert these positions in in-house conflicts. This chapter also emphasizes the number of diverging positions and the amount of conflict inside the EU Commission as one major finding of the book—underlining the fact that the EU Commission is anything but a unitary actor. Building on this comparative overview, Chapter 12 captures the essential features of position formation in the EU Commission in a threefold typology of stylized process models. Why the Commission frequently proposes policies that contradict one another or that meet vehement opposition from the member states is explained by variation in these process types, where position formation either follows the logic of technocratic problem-solving, of bureaucratic competence maximization, or of ideologically motivated policy-seeking. Within these types, different sets of factors and most importantly different mechanisms linking factors and policy choices contribute to explaining the outcome of position formation inside the EU

Commission. Ultimately, these models also hint at different directions for reform that would be necessary to produce different policy outcomes at the EU level. Chapter 13 concludes and summarizes how different interests emerge and aggregate in the early phase of EU policy-making. The argument returns to the main themes elaborated in this introduction and indicates avenues for generalizing from the findings by reference to related research and likely developments in the EU itself.

NOTE

1. The EU has grown to 28 member states in the meantime. However, whenever referring to unspecified member states in this book, we refer to the set of 15 or 27 member states, respectively, that made up the EU during our investigation period.

2

Position Formation inside the EU Commission: An Analytical Framework

The analyses in this book start with an empirical puzzle. The EU Commission sometimes proposes policies that are astonishingly far-reaching, that induce vehement opposition in the Council of Ministers and the European Parliament, or that contradict each other in terms of policy substance. Such observations stand in stark contrast to a naïve view on the European Commission as a collegiate actor whose diverging views should never lead to controversial policy decisions. A technocratic body's own interests should be limited to promoting the goals of the Union within the remit of the common interests of the European member states. On the basis of this naïve view, the null hypothesis is that positions on a specific policy rarely diverge inside the Commission and, even if they do at times, are still "neutrally" aggregated.

However, as pointed out in the introduction, there are grounds to believe that a number of different policy positions exist within the Commission and that the respective internal actors have different degrees of assertiveness when it comes to pushing their preferred policies through. From this point of view, position formation within Europe's central agenda-setter should hold explanatory power for diverging, far-reaching or even contradictory policy proposals. Accordingly we ask: How do power and conflict inside the Commission shape which policy is proposed for the EU?

Among the Commission's manifold obligations defined in Article 17 TFEU, the book focuses on the one most immediately relevant for the 500 million citizens of Europe—its quasi sole right of initiating legislation.[1] We therefore refer to position formation within the Commission as the process whereby the internal Commission actors come to agree on a common policy proposal for binding secondary EU legislation, which is only then fed into inter-institutional negotiations with the Council of Ministers and the European Parliament.

In this chapter, we develop a theoretically informed analytical framework about power and conflict inside the Commission when such legislative proposals are being drawn up. Assuming that the (collective) actors inside the Commission are rational, goal-oriented, and purposeful (Downs 1957), we expect that the Commission's capacity to set the agenda for Europe is guided by the enabling or constraining power of internal and external institutions. Hence, this book subscribes to the heuristics of actor-centered institutionalism (Mayntz and Scharpf 1995; Scharpf 1997). With its strong emphasis on actors, this approach holds that we can only explain the impact of the Commission's internal power and conflict on the policy for Europe if we know what actually drives the Commission and its internal actors when proposing legislation. This is a far from trivial question and it would be ingenuous to expect to find a single rationale that fits all variation within individual policy formulation exercises, let alone across all policies that the Commission proposes.

Regarding its particular role as Europe's main agenda-setter, we can at least identify three fundamentally contrasting types of Commission agency that will serve as the analytical anchors of our analysis. First, the EU Commission is often characterized as a *technocratic* body. This reasoning, which emerged from the seminal works of Mitrany (1971) and Haas (1958/1968), is a cornerstone of functionalist explanations in the literature on European integration. Policies are adjusted in response to new factual challenges and problems, performance crises, or the perception of welfare inefficiencies. Made up of specialized, Weberian-type bureaucrats, the Commission is, in this view, best understood as a neutral clearing-house where actors search for the technically best, that is, the most efficient and effective solution to serve a perceived "common weal" (Mitrany 1971). It is this type of agency that comes closest to the naïve view and the null hypothesis set out above.

Second, the EU Commission is also often characterized as a *competence-seeking* bureaucracy. In this view, the Commission is made up of inherently political actors who strive for influence and are aware of the political implications of their policy decisions (Pollack 1997b; Haller 2009). The Commission's DGs may be seeking growth in competences and/or budget vis-à-vis the national level and/or vis-à-vis other DGs: "With most Commissioners wanting to be responsible for as much as possible, 'turf disputes' can sometimes become decidedly sharp" (Nugent 2000b: 9). More generally, actors inside the Commission may be striving for personal and, more importantly, for organizational well-being (Downs 1966/1967; Niskanen 1974; Dunleavy 1991). A growing bureau can better attract capable personnel, provide its leaders with increased power, income, and prestige, and simply generate more leeway from member states in policy-making and implementation.

And, third, more recent accounts imply that the Commission can also be understood as a *policy-seeking* actor. This perspective is grounded in trends towards the more general politicization of European integration (Hooghe and Marks 2009), in the degree to which choices by the Commission are publically contested in political terms (Grossman and Woll 2011), in scholarly and public debates on the partisan coloring and political experience of Commissioners (Döring 2007; Wonka 2007), and in the fact that Commission officials themselves might bring strong political convictions to the drafting table (Hooghe 2000). In such a politicized context, the Commission can be expected to behave politically too. Actors within the Commission may indeed seek specific policy substance for ideological reasons. Unlike for competence-seekers, for policy-seekers office is not an end in itself but rather a means to realize what is perceived as normatively right. On this view, the Commission and its internal actors might therefore also be understood as being motivated by specific normative policy goals or values.

These three ideal types of Commission agency may overlap or even clash in the practice of policy formulation. They evoke distinct rationales when drafting legislation, but looking at the policy outcomes alone does not tell us whether the

Commission is best described as a neutral technocrat, a competence-seeker, or a pursuer of normative policy goals. Rather than imposing one of these models a priori, we need to look into the policy-making process in order to understand what kind of animal the Commission actually is. In other words, a thorough analysis of position formation inside the Commission prior to the presentation of an official legislative proposal is required. Thus, the question as to what drives the Commission when setting Europe's agenda can only be answered if we understand *how* the Commission processes the different external constraints and resources it faces.

First, such an analysis necessarily has to start with specifying the actors involved and the basic elements of the process we want to analyze, which we provide in Section 2.1. This results in a clear analytical focus for the book, specifying two research questions. Second, actor-centered institutionalism requires spelling out the institutions that limit and enable actor behavior. Accordingly, in Section 2.2 we identify the legislative status quo, the internal coordination, the inter-institutional system of the EU, and optional power resources deriving from the EU multi-level system as the major institutional contexts of position formation within the Commission. From these contexts, we derive particular constraints and resources that can be expected to influence positions and power within the Commission. This set of factors provides the major grid within which we later study *how* and along which type of Commission agency they are used in the internal process. Third, and finally, Section 2.3 highlights two policy-specific context factors—salience and uncertainty—that may mediate the logics of agency in internal position formation. This completes the conceptual framework, which is summarized in Section 2.4 and guides all the empirical analyses presented in the remainder of the book.

2.1 UNPACKING THE MULTI-ACTOR CONGLOMERATE: INTERNAL ACTORS AND THE POSITION-FORMATION PROCESS

In specifying the actors involved and the basic elements of the process to be analyzed, we can broadly distinguish between two sets of internal organizational dividing lines. On the one hand, the existing literature focuses on the interface between the Commission's political arm and its administrative level (Peters 1994: 17; Christiansen 1996: 80; Lequesne 2000). Following this hierarchical conceptualization, the political arm comprises the President as well as the Commissioners—making up the collective College of 27 Commissioners—including their personal cabinets.[2] However, much of the substantial work of policy formulation is done at the administrative level in the DGs, each headed by a Director-General (Cini 1996: 154). Recent studies show that only 13.2 percent of all Commission proposals between 2004 and 2008 were actually subject to decision-making at the political level (Kurpas et al. 2008: 36; Hartlapp et al. 2010a; Wonka 2008: 148 reports 17.4 percent for the period 1999–2004), leaving the rest to be negotiated and decided in the administration proper.

On the other hand, scholars underline tensions and fragmentation along sectoral lines, a well-known feature in other political systems (Bulmer 1993: 361; Peters 1994: 14; Peterson 1995: 475; Christiansen 1997: 78; Harcourt 1998; Mörth and Britz 2004). In the EU Commission, sectoral dividing lines run between the 40 DGs and services that make up the organizational map. They mainly group together specific policy interests, but also include horizontal services, such as translation, budget, and legislative advice, which often also have a management function. Different positions and overlapping competencies among the DGs have been blamed for creating an "inefficient and fiefdom-riddled bureaucracy" (Peterson 1995: 475), but are also considered "a source of diversity and inventiveness" that enhances their problem-solving capacity for EU policies (Lequesne 2000: 45).

We thus take hierarchical as well as sectoral dividing lines as the starting point for analyzing how these dynamics influence the substance of policy. Whatever their empirical prevalence will prove to be, the institutional structure of policy formulation within the EU Commission stylized in Figure 2.1 requires repeated coordination between sectors. Consequently, we treat the DGs, which conceptually link individual actions to organizational behavior, as the most relevant actors in the internal preparation of a Commission proposal.

When a policy proposal is drafted, one Commission DG takes the lead.[3] Within this lead DG, one or a number of middle-ranking officials draft the concrete proposal. The lead DG collects the necessary legal and practical information, contacts any relevant external stakeholders and sets up the first legal drafts representing a political position on the issue in question. This informal stage may take up to several years (Jordan and Schout 2006: ch. 9). The draft is processed up the hierarchy to the Commissioner and his or her Cabinet (stage I in Figure 2.1) with a request for horizontal consultation among "all the departments with a legitimate interest in the initiative by virtue of their powers or responsibilities or the nature of the subject" (Commission of the European Communities 2005a: Art. 23.2). The internal horizontal services also have to become involved at this stage: Consultation with the DGs for Personnel and Administration, Budget and Communication, and with the European Anti-Fraud Office (OLAF) and especially with the legal service and the Secretariat-General (SG) are obligatory in many cases. In practice, the administrative inter-service consultation (stage II) is executed via the internal document base

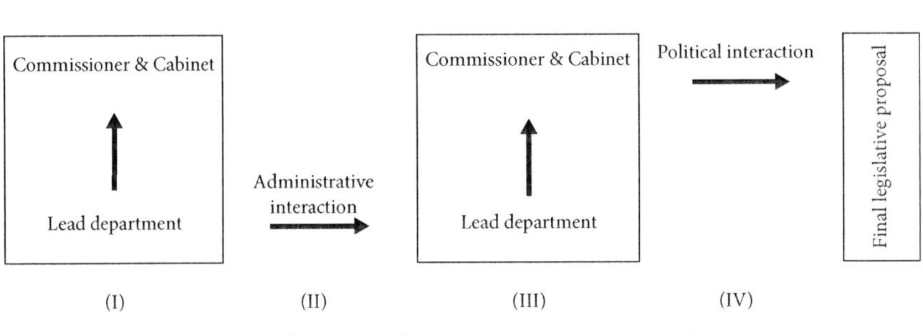

Fig. 2.1. The internal process of position formation in the EU Commission

CIS-Net, through which the draft proposal as well as an explanatory memorandum are circulated among the other DGs. Consulted DGs usually have to respond within four weeks and may express one of three opinions: (1) a disapproving "*avis négatif*"; (2) an agreement; or (3) an agreement subject to certain substantial comments. Once the consultation period has expired, the proposal is revised in the lead DG, which again sends it to its Cabinet and to the Commissioner (stage III). At the political level, remaining sectoral conflicts can be negotiated and agreed horizontally among consecutive negotiation forums of different Cabinet members (the so called Special Chefs and Hebdo) and ultimately among Commissioners themselves in the College (stage IV).[4]

Cutting across hierarchical and sectoral dividing lines, the formation of the overall EU Commission position can be broken down into position formation at the administrative and political levels of *individual DGs* (Stages I and III), and administrative and political coordination *across DGs* (Stages II and IV). To explain the contents of a common proposal of the EU Commission, we not only need to comprehend why and how individual DGs have adopted their specific positions, we also have to combine this with an understanding of the interaction among DGs. We therefore divide our overarching question on position formation in the EU Commission into two analytically separate research questions.

> DG position: *How is the policy position of a DG formed with regard to a specific legislative proposal and how can the DG's policy choices be explained?* (Research question 1)
>
> DG interaction: *How are different DG positions coordinated and how can the assertiveness of a DG in forming the final Commission proposal be explained?* (Research question 2)

Analytically, we treat position and interaction as two distinct, successive processes. Arguably, DGs may interact far earlier than required by the formal rules. A DG may also adapt or reformulate its position during the interaction process. Thus, in practice, these two steps may occur in parallel. However, aiming to explain the Commission's final policy position and knowing that the DGs are the central actors requires us to disentangle a DG's individual process of taking a policy position, on the one hand, and the interaction required by DGs in order to take a common position, on the other.

Our first research question thus inquires into the policy positions of individual DGs with regard to a given legislative proposal. Building on the actor-centered institutionalism set out above, we next derive the institutional constraints and resources that might explain a DG's policy choices while scrutinizing *how* these factors actually exert influence in subsequent chapters. Once a DG has successfully established its desired position in a final Commission proposal, we then ask: How can the relative success of a DG in forming the respective legislative proposal be explained? Thus, our second research question addresses the power of DGs and respective Commissioners during their interaction.[5] Following Weber ([1925] 1978: 53), we define power as "the probability that one actor within a social relationship will be in a position to carry out his own will despite resistance, regardless of the basis on which this probability rests."[6] Accordingly, our second research question focuses particularly on the bases that are used by individual DGs and their Commissioners to carry out their will. Again following actor-centered institutionalism, we derive respective factors from the institutional constraints and resources in order to study the actual mechanism linking them to internal power in the empirical chapters.

2.2 THE EU COMMISSION'S INSTITUTIONAL CONTEXT: FACTORS IMPINGING ON INTERNAL POSITION FORMATION AND INTERACTION

Neither position formation within a DG nor the coordination of different positions across DGs takes place in an institutional vacuum. On the contrary, the institutional context in which the Commission operates will either narrow or broaden the room for maneuver for specific internal policy positions and thus affect their chances of being fed into the EU's inter-institutional decision-making process. Most notably, the relevant literature points to three institutional factors that the Commission as a whole has to deal with: the legislative status quo *ante*, the Commission's need for internal coordination, and the EU's inter-institutional decision-making system. In addition, the EU's complex multi-level system offers a fourth set of more optional power resources that internal Commission actors can draw on during position formation. Factors in these four groups might constrain or enable specific policy positions and interaction strategies on the part of the Commission's internal actors.

These four sets of factors flowing from the Commission's institutional context are not exclusive, instead they operate in parallel. Although some of the factors bond more easily with one or the other of the conceptions of Commission agency sketched above, we refrain from a priori linking them exclusively. The question as to which factors ultimately come into play and how they do so depends on the type of Commission agency that internal actors pursue and this will therefore be an empirical issue. Nonetheless, the derived factors structure our analyses and provide a basis for comparative insights over a medium number of cases (see Chapter 3 for the actual research design). This leads to 25 factors of position formation and interaction in the EU Commission which we define in the following.

2.2.1 Legal Status Quo

The legal status quo has been identified as a powerful constraint for European policy-making. Important sections of the literature on European integration deal with the question of EU institutions (especially the EU Commission) using their discretion to extend competences granted through treaties or other secondary legislation (Pollack 1994; Brent 1995; Rhodes 1995: 100; Dunleavy 1997; Smyrl 1998; Rittberger 2003; Farrell and Héritier 2007). These arguments are all based on the assumption that existing law typically constrains the options for EU policy-making. Creeping competences, in contrast, are expected under specific conditions, empowering the Commission to move away from the status quo. The strong emphasis in EU studies on the category of existing law, both at the theoretical and empirical level, underlines the importance that must be attributed to this factor when studying position-formation processes inside the EU Commission.

We accordingly expect existing legislation to impact on the DGs' scope for proposing policies, through mechanisms either of path dependency or learning. In line with Pierson's (1996) argument on sunk costs, existing legislation constrains internal actors where they are driven by an interest to diminish the need for change or avoid the internal frictions that would be related to new legislation (Pierson 2000). Challenging existing policy involves costs—both political and substantial—for those actors who have adapted to the existing policy path over the course of time. *Ceteris paribus*, the greater the amount of secondary legislation adopted during the integration process, the more costly policy change will be. Applying a constructivist perspective, by contrast, existing legislation might also be an indicator of experience or best practice in an area. Particularly if legal consistency is a shared norm, existing legislation constrains position formation because it may decrease the likelihood of finding a workable new solution to a given regulatory problem. Not surprisingly, crises that challenge existing legislation are perceived as triggers for far-reaching learning processes in the political science literature (Heclo 1974; Rose 1991: 11–12). Disregarding whether the expectation rests on a historical institutionalist reasoning or on softer mechanisms of learning, the further away a DG's policy proposal is from the *status quo ante*, the greater the constraints it meets.

Our baseline expectation is that the position proposed by a DG is shaped by existing policy—the legislative status quo. In conceptual terms, this means that we can only estimate the power and conflict within the Commission if we understand the legal context in which a particular policy-making endeavor began. Establishing both the status quo and the ideal position of a DG in a detailed manner is crucial for the analysis of position-formation processes in the Commission (see also Chapter 3.4.1). The legislative status quo includes extant primary and secondary legislation in the same portfolio or under the leadership of another DG, as well as member states' legislation in cases where no supranational legislation exists.

From this point of view, a first factor impinging on the policy positions of individual DGs should be the *extant acquis* at EU level. In particular, specific articles in EU treaties or distinct secondary-level EU law might enable or constrain a DG's policy position, be it through mechanisms of regulatory consistency, avoidance of conflicts or costs, or their fit to normative policy goals. A similar logic should apply where seminal *ECJ jurisprudence* has shaped existing policies, which is accordingly treated as another factor of position formation. In extreme cases, the EU Commission has been described as being fully captured by extant law and as merely executing ECJ case law without having its own "political aims or visions" (Martinsen 2009: 795). In this sense, the Commission's ability to set the agenda is considerably affected by the legal status quo ante.

While the legal status quo should particularly impact on a DG's policy position, we can also derive a factor for interaction patterns from this institutional constraint. When it comes to internal conflict, a DG's specific *supranational competence* may become a relevant source of power. For example, where a DG can resort to treaty bases that allow for more promising decision-making rules in the inter-institutional process, that is, qualified majority rather than unanimity voting, it should be more assertive in internal interactions that follow a competence-seeking rather than a technocratic logic. Besides the empowering effect of formal rules, a policy portfolio's degree of supranational competence often correlates with its age at EU level (Chapter 4, also Franchino 2009). DGs with greater supranational competence are thus expected to have more experience of practical stakeholder interaction and policy-making and therefore to have a broader knowledge base and informational advantage over other DGs (March and Olsen 1998). It is particularly interesting that the blurring and extension of supranational competences has been the topic of a number of publications on EU policy-making dynamics (e.g. Rhodes 1995: 100; Dunleavy 1997; Smyrl 1998; Farrell and Héritier 2007). In any case, the legislative status quo provides several factors that may impinge on policy choices and interaction patterns within the Commission.

2.2.2 Internal Coordination

From a classical organizational studies perspective (Weber [1925] 1978; Allison 1969; Simon 1970; Olsen 2006), bureaucratic structure "influences which options are to be compared, in what sequence, and by whom" (Hammond 1986: 381). Accordingly, the existing literature on the EU Commission implicitly or explicitly attaches great importance to bureaucratic structure (see Coombes 1970; Page and Wouters 1994; Christiansen 1996: 80; 1997; Lequesne 2000; Nugent and Saurugger 2002; Kassim 2004). It is assumed that actor preferences, contact patterns, and exchange of information, as well as conflict solutions and coordination in an organization, largely follow the formal structure (Egeberg 1994: 88). A satisfactory explanation of the overall policy positions of the Commission must therefore take the organizational structure of internal decision-making into account. In a multi-actor conglomerate, in particular, the internal structure that forms and aggregates positions across the organizational dividing lines sketched out above is extremely relevant (also see Mayntz and Scharpf 1975).

Historically, the EU Commission has been seen as characterized by an "absence of coordination" (Peters 1994: 15; Middlemas 1995: 242). Coordination failures are highly relevance, as has become evident in discussions on internal Commission reform (Jordan and Schout 2006; Schön-Quinlivan 2006, see also Chapter 10). In addition, since the last enlargement, having Commissioners from 27 different member states has been perceived as making formal coordination more burdensome (Kassim et al. 2013). Coordination in the EU Commission is not only important empirically but also conceptually, because a body talking with a common voice has a stronger capacity to shape policy-making and lock out other interests.

In light of these premises, the coordination procedures that exist to aggregate positions within the Commission may clearly constrain some DGs while enabling others in the process of policy formulation. Chapter 10 explicitly discusses the policy implications of varying DG roles and presents the layered structure of inter-departmental coordination at the Cabinet and Commissioner level. These analyses are combined with insights on the enhanced powers of the Commission President and the Secretariat-General (Kassim 2006; Braun 2009), as well as the coordinative effects of formalized inter-service groups and impact assessments (Ludlow 1991: 120; Cecot et al. 2008; Schout and Jordan 2008; Radaelli and Meuwese 2010: 146–9).

Several factors for position formation can be derived from the institutional context of internal coordination. While most of them matter for interaction patterns, structure may also impinge on the policy position of individual DGs. Under the predominance of the technocratic or competence-seeking types of Commission agency, *organizational restructuring* of the Commission's administration, such as the reshuffling of DGs and their responsibilities, may influence a DG's policy preferences. Organizational restructuring is a common practice at the beginning of a Commission term or when a new Director-General assumes office (see Chapter 4). The layout of responsibilities may influence what issue a DG wants to regulate and how it wants to regulate it. Likewise, the anticipated implications of specific policy choices for future organizational changes in the Commission might inform the policy choice of a particular DG.

When DGs have formed their individual positions and come to interact, the Commission's internal coordination rules privilege the DG that holds the lead for drafting a proposal. Being the *lead department* is a factor which affects internal assertiveness because this actor has both an informational advantage about policy substance and a strategic advantage in that it sets the internal agenda and acts as a gatekeeper for deviating positions (Hartlapp et al. 2013). This shows that being the lead DG might be an asset independent of the type of Commission agency being pursued by internal actors.

We also see another factor arising from the need for internal coordination and the collegiality principle at the political level of the College. The ability of DGs to build *alliances* with other DGs should be an asset in pushing a particular policy through (Bailer 2004; Alesina et al. 2005). Where a group of DGs hold the same position, this should strengthen the bargaining position against an opposing, isolated DG. Closely related to this, support from the *horizontal services* such as the Secretariat-General, the Legal Service, or DG BUDG should be a factor that increases a DG's internal power. In formal terms, these services hold internal veto powers that might be important for competence- or policy-seekers, while their assent may also signal the high technical quality of a proposal in terms of legal and financial expertise, which is important for technocratically oriented actors (Radaelli 1999b).

A DG's power to fight against provisions they oppose may be further influenced by *workload* factors. If the workload is high, a DG will be dealing with a number of issues at any one time. It is thus less likely to engage in careful scrutiny of other DGs' proposals and also less likely to be successful in time-consuming internal interaction processes. Consequently, a DG with more personnel available to work on a specific initiative should be at an advantage when compared to others with fewer personnel.

The fact that not all DGs can work on all on-going Commission proposals at a given point in time can be linked to two additional, less directly tangible factors of internal interaction. In tackling large workloads, actors may resort to a "logic of appropriateness" whereby they rely on unwritten but commonly accepted standards as opposed to formal rules and a rational assessment of a situation (March and Olsen 1996). With regard to Commission DGs, we assume two central, unwritten norms that may allow DGs to accept the claims of deviating DGs as legitimate grounds for positions: a bureaucratic norm and a democratic norm. A bureaucratic norm refers to the idea that within the Commission each DG should serve its specific mandate, defined by the Commission's formal internal organizational structure; in other words, it should act within its portfolio boundaries. *Bureaucratic legitimacy* thus rests on services' perception of a DG as the appropriate and authoritative actor on a specific issue that is clearly located within its portfolio. Employing this norm in conflictual interaction may render a particular actor assertive. A democratic norm, by contrast, refers to the common understanding that the Commission should serve the interests of citizens and the general public. *Public legitimacy* therefore stems from a DG's position being backed by public sentiment or the current political climate. Invoking the public acceptability of a particular position in conflictual interactions may also explain a DG's assertiveness.

Lastly, another factor linked to internal assertiveness in interactions could be the *origin of an initiative*, in other words, whether it originated from the administrative or the political level of the Commission. A proposal drafted at the administrative level may benefit from the knowledge of the responsible desk officers and therefore convince others on the basis of its high technical quality, particularly where the predominant type of Commission agency follows a technocratic model. Alternatively, a DG defending a proposal originating from the political level may benefit from support in the form of political firepower in "turf" conflicts or ideological battles.

2.2.3 The Inter-institutional System of the EU

The EU Commission acts as the formal agenda-setter in an open political system of checks and balances with unstable majorities, which encourages coalition-building among formal and informal veto players. The Commission's policy-making capacity therefore not only depends on internal rules, but crucially also hinges on actors and interests in the wider EU political system. Some authors are optimistic in claiming that the fluidity and the openness of the external political system render the EU "the prospective agenda-setter's paradise," as the agenda-setters can choose from a broad range of solutions offered (Peters 1994: 21). More skeptical accounts see decision-making in the EU as being trapped in the difficult institutional conditions of political policy choices and consequently highlight the heterogeneity of actors' interests as a major constraint (Scharpf 1999, 2006). From both perspectives, the anticipation of future decision-making and the Commission's need for external support and acceptance for a proposed policy affects the internal drafting process. These constraints are further reinforced by the demise of the "permissive consensus" and the growing politicization of EU integration, which has increased the need to legitimize political choices not only through the delivery of efficiency in outcomes but also through voter preferences and wider public concerns (Zürn 2006; Hooghe and Marks 2009). When forming its position, the Commission therefore takes into account the possible consequences with respect to the external political system and considers whether its proposal may not be adopted, or may lose legitimacy or support, which is undesirable for the Commission in the long run.

Inter-institutional decision-making is the main battle ground of the EU, where political relationships have evolved over time. The dominant role of the Council has been the subject of scholarly debate since the emergence of the early grand theories of European integration (Hoffmann 1966; Moravcsik 1998). National interests may thus enter position formation through the Commission's anticipation of the relative interest constellation in the Council (Thomson 2008). Today, with the majority of EU legislation adopted under co-decision procedures, the European Parliament's vote may produce a similar national influence on the drafting of legislative proposals (Hix et al. 2005).[7] Thus, depending on the legislative procedure and the voting rule applied, the Commission has to anticipate and accommodate opposing national or partisan interests in the Council and Parliament. The *anticipation of Council and EP majorities* should thus be a relevant factor for the policy positions of individual DGs. When forming their positions, DGs are expected to anticipate the preferences of majorities in Council or in Parliament, in order to prevent their proposal being beaten down in inter-institutional decision-making.

In a similar manner, the inter-institutional process may have a bearing on the power relationships and interaction patterns among DGs. The internal assertiveness of a DG may be determined by the relative *proximity* of its position to a perceived Council or EP majority (Schmidt 2000; Elgström and Frennhoff Larsén 2008). Here, the assumption is that the internal assertiveness of a DG is stronger if the policy area it is responsible for comes with lower thresholds in the inter-institutional process (i.e. if qualified majority voting applies) or if it can claim that its preferred policy choice better reflects the interests of inter-institutional players.

In addition to the Council's or the EP's aggregate position influencing the positions adopted inside the Commission, particular *national positions* may also impact on the policy positions of individual DGs. The role of national interests in European decision-making has also been debated since the start of theorizing about European integration (Hoffmann 1966; Moravcsik 1991; Hug 2003). Apart from governments' interests finding their way into a Commission proposal via the shadow of the Council, specific interests or policy models existing at member-state level may also enter Commission positions via alternative routes. Specific national interests may have an influence on DG positions when national actors lobby the EU Commission directly, for example (Panke 2012). Alternatively, individual Commissioners and DG officials may act as a channel for particular national preferences (Egeberg 1996). With respect to this line of reasoning, case study evidence is more prominent in some policy areas than in others, notably those linked to distributive policies or to policies that interfere with national varieties of capitalism: "Every Commissioner is prepared to support his or her country vis-à-vis the college when it deals with competition rules affecting a national enterprise, for example, or a transfer of funds from the EU budget" (Lequesne 2000: 48; also Schmidt 2000; Christiansen 1997: 78). Finally, individual policy models existing at the national level may also find their way into Commission proposals when they provide efficient templates for specific regulatory problems at the supranational level. According to the technocratic view and the more political models of Commission agency, national positions should matter for internal policy choices while the way in which they matter should differ.

Likewise, national interests may also impact on the interaction process among DGs. Here, in particular, the *size of a member state* supporting a DG's position should represent a power resource for this DG. This may either follow classical realist reasoning relevant to a politically acting DG (Morgenthau 1963), or come about indirectly in a technocratic Commission via nationality-based networks of highly specialized bureaucracies that provide a head start in terms of informational advantages (Joana and Smith 2006: 39).

A further factor deriving from the Commission's external political system that impacts on position formation within the Commission is that of *partisan ideology*. Although no unified supranational party-political system exists, the impact of party-political interests on decision-making has been widely claimed to matter for the EU system (for the EP: Hix et al. 2005; for the Council: Mattila and Lane 2001; Tallberg 2008). Party cleavages may also structure the positions of individual DGs. As with individual national interests, party-political interests may enter the EU Commission through earlier socialization and individuals' underlying beliefs (e.g. Hooghe 2001, 2005; Egeberg 2006a), or through delegation chains at the Commission's political level (Döring 2007; Wonka 2007). Accordingly, we expect the party-political influence to be exerted particularly successfully at the higher echelons of the DGs studied. Clearly, this factor should figure more prominently where Commission agency is rooted in a policy-seeking, rather than in a competence- or efficiency-oriented rationale.

2.2.4 Additional Power Resources in a System of Multi-level Governance

In addition to the three categories of formal institutional constraints impacting on position formation in the Commission, we also identify a fourth category of optional resources that the Commission and its internal actors can draw on. This category emerges from the view of the EU as a more complex decision-making system, which involves multiple actors and governance levels pushing for different policy choices. The existing literature has shown that Commission agency may sometimes be constrained by such external demands, but that it may also use and respond to them selectively when setting the agenda for Europe. Thus, we systematically consider a number of additional factors that decisively impact on the EU policy process and have been subject to extensive scholarly work, but that do not formally belong to the other categories introduced in the preceding sections. Most importantly, this concerns the role of (organized) societal interests that are active at the EU level, the influence of experts and expertise from the Commission's environment, individuals engaging in entrepreneurial policy-making, and consistency with international policies.

In his account of the High Authority—the predecessor of the European Commission—Haas (1958/1968: 460) stresses that it "seeks to organize a general consensus among its subjects before embarking on any policy. Continuous consultation with all interested parties . . . is its watchword." Crucial integration steps such as the Single Market have been explained in terms of the force of organized societal interests mobilizing relevant segments of the public or powerful economic interests (Sandholtz and Zysman 1989; Moravcsik 1993; Stone Sweet and Sandholtz 1997; Coen 1998). Scholars have extensively analyzed the influence of corporate lobbying and civil society forces on EU policy-making (e.g. Mazey and Richardson 1993; Eising 2007), while we also find accounts of how the Commission itself has assisted the organization of societal interests when this benefited its goals (Pollack 1997c; Young 1997a).

Accordingly, the role of *organized interests* requires attention when explaining the policy positions of individual DGs within the Commission. Organized interests can be expected to play a pronounced role in a technocratic rationale as providers of knowledge—the bureaucrats' most important commodity for drafting efficient proposals (Weber [1925] 1978). In the more political models of Commission agency, however, organized interests may also be important where they are used selectively to support competence expansions or ideological goals. In addition to their influence on DGs' policy preferences, stakeholder interests may also be a factor in the interaction among DGs with differing policy positions. DGs may base their power on information or support provided by organized interests. It is not only the information provided but also the type of stakeholders consulted that may convey power to a DG: if DGs can demonstrate that they have consulted broadly—and can thus base their positions on a plurality of interests involved—this may also serve as a source of power.

Similarly, technical or practical *experts* should be relevant for the position formation of Commission DGs. Internal actors may draw on knowledge provided by experts who are internal or external to the Commission, such as seconded national experts and expert groups, or through the submission of reports and studies. When DGs interact, we can expect that the action capacity of one DG will be increased by informational advantages about technical solutions and strategic preferences or causalities in political systems (Mayntz and Scharpf 1975: 8–20). However, expert knowledge can also be used to augment legitimacy and support, or to assess the policy in terms of normative standards (Feldman and March 1981; Metz forthcoming; see also Chapter 8).

Besides organized interests and experts, the *influence of individuals* may also impact on the policy positions the EU Commission proposes. This view builds on prominent studies of the EU Commission that highlight the decisive role of individuals in the Commission in driving the direction of European integration (e.g. Ross 1994). We therefore expect that individuals convinced either by entrenched values or by the desire to expand their competences may also play a role in explaining the Commission's position. Moreover, in addition to influencing DGs' positions, they may also account for a DG's success in internal interaction. DGs may build on individual *entrepreneurs*, meaning "advocates who are willing to invest their resources—time, energy, reputation, money—to promote a position in return for anticipated future gain in form of material, purposive, or solidary benefits" (Kingdon 1984: 188; similarly Fiorina and Shepsle 1989: 32–3; Peters 1994: 13). How and under which type of Commission agency such individuals matter for position formation and interaction is an empirical question, however.

Lastly, position formation in the EU Commission does not occur completely independently of policy developments beyond the EU borders or at the international level. In many cases, a DG's position may be influenced by policies emerging beyond the EU political system. Such blueprints may be provided by *policy transfers* from international templates, for instance. Analytically, the reach of such international policy models is captured by concepts of diffusion or policy transfer (e.g. Braun et al. 2007). In a technocratic model, learning and emulation can be explanations for "general patterns characterizing the spread of innovations within or across political systems" (Knill 2005: 767). Where they provide viable policy models or where they serve competence-seeking or normative motives, a DG might adopt them into its position on the policy at hand.

Likewise, where a DG's position supports the EU Commission's joint interest at other levels of the EU multi-level system, this should strengthen its position internally. Thus, internal position formation in a politically acting Commission can be understood as being nested in a *meta game* (Putnam 1988). A DG's specific position might be internally powerful because it facilitates endeavors towards an effect desired at another level, for example by giving the EU Commission a higher profile in the UN.

In sum, working back from the Commission's institutional context, we find a broad range of external interests and templates that may inform a DG's position, as well as a plethora of power resources that can be expected to matter in internal interactions. What is more, the discussion of these individual factors highlights the fact that they may impinge on the overall Commission position via various mechanisms—depending on whether the Commission is operating through technocratic, competence-seeking, or policy-seeking types of agency. Thus, we argue that a combination of different factors is needed to satisfactorily explain the contents of the common policy proposals we observe. Rather than expecting a stable formula of position formation in the EU Commission, this book is interested in the relative weight of a factor or set of factors and in the logics of their inter-play, which should certainly vary with the context of the policy proposal under analysis.

2.3 POLICY CONTEXT

There are at least two major dimensions that mediate the relevance of external interests and policy templates, as well as the power resources employed in line with technocratic, competence-seeking, and policy-seeking rationales. They act at a distinct level and vary according to the specific issue at hand: (a) uncertainty about the factual consequences of the policy choices involved and (b) the salience of the issue in terms of public politicization (Gormley 1986; Radaelli 1999b; Elgström and Jönsson 2000).

An issue is defined as *uncertain* if "decision makers cannot assign definite probabilities to the occurrence of particular consequences" (March and Simon 1993: 137). In such situations, the cause–effect relationship of policies remains ambiguous and it is difficult for actors to anticipate or accurately predict the policy outcomes of certain choices. This should be the case when DGs lack adequate information about a situation to be tackled. Uncertainty about policy outcomes may, however, be induced by uncertainty about policy output. Generally, uncertainty should decrease where a DG has substantial implementation experience in a particular area, since this should help in assessing "the expected outcomes of different courses of action" (George 1980, in Haas 1992: 14).

Salience refers to the extent to which people care about political issues or hold opinions about them (Franklin and Wlezien 1997) and is understood here as the contemporaneous public attention or public visibility attached to a proposal or a particular issue of that proposal (Epstein and Segal 2000; Mahoney 2008). Looking backwards from the inter-institutional process, Häge and Toshkov (2011: 3) have shown that "public support for European integration . . . increases the Commission's agenda-setting activity." We build on their finding, but also go beyond the expectation that salience matters only where it relates to more or less integration, positing that salience might also influence which policy is proposed for Europe (see Chapter 9).

Turning to what these factors do to our expectations, we can expect that low uncertainty and/or high salience will push position formation in the direction of the factors that correspond to a power-based agency of the Commission. The actors have a clear perception of both their interests and the potential pay-offs. Here, we can assume that actors exploit "hard" power resources—such as size of the home country or the set of procedural factors—in a strategic manner. Where high uncertainty prevails and/or the issue does not significantly mobilize the public, the literature expects more integrative negotiations in a bureaucracy, creating an opening for knowledge or value-driven interaction that helps to shed light on hitherto unknown aspects (Radaelli 1999b). Accordingly, informational sources of power, such as the involvement of experts, can become more relevant. Drawing on the concept of rationally bounded actors, uncertain situations can further facilitate position formation along a value-driven rationale, where "Commission officials use their beliefs as heuristics to judgement" (Schäfer 2012: 7; see also Gormley 1986: 597–8).

2.4 CONCLUSION: AN ANALYTICAL FRAMEWORK TO CAPTURE POSITION FORMATION IN THE EU COMMISSION

Summing up, we expect the policies proposed by the European Commission to depend on power and conflict within the Commission, which, in turn, is structured by the type of Commission agency in play and is determined by the institutional context surrounding Commission actors. We identify four major categories in the Commission's institutional context that may constrain or facilitate policy choices and interaction patterns in the Commission: the legal status quo, internal coordination, the EU's inter-institutional decision-making system, and additional resources of power deriving from the EU's multi-level system. From these four categories, we deduce a number of factors that influence the positions of Commission actors and the interactions between these actors as power resources (Table 2.1).

The following chapter describes in greater detail how these factors and the type of Commission agency guide the empirical analyses conducted in this volume. As

Table 2.1. Overview of factors enabling and constraining position formation

Legislative status quo
• Extant acquis • ECJ jurisprudence • Supranational competence
Internal coordination
• Organizational restructuring • Lead department • Horizontal services • Workload • Bureaucratic legitimacy • Public legitimacy • Initiative's origin • DG alliances
EU inter-institutional system
• Anticipation of/proximity to Council majority • Anticipation of/proximity to EP majority • National positions/member state size • Partisan ideology
Additional resources
• Organized interests • Experts and expert groups • Individuals' influence/entrepreneurship • Meta game • International policy transfer

indicated in this chapter, the explanatory power of the individual factors for specific position formation processes may vary according to the type of Commission agency at play in a specific process. By tracing the position-formation processes and the mechanisms through which these factors play out, we seek to specify the respective type of Commission agency more precisely. This should ultimately provide us with a more conclusive picture of how the Commission forms its positions and, therefore, how the policies it proposes for Europe are shaped.

NOTES

1. In some policy areas, the Commission shares the right of initiative with the Council. In addition, one of the major innovations of the Treaty of Lisbon was to extend the public's right to ask the Commission to come forward with proposals from the Parliament and Council (Art. 225, 241 and 11 TFEU, respectively). Under the European Citizens' Initiative (ECI), one million citizens who are nationals of a significant number of member states can ask the Commission to submit a proposal. These more recent rules curtail the Commission's monopoly of initiative but still rely on Europe's central agenda-setter when it comes to formulating the actual contents of policies. Without doubt, then, no other body determines the substance of EU legislative proposals in the way that the Commission does.

2. We believe there are good grounds for aggregating Commissioners and their Cabinets into political leadership and for assuming common interests and information, for Cabinet staff are at the personal disposal of Commissioners. Given the hire-and-fire autonomy of the Commissioners, Cabinet members are directly dependent on them and typically leave together with their Commissioner once a Commission term is over (Spence 2006b: 60–3).
3. These assignments are part of the long-term planning and programming efforts of the Commission, as expressed in its five-year objectives, in the Annual Policy Strategies, and in Work Programmes (see Tholoniat 2009). Although the explanation of long-term priority-setting is a valuable question in its own right, this book focuses on the more narrow process of proposal preparation.
4. For a detailed account of the internal coordination structures and their usage, see Chapter 10.
5. Without deviating from the conceptual definition specified here, we use the terms assertiveness, power, or punch inter-changeably throughout the remainder of the volume.
6. Although scholars often link the Weberian notion of power to rational-choice approaches and strictly resource-based thinking (e.g. Bailer 2004), we do not impose such strong theoretical limits here. We assume that different logics of interaction—be they rooted in rationalist, sociological, or even constructivist explanations—are at play with varying degrees of importance (cf. Elgström and Jönsson 2000; Scharpf 1997a). Even if endogenous preferences are assumed, the Weberian concept holds because some actors can be expected to have more “persuasive power” than others in such settings (cf. Risse 2003: 16).
7. Votes in the European Parliament have been shown to often (but decreasingly) reflect national dividing lines (Höpner 2005; Hix and Noury 2009).

3

Studying Internal Dynamics

Position formation in a multi-actor organization is a complex process to study. Up until now, analyses of the Commission as an agenda-setter have commonly drawn either on case studies, abstract theorizing, or large-scale analysis of individual-level data. Our research design differs from these approaches and is innovative in several respects. With the intention of bridging the gap between qualitative and quantitative research, this book presents a medium-n design. It expounds in-depth analyses of 48 concrete position-formation processes and systematically compares relevant factors and mechanisms across these processes. It also brings together a particularly broad range of information sources, notably 153 interviews with experts and an original database on personal and structural features of the European Commission since its founding days. We draw on different quantitative and qualitative analysis techniques to shed light on the "black box" of position formation within the EU Commission. This chapter describes our research design in more detail, provides the rationale for selecting the 48 cases, and introduces the empirical material and the operational indicators that link the design to the two analytical research questions derived in Chapter 2.

3.1 A TWO-STAGE RESEARCH DESIGN

The basic rationale of the research design guiding the analyses summarized in this volume is informed by (a) the state of the art of research on decision-making inside the Commission and (b) the high demands on data collection and interpretation.

With regard to (a), the existing literature lacks conceptual clarity on "what kind of animal" the EU Commission actually is. Most theoretical accounts of European integration handle the policy position of the Commission simply as given, implicitly or explicitly settling for the assumption of a unitary Commission. The analytical literature on policy, by contrast, provides us with a complex set of potentially interacting factors that may reasonably be assumed to structure internal position formation to varying degrees. The scant amount of generalized knowledge—in combination with the large number of causal factors, interaction effects, and context conditions—necessitates a more systematic analysis of power and conflict inside the EU Commission.

With regard to (b), the conception of a research design is further informed by greatly limited data availability of episodes of strife inside the Commission. This is no surprise, given that the Commission generally acts on the principle of collegiality and seeks to uphold consistent positions providing it with strategic advantages vis-à-vis the other actors in inter-institutional decision-making. Consequently, information on internal position formation is less than readily available and can even be legally withheld from the public on the grounds that such information was meant for internal use only and that disclosure would undermine the institution's decision-making activities (Regulation [EC] no. 1049/2001, Art. 4, Para. 3). In sum, the absence of systematic preference data in combination with the lack of systematic knowledge about relevant causal mechanisms renders a *two-stage research design* advisable, which combines thick analysis from case studies with a systematic cross-case comparison.

First, a "systematic process analysis" (Hall 2008) of single cases will provide insights regarding proposed causal mechanisms, while also leaving enough room to provide the best possible fit for each case under scrutiny along a y-centered logic (Ganghof 2005). Hall's concept is closely connected to (and in some respects a refinement of) the seminal writings on "process tracing" by George and Bennett (2005, esp. ch. 10). Rather than establishing parametric input–output relationships across cases, the analysis in our first stage covers the mechanisms that link the theoretically proposed explanatory factors with the explanandum, that is, the final position of the EU Commission. Second, the overall research follows the logic of a "structured focused comparison" (George 1979). The empirical results from the single case studies on conflict and power in the Commission are compared systematically so as to allow judgments on the cross-case relevance of causal claims. The great advantage of our medium-n set-up is that we actually evaluate the plausibility of an argument that emerges from a single case with the rest of the n–1 number of cases at hand. Although we cannot lay claim to an ultimate testing framework at this stage, our contribution to theory development comes close to what Eckstein (1975) has labeled a "plausibility probe." Under the theoretical and empirical research constraints set out above, this approach provides the best possible contribution to a systematic understanding of how internal conflict and power shape the individual policies the EU Commission proposes for Europe.

3.2 CASE SELECTION: THE SAMPLE OF POSITION-FORMATION PROCESSES UNDER ANALYSIS

We selected 48 legislative proposals for the medium-n design, a sample size that balances the number of observations with the high data-collection demands. Given the theoretical interest and the questions raised in Chapters 1 and 2, we constructed the sample in accordance with six basic choices.

First, the book's basic question about which policy the EU Commission selects for Europe implies that the universe of relevant cases is given by *all original Commission proposals aiming at the enactment of binding secondary EU legislation with universal entitlement within all member states of the European Union*. Accordingly, a proposal for a regulation, a directive, or a decision, as the most common legislative instruments, represents a case. To identify this basic population and to build an initial selection basis, we relied on data from EUR-Lex and PreLex as the major publicly available databases on EU legislation (König et al. 2006).[1]

Second, in order to arrive at contemporaneously meaningful results while allowing variation on some basic factors of position formation, our *investigation period* starts with the inauguration of the Prodi Commission in September 1999 and ends with the first Barroso Commission in February 2009. This book therefore covers two recently completed Commission terms, while also having regard to intra-institutional developments and shifting policy responsibilities. Furthermore, we selected initiatives tabled by the Commission within these two Commission terms, independently of their state in the inter-institutional process, thereby including cases that were still pending in the Council or might even have been withdrawn at later stages. This selection criterion allowed us to include initiatives that have never materialized as EU legislation and that would have been overlooked by studies that focus only on the inter-institutional process of European policy-making.

Third, our interest in conflict and power inside the European Commission and its problem-solving capacity in the context of increasingly differentiated modern societies warrants a concentration on portfolios with overlapping internal policy competences. Thus, we chose *three policy areas* that fall within the responsibility of two or more Commission DGs.

In practice, each author focused on one policy area. We chose to analyze the intersection of common market and social policy, as well as research and innovation policy, and consumer policy. Apart from the fact that these policy areas touch on the interests of many different segments of society, we also selected them because of presumed diverging policy focuses on the conflict dimension of market-liberalizing and market intervention, which we see as being particularly important for the EU integration project. Treating the Commission's DGs as the most relevant actors in the internal preparation of Commission proposals, we found that both more market-liberalizing and interventionist DGs co-exist within the Commission. Next to the usual suspect for deregulatory policies (DG MARKT, the DG for the internal market),[2] the chosen policy areas involve actors with mandates that are usually based on regulatory or even distributive interventions. Some prominent examples in this respect are the DGs for Employment, Social Affairs and Equal Opportunities (DG EMPL), for Health and Consumer Protection (DG SANCO), and for Research (DG RTD), but also for Enterprise and Industry (DG ENTR).

We define policies at the intersection of *common market* and *social policy* as comprising all EU policies that directly or indirectly concern public policy aiming at changing, maintaining or creating living and working conditions that are conducive to social justice and human welfare. So far it remains an open question how far a social dimension of the EU has developed in its own right or whether interaction between the two lead departments, DG EMPL and DG MARKT, mainly produces market-liberalizing policies (see Chapter 5). The second area is *research and innovation policy*, defined as all measures that aim at producing knowledge, new products, and processes, and enhancing the competitiveness of a specific sector or the market in general. During the investigation period, research policy was predominantly the responsibility of DG RTD, while innovation policy was part of DG ENTR's broad portfolio.[3] In addition, sector-specific DGs are responsible for the research and innovation measures within their respective domains, such as DG INFSO for information technology, DG TREN for aspects of energy activities, and DG ENTR for space and security. The third sub-sample covers *consumer policy*, which is aimed at protecting the end users of products or services against risks and disadvantages in economic life that may preclude her benefiting from the full choice offered in a perfect market. The DGs typically involved in such interactions are DG SANCO, on the one hand, and DGs ENTR and MARKT, on the other. Having demarcated these three areas of interest, we then selected all relevant Commission proposals during the investigation period according to their classification in the *Directory of Community legislation in force* ("directory codes"), which resulted in an initial dataset of 665 observations.[4]

Fourth, in order to reduce this sample further, we excluded all cases that were of no direct or of strongly limited *theoretical interest* for the questions covered in this volume. This involved rejecting Commission proposals addressing external relations, enlargements of the EU, and administrative issues. We further excluded acts that were closely linked to other analyzed pieces of legislation, as well as proposals re-introduced from the inter-institutional process, as we assumed they would feature only minor adjustments.[5] We further excluded a minor number of proposals prepared under rather atypical internal decision-making procedures because their rare occurrence endangered the comparability of cases in our final sample.[6]

Fifth, our choice was guided by an interest in covering all important (not only exposed and highly contentious) instruments and in systematically varying some of the explanatory factors (Seawright and Gerring 2008). To avoid a selection bias along a specific Commissioner set-up or specific internal procedures, we employed additional case-specific PreLex data to distribute cases equally across both the Commission terms covered and across decision procedures in the College of Commissioners. The adoption date provides us with control over potential differences in presidential leadership and—more importantly—guarantees variance on the independent variables that are directly related to a specific Commissioner. The decision procedure in the College, in turn, ensures that we have a roughly equal number of cases in which diverging positions actually reached the political level of the Commission (oral procedures) and those most likely to be resolved at lower echelons (written procedures).[7]

Sixth, and finally, the immense data-collection efforts required for the envisaged medium-n research design necessitated a further systematic reduction of the cases analyzed. In line with our claim regarding the societal relevance of common Commission decisions, we selected the proposals with the *broadest scope*, as indicated by the subject matter in the title, from each cross-table cell, while ensuring variation on the DGs that acted as the lead.[8]

Ultimately, this selection process resulted in 48 position formation processes in the European Commission, where 16 deal with the intersection of the common market and social policy, 14 fall in the area of research and innovation policy, and 18 cover consumer policy issues. Table 3.1 summarizes the distribution of cases across policy areas, Commission terms and internal procedures, while the policy-specific Chapters 5–7 discuss the substantial legislative content in greater detail.

Table 3.1. Case distribution over Commission term and procedure in College[a]

	Prodi (1999–2004)	Barroso (2004–2009)	Total
	M&S/R&I/C	M&S/R&I/C	M&S/R&I/C
Written	6/2/4	1/2/6	7/4/10
Oral	6/6/5	3/4/3	9/10/8
Total	12/8/9	4/6/9	16/14/18

[a] Numbers refer to the areas of the intersection of common market and social policy (M&S)/research an innovation policy (R&I)/consumer policy (C), respectively

In sum, this purposeful sample construction maximizes the theoretical leverage in answering the research questions raised in Chapter 2. And while it does not present all features of a random sampling procedure, the six selection steps outlined in this section provide a clear guideline on the extent to which the subsequent results can be generalized.

3.3 DATA SOURCES: BRINGING EMPIRICAL INFORMATION TO BEAR ON THE ANALYTICAL FRAMEWORK

As for the overall research design, our data-collection strategy is determined both by the complexity of the analyzed processes and by the lack of public access to systematic information on power and conflict within the Commission.

Where access to primary documentation is restricted, relying on expert or elite interviewing is a highly promising approach for maximizing the amount of available information (King 1995; Aberbach and Rockman 2002; Dexter 2006 [1970]; Littig 2008). For our purposes, clearly those Commission officials who took part in the 48 drafting processes are the most knowledgeable experts, and their information constitutes the core of our empirical data. Between May 2009 and January 2010, we conducted 137 semi-structured expert interviews in Brussels and Luxembourg.[9] Because personal responsibilities for particular legal acts are most often not public knowledge, and because we are not interested in making inferences about officials themselves, we relied on a non-probability sampling (Goldstein 2002; Tansey 2007) in identifying the relevant interview partners in the Commission based on (a) the officials' formal positions and (b) reputational information gained during initial research. In order to avoid biased conclusions, our strategy cross-validated information obtained from individual contacts (cf. Berry 2002). The interviews in the Commission span different hierarchical levels, ranging from the desk officer who drafts a specific provision to the Commissioner who defends the proposal in the College, including officials from the coordinating units in the Secretariat-General. We interviewed officials from the lead DG as well as from other DGs involved in each case, and also added 16 further views from outside the EU Commission (participants of expert groups, representatives of organized interests, and former Commission officials), resulting in a total of 153 interviews.

Each of the interviews followed a semi-structured guideline with open questions, was based on a solid preparation of each proposal under analysis (cf. Leech 2002) and lasted between 30 and 90 minutes. The questions were constructed with a view to capturing process information and insights on the theoretically informed factors and mechanisms in our analytical framework (see Appendix A1 for the complete list of questions). All interviews were transcribed and deductively coded with the software Atlas.ti, which allowed systematic searches for specific issues covered in the book.

Table 3.2 lists the distribution of our 137 contacts from within the Commission. We see that the interviews are clustered in DGs SANCO (20), RTD (18), and EMPL (14)—the DGs with the main responsibility for the policy areas under analysis—but are equally well distributed across DGs with overlapping competences, such as DGs MARKT (22), ENTR (16), and INFSO (12), as well as the central coordinating services SG and SJ (15) and other DGs (18). The cluster along the lower ranks of the Commission's hierarchy is partly explained by the limited time those in leading positions can dedicate to interviews, but also by the fact that the relevant officials in the higher echelons often held responsibility for several cases in our sample.

Given the absence of systematic preference data, a second data source of particular value to our research is documentation from the Commission's internal CIS-Net database. In operation since 2001, this electronic database circulates draft proposals to the DGs concerned; coordinates DGs' formal exchanges; and registers their agreement, opposition, and comments. Typically, a number of DGs reply, ranging from lengthy observations to editorial remarks. This database therefore allows us to control and to complement our interviews in a most fruitful way. We requested access to CIS-Net documentation for all our 48 cases and received replies from the Commission in 46 cases. For reasons of data confidentiality or technical difficulties in tracing old files, however, in 15 of these replies the

Table 3.2. Expert interviews conducted in the Commission (May 2009–Jan. 2010)

Directorates-General and services	Policy officers	Heads of unit	Directorate and Staff	Commissioner and Cabinet	Total
Employment and social affairs (EMPL)	7	5	1	2	**15**
Internal market and services (MARKT)	15	4	1	2	**22**
Research (RTD)	6	6	4	2	**18**
Secretariat-General (SG) and Legal Service (SJ)	11	1	1	2	**15**
Health and consumers (SANCO)	7	8	3	2	**20**
Information society (INFSO)	9	1	3		**13**
Enterprise and industry (ENTR)	8	4		4	**16**
Other DGs and services	10	4	2	2	**18**
Total	**73**	**33**	**15**	**16**	**137**

Commission neglected to provide insights and for 28 of the 46 cases we were granted only partial access. In these cases, we were provided with some but not all of the comments issued by the DGs involved at the time, while some documentation contained blacked-out sections.

Besides these two internal sources, we also traced position formation on the basis of published primary documents from PreLex and EUR-Lex that record the Commission's final position as well as (earlier) Communications and consultation documents. This endogenous process documentation is complemented and cross-validated by externally published information. Here we focused in particular on *Agence Europe*, a daily news service targeting mainly EU practitioners, as well as other media information (e.g. *EUobserver*, *European Voice*, and the *Financial Times*) to capture the wider policy context and the salience of an issue, in addition to position papers summarizing the demands of external stakeholders. Moreover, some of the factors in our analytical framework point to operations that combine this qualitatively gained knowledge with other data sources, for example, the publicly accessible expert-group register of the EU Commission, public-opinion data from Eurobarometer, and, finally, our original database on personal and structural Commission features since its founding. Some of these sources were used for particular operational indicators described in the next section, while all of them will be individually referenced in the corresponding empirical chapters.

3.4 CASE STUDY STRUCTURE AND OPERATIONAL INDICATORS

The narratives of our cases studies are guided by our theoretically informed analytical framework. They are not designed to test competing hypotheses against one another, but to provide the best possible explanation following the logic of a y-centered research design (Ganghof 2005). The cross-case comparison allows inferences to be drawn about the relative explanatory power of the factors and mechanisms identified as relevant. Necessarily, this required definitions and operationalizations of core concepts that are amenable to systematic comparison.

3.4.1 Policy Substance

The analysis of power and conflict in the Commission not only requires the identification of (diverging) actor preferences that exist in the Commission, but also an assessment of the policy substance, that is, what are the issues to be regulated and what precisely are the DGs quarrelling about? We therefore start our case studies by describing and categorizing the content of the particular legislative draft. Obviously, not all the issues addressed in a specific case are equally important. When looking at the legal substance of our cases, we identify their key provisions (KPs). A key provision in a legislative draft is defined as a provision that is of either high or medium material relevance, has substantial scope of application, has a financial impact or involves an important institutional dimension. Our categorization of KPs is derived from an analysis of the legal text adopted by the Commission. KPs are often found at the level of individual articles, but they may vary in breadth. In addition, provisions that were identified as important on one of these dimensions through other data sources but did not make it into the proposal are equally considered to be KPs (Bachrach and Baratz 1962). Thus, we also capture the "non-issues" that do not appear on the EU's decision-making agenda. The 48 sampled acts contain seven KPs, on average.

In substantial terms, regulatory key provisions can often be linked to known EU regulatory concepts, such as minimum harmonization, mutual recognition, and the country-of-origin principle. The concept of EU "minimum harmonization" refers to agreed thresholds that member states must meet. While complex negotiation dynamics typically impede agreement on more far-reaching standards, member states are free to maintain or to raise national standards above these minima. "Mutual recognition" is inherently linked to the famous *Cassis de Dijon* case (C-120/78) and allows products lawfully marketed in one country to be marketed throughout the Common Market—even though they might not fully comply with other countries' specific national regulations. Although often used interchangeably, the "country-of origin-principle" does not focus on products, instead it regulates which law is applicable for services or actions performed in one EU member state but consumed in another.

For each particular KP, we construct the fall-back option (FBO), defined as the outcome that would prevail if the EU Commission did not adopt the proposal in question (Thomson et al. 2006: 39–40; see also Schmidt 2000). This reference point—indicated at the beginning of each case study—enables consistent judgments to be drawn on the extent to which the Commission proposal in question actually brings about political change in Europe and also allows an objective classification that transcends political rhetoric. Furthermore, we used the FBO as a reference point to assess the relative power of Commission DGs in the interaction process (see Section 3.4.3). The FBO is easily identified where secondary EU legislation on the same or a closely related issue already gives a precise definition of the rules that would prevail if no proposal were brought forward. In all other cases, we constructed the FBO from what we know about interpretations of primary law, ECJ rulings that introduced legal uncertainty, and, in some cases, relevant national legislation. Thus, the FBO and the legal status quo ante were often one and the same (cf. Chapter 2.2.1).

3.4.2 Operationalizing Research Question 1: DG Policy Positions

The next crucial part of the empirical analysis concerns the drafting process. We describe what motivated the drafting unit in the responsible DG to come forward with the proposal, considering bottom-up and top-down processes between the administrative and the political levels in the DG in question. The timing and the nature of the involvement of organized interests is assessed, taking into account not only the substantial positions voiced, but also the nature of consultation and the resources acquired (e.g. factual expertise or quantitative data). Public consultations typically take the form of a Green Book or other document inviting the *general* public to comment (on the Internet), with the results being made public in a report, typically accompanied by a press release. Specific consultations refer to activities whereby a DG approaches a *specific* audience, for example, by inviting particular interest groups or attending specific meetings and consulting the audience present on the issue.

Subsequently, our case studies turn to a discussion of the lead DG's ideal position and its relationship to the FBO, as well as of the ideal positions of other DGs. Where possible, we differentiate between the general position on the act and positions on specific KPs, and also specify changes over time. Explanations are assessed according to the factors derived in the analytical framework in Chapter 2 and following the application of the operational indicators and data sources summarized in Table 3.3. Whether or not a particular factor had explanatory power for a DG's ideal position is established by a respective counterfactual argument. For each factor, we can argue that a DG's ideal position would have looked different had the factor been absent.

Table 3.3. Operationalizing factors affecting DG positions

Analytical factor[a]	Operational indicators	Data sources
Extant acquis	Proposal or interview references to extant EU law	Interviews, proposal preamble, EurLex database
ECJ jurisprudence	Proposal or interview references to extant jurisprudence or ongoing procedures	Interviews, Proposal preamble, CURIA database
Organizational restructuring	Recent changes in internal responsibilities conform to voiced positions	Interviews, own historical database on internal portfolios,[b] proposal text
Anticipation of Council or EP majority	Position conforms to voiced Council/EP interests	Interviews, consultation documents, Council/EP communications
National positions	Nationality of Director-General/Commissioner, member-state preference reflected in DG position	Own historical database on Commissioner characteristics,[b] interviews, *Agence Europe*, position papers and consultation documents
Partisan ideology	Partisan orientation of Director-General/Commissioner, partisan preference reflected in DG position	Own database on Commissioner characteristics,[b] interviews, *Agence Europe*, position papers and consultation documents
Organized interests	Interest-group position reflected in DG position	Position papers and consultation documents, interviews, *Agence Europe*, proposal preamble
Experts and expert groups	Expert position reflected in DG position	Expert group documentation, and expert interviews, consultation documents, external studies, and reports
Individual's influence	Individual official held strong individual stakes in a DG's position	Interviews
International policy transfer	Position of international organization/third country regulator in the area reflected in DG position	Interviews, existing international regulation, proposal preamble

[a] For detailed information on the derived factors see Chapter 2.
[b] For detailed information on this database see Chapter 4.

3.4.3 Operationalizing Research Question 2: DG Assertiveness

The analysis continues with a description of the internal *interaction process*. We systematically trace between whom and on which issues conflicts emerged, describe at which hierarchical levels and at which stages of the process inter-DG contacts occurred, and examine whether they were defined and prescribed by rules or were of an informal nature. Where possible, we record whether this concerned the whole directive or specific provisions.

One crucial aspect in the analysis of position-formation processes in the Commission is the conflict intensity of DG interaction, which we break down into two distinct components. First, based on interview and CIS-Net data, we assess differences in DG positions on the analyzed KPs ("objective" or position-based conflict dimension). Our scale ranges from 0, where no differences on KPs were visible between DGs, to 3, where we found opposing views regarding the overall act, its overall approach, or the very necessity to regulate the particular issue area at all. Second, we record the degree to which the involved actors perceive and describe the interaction process itself as conflictual ("subjective" or process-based conflict dimension). We assess all cases ranging from 0, where all interviewees on the case qualified the process as non-conflictual or none of them made particular reference to the intensity of inter-DG conflict, to 2, where all interviewees agreed that the case at hand was particularly conflictual. We also include in this category conflicts between DGs that are not position-based, but reflect institutional interests such as turf battles. Obviously, the value for both dimensions of conflict intensity may vary along the different bilateral interactions the lead DG has with other participating DGs.

Within each case study, we then discuss for each key provision whether a DG was (1) successful and (2) powerful. Taking the "neutral" fall-back option as a reference point enables consistent judgments on the relative power of Commission DGs. Bargaining theory holds that the success of an actor must be evaluated in relation to his or her best alternative to a negotiated agreement (BATNA), which often represents the status quo (Scharpf 1997). In line with this idea, we can express each DG's ideal position relative to the FBO and then assess whether the final Commission proposal benefits or disadvantages each DG in question. First, we define a DG as *successful* where it made a gain in the final text of the legislative proposal compared to the FBO. Technically, being successful is understood as (the absolute value of) the difference between the DG's ideal position and the FBO, minus (the absolute value of) the difference between its ideal position and the final outcome (reflected in the legislative proposal).[10] Practical limits are set by a lack of information or difficulties in precisely situating qualitative or institutional positions in a multidimensional space. Second, we define a DG as *powerful* only where it was successful vis-à-vis another DG thanks to employing a specific power resource that it controls and not simply because of luck. We follow Weber's ([1925] 1978: 53) resource-based view, which combines actor positions with *process* in capturing power. By providing evidence that a DG has actively and successfully employed one of the derived factors as a resource to overcome opposition, we can show that it was not successful simply because of good fortune (Barry 1980). To come to a judgment concerning the most powerful DG on a case level, we employed a three-stage aggregation rule that considers quantity (number) and quality (relative importance) of KPs in which a DG was powerful.[11] As for the research question on a DG's position-building, explanations are provided according to the factors and mechanisms discussed under the analytical framework and following the operational indicators and data summarized in Table 3.4. Similarly, counterfactual reasoning provides the basis for our judgments on the sources of a DG's powerfulness. For each factor, we can argue that the assertiveness of a DG would have been different in the absence of the respective factor.

For both research questions, we further cross-validated the basis of our respective judgments and counterfactual arguments by means of an inter-subjective review. Following drafting by one author, each case study was reviewed and discussed by the whole research team and revised where necessary.

Table 3.4. Operationalizing factors affecting DG power in internal interaction

Analytical factor [a]	Operational indicator	Data source
Supranational competence	Greater scope and degree of competence (treaty base, age of community policy, quantity of legislation) account for assertiveness	EurLex database, interviews
Lead department	Lead department is assertive	PreLex Database, interviews, CIS-Net
Horizontal services	Support from horizontal services (SG, SJ, DGs BUDG or ADMIN) accounts for assertiveness	College meeting minutes, CIS-Net, interviews
Workload	Lower workload accounts for assertiveness	Number of personnel in unit in relation to other initiatives on the unit's agenda, interviews
Bureaucratic legitimacy	Arguments along bureaucratic norms account for assertiveness	Interviews
Public legitimacy	Arguments along democratic norms account for assertiveness	Interviews, Eurobarometer, *Financial Times*, *Agence Europe*
Initiative's origin	Political/administrative support accounts for assertiveness	Interviews
DG alliances	Alliance among two or more DGs accounts for assertiveness	College meeting minutes, CIS-Net, interviews
Proximity to Council/EP majority	Positions closer to voiced Council/EP preferences are assertive	Interviews, consultation documents, Council/EP communications
Member state size	Director-General/Commissioner from larger member state accounts for assertiveness	Interviews, Council voting rights, population size
Organized interests	Powerful/diversified stakeholder support accounts for assertiveness	Interviews, position papers and consultation documents, *Agence Europe*
Entrepreneurship	Leadership skills and political connections of a particular individual account for assertiveness	Interviews, *Agence Europe*, *Financial Times*
Meta game	Issue linkage and nesting account for assertiveness	Interviews, proposal preamble, consultation documents

[a] For detailed information on the derived factors see Chapter 2.

3.4.4 Contextual Factors

To understand the position formation process on a particular act, we need to consider the broader political environment during drafting, the policy context in the particular policy area and the context factors of uncertainty and salience.

Political context refers to the broader European political environment at the time a proposal was drafted in the Commission. This encompasses broad debates in the other European institutions, Council summits, other salient European initiatives discussed or negotiated at the time (in a policy area other than the issue at hand), referenda or elections on European issues, and trends or swings in general public opinion on the integration process. Both Commission terms studied provide for a general political context that presumably impacted on the interests and processes in position formation. When Prodi was appointed Commission President in 1999, for example, the Commission faced the challenge of introducing the euro in 2002 and negotiating the Convention on the Future of Europe, meant to reshape the institutional architecture of an enlarged Union. On top of this, the Prodi Commission internally engaged in the administrative reform (Kinnock Reform) that, inter alia, introduced systematic impact assessment, put stakeholder consultation on a more systematic level, and pledged loyalty to the banner of "Better Regulation." In 2004, the succeeding Barroso Commission continued with the "Better Regulation" agenda and implemented the Eastern enlargements. Important political context conditions were the (failed) referenda on the Constitution and some highly controversial legislative initiatives, notably the Bolkestein directive and the regulatory agenda on registration, evaluation, authorization, and restriction of chemicals (REACH).

The *policy context* of a drafting process refers more specifically to the environment of the particular policy area to which the analyzed proposal belongs. For example, this encompasses particular discussions prevailing in the respective policy community at the time and other relevant national or international acts that were drafted, negotiated, or concluded in the area. *Salience* refers to the extent to which the wider public cares about political issues or holds opinions about them (Franklin and Wlezien 1997; Chapter 2.3). As we refer to contemporaneous salience (Epstein and Segal 2000), we operationalize it as the presence of an issue or a proposal in the *Financial Times* during the internal drafting process.[12] We assess the *uncertainty* attached to a legislative proposal (March and Simon 1993: 137; Chapter 2.3) by drawing on information collected through our interviews, media coverage, and secondary literature. For the sake of comparison across cases, these two issue-related variables are binary coded. For example, a proposal displaying no or low uncertainty is coded with 0 and one displaying a rather high uncertainty about the policy consequences is coded with 1.

Finally, the individual case studies also contain assessments of the relevance of the act beyond particular KPs—either for a DG, for the EU Commission as a whole or even for the overall process of European integration. In order to capture possible interactions with the following inter-institutional process, we finalized each case study by collecting information on the respective inter-institutional process: Did the Council and Parliament discuss the same points raised within the EU Commission? Were similar conflict lines visible? Did new issues emerge?

As for the operationalization on DG policy positions and DG assertiveness, these operationalizations of context factors were also inter-subjectively reviewed by the whole team of authors.

3.5 CONCLUSION

This chapter unfolds a consistent empirical strategy for studying position formation in the multi-actor conglomerate that makes up the European Commission. Clearly, the complexity of the processes under analysis is mirrored in the research design. Nonetheless, a replication of our findings on and beyond the cases we cover should be possible along the lines we have presented here. Moreover, our choices transparently reveal the standards by which generalizations can be judged.

In sum, our case studies provide a rich empirical base regarding power and conflict in individual drafting processes inside the Commission, which will be presented in greater detail in Chapters 5–7. These chapters serve as a solid basis for a systematic cross-case comparison. By combining our case study knowledge with a visualization of distributions across cases, we are able to assess the relative importance of individual factors in the internal position formation processes (Chapters 8–11). This allows us to detect patterns of position formation and to arrive at a more encompassing typology of the agency that drives Europe's central agenda-setter (Chapter 12).

NOTES

1. EUR-Lex is the legal information system monitored by the European Publications Office. Commission proposals can be identified on the basis of the type of legislative document (Commission Proposal for legislation, PC). PreLex is the Commission tool for monitoring and tracing the legislative decision-making process between the Commission and other EU institutions; it is run by the Commission's Secretariat-General. We used PreLex as a source of additional information for the later steps of case selection and analysis.
2. Throughout the book, we use the reader-friendly acronyms for the DGs, even though some of the cases and literature stem from times when the Commission's numerical system was still in place (see Chapter 4).
3. Under the Barroso II Commission, these two areas were merged into DG RTD's portfolio, which was then renamed DG for Research and Innovation in January 2011.
4. The great advantage of relying on directory codes (rather than on the Eurovoc thesaurus or the "'subject matter" classification) lies in its non-exclusive use of descriptors, allowing documents to be indexed in several policy areas, and in its hierarchical structure of 20 principal policies, each comprised of several (sub-)headings (Düro 2009: 102). The policy area of common market and social policy was given by freedom of movement for workers (05.10), general social provisions (05.20.05), European Social Fund (ESF, 05.20.10), working conditions (05.20.20), employment and unemployment (05.20.30), social security (05.20.40), approximation of certain social provisions (05.20.50), insurance related to the right of establishment and freedom to provide services (06.20.20.10), self-employed activities (06.20.40), general (public

contracts, 06.30.10), public works contracts (06.30.20), public supply contracts (06.30.30), public services contracts (06.30.40), other public contracts (06.30.50), social conditions of transport policy (07.20.40.20), health protection (15.30), freedom of movement of people (20.10), and European citizenship (20.20). To identify research and innovation policy proposals, we relied on agricultural research (03.30.50), general, supply, and research on fisheries (04.05), nuclear research (12.40.40), general research on industrial policy and internal market (13.10.10), programmes and statistics (13.10.20), research and technological development (13.10.30), general principles of science, information, education, and culture (16.10.10), and research sectors (16.10.20). Finally, consumer policy proposals were defined by directory codes on general consumer policies (15.20.10), consumer information, education, and representation (15.20.20), protection of consumer health and safety (15.20.30), and protection of economic interests (15.20.40).

5. Technically speaking, this exclusion covers proposals that were formally marked as codifications, recasts or repeals of existing EU legislation, as well as amendments, supplements, corrections, extensions to existing EU legislation and proposals formalizing autonomous social-partner agreements (Art. 155 TFEU).
6. This exclusion concerns "joint responsibility" of two or more DGs and "empowerment procedures", which are technical or routine issues consigned to the responsibility of a single Commissioner.
7. In the latter case, a proposal is distributed among Commissioners and their cabinets in written form and their non-response is interpreted as agreement. In the former case, verbal negotiation among the members of different cabinets and possibly also Commissioners takes place and the proposal can only pass on the basis of express agreement (see also Chapter 10).
8. While the judgment on scope is inherently subjective in nature, an independent replication of the procedure is very likely to result in a similar sample because the universe of cases contains a huge number of proposals with a very limited scope. In consumer policy, for example, the original sample contains a range of regulations on individual chemical substances in foods, but it contains only one proposal for a general framework on the regulation of food additives in the Union. Since this is a much more relevant choice regarding which policy should be proposed for Europe, we always preferred the broader acts.
9. To preserve anonymity, we refer to the interviews as COM1, COM2, etc. Throughout the book, the codes include consecutive numbers and a number referring to the relevant passage in the transcript.
10. In other words, in a one-dimensional world, DG influence would be captured as ||DG—FBO|—|DG-PROPOSAL||. In some rare cases, it was not possible to define the FBO. In these cases, success was assessed relative to the lead's ideal position in a dyadic relationship.
11. On KP level for every DG involved, success is assessed in relation to the FBO. For the lead and each deviating DG, we assess whether they have been powerful. We consider powerfulness at the level of KPs and on this basis come to a conclusion about powerfulness in a bilateral DG relationship. Finally, for each case, the most powerful DG in quantitative and qualitative terms is assessed.
12. The *FT* addresses a transnational audience, provides news on international business and finance as well as on international politics, and is the largest daily newspaper that has a European-wide outreach (Pearson plc 1998). Given the complexity of the EU's 23 official languages and 27 national media systems, relying on the *FT* is thus deemed the most adequate option for operationalizing the salience of an issue (cf. Mahoney 2007).

4

Connecting Personal Characteristics and Organizational Structure

Commissioners, Directors-General, and Services

Before delving into our case studies of specific position formation processes, we will describe the historical evolution of the multi-actor conglomerate that is the EU Commission. More precisely, the chapter connects the formal layout of the organization's major internal units—the Directorates-General (DGs)—with the personal characteristics of their leaders—the responsible Directors-General and Commissioners. In this sense, the chapter prepares the ground for the subsequent analyses by providing some of the basic parameters needed to locate the Commission between the poles of purely technocratic and essentially political decision-making. In assessing the congruence between policy portfolios and leadership characteristics, we highlight here how keenly different logics of position formation—ranging from bureaucratic portfolio logics over national interests to party politics—have inter-related and still do inter-relate within the Commission. In order to track this complexity over time and across DGs, we draw on comprehensive descriptive data from a newly established database (1958–2010).[1] In this chapter we take a longitudinal perspective, which is particularly warranted if we want to understand whether and how today's policy choices are influenced by institutions that have built up over time.

From studies at the national level, we know that the personal characteristics of organizational elites, such as geographical origin, prior employment, and party membership, are important factors in explaining the policy choices of administrations (Aberbach et al. 1981; Page 1987; Aberbach et al. 1990). It is reasonable to assume that such factors likewise matter for position formation in the EU Commission, so that we can argue that the way a policy field is approached, the importance attached to an area, the favored problem solution, and the final position adopted in the College can vary in accordance with the personal characteristics of the administrative and political leadership. However, compared to national governments, the diversity in the individual backgrounds of the Commission's internal leadership is much broader.

Nevertheless, research focusing on individuals inside the EU's central administration is a recent, though now growing phenomenon. This is unsurprising given that a technocratic actor perspective often prevails in this field. In the relevant accounts, individuals are considered to be "neutral" actors. After the end of World

War II, the Commission's predecessor, the High Authority, had been designed as a body composed of impartial people who were independent of national governments and ideological disputes (Haas 1958/1968: 452ff). To the present day, the Treaty establishing the European Community prescribes that Commission members "shall be chosen on the grounds of their general competence and their independence shall be beyond doubt. In carrying out its responsibilities, the Commission shall be completely independent. . . . the members of the Commission shall neither seek nor take instructions from any Government or other institution, body, office or entity" (Article 17 TEC). However, when we look at EU policy analyses, the view of a value-neutral elite heading the EU Commission hardly seems to be an accurate description of reality.

A first group of relevant studies shows that Commissioners tend to act as agents of their national governments and therefore defend prevailing governmental or party-political interests. The focus in these studies lies on the party-political orientation of Commissioners and its link to national governing parties. Researchers in this field are interested in whether the Commission can indeed be considered an independent "preference outlier" or whether positions will be in line with government interests (Crombez 1997; Hug 2003; Döring 2007; Wonka 2007). In this setting, personal characteristics are expected to be of relevance in principal–agent relationships and party-political chains of delegation.[2] Where Commissioners are understood to be member-state or party-political agents, they can be expected to pursue the interests of the respective member state or political party. They act on the basis of a cost–benefit calculus and respond to a range of *ex ante* and *ex post* mechanisms. For example, Commissioners who act in line with their party's preferences could be rewarded with party offices at a later time.

From a different theoretical perspective, the view of a value-neutral Commission is challenged by a second strand of the literature that analyses the socialization of individuals inside the Commission. Looking at the beliefs of EU Commission's top staff, this perspective is interested in explaining the origins of those beliefs and in identifying the formative power that can be attributed to the European institution, for instance compared to previous socialization at the national level (Egeberg 1996, 2006a; Hooghe 2000, 2001, 2005; Suvarierol 2007; Trondal 2010; Ellinas and Suleiman 2012; Kassim et al. 2013). Here, earlier affiliations are considered formative for position-taking inside the Commission. Once certain ideas or beliefs have been established, positions that correspond are considered appropriate when deciding new policy substance. "National norms, originating in prior experiences in national ministries, loyalty to national political parties, or experience with one's country's organization of authority, decisively shape top officials' views on supranational norms" (Hooghe 2005).

The two schools of thought disagree on the relevant causal mechanism, but they both uphold the view that the characteristics of individuals in the Commission impinge on the organization's policy choices (Wonka 2007; Bauer and Ege 2012; but see Peterson 2008: 765). Both obviously support a perspective that understands the Commission as a political rather than a technocratic or ideology-free institution. Our subsequent cases studies will also return to the influence of individuals on policy positions.

For now, however, we are interested in the descriptive patterns over time, while also extending the existing approaches along three empirical dimensions. First, we are interested in the congruence between formal portfolios and leadership characteristics. Second, we include and compare both administrative and political leadership. While it is true that many policies are signed and sealed only in the College of Commissioners, Chapter 2 pointed out that the administrative level can have a substantial influence through internal agenda-setting, strategic interaction, and bureaucratic drift (cf. Schnapp 2004: 331–7), so that this level also requires attention. Third, we map these internal leadership characteristics over all Commission terms since the EC's founding. In line with the existing literature, we concentrate on the nationality, party-political background, and prior professional activity of Commissioners, and on the nationality of the Directors-General. Taken together, this approach permits a more comprehensive and long-term view on how potentially relevant factors of position formation are distributed inside the Commission.

4.1 THE DATA: SOURCES AND STRUCTURE OF PRESENTATION

The data presented in this chapter cover the period from the first Hallstein Commission, established in 1958, to the first Barroso Commission, which held office until 2010. We drew on and combined three sets of data sources.[3] First, we relied on the official organigrams of the Commission. For more recent periods, these are available on the Commission's websites, but most of those we used had to be retrieved from the institution's Historical Archives in Brussels. Second, we combined these data with Fabio Franchino's dataset on Commission portfolios (Franchino 2009). Third, we coded data from the CVs of the individuals of interest, which were provided by the Commission's or personal websites.

The presentation of these data is structured in accordance with our interest in the Commission's Directorates-General, which, as outlined earlier, represent the major organizational units for position formation. The database covers all DGs, but the remainder of this chapter will focus only on those that are relevant for the empirical material presented in this book. Thus, most of the graphs in this chapter present sub-samples of DGs that are potentially active in the areas of consumer policy, research and innovation policy, and the intersection of common market and social policy. Three more specific remarks are required in order to facilitate interpretation of the figures that follow in this chapter.

First, not all Commissioners stay in office for the entire term of their Commission. Sometimes a new face may enter the Commission during a term, for example in the event of illness or when a Commissioner decides to return to his or her national political scene. In these cases, the departing Commissioner is replaced by a Commissioner of the same nationality. However, if the national government has since changed, the likely result is a change in the partisan orientation of the respective Commissioner. In order not to bias our data given such staff turnovers, we rely on the actual number of months each Commissioner spent in office.[4] The analyses regarding the Commission's Directors-General, by contrast, rely on Commission terms. Given the substantially longer time period these officials serve in office (an average of 2.29 terms) and the less frequent turnover during terms compared to Commissioners, this choice seems unproblematic. However, whenever we encountered a Director-General turnover at any point during a term, we assigned the entire term to the Director-General with the greater share of office during the term in that particular DG.

Second, we present relative data, that is, the shares of each individual characteristic within the Commission or within DGs over time. While this allows us to analyze possibly biased distributions within the Commission, the reader should bear in mind possible distortions in the case of more recently founded DGs for which the basis is a relatively small number of total months (e.g. DGs INFSO, JLS, and TAXUD).

Third, the number and the names of DGs have changed over the course of the integration process. Similarly, the layout of portfolios has seen changes. In order to track the data consistently over time, we refer to the names used during the Barroso I Commission throughout the chapter. In some cases this required us to make adjustments to the DG names that were used at the time of concrete drafting processes. An example is the social affairs portfolio covering Employment, Industrial Relations and Social Affairs (DG V) under Delors, which was renamed Employment, Social Affairs and Equal Opportunities under Barroso I (DG EMPL). However, making the DGs comparable also meant dealing with substantial changes in the organization's portfolio structure over time.

4.2 THE EU COMMISSION'S PORTFOLIO STRUCTURE OVER TIME

Before discussing the personal characteristics of the EU Commission's administrative and political leadership, this section describes the development of the Commission's organizational structure over time. This outline serves as a preparation for our in-depth case studies, with the Commission DGs as our central administrative unit of analysis. In addition, it must be remembered that the Commission's leadership is mutually dependent on the organization's portfolio structure. On the one hand, the number of member states has, to date, determined the number of Commissioners, which in turn has influenced the number of portfolio responsibilities. On the other hand, the leadership's, and, in particular, the Directors' General areas of responsibility depend on a number of other factors.

Thus, Figure 4.1 shows the EU Commission to be an evolving organization. First, new areas of activity have constantly been added since the founding days. This partly reflects the ongoing transfer of competences to the supranational level, but also the demand for more portfolios in association with enlargement rounds that have increased the number of Commissioners seeking to be head of "their own house." The growth in the number of areas may also reflect administrative changes (e.g. from in-house accounting to central accounting through a separate service, Bauer et al. 2008), a new President's own political priorities, or functional

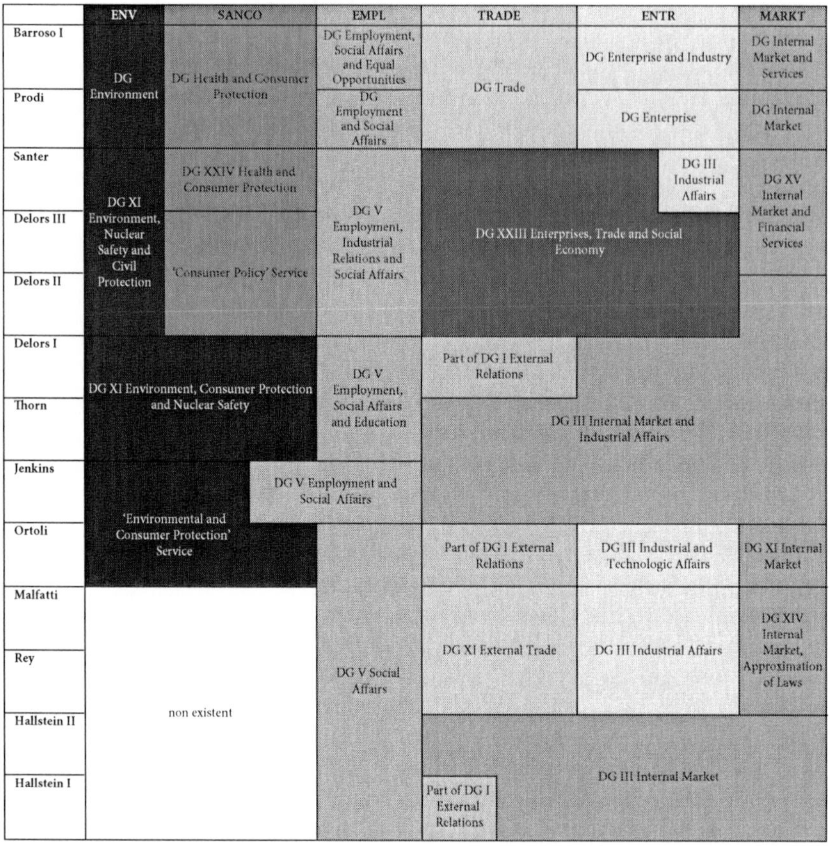

ENV
SANCO
EMPL
TRADE
ENTR
MARKT
Barroso I
Prodi
Santer
Delors III
Delors II
Delors I
Thorn
Jenkins
Ortoli
Malfatti
Rey
Hallstein II
Hallstein I
DG Environment
DG Health and Consumer Protection
DG Employment, Social Affairs and Equal Opportunities
DG Employment and Social Affairs
DG Trade
DG Enterprise and Industry
DG Enterprise
DG Internal Market and Services
DG Internal Market
DG XI Environment, Nuclear Safety and Civil Protection
DG XXIV Health and Consumer Protection
'Consumer Policy' Service
DG V Employment, Industrial Relations and Social Affairs
DG XXIII Enterprises, Trade and Social Economy
DG III Industrial Affairs
DG XV Internal Market and Financial Services
DG XI Environment, Consumer Protection and Nuclear Safety
DG V Employment, Social Affairs and Education
Part of DG I External Relations
DG III Internal Market and Industrial Affairs
DG V Employment and Social Affairs
'Environmental and Consumer Protection' Service
Part of DG I External Relations
DG III Industrial and Technologic Affairs
DG XI Internal Market
non existent
DG V Social Affairs
DG XI External Trade
DG III Industrial Affairs
DG XIV Internal Market, Approximation of Laws
DG III Internal Market
Part of DG I External Relations

Fig. 4.1. Organizational evolution of the EU Commission: selected portfolios by Commission term

Source: Authors' compilation on the basis of official organigrams from the Commission's historical archives in Brussels (accessed in March 2010).

differentiation and policy developments, such as in the area of environmental policy. Second, the boundaries between different portfolios are anything but stable. Most "new" areas originally belonged to established portfolios before they became independent services. A particularly relevant case in our sample is the birth of DG SANCO after the BSE scandal—it developed out of the Consumer Policy Service, which itself was previously part of the responsibilities of DG ENV (see also Chapter 7). In other cases, units have shifted back and forth between two DGs, depending, for example, on the relative strength of the Commissioners or on negotiations by their respective national governments regarding portfolio allocation. Examples are the interfaces between DGs ENTR and MARKT when it comes to industrial affairs and between both the former and the latter and DG TRADE on trade issues. There was a period when all three of these portfolios were actually handled in one joint DG. This was during the Thorn and Jenkins Presidencies when DG III on 'Internal Market and Industrial Affairs' was the all-embracing

Commission entity for market, enterprise, and trade issues. In the aftermath of the Santer crisis, in particular, the Commission's reorganization under Kinnock brought about a shift in the portfolio structure. One example in this regard that has affected some of the drafting processes discussed in this book is the reorganization of DG ENTR (see Chapter 6.2). The following chapters will show that these organizational dynamics between portfolios over time are of great relevance in explaining contemporary Commission positions.

4.3 PARTY AFFILIATION

The following graphs allow us to identify possible ideological or partisan biases on the part of the various Commissions and DGs. Figure 4.2 shows the composition of the particular Commissions regarding their Commissioners' party affiliation from the first Hallstein to the first Barroso Commission. Every Commissioner who ever served in the listed Commissions was assigned to one of the following party families: Conservatives/Christian Democrats, Social Democrats, and Others (Liberals, Greens, and Communists). The party families are based on the EP group to which the Commissioner's party in question belonged at the time of observation. To this end we use party family groupings that built on and develop further Hix and Lord (1997). Other than for the Commission's political leadership, little information is recorded about the Commission bureaucrats' party-political preferences and membership. Thus, a corresponding analysis of the Directors'-General party affiliation could not be carried out.

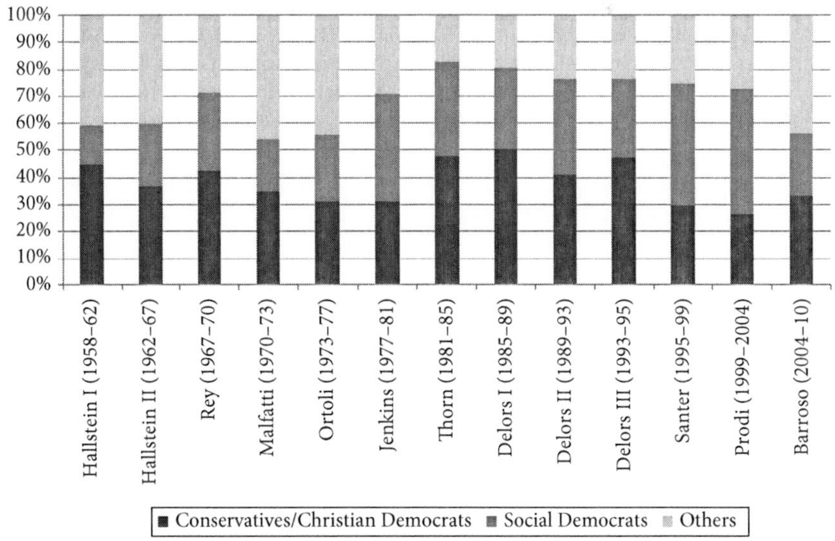

Fig. 4.2. Party affiliation of Commissioners by Commission term (months in office)

Source: Authors' compilation, updating Franchino (2009).

At first sight, the relative dominance of conservative as compared to social-democratic dominated Commissions catches the eye. However, alternating dominances between the two big parties become evident over time. The chart shows relatively more social-democratic Commissions during the late 1970s and early 1980s (Jenkins) and from the mid-1990s to mid-2000s. In line with public perception, the Prodi Commission was the "least conservative" (26.4 percent Commissioner months in office), while Barroso assembled a strikingly liberal Commission. Hallstein I was the "least social-democratic" Commission (14.6 percent of terms of office). Surprisingly, the Delors Commissions were not among the most social democratic, although they are typically associated with the regulatory "social" dimension of Europe (Falkner et al. 2005: 47; also Ross 1994). The Santer and Prodi Commissions, by contrast, which appear as being dominantly social democratic according to Figure 4.2, are actually associated with "only" soft social-policy measures under the Open Method of Coordination. A possible explanation is that single individuals—such as the social democrat Delors—matter more than the "party political centre of gravity" (Manow et al. 2007) inside the Commission.

The two largest party families (conservative and social democratic) combined were most powerful in the Thorn Commission (82.7 percent) and the Delors Commissions (80.6 percent, 76.4 percent, and 76.5 percent), reflecting relative ideological homogeneity in the sense of a grand coalition in the College of Commissioners. This matches the decision period of the (probably) most important integration project: The Single Market Project, "project 1992." In this wave, the member states agreed on the Maastricht Treaty, which dealt not only with EMU, but also with foreign and security policy and political union. In contrast, a relatively heterogeneous Commission under Malfatti and Ortoli coincided with the period of Eurosclerosis in the 1970s when the Commission made few far-reaching attempts to use its powers; in fact, in those years it made little effort to push or drag member states, to extend competences or to develop important policy projects. The Commission was less mixed during the last decade than in the 1970s, but more so than during the 1980s and early 1990s. During this most recent period, integration developments can be described as very active, but also increasingly contested (Hooghe and Marks 2009). Overall, the College of Commissioners has grown more political in that it has fewer independent Commissioners, but there is no evidence of a clear pattern of becoming more right or more left wing over time.

Administrations' policy portfolios are often associated with different ideological orientations (e.g., Budge and Keman 1990). Whereas economic and industrial portfolios are often attributed with a liberal or conservative world view, social-policy portfolios are generally considered to be influenced by a social-democratic view. This point has also been made in case studies on the Commission's DGs (Cini 2000; Beyers and Kerremans 2004). However, does it also hold on the aggregate level when we consider the distribution of Commissioners' partisan ideology across DGs?

Figure 4.3 presents stark differences in the ideological backgrounds of the DGs' political leadership.[5] Some DGs display alternating party political "flags" over time, while others have been dominated by a specific ideological orientation. Social democrats have indeed often headed some of the more interventionist

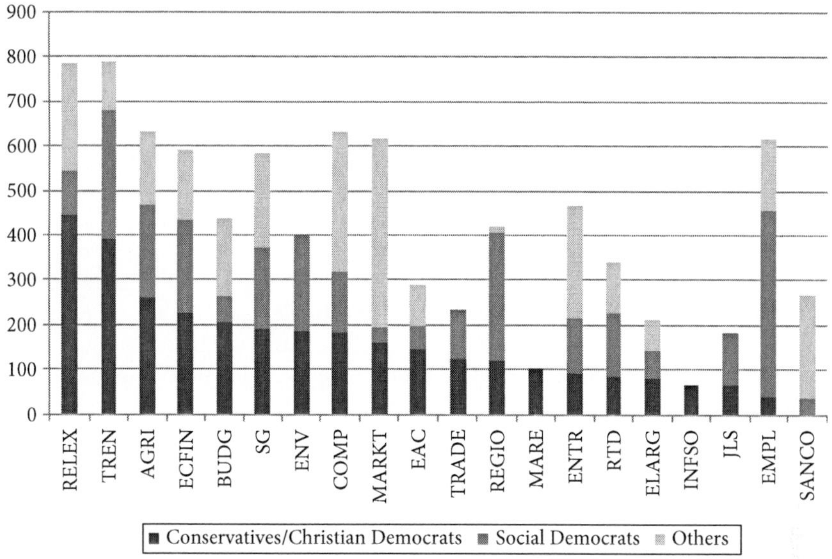

Fig. 4.3. Months spent in office by conservative, social-democratic and other Commissioners by DG, 1958–2010

Source: Authors' compilation, updating Franchino (2009).

DGs, such as DGs EMPL, REGIO, and TREN. Likewise, members of conservative or liberal parties are found more often at the helm of the economic portfolios DGs MARKT, BUDG, and even COMP (but also RELEX) than their social-democratic colleagues (the "others" category largely contains liberal Commissioners). Three portfolios, DGs TRADE, ECFIN, and ENV, stand out as being balanced with respect to the party-political orientation of their leaders. This can be explained by considering that the environmental portfolio, especially, does not lend itself easily to exclusively left-wing or right-wing interests. Green parties are typically most closely associated with environmental policies, which cut across the traditional left–right dimension (Hooghe et al. 2002). With respect to trade, economics, and finance, we may consider this picture in the light of the different approaches a party may take towards the policy—as an interventionist public-utility policy or as a privatized competition policy. Our findings on party-political orientation and administrative structure are in line with an analysis by Franchino (2009), who stresses that "left (right) leaning commissioners are significantly more likely of being assigned portfolios with a left-(right-)wing ideological profile."[6] And they also fit a characterization Hooghe has proposed drawing on insights from the political economy literature for portfolios adhering to "regulatory capitalism": DGs EMPL, COMM (previously Culture), ENV, EAC, SANCO, AGRI, DEV, FISH, and REGIO (Hooghe 2001; Chapter 5 and appendix). In line with existing research, our findings show that, overall, DGs with such interventionist policies are often found to be headed by Commissioners belonging to the social-democratic party family. DGs with a largely economic outlook, by contrast, are more often headed by Commissioners from conservative and liberal parties. It will thus be interesting to see if and how the structural congruence of party politics and sectoral policies translates into concrete policy output. This may happen directly when the policies proposed are in line with the ideological orientation of the political leaders in the respective portfolio at the time. Alternatively, we may observe a cumulative effect, where the party-political orientation of the person at the helm has shaped the existing acquis in the area over time and thus indirectly the positions on concrete initiatives.

4.4 NATIONALITY

Existing research also argues that the Commission's policy portfolios have been dominated by specific nationalities, which has contributed to the creation of DG-specific cultures (Ross 1994; Cini 2000; McDonald 2000). Our data only partly confirm this view. On the one hand, we do note that some of the most important policy DGs have been headed over a large proportion of time by Commissioners from the same member states. Put differently, most countries tend to focus on specific issue areas, so it is likely that certain member states will have left a footprint on certain policy outputs. On the other hand, this is by no means the case for all portfolios, given the complexity and diversity of the links between up to 40 DGs and up to 27 member states—a complexity and a diversity that increased during the period of investigation.

Figure 4.4 shows the national homogeneity of Commission portfolios. The values were obtained by dividing each DG's age (Commission terms) by the number of states having appointed its Commissioners. The higher the attributed value, the smaller the number of member states that were able to leave their footprints on the portfolio, taking the age of the DG into consideration.

The examination of the link between nationality and particular DGs revealed that France focused on DG ECFIN and provided the Commission's President no less than 26.9 percent of the time since the founding of the institution (with Delors

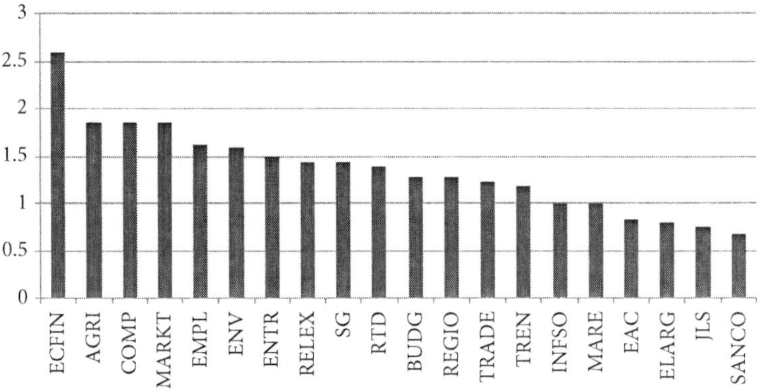

Fig. 4.4. National homogeneity of Commissioners by DG, 1958–2010

Source: Authors' compilation, updating Franchino (2009).

accounting for 19.2 percent). DG ENTR has been under the influence of German Commissioners for most of its existence. DG COMP—one of the other DGs with a high value in our graph—has been dominated largely by the Netherlands. DGs MARKT, EMPL, and ENV have been led most of the time by Commissioners from Italy. DG RELEX has been over-proportionally in the hands of Belgian Commissioners, and Belgium has also so far been the nation most often in charge of DG RTD. Thus, there is some evidence that large member states show a particular inclination to concentrate on "old" DGs, but also on those responsible for areas with a substantial transfer of competences.[7] The United Kingdom, by contrast, shows a fairly balanced personnel placement, with DGs TRADE, REGIO, RELEX, and BUDG being the DGs often occupied by British Commissioners. This is in line with earlier observations by Page (1985), who found the UK to be a prime example of a career-system administration where political appointment is rare and posts are instead filled on a merit-based system. If we assume this cultural pattern to matter for appointments at the EU level, too, then finding UK flags above certain DGs should be highly unlikely. These findings are extremely relevant for our research question, where we assume that portfolios are pitted against each other in terms of national approaches and cultural differences, so they will be considered carefully as explanatory factors in the case studies.

One surprising finding is the Dutch focus on agriculture. Over 40 percent of the total months spent in office by Dutch Commissioners were completed in DG AGRI. We would have expected a French dominance in this DG, given the national importance of the agricultural sector. In case of the Netherlands, this country's prominence in DG AGRI is not matched by a particular salience of the policy area at the national level according to the data presented by Druckman and Warwick (2005: 40). One explanation may be that national-level and EU-level salience may matter differently. A policy that has little importance at home might nevertheless still be of great importance at EU level. A further explanation emerges from our analysis of the national distribution of the administrative leadership—the Directors-General—across policy portfolios, where DG AGRI proves to be clearly dominated by the French.

Examining these data more systematically, Directors-General typically occupy their posts longer than Commissioners. They serve in their respective positions for an average of 2.29 Commission terms, while Commissioners stay in office for an average of 1.67 Commission terms. Other than in the College of Commissioners, where old and new member states have an equal voice today, even since 2004 these posts have been dominated by the old member states in terms of their national composition. All of the 44 persons having served as Director-General under the first Barroso Commission came from EU-15 member states. Bearing in mind the bias resulting from our descriptive longitudinal analysis, 128 of the total 176 Directors-General who served from 1958 to 2010 were nationals from the Community's founding states or from the United Kingdom.

In line with Figure 4.5, we find DGs that have mostly been led by Directors-General from one member state (DGs AGRI, ECFIN, COMP) and DGs with changing nationalities at the administrative helm (DGs ENTR, REGIO, or ELARG). With respect to Directors-General, national strongholds are DGs AGRI, BUDG, and the SG for France; DGs COMP, DEV, and RELEX for Germany; DG ECFIN for Italy; and DG EMPL for Belgium. Given that some of

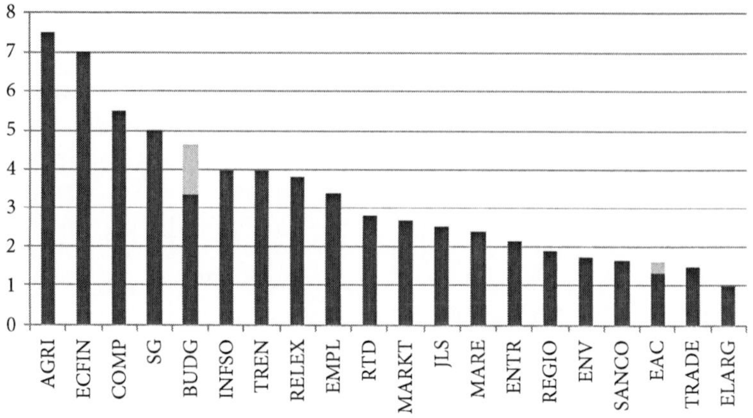

Fig. 4.5. National homogeneity of Directors-General by DG, 1958–2010

Source: Authors' compilation. In the cases of DGs BUDG and EAC, we could not ascertain the nationality of all the Directors-General: the potential deviance is marked by the areas in light grey.

these are portfolios have existed since the founding days—for example DGs AGRI, COMP, and ECFIN—the figures are remarkable. DG AGRI, for example, has been headed for about 45 years by French Directors-General.

Comparing national portfolios at Directors-General level with the Commissioner level, we mostly observe deviations with respect to the national focuses. This could have implications for differences in positions between the political and administrative level of a DG and thus was carefully considered as an explanatory factor in the case studies presented in the following chapters. In any case, it already anticipates the complexity involved in the identification of influencing factors on position formation between DGs in the EU Commission.

4.5 PROFESSIONAL BACKGROUND

Indices and assessments of the politicization of administrations vary substantially (Peters and Pierre 2004; Schnapp 2004; Bauer and Ege 2012). Guided by our interest in understanding position formation in the EU Commission, we opt for a view that combines a power logic and a legitimacy logic of politicization. In a first step, Commissioners who served between 1958 and 2010 were grouped according to their former professions. In a second step, we built two indices of politicization for each Commission and portfolio, respectively (for details of index construction see Appendix A2).

Our first index measures political power and assigns a numerical value to each position, as defined by Druckman and Warwick (2005) and by Druckman and Roberts (2008) and extended by Döring (2007, 2013).[8] Our second index measures how strongly a Commissioner relied on democratic legitimacy in his former career and differentiates between "democratic" and "technocratic" credentials on the part of persons who have served in the Commission. Drawing on

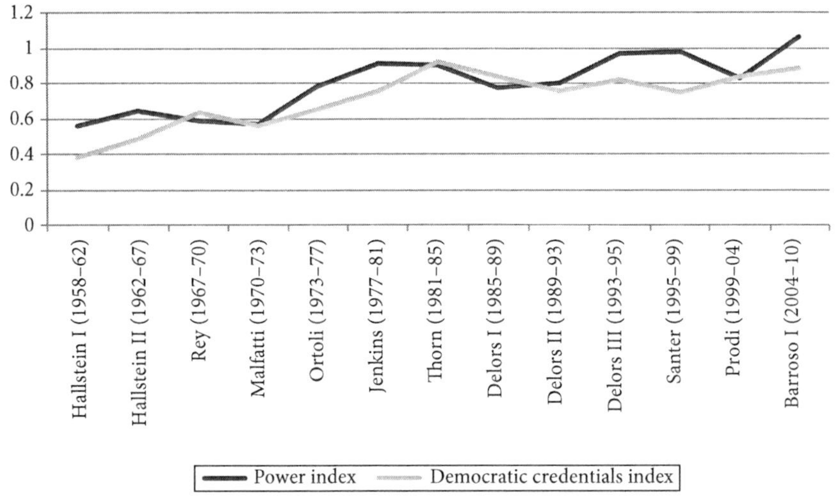

Fig. 4.6. Indices for power and democratic credentials in the Commissioners' professional backgrounds over Commission terms

Source: Authors' compilation based on Schnapp (2004), Druckman and Warwick (2005), Döring (2007, 2013), and Druckman and Roberts (2008).

Schnapp (2004), we assign a positive value of 1 to "political" positions, understood as those offices that are filled and legitimized by democratic elections, and a value of 0 to all "technocratic" posts that do not fulfill this criterion. Figure 4.6 shows the composition of the individual Commissions on both indices.

Our analysis shows the growing importance of politics (i.e. governmental and political positions) as Commissioners' former field of activity over time. An increase in former partisan posts is in congruence with the observation already made about an increasingly party-political College of Commissioners. What is more, our database reveals a trend towards higher previous positions (e.g. Prime Ministers) within this group. Evidently, Europe has gained in importance both for individual careers and for national governments who are willing to send highly qualified (party-political) personnel to the European level. This is in line with earlier findings by Döring (2007) and Wonka (2007).

Providing a nuanced view on different categories of non-political prior positions, our data reveal that other party-political positions (National Prime Minister, National Minister, Regional Government, Parliamentarian, or Party Leader) are also increasing, to the detriment of former administrators and especially diplomats, who accounted for roughly one-third of the College in the early decades.[9] There are also fewer academics today than in the early decades of the Commission. A possible explanation is that, as opposed to the early days, when European politics were perceived as some kind of external affair, the increasing transfer of competence has heightened the understanding that decisions taken in Brussels affect many "national" policies—hence staff should not be limited to diplomats trained in the "external" view. In almost all portfolios, in fact, decisions are political in the sense that they have distributive outcomes. Therefore here, as

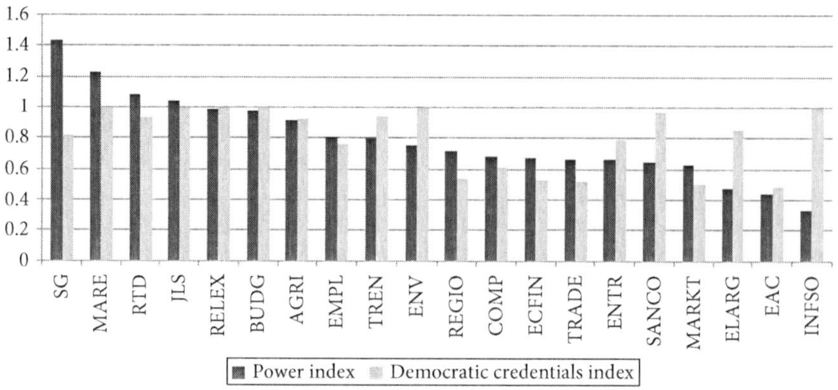

Fig. 4.7. Indices for power and democratic credentials in the Commissioners' professional backgrounds over DGs (1958–2010 averages)

Source: Authors' compilation based on Schnapp (2004), Druckman and Warwick (2005), Döring (2007, 2013), and Druckman and Roberts (2008).

well, a politicization of the EU Commission's leadership goes hand in hand with a politicization of European decision-making.

The figures show that the indices are analytically closely related and correlate strongly (Figures 4.6 and 4.7). Thus, the evolution of both indices over time clearly supports views that the Commission is being increasingly politicized as regards the professional background of its personnel. While the Secretariat General and DGs that deal with traditional areas of state sovereignty such as foreign policy, and justice, freedom and security (RELEX, JLS) appear to be led by particularly "powerful" personnel, the opposite is true for "soft" policy fields such as education and culture (EAC), information and media (INFSO), and DG ELARG. Regarding the democratic credentials index, the differences are less pronounced. No DG has an average value under 0.4—meaning that each DG was led by a democratically experienced individual at least 40 percent of the time it has been in existence—thus confirming the trend towards an increasingly politicized Commission. All in all, the tendencies of the indices overlap. The reason is that most positions that have been encoded as "powerful" are political positions that have been filled and legitimized by democratic elections. The most striking outliers—such as DGs SANCO and INFSO—can be explained by the fact that these are relatively "young" DGs where only a few people could be appointed as Commissioners.

4.6 CONCLUSION

We argued that as soon as one abstains from the null hypothesis defining the European Commission as a neutral, technocratic clearing house, the personal characteristics of the Commission's administrative and political leadership, their evolution over time, and their link to the Commission's administrative structure should be given greater relevance. Variation in these characteristics might indeed provide some of the answer to our initial puzzle as to why the Commission produces sometimes innovative, sometimes controversial, and sometimes inconsistent policies.

The empirical view on the historical development of the Commission's organizational make-up suggests that this body is indeed an evolving institution (Olsen 2010) whose central administrative structure of policy DGs has changed significantly over time. Rather than being an insulated monolith, the Commission's organization has clearly responded to a number of internal and external needs. Functional differentiation—and with it the likelihood of different perspectives clashing in individual position formation processes—has increased. Whether one assumes that the Commission operates in line with a technocratic or a competence-seeking type of agency, the consistency of its policy output still increasingly depends on internal coordination.

What is more, the historical overview of personal characteristics also indicates a likelihood that Commission agency of the policy-seeking type will strengthen in the future. We found strong support for the politicization thesis put forward in the contemporary literature: Over time, the Commission's top leadership has become increasingly partisan and has progressively been recruited from the sphere of politics rather than from the administrative, diplomatic, and academic backgrounds seen in the past. The College of Commissioners has also grown more politicized in that it has fewer independent and more partisan Commissioners.

Again, this exacerbates the potential for inconsistencies in the policies proposed by Europe's central agenda-setter because there is no clear pattern of it becoming either more conservative or more social-democratic over time. In fact, we find that functional differentiation often coincides with partisan cleavages. In agreement with existing policy and administrative studies, our findings imply that the DGs with more interventionist policy mandates are more frequently headed by Commissioners adhering to a social-democratic party family. DGs with a largely economic outlook, by contrast, tend to be headed by Commissioners from liberal or conservative party families.

Another source of inconsistency in the policy agenda drafted by the Commission might be varying national demands. Regarding nationality, interestingly, most countries tend to maintain a particular focus on specific issue areas when it comes to the Commission's internal make-up. Thus, there is systematic evidence for the claimed existence of national flags inside the Commission, although this is far more noticeable at administrative leadership level and often differs from the political level.

In addition to other factors, therefore, the following chapters on individual position-formation processes in the Commission's day-to-day policy-making will systematically consider whether and how variations in organizational structure and the corresponding personal characteristics of the internal leadership matter for power and conflict over policy positions inside the European Commission.

NOTES

1. The database contains information on Commissioners' and Directors'-General nationality and on Commissioners' party affiliation and pan-European party attachment, positions held in the Commission, dates of entry and departure, prior and successive career positions, dates of birth and gender. In addition, the information on the evolution of the Commission as an organization contains the number of Directorates and the number of Units, as well as the number of A-level bureaucrats where comparable data are available. The full dataset is available at <http://www.wzb.eu/en/node/19782> (last accessed: December 9, 2013).
2. In a principal–agent relationship, the agent is authorized to act in pursuance of the principal's interests, and in the case of asymmetrical information, the agent is endowed with substantial discretion to do so (Kiewiet and McCubbins 1991: 5; Shepsle and Bonchek 1997). With regard to parliamentary politics at national level, Strøm et al. (2003) argue that voters delegate via elected representatives to chief executives and civil servants (also Bergman et al. 2000). In the EU, however, the Commission lacks a direct delegation chain to the people and party politics instead take effect through links with national governments.
3. Here we are particularly grateful to Holger Döring and Fabio Franchino who generously shared their data.
4. Every month affected is assigned equal value. Thus, a Commissioner who served from January 1, 2009, to February 2, 2009, is assigned two months, as is a Commissioner who served from January 31, 2009, to February 1, 2009.
5. In the interest of readability, the sectoral perspective on Commission members' party-political orientation only contrasts social-democratic with conservative parties. The "others" category contains all other parties, with liberals and independents being most strongly represented. Commission presidents are listed under SG (Secretariat General) because they do not have a specific portfolio. Note that the values for DGs INFSO and MARE have to be considered particularly carefully because they are based on one (DG INFSO: Reding) or two people (DG MARE: Cardoso e Cunha and Borg) only.
6. Note, however, that he finds a Commissioner's (supranational or national) experience in the relevant portfolios to be the dominant explanation for portfolio assignment.
7. Note that the relative ascendancy of long-standing EU member states in several DGs is not only a matter of preference or *flag*, but also of EU membership duration. Founding members are more likely to have dominated simply because newer members were not yet present.
8. Based on expert surveys in 28 European countries, these authors developed a ranking of portfolio salience in European parliamentary democracies. We added Junior Ministers/ Secretaries of State and Parliamentarians, as well as new scores for a number of positions that had not been considered in detail in existing works (see Appendix A2 for details).
9. Recent Eastern enlargement is said to have produced a more "technocratic" Commission (Peterson 2008: 765). With a view to the College, we found that enlargement rendered College members somewhat more technocratic, but not substantially so.

5

Intersection of Social and Common Market Policies

Dealing with one of the three chosen policy areas at a time, this and the following two chapters will summarize the 48 individual case histories in accordance with the process-tracing design we developed in Chapter 3. While systematically considering the most relevant factors behind internal position formation and interaction, as derived from the analytical framework in Chapter 2, the case studies will also present the idiosyncrasies and particular logics of each process in as much detail as possible. This makes our findings accecssible for readers interested in particular Commission policies, and also serves to render reproducible the more inductive conclusions in the later parts of the book.

5.1 INTRODUCING THE POLICY AREA

This first case study chapter focuses on internal drafting processes at the intersection of common market and social policies. These two policy fields, despite their very different histories and their very distinct regulatory approaches, are intricately interwoven at the EU level. Unlike classical national welfare-state policies, which are based on the distribution of financial resources and have been essential to state-building, the treaty founding the EU included few explicit social policy provisions. The dominant philosophy was that welfare would be provided through economic growth stemming from the liberalization of the common market (Leibfried and Pierson 1995). There were two major exceptions, however: the coordination of the member states' social security systems was considered a precondition for the free circulation of people (Art. 352 TFEU/308 TEU); and the principle of equal pay for male and female workers was introduced to prevent competitive disadvantages for countries with higher standards (Art. 157 TFEU/141 TEU, originally Art. 119). In the following decades, more and more competences were transferred to the EU, broadening the areas of EU social policy and allowing increasing numbers of decisions to be taken under a qualified majority (Falkner 1998: 56–77). This trend has continued in the Amsterdam Treaty, which contained, inter alia, a new anti-discrimination Art. 13 TEU (Art. 19 TFEU). Particularly under the Delors presidency of the Commission, and as a consequence of newly transferred social policy competences, increasing numbers of secondary social policy acts were adopted (Ross 1995), resulting in a *social acquis* of about 200 acts today. Legislation is quantitatively most important in the area of occupational health and safety, followed by general working conditions, such as working time regulation and equal treatment policies (Falkner et al. 2005: 49). And while social policy *acquis* "has quite a . . . history of being interventionist" (COM86:181), some of the classical national social policy areas to remain explicitly excluded from harmonization in the EU treaties are those of pay and the right of association, the right to strike, and the right to impose lock-outs. Spending policies—the classical instrument of social policy at national level—are limited and appear only in the context of the Union's cohesion and structural policies in Art. 159 TEU (Art. 175 TFEU).

Common market policy, by contrast, was able to draw on a strong treaty base from the outset. Regulatory initiatives concerning the common market far outnumber social policy initiatives (Young 2010: 110), particularly since the ambitious 1992 white paper on "Completing the Internal Market" (Egan, forthcoming). The most important treaty bases for our study concern mutual recognition of diplomas, certificates, and other evidence of formal qualifications for the self-employed (Art. 47 TEU/53 TFEU); the free movement of services in the internal market (Art. 55 TEU/62 TFEU); and the so-called "catch all Article" 95 TEU (Art. 114 TFEU), which provides EU rules that regard the establishment and functioning of the internal market. Today the common market *acquis* covers a broad range of issues, including the regulation of professions and services, company law and corporate governance, public procurement, intellectual and industrial property, and postal services. Built around the four freedoms, the regulatory impetus of common market policy is liberalization, in particular by means of a reduction of barriers to trade in commodities, services, and capital. Where market efficiency is sought through regulation, minimum harmonization is often combined with control of standards in the home country. Once common standards have been agreed, free operation throughout the market is allowed (e.g. Young 2010: 112–13). Regulations aimed at greater market efficiency on these bases will invariably touch on and often clash with social regulation. This is particularly the case where the social regulation seeks not only to correct market failures but also to countervail market forces so as to reach "outcomes different to and better [more just, fair, equal or socially cohesive, MH] than those produced by efficiently operating markets" (Windholz and Hodge 2013: 4).

Despite these differing regulatory points of departure, EU common market and social policies are intricately interwoven. First, market developments have driven social policy advances, for instance where the free circulation of labor required active EU coordination of national security systems (Leibfried and Pierson 1995; see Chapter 5.4.3). Second, and more recently, the other side of the argument has become more visible: the realization of the common market has led to the dismantling of national welfare states (Leibfried 2010). Finally, and related to the latter development, the intersection of common market and social policies is relevant where the extant EU social policy *acquis* collides with or is undermined by EU common market regulation, which is a perspective that is at the forefront of discussions on the directive on the liberalization of services vis-à-vis the directive on posting of workers (cf. Chapter 5.4.2). So far it remains unclear whether interaction between departments within the EU Commission produces mainly market-liberalizing policies or whether a social dimension of the EU exists in its own right. Table 5.1 details the cases considered in this chapter at the intersection of social and common market policies.

Table 5.1. Sample of cases at the intersection of social and common market policies

Proposal number	Contents	Lead DG	Type of instrument	Treaty base (TEU)	Commission adoption date	Commission adoption procedure	Council procedure	Sub-group
COM[1999]565	Equal Treatment Employment Framework	EMPL	Directive	Art. 13	Nov. 25, 1999	Oral	Unanimity	Individual rights and entitlements
COM[1999]566	Equal Treatment Race Equality	EMPL	Directive	Art. 13	Nov. 24, 1999	Oral	Unanimity	Individual rights and entitlements
COM[2000]275	Public Supply Contracts	MARKT	Directive	Art. 95, 47(2), 55	May 10, 2000	Oral	QMV	Right of establishment and services
COM[2000]276	Public Supply Contracts in water, energy and transport sectors	MARKT	Directive	Art. 95, 47(2), 55	May 10, 2000	Oral	QMV	Right of establishment and services
COM[2000]511	Insurance Mediation	MARKT	Directive	Art. 47(2), 55	Sep. 20, 2000	Written	QMV	Right of establishment and services
COM[2001]213	Supervision of Financial Firms	MARKT	Directive	Art. 47(2)	Apr. 24, 2001	Written	QMV	Right of establishment and services
COM[2001]449	Common Procurement Vocabulary	MARKT	Regulation	Art. 95, 47(2), 55	Aug. 3, 2001	Written	QMV	Right of establishment and services
COM[2002]119	Recognition of Professional Qualifications	MARKT	Directive	Art. 40, 47(1 & 2), 55	Mar. 7, 2002	Written	QMV	Free movement of people and services
COM[2003]657	Gender Discrimination in Services	EMPL	Directive	Art. 13	Nov. 5, 2003	Oral	Unanimity	Individual rights and entitlements
COM[2004]2	Services in the Internal Market	MARKT	Directive	Art. 47(2), 55, 71, 80(2)	Jan. 13, 2004	Oral	QMV	Free movement of people and services
COM[2004]273	Reinsurance	MARKT	Directive	Art. 47(2), 55	Apr. 21, 2004	Written	QMV	Right of establishment and services

(continued)

Table 5.1. Continued

Proposal number	Contents	Lead DG	Type of instrument	Treaty base (TEU)	Commission adoption date	Commission adoption procedure	Council procedure	Sub-group
COM[2004]279	Recast Equal Opportunities for Men and Women	EMPL	Directive	Art 141(3)	Apr. 21, 2004	Written	QMV	Individual rights and entitlements
COM[2006]16	Coordination of Social-Security Systems	EMPL	Regulation	Art. 42, 308	Jan. 31, 2006	Written	Unanimity	Free movement of people and services
COM[2006]91	European Globalization Adjustment Fund	EMPL	Regulation	Art. 159	Mar. 2, 2006	Oral	QMV	Individual rights and entitlements
COM[2008]414	Cross-border Healthcare	SANCO	Directive	Art. 95	.Jul. 2, 2008	Oral	QMV	Free movement of people and services
COM[2008]426	Equal Treatment General Framework	EMPL	Directive	Art. 13	Jul. 2, 2008	Oral	Unanimity	Individual rights and entitlements

DG EMPL and DG MARKT are the two central DGs involved in these policy areas. They both belong to the Commission's administrative set-up since the Union's founding days and their organizational boundaries have remained fairly stable during the period covered in this book (Chapter 4).

Both DGs are among the larger portfolios, but while DG MARKT is often seen as one of the prestigious powerhouses in the Commission, DG EMPL has lost much of its standing inside and outside the Commission in recent years. DG MARKT has strong links with industry and other stakeholders that traditionally assist the DG in highly technical issue areas. Historically, this portfolio has been headed mostly by liberal and independent Commissioners (Chapter 4). During our investigation period, Commissioners Bolkestein (Netherlands, Liberal) and McCreevy (Ireland, Liberal) led DG MARKT together with Directors-General Mogg (until 2002, UK), Schaub (2002–04, Germany), and Holmquist (since 2004, Sweden). DG EMPL, by contrast, "is a huge DG, it has a huge agenda, it has quite a reasonably good history of being interventionist" (COM86:181). It has been characterized as the hub of a corporatist policy community that traditionally gave much weight to social partner involvement (Falkner 1998), but increasingly also to NGOs representing other societal interests. Since 1999, DG EMPL has been headed by Commissioner Diamantopoulou (Greece, Socialist) and Director-General Quintin (France) and then by Commissioner Spidla (Czech Republic, Socialist) and Director-General Van der Pas (Germany) under Barroso's presidency from 2004. Besides DGs MARKT and EMPL, DG ENTR is also relevant as the body defending the other side of the labor-capital relationship. Other DGs concerned by the policies examined in this chapter are DG SANCO, whose consumer-oriented perspective resonates with welfare considerations, and portfolios involved through their sectoral interests such as DG TREN (social aspects of transport and energy for services) and EAC (educational issues for workers and qualification).

The proposals studied here are mainly directives, but three regulations will also be examined. The distribution of cases over Commission terms shows a bias to the Prodi Commission (12 cases, against 4 cases under the Barroso Commission), reflecting a trend towards adopting less new binding law (Kurpas et al. 2008: 19). The cases are roughly equally distributed between oral and written procedures in the College (9 and 7 cases, respectively) and can be grouped into three policy subfields. The proposals on *individual rights and entitlements* (6 cases) cover almost all the original and binding social policy legislation in the period studied, mainly consisting of anti-discrimination initiatives. Next, under the heading *right of establishment and provision of services*, six acts implement entrepreneurial freedoms to operate in the common market, which often collide with other political aims such as justice, equality, and social cohesion. The acts concerned regard financial services (which increasingly impact on the bases for many welfare products) and public procurement policies regulating the role of the state as an economic operator. In the third sub-group, *free movement of people and services*, all four acts deal with the question of how the market freedoms affect national welfare solutions when services are provided or consumed across borders.

With respect to decision rules in the Council, the sample reveals a striking difference between proposals concerning the responsible lead department and the legal basis applied. Where DG EMPL was the lead (7 cases) and applied social policy articles, unanimity was required in all but two cases. By contrast, the processes led by DG MARKT (8 cases) and the Cross-border Healthcare Directive drafted by DG SANCO came under qualified majority—the less demanding inter-institutional decision-making rule. This situation mirrors the differences described above between these two policy areas in the EU integration process and the asymmetrical treaty bases they draw on. However, as will become evident in the following discussion as the individual position formation processes are traced along the lines set out in Chapter 3, the internal Commission actors have a good deal of leeway in tilting regulation towards either market liberalization or intervention in all three sub-fields.

5.2 INDIVIDUAL RIGHTS AND ENTITLEMENTS: ANTI-DISCRIMINATION AND SPENDING POLICIES

Gender equality had been on the EU's legislative agenda since the 1970s (Mazey 1995: 598). DG EMPL has proactively and successfully generated and shaped EU equal-treatment law into one of the "success stories" and "one of the central pillars of EU social policy" (Caporaso and Jupille 2001: 21; for a quantitative analysis, cf. Falkner et al. 2005: 48–9). Most notably, the Amsterdam Treaty introduced a new general anti-discrimination Art. 13 TEU. Thus, while EU equal-treatment policies originated in employment issues, during our investigation period they were increasingly framed as a fundamental right of all citizens. Similarly, DG EMPL's experience with spending policies dates back to the origins of the integration process. Similar to other cohesion instruments (e.g. managed by DGs AGRI and REGIO), they distribute EU money indirectly via national governments. The European Globalisation Adjustment Fund (EGF), however, which was proposed in 2006 and operates with a budget of up to €500 million a year, newly establishes a truly redistributive instrument directly providing individual entitlements. Tables 5.2 and 5.3 detail proposal and process characteristics relating to position formation and interaction on individual rights and entitlements.

Conceived as less abstract issues that address individuals directly, the proposals discussed here attracted considerable public attention. The related position-formation processes reveal sensitivity to national and wider public concerns, particularly after the "No" in the 2005 referenda on the European Constitution had signaled the end of the permissive consensus (Hooghe and Marks 2009). Reflecting their political dimension, these drafting processes involved not only the Commission's administrative, but also its political level. Particularly in the area of equal treatment, organized interests played an important role, too.

5.2.1 Employment Equality Framework and Race Equality

The first two cases were aimed at extending existing principles of equal treatment regarding gender equality to new areas of application and addressees by

Table 5.2. Position formation on individual rights and entitlements

Proposal number	Contents	No. of key provisions	Main line of proposal (content)	Uncertainty	Salience	Origin (hierarchical level)	Process duration (months)	External consultation	Main position-formation factors
COM[1999]565	Equal Treatment Employment Framework	8	Equal treatment in employment on new discrimination grounds	Yes	Yes	Administrative	29	Specific	- Extant *acquis* - Anticipation of Council majority - Individuals' influence - Organized interests
COM[1999]566	Equal Treatment Race Equality	7	Race equality in new areas (including services)	Yes	Yes	Administrative	29	Specific	- Extant *acquis* - Organized interests - Individuals' influence - Anticipation of Council majority - National positions
COM[2003]657	Gender Discrimination in Services	7	Equal treatment of sexes in new areas (including services/insurance)	No	Yes	Political	12	Specific	- Extant *acquis* - Anticipation of Council majority - Individuals' influence
COM[2004]279	Recast Equal Opportunities for Men and Women	10	Consolidation of equal-pay *acquis*	No	No	Administrative	13	Public	- Extant *acquis* - ECJ jurisprudence - Experts
COM[2006]91	European Globalisation Adjustment Fund	5	Support for redundant workers affected by trade adjustment	Yes	Yes	Political	7	No	- Anticipation of Council majority - International policy transfer - Extant *acquis*
COM[2008]426	Equal Treatment General Framework	8	Equal treatment in new areas (including services) and on new discrimination grounds	No	Yes	Political	15	Public	- Extant *acquis* - Anticipation of Council and EP majorities - Council anticipation

Table 5.3. Interaction on individual rights and entitlements

Proposal number	Contents	Deviating DGs	Informal interaction	Position-based conflict	Process-based conflict	Main line of conflict	Most powerful DG	Main power resources
COM[1999]565	Equal Treatment Employment Framework	ENTR ECFIN ELARG	Medium	3	1	Inclusion of age and disability as expensive grounds	EMPL	- Lead department - Supranational competence - Support from organized interests - Entrepreneurship
COM[1999]566	Equal Treatment Race Equality	ENTR REGIO MARKT EAC SG SJ	Medium	3	1	Coverage of services and private contracts	EMPL	- Lead department - Supranational competence - Entrepreneurship
COM[2003]657	Gender Discrimination in Services	MARKT COMP EAC ELARG SG TRADE	Intense	3	2	Coverage of services and private contracts	EMPL	- Lead department - Entrepreneurship - Support from SG - Public legitimacy - Proximity to EP majority
COM[2004]279	Recast Equal Opportunities for Men and Women	SJ SG MARKT	Medium	2	1	Instruments formed as recast and extension to occupational social security schemes	EMPL	- Lead department
COM[2006]91	European Globalisation Adjustment Fund	BUDG REGIO ENTR ECFIN SJ	Intense	3	1	Workers as target rather than companies, delineation from ESF, strictness of intervention criteria	EMPL	- Support from SG - Lead department - Public legitimacy
COM[2008]426	Equal Treatment General Framework	ENTR MARKT SG TRADE	Intense	3	2	Coverage of private sphere, inclusion of disability and insurance	EMPL	- Support from SG - Proximity to Council and EP - Lead department - Stakeholder support - Supranational competence

employing the new Treaty Art. 13 (TEU) on anti-discrimination.[1] According to the proposal for a general framework for equal treatment in employment and occupation (Employment Equality Framework, COM[1999]565), employers have to ensure that they do not discriminate on the basis of a person's religion or beliefs, disability, age, or sexual orientation. This applies from recruitment to the termination of an employment contract, including promotion, training, and employment conditions. For persons with disabilities, equal treatment means providing specific accommodation unless this creates "undue hardship" (Art. 2.4 of the proposal). The second proposal for a directive on equal treatment between persons irrespective of racial or ethnic origin (Race Equality, COM [1999]566) is limited to race as a ground for discrimination, but embraces a much broader area of application. Extending substantially beyond employment, the proposed directive also covers the area of social protection, including health-care and social advantages, as well as goods and services available to the public—notably housing, culture, and education.

The real force of the proposed acts lies in a number of cross-cutting provisions that define core concepts underpinning the principle of equal treatment and had been a response to evolving ECJ jurisprudence. Case law had led to legal uncertainty about the actually applicability of the equal-treatment principle when it came to questions such as how to improve employment opportunities for women without putting men at an unfair disadvantage (*Kalanke* C-450/93, AE October 17, 1995, May 14, 1996) and under which conditions the burden of proof would shift to the employer (C-109/88 *Danfoss*, C-127/92 *Enderby*, C-400/93 *Royal Copenhagen*, cf. AE September 13, 1996). Against this background, the proposed directives clarify the notions of positive action and the transfer of the burden of proof to the employer (cf. Alter and Vargas 2000). Moreover, both acts explicitly define harassment, as well as direct discrimination (less favorable treatment) and indirect discrimination (the adverse effect of an apparently neutral provision or practice) (cf. IA SEC[2004] 482: 6 and Bell 2002: 385). A second group of cross-cutting provisions targets enforcement and goes much further in prescribing to member states not only what rights to guarantee but also *how* to do so: Effective, proportionate, and dissuasive sanctions have to be put in place, as well as effective judicial and administrative procedures for remedying that can now also be invoked by associations or organizations (*locus standi*[2]). In sum, to ensure the application of individual rights, the proposed directives apply existing equal-treatment principles to a much broader area and make recourse to a substantial degree of institutional embedding. For the Commission, and particularly for DG EMPL, the acts mark the change from considering equal treatment only in terms of labor law to its consideration as a more general issue of individuals' fundamental rights. Strategically, the proposals gave life to the new Treaty article and set the scene for later equal-treatment initiatives.

The two drafting processes were closely intertwined in DG EMPL and were initiated within a wider policy context that was beneficial to equal-treatment legislation. Equal chances in labor-market access had become an important discourse, with the European Employment Strategy (EES, 1997) calling for a 70 percent overall employment rate by 2010—a significant challenge in the light of the low employment rates among the older workforce (Hartlapp 2012). In December 1995, the Commission published a Communication on racism, xenophobia, and anti-Semitism (COM[95]653final). In 1997, a broad range of activities had made up the European Year against Racism, an instrument typically followed at the time by legal projects and which had also created "a race-awareness attitude" (COM39:176) in the public and among governments. In addition, regular newspaper coverage signaled to the drafting officials that the discrimination issue had a "wider public profile," which was deemed beneficial for regulation (COM21:159).

Once it had become clear that the Amsterdam Treaty would contain a new Art. 13 TEU on anti-discrimination, drafting began in 1997. The wish to make use of the new article was visible at all levels in the Commission (COM39:112). Officials in DG EMPL's unit for Labour Law, Fundamental Social Rights and Anti-discrimination took the lead and wanted to show that "we are not doing this just because people cross borders, but because it is a fundamental part of EU membership that countries protect the rights of their citizens and others from discrimination" (COM21:51). In 1998, Commission President Santer provided his political support when he recalled his "personal commitment to the promotion of equality between men and women" and stressed that "[e]quality is the future . . . , a fundamental ambition to which the Commission gives its full support and which it hopes to pursue without respite" (cited in: AE 1998, also COM38:145, COM39:72, COM21:51). When Social Affairs Commissioner Diamantopoulou took over in 1999 with the incoming Prodi Commission, she continued to invest considerable energy in the issue, actively promoting the cause internally, at public events and in the media (cf. *FT*, November 3, 4, 10, 24, 1999, AE, June 6, 2000). Resources were invested at the administrative level to boost expertise in the drafting unit: a new official was recruited from the UK—one of the countries with particularly advanced legislation in the area (COM21:12).

Extremely eager to put the new article into practice, DG EMPL strove for the broadest possible coverage of discrimination issues (COM39:132). This entailed a conscious choice to expand the scope of application of existing principles in two different directions: discrimination grounds and discrimination areas (as visible, respectively, in acts COM[1999]565 and COM[1999]566). As one DG EMPL official reflected: "There were plenty of different possibilities. . . . we choose one, but we could have obviously taken another decision. We could have decided to come only with one directive, only the race and maybe not covering these areas" (COM39:132). The two acts were publicly announced towards the end of 1998 (COM21:48, COM39:68) and finally adopted in the College at the end of November 1999.

Whereas the member states had welcomed the new Treaty article, they were reluctant about the EU Commission deciding on concrete regulatory measures. Powerful governments such as those of Germany and the UK, especially, would have preferred the new article to be directly applicable rather than adopting secondary legislation (*FT*, November 24, 1999). Given that the Treaty article demanded a unanimous member-state position and the proposals were therefore considered to be "sensitive," DG EMPL applied a "very pragmatic and realistic [drafting] approach" (COM39:132). In order to curb opposition in the Council, member-state representatives were given the opportunity in expert committees to explain to DG EMPL "why this [national] legislation existed or not, what was behind it, how public opinion could react" (COM39:168). Vice versa, the DG also used these committees as an arena to explain its "rationale" (COM39:172) for proposing the acts.

In addition, the influence of national interests via nationally flagged portfolios inside the Commission can be directly identified in the case of the Employment Framework proposal. Governments were particularly unenthusiastic about regulation of equal treatment on age and disability, given the associated high implementation costs for the member states (COM151, COM39:80). The German Commissioner Verheugen (DG ELARG)—despite being a social democrat—took a critical stance on the proposal because his home country would be particularly strongly affected by the directive's implementation costs (*FT*, November 24, 1999). The Spanish Commissioner Solbes (DG ECFIN) was "not too enthusiastic either" (COM151) about the inclusion of age discrimination. Besides national interests, his critical stance is likely to have also been related to active lobbying by the Ford motor company, which has large automobile plants in Spain. When Ford opened its Spanish plants, the workers had all been recruited from the same age cohort. Now the company saw a need for a more age diversified workforce and planned redundancies for reasons of age—a strategy that would be constrained by the directive (COM151).

Likewise, DG ENTR, voicing its stakeholders' concerns, considered legislation with "a potential impact especially on SMEs" (COM151) to be a burden for business. Advocacy by other organized interests, however, contested this view. Untypically for a social policy initiative, the Commission did not grant privileged access to social-partner organizations, which had by and large been conservative on equal-treatment policies and showed little inclination to shift the anti-discrimination issue from labor law in the direction of an individual fundamental right (COM21:57, Hartlapp 2012). Consequently, they were "marginalized" (Bell 2002: 394) in the drafting process, while civil-society organizations were granted both a voice and influence in "a constant conversation" (COM151, also COM152). DG EMPL strategically built up alliances with NGOs concerned with equal-treatment issues and "shifted them to be interested in rights questions" (COM21:57). The DG even encouraged existing national organizations to come together under one umbrella and provided financial support to this end (COM152). The strategy paid off when "very powerful" NGOs (COM39:52, also COM21:48) publicly pushed for the application of individual rights and inspired legal provisions on "disability [which] requires not just not discriminating but actually making positive steps—that was the big new element" (COM19:33, also COM39:152).

With the race equality proposal, DG EMPL sought to cover areas of application that were not touched on by the extant equal-treatment *acquis*. In this case, too, the unanimity requirement in Council was the reference point for the lead DG's legal approach: it had strategically singled out race as the ground for discrimination on which member states showed a willingness to go further compared to other grounds (COM21:48, COM39:52). In fact, the 1997 European Year against Racism had provided actors inside the drafting unit with a platform to test member-state dispositions for EU actions. The DG recognized that "nobody would be going to stand up and say: Europe should not have anything to do with the fight against racism" (COM151). DG EMPL proceeded with collecting ideas and information about the *de facto* situation in member states and on countries with advanced legislation (USA, UK, Ireland, Canada, and South Africa,

COM39:32, COM21:60). The concrete proposal was, however, substantially influenced by an innovative draft law produced by the NGO network *Starting Line*.[3] This document took the form of a complete legal instrument, including much-welcomed technical information on the situation in the different member states, and overall substantially influenced the Commission's proposal (Tyson 2001: 200). For DG EMPL, furthermore, this text had the advantage that it had the support of the network of NGOs.

The motivation to legislate on the basis of a fresh supranational competence carried over into the interaction process, where it cushioned differences in positions with a view to achieving a proposal that had "real possibilities to be adopted" in the inter-institutional process (COM39:136). Nonetheless, intensive, though not "over exaggerated, or complicated" (COM39:140) interaction between portfolios with persistently different views took place during the inter-service consultation, including discussions "particularly at the very final stages" (COM151). Officials from the drafting unit and the Diamantopoulou cabinet "spent a lot of time going round to other cabinets" (COM151), proactively approached "all the different Chef de Cabs who were difficult" and "tried to answer the questions," investing much individual effort and showing their conviction for the cause (COM39:80). However, controversies remained, and in a first College meeting on November 3, 2003, a decision was postponed. This was a very unusual development and the press reported extensively on the "orientation debate," noting the reservations of some Commissioners, while some member states and many MEPs were "enthusiastic about the proposals" (Smith 1999, also AE November 3, 1999). Surprisingly, only three weeks after the College fiasco, the anti-discrimination package was adopted on November 25, 1999 without further ado (COM21:121). In the meantime, DG EMPL had used its position as lead DG to see "four or five cabinets . . . try[ing] to find a compromise" (COM39:80). Here, discussing a double package rather than a single act allowed DG EMPL to increase the chances that "inevitably [DGs'] attention is drawn to particular aspects and they miss other things which they might otherwise see if there were individual proposals" (COM21:168).

Interaction on the race equality proposal was dominated by the controversial question as to which goods and services should be covered. DG EAC feared coverage of religious schools that by denomination discriminate on the ground of religion (COM21:132) and was in fact accommodated by means of a more flexible formulation that circumvented conflict with the national traditions of religious schools (COM39:92). DG REGIO, in charge of EU policies on housing, "was pretty unhappy about" (COM21:153) DG EMPL's attempt to make the choice of tenants in an apartment block subject to the new equal-treatment rules. Here, too, DG EMPL responded with a compromise (COM21:153). Meanwhile, the Secretariat-General and the SJ did not favor the inclusion of sports initially envisaged by DG EMPL (COM21:153). In all three cases, DG EMPL willingly listened to the others' objections, well aware that supranational competences were too weak to risk conflictual policy-making under unanimity later on in the process and create "tensions between the institutions for nothing" (COM39:136).

On other provisions, DG differences in positions were more persistent and conciliation was "really difficult" (COM39:132), particularly where portfolio interests were aligned with national concerns, such as with DGs ENTR, ELARG, and ECFIN vehemently opposing age and disability coverage in the Employment Framework proposal (COM39:80, 164, COM151). Similarly, on the race equality proposal, DGs ENTR and MARKT were concerned about the costs for industry and business, particularly for SMEs (COM39:94). The fact that DG EMPL's proposals were considered "political" and had created "a lot of emotion" (COM21:168) worked both for and against DG EMPL's position and was now used by Commissioner Diamantopoulou in the last round of negotiations. The "overall political weight" (COM151) of the issue, the general interest in using competences newly transferred to the supranational level and the substantial media interest made it "difficult for one cabinet to block [while] some cabinets were very supportive" (COM151).[4] This raised the pressure on the Commission to adopt a compromise act, and DG EMPL profited enormously from having laid the foundations for support for its position earlier in the drafting process. As lead DG, it had armed itself with reports and "very clear figures." As conceded by one DG EMPL official, "more than [anything else it is] a huge resource sometimes to come with figures and say 'okay we know that this percentage of people are discriminated and we have this percentage of case law'" (COM39:60). This proved particularly helpful for working out a compromise allowing for unequal treatment of age only where objectively and reasonably justified, such as for special working conditions or professional experience. What is more, by funding an umbrella organization of anti-discrimination NGOs, the DG had created a united front that was decisive at this stage of political negotiations to keep opposing interests from publicly contesting the most expensive discrimination grounds, such as age (COM151, COM152). Consequently, the lead DG managed to save a clause on an employer obligation to accommodate disabled people unless—and this exemption can be credited particularly to DGs ENTR and ELARG's objections—this creates undue hardship.

Summing up the processes, a clear political agenda enforced by individual actors who were convinced by the cause and were able to build on extant *acquis* is important in explaining the proposal. To understand why and how national opposition inside the Commission could be overcome, political games are central. They allowed the lead DG to strategically employ the new supranational competences in Art. 13 and also the knowledge and support from organized interests it had constructed and shaped to its benefit earlier during the drafting process.

5.2.2 Gender Discrimination in Services

Having expanded its equal-treatment regulation in the areas of employment and race, the next logical step for DG EMPL was to return to its classical area of gender discrimination. As the most developed area of EU equal-treatment policy, gender had been intentionally kept out of the first Art. 13 TEU directives for fear of regressing behind standards that had already been achieved. However, once the 1999 proposals had been negotiated in Council, in June 2000 the EU's New Social Policy Agenda (COM[2000]379) announced a proposal based on Art. 13 TEU for equal treatment between women and men in the access to and supply of goods and services (Gender Discrimination in Services, COM[2003]657). This proposal covers financial services and banking, leisure facilities such as pubs and clubs—unless designed for one sex only (e.g. saunas)—entertainment and transport. DG EMPL was very certain that positive effects would be achieved by raising the standards "provided against discrimination on [the] ground of sex to the level covered by the Race Directive" (COM21:26) and therefore framed its new proposal on the basis of the extant *acquis*. Moreover, the proposal goes a step further than the enforcement standards stipulated in the earlier directives by prescribing the establishment of one or more bodies to promote, analyze, monitor, and support equal treatment and to encourage non-governmental organizations to assist with implementation.

Political demand for legislation intensified in December 2000 when member states called for an act at the Nice Council. However, inside DG EMPL, the actual preparation of the act was thwarted by a combination of work overload and the question of which unit should be in charge of an issue found at the crossroads between classical gender policy, based on Art. 141 TEU, and the recent change in direction towards fundamental rights, which drew on the new Art. 13 TEU (COM21:18). Drafting started only at the end of 2002, but the process was concentrated and the first ISC took place only half a year later in June 2003. DG EMPL had been able to easily exploit existing structures, thick knowledge, and reporting practices that stemmed from decades of EU policy-making and implementation supervision (COM125:71). Again, the drafting unit drew on external actors "all convinced already of the arguments for further legislation" and "pushing in the direction of more legislation" (COM21:42). Although there was general support, external interests and reports still revealed that the member states were split on the issue and that the default condition for legislation was changing. First, the lead DG used two expert networks on "Employment and Gender Equality" and "Gender Equality, Social Inclusion, Health and Long-Term Care" to test "the ground . . . so you could see that there were some member states who were actively encouraging the Commission to go down this route, while others were either a little more cautious or not convinced that there was really a need" (COM21:39). Second, regulations on gender discrimination had persistently been accompanied by implementation deficits, and this problem was likely to worsen. A Eurobarometer survey commissioned by DG EMPL in 2002 revealed that about one-quarter of the discrimination experienced in the area of goods and services was based on gender (COM[2003]657: 5), a figure that was expected to rise as social security was increasingly privatized across the member states (creating conditions equal to those in the private insurance sector, see the next paragraph).[5] Against this background, DG EMPL's hierarchy urged its service to "deliver" a broad proposal (COM21:30) that would go substantially beyond the legal status quo and comprehensively address equal treatment of the sexes in both access to and supply of goods and services.

The abolition of unequal treatment of men and women in the private insurance sector was the politically most important key provision. Here, actuarial factors are typically employed to calculate differences between men and women in terms of life expectancy, behavior (e.g. car insurance) and consumption (e.g. health insurance). No EU regulation had existed before in this area, although "distinctions were made on [the] ground of sex all the time"(COM21:26). The Commission's approach of deeming it discriminatory to separate women and men into different pools for the calculation of premiums broke with the deeply ingrained practices of the insurance industry (*FT*, May 31, 2003). Not least because of this substantial market intervention, the directive was highly relevant for DG EMPL as a sign that Art. 13 TEU was being consistently applied by following up on the 1999 acts discussed earlier in this chapter.

Commissioner Diamantopoulou, who had a personal background in the Greek Women's Movement, "believed in gender equality and wanted to be able to show that she had done as much for gender equality as she had for race equality at the beginning of her mandate" (COM21:30, also COM125:183). This line was willingly adopted by Director-General Odile Quintin (COM21:33). The two officials justified their joint—and decisively political—commitment on moral grounds. Arguing provocatively on the basis of the Race Equality directive that had just been adopted, Commissioner Diamantopoulou asked whether it would be "acceptable to fix higher life insurance premiums for black people if statistics were to show that their life expectancy is shorter than that of white people?" (AE 2003a) and stressed that "[w]e cannot punish or reward somebody because he or she happens to be born in a particular group, whether race or gender" (cited in: Minder 2003). Ultimately, the objective was to deliberately accept short-term economic costs (mainly for the insurance industry) in order to reach a long-term political goal that would benefit the individual and render European societies more just.

The insurance lobby was shocked (AE, October 4, 2004). In a number of bilateral meetings, representatives of the major European, British, French, and German insurance associations (IA SEC[2003]1213: 23) argued that Commissioner Diamantopoulou would not decrease, but "only increase sexual discrimination—in some cases [of] men, and in others [of] women" (*FT*, 2003). Industry found their cause better presented through DG MARKT, which was "very, very strongly opposed to any intervention at all" and wanted "insurance to be [kept] completely out" (COM21:75). Lining up with this opposition, DGs COMP and TRADE questioned the need for the act at all (COM125:211, *FT*, June 24, 2003, DG COMP's response to CIS-Net consultation no. 6474) and opposed aspects of the proposal as "burdens on business" (COM21:75). German Commissioner Verheugen, heading DG ELARG, was described as "militant against Mrs. Diamantopoulou" (COM125:103). Taking up the same lines of conflict that had already characterized the debate around the race equality directive, and giving voice to the concerns of the strong insurance industry in his home country Germany, Verheugen called for a separation of public and private law that would limit the scope of the directive (COM125:103). The Secretariat-General, fearful of further increasing rather than reducing legal uncertainty, questioned the composition of the act (responses to CIS-Net consultations no. 6474, 13264). Finally, other portfolios contested the inclusion of taxation (DG TAXUD) and education and media (DG EAC). Particularly DG EAC carefully watched the implications for its area, with an eye on potential overlaps with the "TV without Frontiers" directive (89/552/EEC), which was undergoing revision at the time (DG EAC's response to CIS-Net consultation no. 6474).

Given such numerous and deeply entrenched internal differences, it is not surprising that the proposal created much more internal difficulties than the two 1999 acts (COM21:75) and was internally and externally one of—if not the most—controversial social policy acts under the Prodi Commission (COM125:115). Unsurprisingly, the proposal received a negative opinion in the formal ISC (COM21:87) and came close to being buried altogether.[6] Even the *FT* reported publicly on the conflicts inside the Commission, writing that no decision has been taken "on how and whether to proceed" (Burt and Parker 2003, also *FT*, June 11, 2003).

Consequently, DG EMPL pursued a double strategy of fostering a debate that evaluated the issue from a political rather than a technical perspective, at the same time preparing compromises to ensure that the proposal would make it through the College. First, it mobilized actors who would benefit from the proposal, particularly when insurance would be made subject to equal treatment. Using reports and knowledge created during the drafting process, the DG demonstrated that unequal treatment in services was indeed a problem (COM21:105, COM [2003]657), which in turn helped to trigger reactions in the Commission and to spark a public debate (COM125:71). It bears noting that the salience of the proposal exceeds that of any other social policy case in our sample, with DG EMPL actively engaging in the media to make sure that discourse would account for the political benefits. When the *FT* reacted critically to the intended coverage of media and featured the front-page headlines "Media dismay at EU sex bias bill" (Burt and Parker 2003) and "Ambitious move to enshrine 'respect for human dignity' could force up premiums" (Parker 2003), Commissioner Diamantopoulou provokingly responded with her own piece in the same newspaper: "Europe is a long way from a sexism directive" (*FT*, June 27, 2003, COM21:159). Finally, DG EMPL prompted a public hearing in the European Parliament on the controversial issues of insurance and the media in early September and thus proactively "used the EP to make sure that they told [reluctant] Commissioners to create the right environment" (COM21:113). Second, and similarly to the 1999 proposals, officials from the drafting unit and a member from the Diamantopoulou cabinet set forth to meet their counterparts from DGs MARKT, ELARG and other opposing portfolios (COM21:75, 115). Only after most of the details had been cleared up did DG EMPL send the proposal into a second ISC on 24 October 2003—still anticipating that discussion on political questions would continue at College level (COM21:115, COM116:194).

In this debate, Diamantopoulou stressed "political reasons for not accepting gender as an element justifying a differentiation of the treatment of individuals in the access to the supply of goods and services" (Secrétariat Général 2003:21). Nonetheless, DG EMPL still faced "reservations at the College, notably on Article 4" dealing with insurance (AE 2003b), and "hostile reaction from other Commission departments" continued (Burt and Parker 2003, COM21:78). But now DG EMPL had strong political support and was able to push through the technical compromises it had hammered out in the bilateral meetings over the summer. Launched in a context of Treaty reform and upcoming referenda, this decidedly political stance on the desirable quality of European market integration could not be ignored by Commission President Prodi—both in his role as President of the Commission and for personal reasons, since he was a social democrat and "a man of principle" (COM125:55). In the end, political negotiations resulted in a legislative text that contained almost all of DG EMPL's original ideas on regulating anti-discrimination. In the light of the tension between market and social policy outlined above, the proposed act clearly aims at rendering societies more equal, deliberately accepting disadvantages for markets that had worked efficiently for enterprises and service providers.

> We won just because of the politics of it really. That it is difficult politically to make the speech, to stand up and make a speech, to say it is right [that] women should pay more for their health insurance.... And so we knew that once we got to the level of the Cabinet we would be able to win the argument on political grounds. What we have prepared to do was to consider compromises which would come later on, in terms of how you calculate the premiums and what justifications you could have for differences in the treatment (COM21:75, also COM125:55, 147).

The final draft acknowledges DG EAC's concerns about overstepping EU competences by completely excluding education (COM21:132). DG ELARG and its Commissioner Verheugen were presented with a formula that exempts from the proposal transactions that take place in a purely private context—such as letting a room in a private house. Finally, even for financial services, which were the most fiercely debated issue, a compromise was reached. The proposal in principle covers insurance, but moves towards DGs ELARG's and MARKT's position by applying the provision to new contracts only and by allowing member states to apply a longer transition period of up to six years (COM21:75). In this case, however, they have to inform the Commission and provide continuous data collection on the most recent actuarial and statistical figures—ultimately increasing the Commission's discretion in implementation.

Overall, position formation in this case resembles the 1999 acts in substance and process. The individual initiative of Commissioner Diamantopoulou was even more evident and appeared as anathema to national reluctance to extend the extant *acquis* to new areas. Against opposition from other Commission DGs, DG EMPL's strategy of playing a political game of supranational legitimacy and political alliances (particularly with the President) and its advantage of being lead and having related knowledge gave it the edge over the internally opposing portfolios.

5.2.3 Recasting of Equal Opportunities for Men and Women

At the same time, albeit in a largely separate process from their role as clients or consumers, the equal treatment of men and women in matters of employment and occupation (COM[2004]279) was recast. The consolidation of the five original directives (75/117/EEC [equal pay]; 79/7/EEC [social security]; 86/378/EEC, as amended by 96/97/EEC [occupational social security schemes]; 76/207/EEC, as amended by 2002/73/EC [relating to access to employment, vocational training and promotion, and working conditions]; and 97/80/EC, as amended by 98/52/EC [burden of proof]) was considered a technical process with little connection to the ongoing debates on EU anti-discrimination directives. Preparation for the act started in spring 2003 in DG EMPL's unit on Equality for Women and Men (COM48:24). A public consultation took place in July (IA SEC[2004]482: 24) and, following meetings with stakeholders, experts, and national interests (COM48:84, COM131:68, 160) and intensive drafting over the summer (COM131:76), the proposal was "already almost ready in October" (COM131:148). While the broad consultation indicates a politically inclusive process, DG EMPL was actually pursuing a technical "better regulation" strategy, the "general approach in the Commission at this moment" (COM131:44). Adhering to the Commission's Better Regulation Agenda (COM[2002]275), the drafting officials emphatically argued that they had only systematized established provisions and aligned differential concepts that had led to misunderstanding and confusion in the area (COM48:36, COM131:44, AE, October 5, 2004), and "did not introduce a measure [or] new provisions" (COM131:176). In line with this approach—and unlike the previously discussed acts on equal treatment—the act attracted little political or public attention (COM48:76).

The technical emphasis could not, however, entirely conceal the fact that the integration of five directives entailed the systematic application of concepts and definitions that hitherto had regarded only specific areas to other sectors, and, thus, on a much broader scale. DG EMPL claimed that moving from the legal status quo implied a "small parameter adjustment on two or three substantial issues, but *clarifying* really rather than anything else" (COM48:36, authors' translation). Still, the Secretariat-General and the SJ kept a close eye on this regulatory expansion, reminding DG EMPL that "this kind of horizontal provision" (COM131:108), such as the burden-of-proof approach, were "really for equal treatment on working conditions and not for social security" (COM131:36). This position was embedded in wider criticism by the Secretariat-General and the SJ on the lead DG's choice of instrument: formally, a "recast" could not sufficiently legitimize advances in the legal substance, so that a different legal instrument was actually warranted (COM131:108, cf. IA SEC[2004]482: 13). In addition, there is some evidence that DG EMPL had opted for a recast for strategic reasons, because this meant it did not have to formally consult the social partners, who interpreted ECJ case law on equal pay more critically than the DG (COM48:48, UNICE 2004: 1–2).

Extending equal-treatment principles from pay and social security to occupational social security schemes had implications for retirement age, survivor benefits and specific old-age benefits, particularly in the public sector. This position met with strong reservations on the part of the social partners and member states (COM48:72, COM131:68) that were not keen on merging occupational social security schemes and equal-treatment issues (COM131:20). This external opposition translated into internal critique from DG MARKT. However, DG EMPL had structurally prepared the fusion of both areas: just before drafting started, Director-General Quintin had recruited an official to the drafting unit who had worked on occupational social security schemes for many years in DG EMPL (COM131:20, 48). Endowed with detailed technical knowledge, the unit now nonchalantly claimed a need to clarify that "Art. 141 applies also to public sector schemes" (COM131:116), pointing to recent ECJ case law (*Evrenopoulos* C-147/95, *Griesmar* C-206/00, *Beune* C-7/93, *Neimi* C-351/00). In addition, the lead DG underlined that the inclusion of public-sector schemes had been an unfulfilled request from the European Parliament since directive 76/207/EEC had been amended at the beginning of the century (COM131:36).

Shortly before the ISC was launched on November 20, 2003, DG EMPL organized two multilateral meetings where remaining differences between the dissenting portfolios were easily surmounted (COM131:120). DG EMPL successfully pushed coverage of the public sector, while DG MARKT was successful in its quest to allow sex-based differences where they simply reflect actuarial differences. Thus, "at the end there was a consensus" (COM131:124).

Overall, despite its technical approach, this act nevertheless shows a strong disposition on the part of the lead DG to advance EU anti-discrimination policy. In particular, extant legislation and ECJ case law were influential since they were in line with a broader strategy to simplify existing rules. Although empirical information on interaction is rather meager, the lead DG exploited its advantage to assemble provisions from different acts and also to rely on intentionally introduced expertise and the wider policy context of simplification.

5.2.4 General Framework for Equal Treatment

The act on equal treatment between persons irrespective of religion or belief, disability, age, or sexual orientation (General Framework, COM[2008]426) combines all the grounds that had been subject to EU equal-treatment legislation with all the areas regulated so far, and thus covers social protection (including social security and healthcare), social advantages, education, and access to and supply of goods and services. Moreover, it extends existing definitions and means of enforcement to a much broader area. Once more, the proposal substantially departs from the status quo of existing directives (most notably, those discussed so far) and intervenes more strongly in European markets. This should not be taken too seriously, however, because the proposal actually contains some far-reaching exemptions.

Initially, it was the newly elected Commission President Barroso who had given the equal-treatment agenda a—more or less deliberate—boost, largely compelled to do so by the Buttiglione scandal in 2004. Buttiglione, an Italian Commissioner nominee, had to step down from the Commission-to-be in October 2004 after he had expressed outright homophobic views in a European Parliament hearing. In response, Barroso pledged to the European Parliament that he would put forth a General Framework directive on equal treatment (AE, October 26, 2004). Several years later, in the run-up to his re-election in 2008, the European Parliament reminded Barroso to display "more political courage, as this is very much lacking" (AE 2008, also COM38:42). This half-hearted commitment from the Commission's political apex was met by the expertise of services that had gathered substantial experience in advancing EU anti-discrimination legislation over about 30 years. However, DG EMPL recounted the process as follows: "Whether we would have introduced it otherwise or not, I do not know, but at that point we were pretty much obliged to do so, because if we do not, we will get an increasing amount of pressure" (COM86:167, also COM84:77).

Concrete preparations started in spring 2007, the act was officially announced as part of the Commission work programme in October (COM[2007]640) and it was finally adopted in the College in July 2008 as part of the Renewed Social Agenda (COM[2008]412). A core team of four persons in DG EMPL's Equal Treatment unit collaborated closely with the DG's Disability unit and the SJ (COM19:213, COM38:106), while at the same time running the European Year of Equal Opportunities for All in 2007. The responsible officials approached drafting with the "straightforward conviction [that] it was morally right" (COM19:48, also COM38). Unsurprisingly, the topoi resembled that of the earlier acts in this sub-sample. The DG EMPL officials evoked the constant technical need to legislate for better implementation (COM107:46, COM19:252).[7] Their Commissioner Spidla stressed that "the same level of protection as for other groups" was needed in order to do away with "inequality in Community legislation itself because people are protected from discrimination outside the workplace only on grounds of gender and race or ethnic origin" (in European Commission 2008). Consequently, regulation would have "to level up but not come down" (COM19:33).

Unsurprisingly, the far-reaching 1999 proposals had heightened sensibility and "member states were at best lukewarm" (COM19:33) about the new framework proposal. Again, Germany, especially, was described as being "openly hostile... and tried to wreck it from the very beginning" (COM19:33, COM107:44, COM84:77). Other member states opposed specific aspects of the act, such as Poland and the Czech Republic with respect to religion (COM84:125). For the services, this translated into considerable caution in carefully screening national and stakeholder interests and in drawing on broad existing or newly generated expertise to draw up an act that would nonetheless aim at "pushing forward the anti-discrimination agenda as much as possible" (COM19:33). The DG opted for an extremely broad preparation and consultation (COM38:109), successively involving member states in a mapping exercise and industry in a European Business Test Panel "to get a feel for what business thought" (COM19:306), as well as cultivating a number of bilateral contacts (SEC[2009]2180: 8). This was followed by what was deemed "the largest response to a public consultation... the Commission had ever had" (COM19:297) and also by exchanges with the DG's "usual suspects," such as European umbrella associations of organized societal interests and its expert groups on anti-discrimination (COM86:143).[8] In the course of the process, however, the need for more public support had become evident and, in a new step, the DG launched a Eurobarometer survey on discrimination in the EU (AE, January 23, 2007). Collecting further supportive data, DG EMPL commissioned the Brussels-based think tank, the European Policy Evaluation Consortium (EPEC), with a study focused on discrimination outside employment and its costs for individuals and society.

The political level in the Commission still remained skeptical regarding the proposal's political viability. In 2008, the Commission had just been heavily criticized for its service directive proposal (COM84:145, see Chapter 5.4.2) and ratification of the Lisbon Treaty was pending. The President, in particular, felt the discrepancy between wanting an act that would pass as favoring a social Europe—particularly in the eyes of the European Parliament—and avoiding a rise in economic costs or provoking member-state opposition, which would have threatened unanimity on the act in Council. In its efforts to square this circle, the President's Secretariat-General proposed a solution to DG EMPL that kept adaptation costs for enterprises low by covering only disability (COM86:71). However, EU-level NGOs, led by ILGA, countered with an active campaign contending that the President had to keep his promise to legislate broadly (COM86:76, COM84:22), while the European Parliament issued a critical initiative report provocatively denouncing that "more than half of the College of Commissioners does not support . . . a general directive" (AE 2008). In this setting, the Cabinet of Social Policy Commissioner Spidla applied the brakes to the services and very actively interfered in the drafting "to counter-steer in order to make the act 'sellable' in both directions" (COM84:141, authors' translation). Consequently, the services "to some extent, lost control at that point," which was considered as something that does not "normally" happen in the Commission (COM19:318).

These struggles within DG EMPL coincided with "intensive" (COM38:106) horizontal intra-Commission dynamics throughout the entire drafting period (COM19:15). Bilateral contacts, perceived as "helpful" (COM19:237) and "all very friendly" (COM42:117), led to the establishment of an inter-service steering group "partly to have discussion, . . . partly to pre-empt DGs" (COM19:111). Interaction at the political level was much more controversial, with actors arguing until they were "blue in the face" (COM19:260). Consequently, two rather unusual moves characterized the subsequent interaction process. First, at the end of May, a meeting between DG EMPL services and cabinet members of the critical DGs was convened, putting the drafters' "technical" knowledge at the same table as political calculus to hammer out solutions directly (COM81:132, COM105:15). Second, just four days after the ISC had started on June 6, Barroso convened a lunch among Commissioners to garner political support and curb fundamental opposition (COM84:22, 241). In order to prevent the entire proposal from crumbling, far-reaching exemptions were offered. Once more, this evidences the conviction that "it was better to have something adopted, which was going to go into Council and be discussed, than not to have a proposal" (COM19:189). This Janus-faced political support was decisive for DG EMPL's securing adoption of the proposal, and a Special Chefs meeting was able to resolve the remaining issues on 26 June (COM38: 97, COM105:189).

The internal lines of conflict substantially replicated those of earlier acts. Again, German Commissioner Verheugen—now heading DG ENTR—"just said no, no way, nothing" (COM19:196). Fearing rising costs for enterprises, DG ENTR called for the exclusion of disability (COM81:32, COM105:64) from the act, but also of tourism and hotels (COM19:243, COM38:53). DG ENTR also opposed provisions that would ease application by empowering organized interests through the *locus standi* and a stronger role for equality bodies, and also called for "an upper limit" for penalties (COM105:144). DG EMPL played up the political valence of the disability issue (COM38:100) and emphasized the link with the UN Convention on the Rights of Persons with Disabilities (2007), which had been ratified by member states anyway. The lead DG forcefully invoked requests by the European Parliament and organized interests—particularly the Social Platform and the European Anti-Poverty Network (EAPN)—for a broad act, as well as the societal demand visible in the responses to the earlier consultation (AE, June 3, 2008). These sources showed that "there was lots of discrimination, lots of complaints [that were brought to the DG's] attention, by individuals, by lobby groups and there was no denying them" (COM19:33). The lead DG further received support from a DG TREN study on the estimated costs of making public transport fully disabled accessible, which allowed DG EMPL to say that "it is not true that this is going to ruin the industry" (COM19:234). Nevertheless, a DG EMPL cabinet member stressed the need "to meet the Germans by moving towards them here and there" (COM84:257). Unsurprisingly, in the final proposal employers were granted more leeway by limiting their duty to provide accommodation for handicapped workers, such as in situations that would "require major changes to the product or service" (Art. 4.2 of the proposal).

This logic of general acceptance—bought dearly by limiting the implementation costs for industry—was implemented regarding other provisions, too. DG MARKT observed critically how unequal treatment in services, which had been included in the 2003 proposal, would translate to the scope of the broader proposal at stake, particularly with regard to age discrimination in insurance services (COM42:39).[9] At the political level, the Irish Common Market Commissioner McCreevy joined forces with the British Trade Commissioner Mandelson in rallying against the provision (COM81:68, COM86:95), viewing such a "damage limitation exercise" (COM19:78) as crucial for their respective national industries. Again, these opposing interests were successful, because the final proposal indeed allows for general exemptions. Similarly, on private-life transactions the German Enterprise Commissioner Verheugen pushed for an "old lady clause" that would keep the equal-treatment principle out of the private sphere (COM105:92).[10] DG ENTR was successful because the proposal *de facto* allows obligations to be easily circumvented "if a small enterprise doesn't have the means" (COM105:164). But overall, DG EMPL succeeded in proposing this act and managed to carefully limit the exemptions required to disarm the German opposition. In this case, DG EMPL obtained power of definition by closely following up on national transposition of the earlier acts and critically questioning member states that had interpreted the private sphere rather broadly. One example is an infringement procedure launched against Ireland because their transposition of the race equality directive had excluded people employed in private households (COM19:255). DG EMPL therewith tried to make the fall-back option for reluctant member states legally uncertain, hoping to garner support for a re-regulation.

Overall, this case largely follows the patterns adhered to for the other anti-discrimination acts. Again, not only the extant *acquis*, but also the lines of conflict and the national and political sensibilities established in the earlier processes shaped the positions adopted. Responsiveness to European Parliament demands can explain why support from the Secretariat-General (albeit Janus-faced) was much more relevant in this case. In addition, DG EMPL made use of knowledge and support generated by reports, studies, and organized interests to push the act through in internal disputes that were significantly shaped by the debates anticipated in Council.

5.2.5 European Globalisation Adjustment Fund

The last case in this sub-field is the European Globalisation Adjustment Fund (EGF, COM[2006]91), which introduces a new type of EU instrument of social policy intervention. It newly establishes the possibility for companies to claim financial assistance for counter-balancing trade adjustment and provides criteria for the relevant intervention. It further proposes two types of intervention targeted at individual workers: active labor-market measures and in-work time-limited income supplements. Unlike the EU structural funds, the EGF is explicitly reactive and flexible and not targeted towards long-term and anticipatory spending. What is more, while these existing community instruments spend EU money via national projects, the EGF redistributes money directly to individuals.

Developments predating the actual drafting are crucial to understanding both the wide political support for and also the rifts regarding the act. As a spending instrument, the EGF is closely linked to future EU cohesion policy, which was strongly debated at the time. A classical perspective advocated cohesion policy largely along the lines established by DG REGIO, thus levelling economic and social conditions within all EU regions through strategic spending (COM44:29). Reformers wanted to reduce regional spending and instead concentrate resources on the least developed member states, particularly the enlargement countries. The transition was to be balanced by a restructuring instrument targeted at the unemployed (Hall 2005: 969–70). The idea was criticized heavily internally (COM78:50) and the subsequently proposed Growth Adjustment Fund was rejected by member states in January 2005 (AE, October 27, 2005). But by then discussions had paved the way for an instrument on restructuring, both inside the Commission and among member states (COM44:47, COM74:49, COM78:134). And it took only a couple of months before a spending instrument on restructuring was back on the table as part of the Financial Perspectives 2007–2013.

The EGF was publicly announced in early October 2005 by Social Affairs Commissioner Spidla and President Barroso (AE, October 7, 2005). "[D]riven by political concern" (COM78:146), they linked the new instrument to public debates that saw the cause of the rejection of the Constitution in the lack of a social dimension to Europe, aggravated by globalization plus enlargement. In this context, the EGF "was just a political gesture . . . to calm down . . . the general opinion in some member states at the time of the adoption of the European Constitution" (COM77:28, also COM67:68). All in all, the Commission started the process with a clear vision in mind. Commission President Barroso stressed his intention that the beneficiaries of an EGF should see the EU as a warrior against painful globalization effects:

> It is nice for national politicians to say "we care and the European Union doesn't care. They just speak about liberalization and they don't think about social responsibilities". We think it's very important to show that we in the EU care. . . . No member state, not even the biggest ones, can respond to globalization on their own. It is a kind of European insurance policy (Barroso quoted in: Browne 2006, also COM43:78).

Unsurprisingly, in this context, officials saw the instrument as having "huge public appeal . . . really responding to citizens' concerns" (COM18:66). The unequivocal commitment from the political apex of the Commission met with division among the member states. Net contributing countries, spearheaded by Germany, voiced doubts about the usefulness of the new instrument (*FT*, October 20, 27, 2005, also COM107:20). But countries that had recently experienced redundancies related to globalization, such as Portugal, France, and the UK Presidency, strongly supported the proposal (AE, October 27, November 10, 2005).[11] And they managed to broker a deal within the context of the Financial Perspectives at the informal Hampton Court Summit on October 20, 2005.

Such general member-state commitment was all Barroso needed to start drawing up a concrete proposal. The drafting process inside the Commission is a prime example of top-down policy-making. Despite DG EMPL being the lead DG, the initial drafting steps were taken in the Secretariat-General in the week following the Hampton Court Summit (COM67:48, COM44:83). More detailed drafting continued at high speed in DG EMPL. A fast-track ISC (with reduced time for comments) was launched on February 7, 2006 (COM74:130, COM67:82), and with adoption in the College due in early March, the entire position-formation process extended over only a handful of weeks. The *ex ante* commitment of the top political level and the unusual time pressure arising from the link to the negotiations on the Financial Perspectives blurred the different formal stages of drafting (COM67:46)—for instance, the political level was involved throughout, not only in the run-up to the ISC; stakeholder involvement was limited (COM18:72, COM43:82, UEAPME 2006; ETUC 2005); and the IA (SEC[2006] 274) was exceedingly slim—a fact critically remarked upon by a number of DGs during the formal interaction (responses to CIS-Net consultation no. 1642).

Internal interactions throughout the process were described as "professional and consensual" (COM74:108) and "little controversial" (COM43:194). In an area characterized by high uncertainty and little experience on the part of DG EMPL (COM43:234, COM67:46), and given the time constraints, the lead department depended on external knowledge from colleagues in other DGs with experience in this area. Consequently, the drafting involved DGs BUDG, REGIO (COM67:100) and "very, very close contacts with particularly TRADE" (COM74:124, also COM77:112). For a crisis intervention instrument, DG REGIO's Solidarity Fund for Natural Disasters (2012/2002/EC) served as the best available example (COM44:93, COM43:96). Moreover, DG REGIO's general experience with structural policy helped in drafting provisions defining the eligible actions for workers (COM78:24, COM43:234). However, the criteria for selecting sectors or regions were particularly perceived as "unexplored ground" (COM74:151). In this respect, two questions were central. First, when do redundancies have a significant adverse impact? In the light of critical member states calling for strict criteria, DG EMPL had initially favored a higher threshold of redundancies. However, an empirical investigation of restructuring data collected by the Eurofound Agency in Dublin had shown that this would lead to the omission of serious cases. DG EMPL thus eagerly reduced the threshold so as to reach more people. DG EMPL officials also looked at the US experience with its trade adjustment assistance (TAA) (SEC [2006]274: 9, COM18:78, COM43:94, COM74:71). Second, how should the causal link between these redundancies and structural changes in trade patterns be captured? Here, support from DG TRADE officials was much valued. Experience from the crisis-shaken textile sector was used "as a template . . . providing concrete data, figures, economic analysis on the impact of globalization" (COM77:34, also COM43:96, COM74:64). DG TRADE, in turn, used the interaction to ensure that globalization, core to its mandate, would not appear in a negative light (COM74:89).

Despite extensive exchange and knowledge-sharing, substantial differences inside the Commission prevailed throughout the process and DG EMPL finished the ISC with a number of critical remarks (responses to CIS-Net consultation no. 1642). The fundamental critique of the general structure of the crisis intervention instrument was re-emphasized by DG REGIO, who advocated a second stream for the EGF that would target enterprises rather than workers (COM78, 74, Hall 2005: 969–70). This DG's criticism was in line with DG ENTR's wish to include companies as applicants (COM74:61), while DGs ECFIN and BUDG once again called for more uniqueness vis-à-vis the European Social Fund (COM76:68, DG BUDG's response to CIS-Net consultation no. 1642).

Besides this debate on the general direction of regulation, much more specific but equally critical comments concerned the intervention criteria, influenced by the anticipation of Council voting and sectoral concerns. Although DG EMPL had tapped external knowledge and expertise from other DGs, political sensibilities proved difficult to surmount. DG ECFIN feared generating rent-seeking behavior by member-state governments and therefore demanded that only "big cases in 'problematic' regions in terms of employment and economic dynamism" should be targeted (DG ECFIN's response to CIS-Net consultation no. 1642, COM74:64). Contrasting with this view, DG ENTR wanted to widen the scope of the instrument and make it available in cases of redundancies resulting from relocation in the EU (COM74:68, COM67:66, DG ENTR's response to CIS-Net consultation no. 1642). Finally, DGs REGIO and BUDG put forward their concerns about equal treatment of countries, considering the likelihood of reaching the thresholds even with small labor markets (responses to CIS-Net consultation no. 1642, COM76:68).

DG EMPL accepted adjustments only as long as they did not interfere with the goal of the EGF that Barroso had followed since the beginning of drafting: a crisis-intervention instrument targeted at individuals to show that the EU cared about the victims of globalization (COM78:90, COM44:83, COM77:134, COM74:43). Consequently, the equal treatment of member states was assured by introducing a reference to the different levels of the European Statistical System (NUTS), but companies were not allowed as applicants, nor could redundancies due to relocation inside the EU qualify for application. Principled support from "the very top" (COM67:22, authors' translation) was particularly important in the struggle with the SJ, which opposed the legal basis envisaged by DG EMPL. Again, DG EMPL was able to secure the initial position since "only the President's cabinet can overrule the legal service" (COM18:94). However, the power of political support was limited when it came to the financial side of the instrument (COM43:234). Initially, the Secretariat-General and DG EMPL had a strong interest in operating the EGF from a classical budget line that would have entailed "a free hand in running" the instrument (COM74:53). DG BUDG, in turn, argued for integrating the new aims into the existing European Social Fund. Both sides had to bow to member states that had conditioned acceptance of the instrument on budget neutrality at the Hampton Court Summit (AE, October 27, 28, 2005, COM78:142, COM44:65, COM18:120, COM107:106). Thus, money that had not been spent in other budget lines had to be used, and spending was made subject each time to a discrete decision by the Council and the European Parliament (COM18:103). Although DG BUDG had provided technical assistance in employing the mechanism of under-spends (COM77:90, COM107:122), in the ISC it issued a negative opinion and DG EMPL had to resolve this controversy "before [it] went to the college. Because not even the President's cabinet can overrule DG BUDG" (COM18:106). Hastily, DG EMPL accepted changes ensuring equal treatment of applications that arrived at different times of the year and a safeguard on how to proceed in cases of financial shortfall.

Overall, the broad lines of the instrument were significantly influenced by net-payer member-state interests, while concrete criteria for awarding money benefited from international transfer and expertise coming from other DGs. In the interactions, DG EMPL was successful in pushing through an intervention instrument targeted at individuals compared to continuing with the European Social Fund. This was based on the ability to manage the time-limited process as agenda-setter and on exceptional political support from the Secretariat-General and the Commission President himself.

Summarizing the findings from this first sub-field, all the acts are strong in creating rights and benefits for individuals. This can be understood as emancipation from the classical national social policy approach targeting the work–employment relationship, which is limited at the EU level by the difficulties of pondering diverging national models. At the same time, even though they were proposed by the social portfolio, these initiatives are also remarkably compatible with the common market project. Thus, controversies with other portfolios and member states *en toto* concerned the question how to integrate human resources into markets (Somek 2011) and thus the "quality" of markets—not the more fundamental conflict as to whether regulation should seek to produce outcomes *other* than those produced by markets. Likewise, targeting individuals rather than the work–employment relationship meant expanding the involvement of organized interests from classical social-partner organizations to those advocating wider societal concerns. This was vital because it provided an important means to justify extension of social-community competences against national interests and industry and business concerns, for which DGs MARKT and partly ENTR proved important access points.

What was striking throughout all the processes studied—including even the seemingly technical recast COM(2004)279—was the lead DG EMPL's agenda of which political goals to achieve with the act. Often this was strongly influenced by extant *acquis* and related experiences with implementation. In some of these cases, the lead DG had benefited from ECJ case law, modifying the fall-back option in its own interest, while almost always opposing national interests had to be outmaneuvered. DG EMPL rarely accepted these as given, rather crafted solutions to circumvent or at least stretch them somewhat. The lead DG with its explicit agenda decided which and when drafting processes should follow either a political or technocratic logic. Importantly, this entailed pre-structuring the influence accorded to external expertise, organized interests, or international policy developments. The positions expressed—both those of the proponents and the opponents of the acts—were remarkably political, and where they gained public visibility this worked to the benefit of market-intervening positions. Interactions became particularly intense between DG EMPL and the economically oriented portfolios of DGs MARKT, ENTR, and ECFIN. Final decisions on the most contentious provisions were mostly fought out at the political level. Here, DG EMPL was powerful when it could gain strength from the drafting process itself by exploiting its lead position and alliances with other DGs strategically, and by employing reports and studies or support from organized interests to its liking.

5.3 RIGHT OF ESTABLISHMENT AND FREEDOM TO PROVIDE SERVICES

The second sub-field concerns the regulation of public procurement and financial services. In both areas, a strong treaty base on common market freedoms regarding the right of establishment and provision of services contrasts with sluggish law development in Europe—either in terms of particularly bad implementation records (public procurement) or in terms of insufficient European regulation (financial services). Consequently, the acts analyzed here aim at improving regulation in the respective common market areas. It was widely believed that their focus on industry and enterprise interests would increase the Union's competitiveness under the Lisbon Strategy. Tables 5.4 and 5.5 give details of the proposal and process characteristics of position formation cases in this subfield.

EU public-procurement legislation seeks to ensure that domestic regimes operate according to common principles on notice procedures, selection, and award criteria. This should open up domestic markets for EU-wide public procurement, which accounts for around 14 percent of GDP in the EU (IP/00/461). In order to prevent government and state-owned bodies from favoring domestic suppliers over foreign rivals, state autonomy in spending had been curbed by EU legislation since the 1970s. Regulatory efforts had built up a quite stable public-procurement policy community, encompassing both DG MARKT and national officials struggling alike with implementation deficits. This community also dominated the three public-procurement cases discussed below. Because it impinges on member states' autonomy regarding spending, public procurement is of importance for local authorities, industries, and labor markets. Unsurprisingly, two of the three acts attracted substantial attention in the media during the drafting period (COM16:209, COM104:70).

EU regulation on financial services is less developed but has experienced a thrust in policy-making activities since the late 1990s (AE August 13, 1997), when the Commission published a Green Paper entitled "Financial Services: Meeting Consumer Expectations" (COM[1996]209), a Communication entitled "Financial Services: Enhancing Consumer Confidence" (COM[1997]309) and a subsequent Financial Services Action Plan (FSAP, COM[1999]232). The policy dynamic emerging from these documents presented a shift "from market opening measures towards common regulatory measures—that is from negative to positive integration" (Mügge 2010: 126; Quaglia 2010a: 1007). All three acts discussed in subsections 5.3.3 to 5.3.5 were announced in the FSAP. Entering new regulatory territory, they were accompanied by substantial uncertainty regarding the effect of the envisaged provisions. While political and public interest in the highly technical regulations was minor (COM36:52), industry interests, stakeholders' expertise, and international developments are core to understanding all three of them.

Table 5.4. Position formation on right of establishment and provision of services

Proposal number	Contents	No. of key provisions	Main line of proposal (content)	Uncertainty	Salience	Origin (hierarchical level)	Process duration (months)	External consultation	Main position-formation factors
COM[2000]275	Public Supply Contracts	10	Specification of common notice, selection and award criteria to implement a pure market logic for public contracts	No	Yes	Administrative	24	Public	- Extant *acquis* - Experts - National position
COM[2000]276	Public Supply Contracts in water, energy and transport sectors	10	Specification of common notice, selection and award criteria to implement a pure market logic for public contracts, exclusion of telecommunications	No	Yes	Administrative	24	Public	- Extant *acquis* - Experts - National position - ECJ jurisprudence
COM[2000]511	Financial Intermediaries	5	Harmonized mandatory registration in country of origin and increased consumer information	No	No	Administrative	42	Specific	- Extant *acquis* - Organized interests
COM[2001]213	Financial Conglomerates	5	Definition of conglomerates, supervision and risk management	Yes	No	Administrative	24	Public	- International transfer - Experts - National position
COM[2001]449	Common Procurement Vocabulary	2	Merger of existing classification schemes in a single vocabulary	No	No	Administrative	6	Specific	- Extant *acquis* - Experts - Anticipation of Council majority - Organized interests
COM[2004]273	Reinsurance	9	Harmonized licensing system	Yes	No	Administrative	51	Specific	- Extant *acquis* - National position - Organized interests - Experts

Table 5.5. Interaction on right of establishment and provision of services

Proposal number	Contents	Deviating DGs	Informal interaction	Position-based conflict	Process-based conflict	Main line of conflict	Most powerful DG	Main power resources
COM[2000]275	Public Supply Contracts	ENV EMPL JLS ENTR	Intense	2	1	Green and social award criteria versus pure cost efficiency	ENV	- Supranational competence - Entrepreneurship
COM[2000]276	Public Supply Contracts in water, energy and transport sectors	ENV EMPL JLS ENTR	Intense	2	1	Green and social award criteria versus pure cost efficiency	ENV	- Supranational competence - Entrepreneurship
COM[2000]511	Financial Intermediaries	—	Medium	0	0	—	—	—
COM[2001]213	Financial Conglomerates	—	Little	0	0	—	—	—
COM[2001]449	Common Procurement Vocabulary	—	Little	0	0	—	—	—
COM[2004]273	Reinsurance	—	Medium	0	0	—	—	—

5.3.1 Directives on Public-procurement Procedures

The first two cases in the sub-field concern almost identical provisions to regulate the procedures of procurement. While one general act covers public supply, service, and works contracts (COM[2000]275), a more specific act addresses utilities in the areas of water, energy, and transport (COM[2000]276). In general, the new utilities directive takes a softer approach to competition, reflecting the authorities' privileged situation or monopoly status in these areas. In both cases, a uniform procedure calls for specification and publication of the tender content in all languages in a supplement to the Official Journal of the European Union (yielding 300–500 calls daily). In principle, the scope of the two acts had been covered by earlier directives on supply (93/36/EEC), service (92/50/EEC), and works contracts (93/37/EEC), and the parallel utilities regime (93/38/EEC), which had "introduced all the basic elements" (COM16:41). However, both acts propose a number of changes to the extant *acquis*.

The major changes do not concern the depth of intervention but shifts in the scope of application. Telecommunications is moved from the utilities regime to the more competitive general public–procurement regime. In addition, more contracts are now covered under the general public-procurement regimes because the financial threshold above which the directive applies has been lowered. Additional changes grant the private sector a larger role in public procurement than was previously the case. Where private capital participates in financing or operating infrastructure and public services, concessions for public-private partnerships are introduced. Whereas the old regimes had prohibited long-term procurement relationships, contracts can now take the form of framework arrangements between the authority and a list of suppliers, for example when it comes to the acquisition of complex computer systems.

With respect to the selection of participants, the new provisions require an explicit fixing and *ex ante* weighting of the criteria in a transparent manner. Core to the directives is the stipulation that contracts can be awarded only to the bidders with the lowest price or alternatively to those who are most "economically advantageous." This includes consideration of the quality, price, technical merit, aesthetic and functional or environmental characteristics, running costs, cost-effectiveness, after-sales service and technical assistance, delivery date and delivery period, or period of completion as justification for a higher price (Art. 53). Highlighting the basic tension between economic and social regulation outlined above, the predominantly economic rationale leaves little room to seek other outcomes such as justice, equity, or social cohesion via EU public-procurement policy. Overall, by exposing sectors hitherto sheltered from competition and by specifying criteria for selecting and awarding contracts, the directives establish a "very purist" (COM104:122) EU public-procurement regime that fosters competition and cost efficiency above other goals in the common market.

Not long after the forerunner public-procurement directives had been adopted in the early 1990s, the European Parliament and Council called for more modernization (COM16:218, Gelderman et al. 2010: 244). It was a time of rapid technological and information-related innovation in telecommunications, electronic commerce, and computerized resources (COM16:41, Erridge et al. 1998: 255). At the same time, the role of the state in the economy was changing, budgetary restraints had become the order of the day, and privatization, liberalization of utilities, and public–private partnerships had substantially altered the context of public procurement (COM[1998]143: 2). The potential of public procurement and the persistent member-state failure to implement existing community standards was increasingly perceived as a mismatch (*FT*, January 14, 2000). Even where member states had transposed the earlier directives, *de facto* the EU legislation contained "so many loopholes that unscrupulous purchasers were able to evade them" (Martin and Hartley 1997: 92). There was widespread agreement on the need to modernize procurement and render it more efficient (*FT*, May 9, 2000, COM16:42; Erridge et al. 1998).

Against this backdrop, DG MARKT had published a Green Paper in 1996 (COM[1996]583). This was followed by a broad public consultation with nearly 300 replies from member states, suppliers, and purchasers, as well as representative organizations from the demand and supply sides. The Commission responded with a further Communication (COM[1998]143). Concrete preparation of the proposals started in spring 1998 in DG MARKT. The drafting unit and their colleagues from the entire Directorate on Public Procurement Policy were able to build on a long legacy and substantial experience in the area, accumulated since the 1970s (COM16:92, COM22:13). Drafting stretched out over two years until the acts were submitted to the ISC in spring 2000 (COM22:77). Throughout the drafting process, DG MARKT and national officials dealing with the existing directives met regularly in different expert groups to discuss the proposal (COM16:188). This exchange helped to "test the waters" and the "likely positions" of the parties concerned (COM16:92, 176), particularly on the issue of thresholds (COM22:104). In addition, the wider circle of external views was also carefully listened to, such as environmental NGOs "proposing more ethics in public procurement, like fair trade" and the associations of engineers and architects, who exerted "a lot of pressure" (COM16:65). Their influence on the "rather technical" legal files "with little outside interference" (COM104:210) is difficult to trace, however, which qualifies the drafting processes as closed overall to external interests that were not central to public-procurement policy.

The influence of external policy developments is more directly visible in other portfolios. Competition Commissioner Monti (Italian, independent) had been actively promoting the liberalization of hitherto state-owned sectors (COM22:32, COM16:123; also Schmidt 1998) and along these lines the ECJ had *de facto* established the exclusion of important sectors from the existing utilities directive (AE, May 12, 1999, *FT*, May 9, 2000, COM[2000]276/2: 12). Thus, at the time of proposing the two directives, the fall-back option had changed, which induced DG MARKT to exempt telecommunications from the scope of the broad regime and apply conditions of full competition to the hitherto sheltered sector (COM[2000]275, COM104:202).

Portfolios did not align so easily on other issues, and a huge number of critical remarks arrived on the desks of the drafting officials through the ISC (COM22:80). Most of these comments were swiftly taken into account in order "to deliver" the act (COM22:179), and problems were simply "ironed out on the level of the services" (COM116:32; also COM104:140, COM16:153). However, where neighboring portfolios challenged DG MARKT's underlying logic of pure market competition, internal debates were fought at the political level between the respective cabinets (COM69:114). A first example was DG JLS's wish to explicitly mention the exclusion of corrupt, fraudulent, or criminal operators from public-procurement procedures, not least to give its portfolio more "standing in the internal market legislation" (COM22:70; also COM16:80). DG MARKT only performed a U-turn after it had been challenged with a negative opinion in the ISC and acknowledged that "it was impossible, in a discussion in College, to say we do not care if a contract is given to corrupt tenderers" (COM22:71). In response to DG ENTR's push for separate thresholds for SMEs, DG MARKT simply referred to the international level and argued that "our obligations in the WTO context . . . do not allow that" (COM16:83).

However, most controversial, by far, was the issue of award criteria (COM22:83, 173). Here, deep dividing lines ran between DG MARKT's approach and DGs ENV and EMPL's positions, which followed different underlying economic principles and highlighted the quest for cost-efficient markets against the wish to reach outcomes that demanded more intervention. DG MARKT officials stood up for their purist view on "perfecting the internal market" (COM116:46):

> On the award criteria, the idea was . . . that we did not really want to open for green award criteria, for instance, and certainly not to social award criteria. Because we thought, this does not respect the objective, which was best value for money . . . we did not want to transform public procurement in a social instrument, or in an instrument to pursue green policies. We thought, it has its own logic, it has its own purpose, and we should not use it as an instrument for other policies (COM22:26; also COM16:68).

By contrast, DG EMPL, supported by the European Parliament and the trade unions, wanted award criteria (especially in service contracts) to include fair labor standards, corporate social responsibility, respect for collective agreements and employment of disabled people (COM64:34; ETUC 1998). Finally, DG ENV openly called for a greening of the common market. Integrating environmental concerns into other policy areas was a general aim that was high on the agenda of Environment Commissioner Wallström and her deputy Director-General Verstringere (COM104:62):

> We were aware that we had a huge market for public goods in the European Union, and we wanted to provide some financial stimulus to green procurement. . . . it was really more about politically pushing open the door, to allow green award criteria without being accused of interfering with the market. . . . Legislation had achieved a lot for the environment, and we would still need legislation, but there was a recognition that you needed to use the market. "To green the market" was one of her [Wallström's] slogans and also to integrate environmental concerns into other policy areas. And so this was in many ways the test case for our ability to do that (COM104:38).

The conflicts underlying the debates on the award criteria spread to other provisions, such as technical contract specification, where DG ENV favored eco labels. DG MARKT felt that this contradicted its objective of criteria that were "measurable, objective, transparent, and which lead to a best value for money result" (COM22:23; also COM104:122).[12] Thus, because it directly addresses the basic conflict at the intersection of common market and social regulation, this case reveals the tensions existing between interests seeking (cost-) efficient markets and those wanting to use the market to achieve broader societal goals.

Anticipating conflictual positions, DG MARKT had already worked with DGs EMPL and ENV "in the preparatory phase . . . very regularly" (COM22:122) on finding a compromise. The final proposal allows environmental criteria to qualify an operator as economically most advantageous even though not lowest in cost. By contrast, social award criteria do not figure among those defining economic efficiency, rather are limited to a non-binding legal act (COM69:102). So what explains the success of DG ENV in pushing through its view compared to the failure of DG EMPL to do the same?

First, DG MARKT evoked the common market consensus as the core of the integration project. "[V]ery good lawyers" (COM64:44) argued that green and social award criteria would be a "danger for the whole internal market" (COM16:119). This line of argument gained the DG much legitimacy in defining award criteria in strictly economic terms and garnered it much support from other DGs, notably DG COMP. In this setting, DG EMPL "fully accepted" (COM64:44) the need for a purist public-procurement regime. DG ENV, by contrast, questioned this position early on and argued that "there is no contradiction between defending an internal market and having ambitious environmental objectives" (COM65:167). It virtually fought its case through, since the decision to include green award criteria was reached in the College only after "a big fight" (COM65:133) and "a huge discussion, between our Commissioner [Bolkestein] and Commissioner Wallström" (COM22:32). In addition to Environment Commissioner Wallström's personal skills, her service's initiative also stands out as the means by which the battle was won against the lead department. The responsible DG ENV desk office was described as being very experienced (COM22:89) and skilful in "very proactive[ly] . . . engaging the Cabinet in quite an early stage" (COM104:132). DG EMPL, by contrast, left the issue to be tackled by the central unit dealing with the coordination of diverse policy issues, which had neither particular expertise nor a particular political interest (COM22:89, COM64:14, COM104:108). Moreover, DG ENV took advantage of pending case law on green award criteria, a resource that was actually considered "the main thing that was driving it" (COM104:216). Clarifying the extant *acquis*, the ECJ had judged that the authorities would be allowed to define which criteria made offers the economically most advantageous (*Beentjes* C-31/87, *Evans Medical* C-324/93) and was also expected to follow this reasoning in a prominent case pending during the drafting period (*Concordia Bus Finland* C-513/99).

Overall, what is striking apart from the influence of the extant *acquis* and the involvement of an existing public-procurement community, is the relevance of internal portfolio logics. These were defined by the problem sets being dealt with by DG MARKT (creating a free market), DG ENV (promoting green issues), and DG EMPL (increasing social cohesion). On the most controversial provision of the acts, it was DG ENV's initiative—with a skilful Commissioner and a dedicated service that became involved early on—in combination with supranational competences from ECJ case law that were the decisive factors in explaining the rare instance of an opposing DG being the most powerful.

5.3.2 Directive on Public-procurement Vocabulary

Similar to the two directives discussed above, the proposal for a Common Procurement Vocabulary regulation (CPV, COM[2001]449) claims to promote openness and transparency in a common public-procurement market. It does so by establishing a multilingual classification system which is compulsory for all contracting authorities in the EU. It also seeks to facilitate searches by entrepreneurs, suppliers and service providers looking for potential contracts. The document merges the EU public-procurement regimes on supply, works and services, each of which previously "had its own classification" (COM63:36; also COM129:41).[13] The descriptors in the annex of 464 pages were newly structured to allow for automatic translation and distribution of notices in all member states—an approach that anticipated the e-Europe agenda in the context of the Lisbon Strategy (COM63:144, COM129:33).

DG MARKT's unit for Formulation and Enforcement of Public Procurement Issues led a swift drafting process starting in spring 2001 (COM129:13). Drafting was done from the bottom up (COM63:152), with the DG's hierarchy showing little interest in the file (COM63:24, COM37:157). Because of conservative national interests who feared a *de facto* extension of supranational powers in the area, substantial innovations were limited. Initially, DG MARKT had wanted to extend the scope of the CPV to boost public procurement in the internal market, but when member states objected in an expert advisory committee, "the Commission backtracked and kept the system as it was (COM63:212), concerned that the conflict would lead to discussions in the Council.

Drafting merely amounted to assembling the numbers from the existing classifications in a single structure. The factual conception of the CPV was outsourced to technical assistance contracts (COM63:36). Moreover, as DG MARKT did not consider itself "sufficiently competent for knowing all the types of purchases" (COM63:144), a very open external consultation followed. Thus, input from stakeholders, national authorities, advisory committees, the relevant professional organizations, intermediaries (Euro Info Centres) and service providers provided external expertise on specific descriptors (COM63:84, COM129:73, IP/01/1189). No conflicting positions existed within the Commission because the CPV proposal was "a rather technical instrument" (COM37:103) and seen "as a proposal which serves everybody's objectives" (COM63:190). Some bilateral informal exchanges took place prior to the ISC. The SJ and the Office for Publications (COM129:83, 67) helped by "giving specific input and expertise in their fields" (COM37:103), while DG ENTR, responsible for publishing defense procurement, ensured that the CPV was delineated from the extant *acquis* in its portfolio (COM129:83).

Overall, the lead DG's position formation on the highly technical CPV shows little innovation in drawing on existing classification schemes and updating them with external expertise within the limits allowed for by member states. No diverging positions existed internally on an act that was considered little more than a small device used in EU public-procurement policy.

5.3.3 Financial Intermediaries

Compared to the public-procurement cases, the following three acts promote the common market from a different angle. All aim to regulate financial services by squaring industry interests through supervision and stabilization of markets. The first case concerns the regulation of financial intermediaries (COM[2000]511), which are private market actors that distribute products from financial institutions in their own name and on their own account. Typical examples are travel agencies, car dealers, insurance brokers, and banks. Particularly in Belgium, the Netherlands, the UK, and Ireland, they sell more than half of all insurance products on the market.

The issue was not new at the EU level, but compared to the precursor directive (77/92/EEC) and a non-binding recommendation (92/48/EEC), the proposed act goes into greater detail to re-regulate the EU insurance market via a single registration system. The act applies to a much larger area than the extant *acquis*, which was limited to insurance agents and brokers. Now all intermediaries have to register in their home country according to common EU criteria. They thereby gain quasi-automatic access to the entire EU market via a simple notification by the respective national authority. In contrast to the previous recommendation, the new standards are binding and also much more detailed regarding the criteria intermediaries have to fulfill both qualitatively (minimum professional requirements and reputation) and quantitatively (minimum financial capacity and coverage by indemnity insurance). The proposed act also moves its focus away from a pure supply-side logic so as to also include consumer-related aspects (cf. Mügge 2010: 93). A number of concrete provisions aim at increasing consumer confidence in cross-national consumption by introducing binding information requirements, for example regarding the identity and address of financial intermediaries and the liable party, and on addressees for potential complaints.

Innovation in this area had been announced by former Internal Market Commissioner Monti in February 1997 (AE, April 1, 1997). The existing interface management between national regimes did not work well and, given an explicit agenda to boost the market for financial services, DG MARKT wanted to improve access to national insurance mediation markets for providers from other member states (COM109:21). Almost self-evidently, national experiences with liberalizing financial services for large industrial and commercial risks served as the regulatory blueprint. Not least, the proposed directive nicely dovetailed with a WTO multilateral agreement on the liberalization of financial services (AE, December 29, 1997). Consequently, DG MARKT put forward a number of provisions of "worth for the industry and also to enforce the internal market" (COM109:82).

However, the proposed directive also goes beyond negative integration and recommends substantial re-regulation. The degree to which this second axis of the proposal was born inside DG MARKT or was brought about by external pressure is difficult to trace. However, we know that initially the Commission had envisaged a less far-reaching act that would have been "limited to an update of the 1976 directive and adaptation of the (non-binding) 1991 recommendation at a later date" (AE 1997). However, both industry and consumer interests objected and forced DG MARKT's unit for Insurance and Pension Funds and External Aspects of Financial Services into a drafting process that stretched over "five or six years" and was subject to "a very, very lengthy discussion with the stakeholders [and] member states" (COM109:82). Although they were not among its core stakeholders, DG MARKT welcomed the views of consumers so as to balance an area that was historically shaped one-sidedly by a small number of industry interests (Mügge 2010: 125) and had not been able to deliver an integrated market (COM109:21).

Both sides, the consumers (represented by the European Bureau of Consumers' Unions, BEUC) and the financial intermediaries (represented by the International Association of Insurance and Reinsurance Intermediaries, BIPAR) successfully "insist[ed] that the new legislation must introduce compulsory requirements" and that smaller intermediaries, in particular, could pose problems for the protection of consumers (AE 1997, COM109:80). In particular, consumer-interest organizations from the most liberal national regimes called for information requirements (cf. Consumers in Europe Group 1997: 385). This demand was taken up by Internal Market Commissioner Bolkestein, who had in the meantime taken over the portfolio and placed particular emphasis on benefits for consumers, arguing that advancing market integration "will increase the choice of insurance products available to customers and help ensure they can trust the advice they are getting from intermediaries" (cited in: AE 2002). Thus, DG MARKT assumed a position typically associated with DG SANCO in the latter's representation of consumer interests. Both DGs had for some time been in an outright turf war on contractual consumer rights in general and consumer credit in particular (cf. Chapter 7.2). The main point of conflict was whether or not consumers were overburdened with choice vis-à-vis professional marketing strategies and thus needed regulatory protection. However, this conflict had tied up significant manpower and neither portfolio wanted to additionally wage war in this drafting process.

In line with this situation, interaction between the lead DG MARKT and DG SANCO was confined to the administrative level before and during the ISC. In a low-profile interaction devoid of political considerations (COM76:52), desk officers had room to thrash out compromises (COM109:70) and make adjustments when taking comments on board (COM109:34). No deviating positions from other DGs were mentioned in our interviews and, because it was a rather technical instrument, the proposal gained little attention inside and outside the Commission.

Overall, in order to boost a single market in financial insurance, the lead DG openly accepted far-reaching input from organized interests from both the industry and the consumer sides when reforming the extant *acquis*. Internal interaction on the act was limited to the administrative level and thus remained in a parallel world to the more fundamental ongoing controversies between DG MARKT and DG SANCO on the role of regulation in financial services in general.

5.3.4 Financial Conglomerates

DG MARKT's wish to boost the internal market for financial services was also the driving force behind the proposal on financial conglomerates (COM[2001]213), that is, companies offering banking, insurance, and securities services at the same time. Well-known examples are Allianz, Deutsche Bank, the ING Group, and Nordea. Growing numbers of such conglomerates and blurred distinctions between the activities in hitherto separate financial sectors had made these "a hot topic" (COM95:31) for financial market stability in the late 1990s (COM76:32). Notably the Scandinavian and the Benelux countries had started to consolidate regulation so as to avoid some of the typically associated risks, such as contagion or the use of the same capital as a buffer in two or even more sub-entities ("double gearing" of equity capital). In such precursor countries, regulation had moved away from simply increasing market efficiency and towards rules that benefited market stability and thereby social cohesion. This often entailed the establishment of a new supervisory authority (cf. Deutsche Bundesbank 2005: 48). At the EU level, however, financial conglomerates had remained an unregulated area (COM76:32, COM95:31). Instead, sectoral regimes prevailed that covered various parts of the conglomerates and created overlaps and inconsistencies, while certain types of financial groups were simply not encompassed at all (COM76:48).[14]

> The supervisors realized that when you look only at a solo license, the solo banking license and the solo insurance licenses, then you missed something. You missed the interaction of the two. And it is exactly the interaction of the two which makes the business opportunity (COM95:71).

In other words, the new regulation on financial conglomerates first had to define the subject matter. The new proposal sets thresholds at which a group is considered financial (versus non-financial) and a conglomerate (versus a homogenous group), and it further assesses the size of the financial sector within the conglomerate. Second, it harmonizes sectoral differences in the supervision of financial conglomerates, including strict solvency requirements, a harmonized internal management policy via annual reporting, and identification, measurement, monitoring and control of intra-group transactions. Finally, it sets rules to promote convergence in national supervisory approaches and between company sectors. Within each conglomerate, the assignment of a competent authority that coordinates, gathers information, and carries out controls within the group is required. At the EU level, a Financial Conglomerates Committee is established to accompany implementation.

EU regulation on financial conglomerates, similar to that on financial intermediaries, was announced from the top down in 1999 by the FSAP. However, DG MARKT had no clear policy vision on how to transpose its interest in a functioning market into substance and concrete standards. The issue was "a good example of a lack of knowledge in the European Commission" (COM76:32). Consequently, a national expert was recruited to the unit for Financial Conglomerates and Cross Sector Issues in spring 1999. His task was to draft and negotiate the act within a period of three years.[15] The national expert recalled that he was able to work extremely freely on the draft from the very start: "the only thing that the Commission wanted was that I came up with something, they wanted a result and then it was up to me" (COM76:50). In this context, his experience of having worked with the Joint Forum on Financial Conglomerates (a body of supervisors who collaborated with the Basel Committee on Banking Supervision [BCBS], the International Association of Insurance Supervisors [IAIS] and the International Organization of Securities Commissions [IOSCO]) considerably influenced the proposal (COM76:36). Standards on supervision requirements and capital adequacy agreed upon in Basel were simply transferred to the EU level and were made "legally enforceable" (COM95:23) in the form of a directive.

However, it was provisions aimed at aligning national supervisory approaches that were the main source of conflict with interests outside the Commission. Therefore, once a first version of the proposal had been drawn up, DG MARKT underwent "a kind of a testing with member states" in an expert group (COM76:52). This exercise brought to the fore substantial resistance from the national sectoral supervisor agencies that feared losing out against the new cross-cutting conglomerate supervisory authorities foreseen in the directive. As a DG MARKT drafting official recalled, "you had . . . banking supervisors that were defending banking regulation and insurance supervisors that were defending the insurances approach" (COM76:36) and "you had to convince the different sectors' supervisors to change their sectoral legislation and that was very, very difficult" (COM76:48). Giving in to the collective resistance from national regulatory authorities, DG MARKT opted to harmonize, while at the same time limiting adaptation pressure. This was achieved by agreeing to retreat regarding the scope of the directive and by defining groups as "financial" if they had 50 percent (rather than 40 percent) of financial activity, which *de facto* kept a greater number of entities under sectoral regulation.

Internally, DG MARKT's main interlocutor was DG ENTR. Looking at the proposal from the perspective of the financial industry, this DG would have liked more far-reaching harmonization and the establishment of a single supervisory authority, but still willingly accepted the appointment of a coordinator among the supervisory authorities as a second-best solution (response to written inter-service consultation no. 12000), and no further conflicts are reported.

In sum, the process very much followed a technocratic logic. Input from a national expert, himself drawing on his experience with national and international regulation, mixed with the resistance from national sectoral regulators, limited the degree of harmonization that could be achieved with the act. Again, the nature of financial service regulation had limited the disputes to technical issues and kept internal interaction at the administrative level.

5.3.5 Reinsurance

Our final case in this sub-field, the proposal on reinsurance (COM[2004]273), was also proposed as part of the FSAP in 1999, but took more time to mature. Reinsurance companies are responsible for about 10 percent of insurance premiums for businesses or individuals, reducing the risks for direct insurers. The risk is transferred to professional partners such as Münchener Re, Allianz Re, Lloyd's, and Axa Re. Much as in the case of the intermediaries (Chapter 5.3.3), an earlier directive had already existed (64/225/EEA) and had prohibited discrimination of reinsurers on nationality grounds. Nonetheless, reinsurance was far from a flourishing and harmonized single market. National rules on the supervision of domestic reinsurers differed and administrative burdens for cross-border operations prevailed (COM76:98, AE, April 22, 2004), *de facto* often escaping prudential oversight (cf. IA SEC[2004]443: 5). Against this background, DG MARKT consciously switched from a negative-integration to a re-regulation approach in order to boost the market, because pure negative integration had proved insufficient.

This agenda was again pursued along a dual line: broadening the area to which common rules would apply and implementing a harmonized authorization scheme with common supervisory rules. The proposal extends from all direct insurers under the old directive to all "pure" life or non-life reinsurers with a head office in the EU. The authorization system would follow a licensing approach rather than a more liberal passport regime when granting reinsurers access to the entire EU market. The license differs from the passport system in endowing supervisors with substantial enforcement powers to freeze assets, request financial recovery plans, or withdraw licenses. The harmonized criteria for licensing are both quantitative (e.g. requirement of a minimum guarantee fund) and qualitative in nature (qualification and reputation of personnel) and entail annual reporting as well as detailed minimum capital requirements. Moreover, implementation is further enhanced by a call for proactive cooperation between the different national supervisors so as to ensure application in transnational activities as well as exchange with central banks and national governments. Many of these re-regulatory provisions were copied from existing EU insurance regimes but newly applied to reinsurance. So how can we understand the process that led to this more interventionist approach in financial service regulation?

Backed by a broad consensus within the Commission concerning the prevailing gap in EU reinsurance legislation (COM36:39) and also by official political commitment expressed in the 1999 FSAP, the decision to start drafting was made in January 2000 (MARKT/2132/00: 7). A "very long reflection and work" process followed (COM76:90) until the adoption of the proposal in the College in April 2004. Rather than a high degree of conflict, this course confirms the increasing complexity of the emerging EU financial service regime and the intrinsic linkage of reinsurance to a number of ongoing EU regulatory initiatives (cf. Mügge 2010: ch. 7; Quaglia 2010b). Most importantly, the coverage of reinsurance under the EU insurance solvency regime was debated for a while (COM36:72, cf. IA SEC[2004]443: 10).[16] In addition, and unlike in the conglomerates case, an international regime was only slowly emerging, so that there was no comparable regulatory blueprint (COM36:37).[17]

In this light, DG MARKT was reluctant to move forward with a strong agenda of its own and was open to external input from whomever was "interested" (COM36:74). The basis for drafting was extant EU legislation on insurance companies, which the DG "fixed" to "fit" reinsurance (COM36:22). Moreover, qualitative registration criteria were copied from the financial conglomerates directive and were further influenced by ongoing discussions on the "prudent person" approach in the pension fund directive (2003/41/EC). On this basis, DG MARKT consulted with member states three to four times a year in the standing Insurance Committee (COM36:202) to "check drafting" (COM36:72) in technical terms as well as to anticipate Council dynamics (COM36:166). The external expertise also included a commissioned study on reinsurance supervision (carried out by the KPMG Deutsche Treuhand-Gesellschaft accounting firm, COM36:132) and the recruitment to the drafting unit of two seconded national experts from the German Bundesanstalt für Finanzdienstleistungsaufsicht (Federal Financial

Supervisory Authority, COM36:156). In addition to the input of national interests and experts, the final proposal was also influenced by the results of industry meetings (COM36:162). This step particularly concerned a large-scale simulation exercise towards the end of the drafting process. The simulation involved around 400 reinsurers, 1,650 direct insurers, 145 pure reinsurers, and 275 reinsurance captives and aimed to assess how to guarantee commitment of reinsurers via provisions. On this basis, industry was able to push through the exclusion of direct insurers (MARKT/2530/02: 9), thus narrowing the scope of application, and a separation of solvency margins for life and non-life insurance (COM36:34, IA SEC[2004] 443: 29). Overall, interaction was transparent, which was deemed "very unusual at the time" (COM36:142) given that impact assessments and public consultations had not yet been made compulsory. Thus, the supply of information from national regulators and industry are important in explaining the strongly re-regulatory approach taken in this case.

Internally, DG MARKT consulted DGs TRADE and RELEX on a very specific aspect of capital requirements known as "collaterals," which can be used as a trade barrier (COM76:56). However, rather than engaging in interaction about different positions internally, these DGs aligned jointly against member-state opposition.

Overall, a lack of an agenda of its own on the part of the lead DG in combination with a strong political commitment in the Commission resulted in a position formation process that drew on related existing directives and close consultations with member states, organized interests and experts. Internal interactions were limited and no conflicts were reported.

The second sub-field differs from the first in that it is predominantly characterized by rather technocratic position-formation processes with low salience and limited uncertainty. The extant *acquis* is omnipresent and particularly important in explaining positions, along with outside expertise, transfer of international templates, and national positions. The member states agreed in principle and—under qualified majority voting—provided templates or exerted influence bilaterally rather than in the shadow of the Council vote. Apart from consumers in the intermediaries case, non-market stakeholders were strikingly absent from the processes and DG MARKT did not actively rope them in. Virtually only (national) authorities and the regulated companies provided input to DG MARKT—despite the huge potential repercussions in social terms.

The standards proposed are important in substance and by and large differ from existing regimes by replacing negative integration with re-regulatory approaches to the common market. However, in most of the cases this seems to result from the lack of a strong DG MARKT agenda and member states' and industry's influence rather than from other services' input. Where interactions occurred, DGs ENV and SANCO were more successful than DG EMPL in linking their cause to the market. Overall and with the exception of the public-procurement cases, the processes studied remained uncontroversial inside the Commission and the interactions are best characterized as exchanges of information on how to advance the common market.

5.4 FREE MOVEMENT OF PEOPLE AND SERVICES

About 2 percent of the EU population live in a member state different to the one in which they were born. 1 million workers are posted each year across EU borders to provide services and over a million people cross borders every day, although the figures are much higher if holidays or business trips are taken into account (MEMO/09/353, EP press release 20.6.2013). At the same time, services and establishment of activities are frequently subject to stringent national rules. Historically, regulations on free movement in the internal market targeted discrimination on grounds of nationality. Today, however, a much broader understanding of what constitutes a restriction has developed and any national rule that hinders intra-Union economic activity, such as administrative requirements, must be proportionally justified by legitimate underlying policy objectives. In this context, all four acts in the third sub-group aim at boosting the *free movement of people and services.* What was at stake was a switch from the prevailing logic of regulated liberalization of services in the common market to a more liberal market approach that would basically prevent national regulations from constituting a hindrance. This, in turn, affects practices aimed at realizing social goals and objectives at the EU as well as at the national level. This tension between market liberalization and social aims is core to cases on the recognition of professional qualifications, liberalization of services, coordination of social security systems, and cross-border healthcare. Tables 5.6 and 5.7 give details of these proposal and process characteristics.

The extant *acquis* in the area provided the Commission with implementing experience. However, ECJ case law had repeatedly engendered legal uncertainty that mattered particularly for cross-border healthcare. The potentially broad appeal of free movement of people and services to any individual in the EU did not necessarily translate into salient proposals. Quite the contrary, strikingly little sensitivity for the fundamental political decisions existed inside and outside the Commission. Only with the extreme public visibility the Bolkestein directive gained during the inter-institutional process (COM40:74, COM70:97) did market liberalization receive more public attention. This in turn substantially altered the drafting context for the cross-border healthcare directive.

5.4.1 Recognition of Professional Qualifications

Workers who want to exercise their profession in another country need to communicate knowledge and skills to a prospective client or employer. Clients and employers are dependent, in turn, on decoding the unknown qualification to match it with their needs. In this context, the proposal for the EU directive on the recognition of professional qualifications (COM[2002]119) aims at facilitating the free movement of (mostly self-employed) workers by granting professionals from other member states access and the same rights as nationally qualified professionals. Compared to precursor directives, administrative burdens are lightened, particularly in the case of professional activity of up to 16 weeks per year (services). Furthermore, the proposal integrates 35 sectoral directives on 800

Table 5.6. Position formation on free movement of people and services

Proposal number	Contents	No. of key provisions	Main line of proposal (content)	Uncertainty	Salience	Origin (hierarchical level)	Process duration (months)	External consultation	Main position-formation factors
COM[2002]119	Recognition of Professional Qualifications	10	Simplifying recognition, mix of mutual recognition and minimum harmonization, separation of establishment and services (with fewer administrative requirements)	No	Yes	Administrative	28	Public	- Extant *acquis* - National position - Organized interests
COM[2004]2	Services in the Internal Market	13	Country-of-origin principle, administrative simplification and horizontal coordination, consumer information and rights	No	No	Administrative	17	Specific	- Anticipation of Council majority - Extant *acquis* - ECJ jurisprudence - Individuals' influence - Partisan ideology
COM[2006]16	Coordination of Social-Security Systems	15	Simplification of implementing rules by deleting exemptions and clarifying responsibilities	No	No	Administrative	21	Specific	- Extant *acquis* - Experts
COM[2008]414	Cross-border Healthcare	10	General non-discrimination and market liberalization combined with patients' rights and state responsibilities	Yes	Yes	Political	43	Public	- Extant *acquis* - Experts - Partisan ideology - Anticipation of Council majority - ECJ jurisprudence

Table 5.7. Interaction on free movement of people and services

Proposal number	Contents	Deviating DGs	Informal interaction	Position-based conflict	Process-based conflict	Main line of conflict	Most powerful DG	Main power resources
COM[2002]119	Recognition of Professional Qualifications	SJ SANCO COMP JLS TREN EAC	Intense	2	0	Keeping sectoral *acquis* intact, introduction of platforms to facilitate practices of compensation measures on a middle ground between automatic recognition and harmonization	MARKT	- Lead department - Supranational competence - Support from SJ
COM[2004]2	Services in the Internal Market	SG TREN EMPL SANCO JLS TRADE RTD RELEX	Intense	2	1	Exemptions (public service, nuclear energy, gambling, transport), collusion with international private law	MARKT	- Entrepreneurship - Supranational competence - Bureaucratic legitimacy - Lead department
COM[2006]16	Coordination of Social-Security Systems	MARKT	Intense	2	1	Prior announcement of posting of workers, prior authorization and reimbursement for hospital care	EMPL	- Lead department - Supranational competence - Support from SJ
COM[2008]414	Cross-border Healthcare	EMPL MARKT COMM	Intense	3	2	Authorization and reimbursement, turf defence of existing *acquis* on the Coordination of Social Security Systems	SANCO	- Bureaucratic and public legitimacy - Support from SG and SJ

professions by re-categorizing them in three groups, each matched by a specific regulatory approach. First, minimum harmonization provides free access across the common market for a group of seven professions of particular public interest (mostly medical professions and architects). Second, automatic mutual recognition is granted to crafts and commercial industry qualifications upon two to six years of practice in the home country, depending on the category. Third, for the bulk of professions, the so-called General System applies. Here, individual requests for recognition have to be made in the host country. Where training and practice completed in the home country is shorter or differs in quality, compensation requirements are made. In this way, at the end of the 1990s about 10,000 individual recognitions were granted annually (AE, March12, 2002).

However, the General System was particularly ridden with implementation difficulties related to intransparent, unpredictable, and idiosyncratic assessments, as DG MARKT's drafting unit knew well from "five or eight years of experience" (COM17:37), as well as daily interactions in expert groups and committees (COM17:189, COM41:54). This knowledge was mixed with fears that further reforms would become increasingly difficult after enlargement, while the implementing situation would deteriorate into "something unmanageable" (COM17:77).

Early in 2000, DG MARKT's unit for Policy Development and Coordination of the Internal Market decided to "put on a couple of pages of paper" (COM17:69) how to improve implementation, simplify recognition, and provide "some ease of operation" (COM17:229, also COM106:27). Reinforced by two additional desk officers, the unit embarked on a process that lasted two and a half years (COM17:69). Although the increasingly popular simplification discourse (cf. White Book on Governance (COM[2001]428) served as the major framework, the member states proved to be hesitant. A number of revisions had already taken place in the 1990s (COM17:197, 245), and it was only when DG MARKT increased pressure by launching a set of infringements procedures that member states submitted an official request for legislative action at the Stockholm Council in May 2001.[18] While the political level had maintained a hands-off stance during initial drafting (COM17:39, COM108:125), it now seized the opportunity to promote the mobility of citizens (COM73:168). In a quite exceptional move, Internal Market Commissioner Bolkestein and Employment Commissioner Diamantopoulou together publicly praised the upcoming initiative in the *FT* (January 29, 2001; also COM108:133, COM24:84) as part of a broader strategy on the emergence of new labor markets (COM[2001]116) and the Lisbon agenda (COM41:48), making it even more difficult for member states to argue against reforms.[19]

Drafting was largely business as usual (COM108:125, COM17:69). DG MARKT contacted the SJ early on for help with integrating the many specific rules for each profession, but the lead DG's cross-sectoral simplification approach still drew opposition. Lobbying by the medical professions at different levels of DG MARKT's hierarchy (COM108:93, COM116:124) and particularly critical responses from the legal and accountancy professions in an open consultation (MARKT/D/3723/2002: 2, COM41:123) secured the continuation of the respective sectoral regimes. But while conflict potential was high internally, too, interaction began only during the ISC and was overall "very constructive . . . sorting things out on a technical level" (COM108:55) and a source of "practical improvements" (COM17:101; also COM41:172). This way DG TREN's request to keep the *acquis* on the transport professions intact was accommodated (COM41:102), while DG JLS was parent to a clause preventing all too easy recognition of doctors who had lost their authorization to practice on the basis of initial qualifications (COM41:69). DG EAC backpedalled on the proposal, blurring the line between the common market and educational matters (COM45:38) and claiming mobility for the latter, too—simply to create room for future policy-making in an area confined exclusively to member-state competences.

But the proposal also engendered "interesting and tough discussions" on more fundamental questions across DGs and within DG MARKT (COM41:126; also COM17:157, COM108:43). The drafting unit had started from the outright interest of shaping the regime on a middle ground between harmonization and mutual recognition (AE, December 7, 14, 2004) and now opposed more extreme positions on either side of the continuum. Conflict centered on the most innovative proposal provision, which advocates intervention through delegation to private actors. Decisions about compensation measures under the General System should be delegated to platforms of European-wide professional organizations. This was perceived as a "pragmatic" solution (COM108:73) that was likely to pave the way for a public–private regime situated "between non-harmonization and non-automatic recognition" (COM41:42; also COM17:245, AE February 28, 2001). Precisely for this reason, the SJ spurned this variable geometry approach and, going "very much into the details" (COM41:131), pushed for a more stringent legal oversight of these platforms (COM17:237). DG COMP feared that this would lead to unequal conditions for recognition across professions, for example, and therefore to unfair competition in the market (COM41:90). However, DG MARKT officials had arranged support from their cabinet (COM108:73) and, even more importantly, they knew that a code of conduct and non-formalized and variable application of platforms (MARKT/D/3723/2002: 13) "had happened in practice" (COM108:39), making it difficult for DG COMP and the SJ to pledge support for a regressive solution. Nonetheless, while they had advocated for more intervention on platforms, DG MARKT—this time supported by the SJ—admonished DG SANCO for overshooting the mark with their quest to particularly protect consumers of health services by regulating these professions (COM41:39, COM106:36, COM17:57). Still, interaction across the DGs was solution-oriented by and large. By contrast, the units inside DG MARKT clashed on specific issues, such as special training requirements for tourist guides in southern Europe (COM69:191; Nicolaidis and Schmidt 2007: 727) and the underlying principles for a common market in services (COM108:43), given that the preparation for the directive on the liberalization of services had started in parallel in the same DG (Chapter 5.4.2) and left its mark on the proposal. As an official remembers, "we had still less burdensome procedures [on services as opposed to establishment] after internal discussions" (COM41:181). The liberalization advocates were "stronger in arguing their case" (COM108:43) and ultimate settlement was reached at the political level (COM106:47). However, much of the interaction with other DGs happened at the administrative level. The proposal was debated neither in the Special Chefs meeting nor by the Hebdo and was adopted in the College on March 7, 2002 by written procedure (COM41:214, COM17:89, 153).

Summing up, the act pushes for more cross-border service liberalization by facilitating recognition. It integrates existing regimes while paying attention to implementation experiences and organized interests. Conflict between DGs was limited and was easily resolved by the lead DG through building on its advantage to structure interactions, using its experience about extant *acquis* and practices, and to obtain support from the SJ.

5.4.2 Services in the Internal Market

The proposal on services in the internal market (COM[2004]2) is a horizontal framework applying the country-of-origin principle to all services.[20] Differing national regimes rendered cross-border provision of services complicated and ridden with administrative challenges. Aiming to enhance the free movement of services, the proposal prescribes single points of contact and horizontal cooperation between national administrations, as well as an *ex ante* screening of national authorization schemes. It substantially departs from existing sectoral EU service regimes, which had mixed elements of re-regulation in the form of minimum harmonization with (managed) mutual recognition (Nicolaidis and Schmidt 2007: 721), for instance in financial services (Chapter 5.3) and in the recognition of professional qualifications (Chapter 5.4.1). Thus, DG MARKT's approach displays a sweeping predominance of a pure market logic. After the proposal had left the Commission, it created a political outcry, closely related to the negative referenda on a European Constitution in France and the Netherlands (Menz 2010).

Drafting started in 2001 with the creation of a new unit working exclusively on services (COM69:143, COM35:18, COM70:19). The unit was well staffed, with 12 officials with "excellent . . . brilliant minds" (COM65:37) who "worked very very hard" (COM 69:143) to "give regulatory impetus to service liberalization" (COM40:23, also COM4:100). Particularly the head of unit, the German Margot Fröhlinger, had a clear vision on how to make services circulate in a market in "utterly devastating" conditions (cited in *Der Standard* January 31, 2003) with "the main obstacle [being] home country control" (COM116:76). Widely perceived as a policy entrepreneur (COM40:92, COM65:37), she provided "mental orientation" and a certain "philosophy" (COM4:100), much shaped on the e-commerce directive (2000/31/EC) she had been in charge of preparing two years earlier (COM118:103, COM40:83; Knill and Tosun 2010: 74). Fröhlinger was supported by a number of "very powerful characters" in DG MARKT (COM108:43) who had long-running stakes in moving service liberalization forward (COM70:100, Wonka 2008: 181; De Witte 2007: 2). Commissioner Bolkestein, in particular, identified strongly with the directive that nicely matched his outspoken liberal orientation (COM108:65, COM65:101, COM70:79, COM40:71, COM69:50).

In its ideal position, the drafting unit clearly sought more liberalized European markets for services, while ignoring wider societal goals that might justify trade barriers. This entailed two crucial regulatory choices. First, by applying secondary legislation, the drafting officials sought to "limit member-state sovereignty [reflected in administrative barriers], even beyond the case law of the Court"

(COM83:42), which was characterized by "1000 judgments that no citizen can read" (COM83:24; also COM70:76, IA; SEC[2004]21: 26; Hatzopoulos and Do 2006: 923). Second, while DG MARKT officials claimed modestly that the act would do nothing but translate the country-of-origin principle (which had already existed in primary and case law) into legislation (COM69:41, 185; also D'Acunto 2004: 201), choosing country of origin as the horizontal principle made future sectoral re-regulation unlikely. And equating the country-of-origin principle with mutual recognition (*Cassis de Dijon*, C-120/78, COM116:72), national governments would lose control over the quality of services provided in their country and would be dependent on administrations in the country of origin instead (COM65:37; also Schmidt 2009).

In preparing this approach, the waters were cautiously tested among external actors. A survey of 6,000 service-related companies in 14 member states was carried out and complemented by meetings with member states and national stakeholder organizations, excluding the usual critics of liberalization strategies, such as organized labor (COM114:275). This served "to find out, whether or not there are some national rules which must be cancelled, or modified" (COM69:41). However, the overall involvement of external interests remained limited (COM40:152, COM70:85), and consultation was biased towards those economic interests that would benefit from service liberalization. On this basis, a report on the State of the Internal Market for Services (COM[2002]441) highlighted existing obstacles and served as a reference point for the concrete drafting (COM70:100; also Knill and Tosun 2010: 70). Member states and other DGs largely supported this diagnosis (Wonka 2008: 182–4; Nicolaidis and Schmidt 2007: 722). They hoped that liberalizing services, accounting for 70 percent of economic activity and a rising proportion of overall employment, would give a "new dynamism" (COM40:23) to sluggish economic growth.

However, quite naturally, DG MARKT's horizontal framework cut across other portfolios (COM70:55). This resulted in "pretty intense" (COM64:132) interactions that remained at the administrative level, however (COM69:158, COM17:161). DG EMPL pointed to the tension with its posted workers directive (96/71/EC)—originally designed to limit unfair competition and protect workers—as the application of home-country labor-law standards on service provision would be made much more difficult without an obligation to carry papers for local controls and without the appointment of national representatives.[21] With a forked tongue, DG MARKT responded that DG EMPL's *acquis* would remain in place in any case (COM70:34, COM40:131). *De facto*, and confirming the basic decision that no administrative burdens should be imposed on cross-border service provision, DG MARKT's proposal would, however, replace controls and monitoring requirements with a loose system of administrative cooperation. But DG EMPL "had to give in" in view of a lack of arguments proving the opposite (COM64:108) and also became more accommodating in the light of DG MARKT's very well prepared text (COM65:77, COM116:80). DG TREN (COM70:112; also COM40:116), in turn, found DG MARKT to be more accommodating when it argued that it would be technically accurate to exempt transport areas with higher levels of regulation (COM64:81, COM70:112, COM40:116). DG JLS feared collusion with parallel initiatives for (international) private-law agreements that regulated litigation between providers and recipients of services (Rome I and later

Rome II). According to the SJ, there was a related risk of legal uncertainty (COM83:39). And again DG MARKT resolved the issue by providing for a special derogation that allows the country-of-destination principle to remain applicable in international private law (as opposed to public law), this time to avoid a conflict of law, for instance with respect to non-contractual liability of the provider in the case of an accident (COM118:103, COM65:41, COM70:58, COM116:180). Finally, having set the political course, and flanked by case-law developments (*Kohll* C-158-96, *Decker* C-120/95), DG MARKT's intention to liberalize cross-border health services by calling for an end to prior authorization for non-hospital care fuelled extensive internal debates. On the one side, DG SANCO stressed the specific characteristics of health services (COM73:51). On the other, DG EMPL pressed for a wording that would ensure legal consistency "but would not destroy the coordination" of social security systems (COM20:68; cf. Chapter 5.4.3). Nevertheless, DG MARKT kept debates at bay by arguing that the act was merely codifying existing case law and was "really a result of the decisions of the Court of Justice" (COM116:128-153). On the basis of this argument, DG MARKT's political choice, which prioritized service providers over consumers and the concerns of public financers, was not further debated and the provision remained part of the proposal.

Remaining minor issues were clarified during the ISC in autumn 2003 (COM83:78, COM69:71). Overall, the informal interaction followed a rather technical logic, with concerns being dispelled at the service level and legal-technical questions dominating the exchange rather than the potentially more controversial political implications. This resonates well with the picture drawn by officials from other DGs of the drafting unit running a subterfuge strategy that kept opposition by other DGs (COM65:33 and 81) and external actors at bay, "with a few people, sort of, making the key decisions and everything being kept on rather tight control rather than the usual" (COM73:197, likewise COM108:51).

This strategy culminated in the usage of internal coordination structures to push the proposal through with as little change as possible at an opportune moment. This moment arrived when the political level was involved only shortly before the Christmas break. With adoption in the College scheduled for early January 2004, the usual preparations and exchanges between cabinets were abridged. The Special Chefs meeting took place in the first week of January—when many people are still on holiday. The proposal itself was adopted during a "Strasbourg week," squeezed in to the Monday meeting just before politicians were due to travel (COM65:33). Given these circumstances, only a few contested issues made it to the College (PV[2004]16141: 14). Opposing DG MARKT's horizontal approach, the Secretariat-General in discussions at political level (see Chapter 10) described in detail the derogation of public services (postal, electricity, gas, and water services) by drawing on its ample knowledge of public-sector regulation, which showed that "it did not make any sense to apply the country of origin to sectors where member states can impose public service obligations" (COM65:69, COM64:84). Further exemptions were granted temporally to industry interests (COM40:38), on gambling and on nuclear power safety, which had been advocated by the French Trade Commissioner Lamy (COM40:59, COM65:109, COM69:65, COM70:52, COM116:172) and the Belgian Commissioner for Research (COM65:37). DG MARKT had proposed a fixed deadline for these exemptions, but as for public services, it acquiesced after debates had highlighted sensibilities that might jeopardize the act in the inter-institutional process (COM69:65, COM70:127). Overall, the act can be considered a resounding success for the lead DG. Even though the Prodi Commission was a relatively left-leaning Commission (Chapter 4), which might lead one to expect more internal resistance to such a liberalizing act, there was a "kind of cohesion of the College in proposing this proposal" (COM40:182) and the final decision was taken "by unanimity, without any discussion" (COM69:44, COM116:72). In light of the fierce debates the act had triggered in the inter-institutional process, this led a high-ranking official to argue that "if there has been one internal problem with this Directive it is that it went so quickly through the Commission that we did not have time to have inside problems" (COM65).

Characterized by a strikingly lengthy preparation within DG MARKT, reference to the e-commerce directive and a very limited involvement of external interests or political actors inside the Commission, the strong liberalization thrust of the proposal is best explained by ideologically motivated actors in the drafting unit. Regarding specific issues and exemption possibilities, national interest via the respective Commissioners can be identified, although the main line of the proposal was not questioned. Finally, while most of the participating actors would stress the act's technical quality, the outside view makes clear that personnel, supranational competence, and lead advantage were used strategically by entrepreneurial actors to overcome or even to avoid internal opposition.

5.4.3 Implementing Coordination of Social Security Systems

The extant *acquis* on the coordination of social security systems balanced the free movement of persons (e.g. tourists, mobile workers, jobseekers, and retirees) with the logic of historically evolved and deeply embedded national social security systems.[22] It allowed member states to stick to their national systems as long as individuals were treated equally regardless of nationality and entitlements were portable across countries.[23] DG EMPL's new proposal on the Implementing Regulation (COM[2006]16) simplifies and modernizes existing provisions by abolishing country exemptions (e.g. various provisions for France), specific treatment of types of diseases (e.g. sclerogenic pneumonosis), and sectoral groups of workers (e.g. transport). With this move, some provisions become more detailed, such as for reimbursement and recovery claims. Likewise, others clarified responsibilities, for instance regarding the competent institution for assisting with the completion of formalities. But none of these modifications shifted the general line of interface management characterizing the EU's regulatory approach in the area.

At the time of drafting in 2004, however, this position was severely under attack. The Commission proposal on the liberalization of services had treated health services much like any other service. And while *de facto* this policy had been curbed in the inter-institutional process by removing the relevant article from the directive, case law by "the European Court [seeming] . . . somehow out of control" (COM73:36) had meanwhile continued to increase legal uncertainty (*Kohll* C-158-96, *Decker* C-120/95, and *Vanbraekel* C-368/98).[24] At the same time, prospects for adoption were gloomy. First, Eastern enlargement had increased differences between member states' social security systems. What is more, the highly controversial service directive was still pending in the inter-institutional process (political agreement was reached on May 29, 2006), which kept Europe divided on the benefits of further market liberalization versus regulation of social service provision.

In this context, three fundamentally different positions on cross-border social service provision prevailed inside the Commission. DG MARKT wanted to enshrine ECJ case law in secondary legislation, sticking to its general position on service liberalization and advocating the country-of-origin principle. Juxtaposing this position, DG EMPL considered itself the guardian of citizen access to (public) social security and argued that the Commission should keep the functioning *acquis* on coordination against the intrusion of market principles. DG SANCO positioned itself right in the middle of these demands by favoring market liberalization while strengthening patients' rights and introducing a broader approach to the health system that takes into account providers, consumers and financers of care. In this triangle, the emerging lines of conflict on the proposal for an Implementing Regulation and a Directive on Cross-border Healthcare (Chapter 5.4.4) broke their ground differently in the respective processes, ultimately suggesting very diverse regulatory solutions albeit roughly at the same time.

Once the Regulation had been modified in spring 2004, DG EMPL's unit for Free Movement of Workers and Coordination of Social Security Schemes turned to the accompanying Implementing Regulation (COM23:58). Receiving "4000–5000 letters a year" (COM23:42) complaining about implementation problems and seeking clarification, the unit's "34 people, 23 lawyers" (COM23:42) were faced with the challenge of beginning to simplify a highly technical instrument that was "absolutely impossible to understand" (COM36:28; also COM23:220, COM20:72). Persistent member-state reluctance to alter existing practices (COM23:162) complicated the task. Thus, DG EMPL opted for early consultation in a well-acquainted policy community to improve the Implementing Regulation in substantial terms while at the same time securing support for an expected difficult inter-institutional process. In order to "get all the information we can" (COM20:120), social security experts were invited who had been dealing with the coordination *acquis* for decades at the national level and could provide information on implementation problems (COM23:286). The consultation results were then further debated in formalized EU bodies, which had developed over roughly 30 years of policy-making in the area: the Administrative Commission composed of national experts from the Social, Labor and Health Ministries, the Social Partner Advisory Committee and the Audit Board formed by social partner organizations (COM23:384).

> We tried to invent a working method, which would make the proposal sort of overall acceptable, ... it is a co-ownership in a way, we are building consensus and we are working through our co-ownership. You are not going to shout at something that you have contributed to create. You will have more, will probably be more indulgent—not in a way that you are going to drop your national interest, which is not the point—but you are going to help, to improve, and to try to get to a better product (COM20:108–124).

This move helped to keep debates about the act in the sectoral logic of social security coordination. However, it could not remedy the fact that the general tension between DG MARKT's emphasis on the freedom of services and DG EMPL's approach of highlighting the specific nature of social services, which developed "rather emotionally" (COM23:116) at the DGs' administrative and political levels (COM23:186, CIS-Net consultation no. 16532).

First, DG EMPL required employers posting workers to inform the relevant institutions in the country of destination before the worker departed. Otherwise they would not be eligible for social benefits. Based on implementing experiences with the earlier Regulation, they feared "unfair competition" (COM23:94). This clashed with DG MARKT's position, which understood *prior* information to be a restriction of the freedom to provide services. The internal process was blocked for "several months" (COM23:94) and, while DG EMPL was powerful in securing the provision, DG MARKT played its part by watering down the requirement of prior notification by the employer to read only "if possible" and thus not in cases of immediate departure (COM23:102).

Second, case-law developments allowed patients to choose from two parallel regimes for non-hospital care. These followed either DG EMPL's favored logic of re-regulation (prior authorization and full reimbursement) or DG MARKT's favored country-of-origin principle (freedom of choice and limited reimbursement). Their relationship, however, was unclear and subject to controversial debates. However, DG EMPL hesitated to run the gauntlet by pushing for a dominance of prior authorization, fearing that this would "contradict" the service directive pending in Council (COM23:90). However, given the principled differences, it could not avoid the two perspectives clashing when defining the scope of social services covered under the Implementing Regulation. DG MARKT pushed for reimbursement for non-authorized care at the level of the treatment country to endow financially worse-off individuals with a right to market freedoms. The crucial point was that, stretching case law (*Vanbraekel* C-368/98), they wanted this provision to apply not only to non-hospital care but also to other social services such as hospital care (COM35:44). In line with DG EMPL, however, the SJ was equally hesitant to follow DG MARKT's legally shaky interpretation (COM23:380). Further backing came from those member states that were little inclined to accept the financial implications this would entail for healthcare (COM23:150). With this support, DG EMPL managed to keep the re-regulatory logic of its system in place. This was agreed upon in a consensual and "very fruitful" manner (COM20:40, also COM23:116) at the administrative level, such that no open points remained for the political process between cabinets and Commissioners (COM20:80), leading to adoption by written procedure in January 2006.

Taken together, this technical proposal largely follows the line of extant *acquis*, complemented with implementing experiences channeled into the proposal from DG EMPL's sector-specific policy community. The lead DG could ascertain its position internally against more liberal positions by drawing on legal foundations and using informational advantages and support from horizontal services, as well as the legal uncertainty attached to the case-law interpretation.

5.4.4 Cross-border Healthcare

The proposal on Cross-Border Healthcare (also: Patient Mobility, COM[2008] 414) supports freedom of movement by combining an explicit right to non-discrimination with patients' rights in cross-border healthcare. It sets up common minimum principles of universality, access to good quality care, equity, and solidarity, and obliges member states to implement and monitor them. DG SANCO formed its position along the proactively shaped health system approach, thereby building on the health Art. 152 established with the Maastricht Treaty and its growing organizational strength (cf. Chapter 4; Hervey and Vanhercke 2010).

> [W]e were trying to establish . . . the notion that we should not be starting either from the single market or from social security. We should actually be trying to start from what is good from a health point of view. But that is complicated, because it is not only what is good from the health point of view for the individual, but what is actually good from the point of view of people actually trying to run efficient health services. And the two may not necessarily always coincide. So we were trying to cover that, a new space [the health-system approach] (COM73:186)

This approach was now used to fill the legal vacuum left by internal struggles in the Commission and divided national interests on cross-border health services in the context of the services directive (see Chapter 5.4.2). The "very painful gaffe" (COM107:60, authors' translation) the Commission had received with the liberalization of services directive, as well as the rejection of the Constitutional Treaty in the French and Dutch referenda and the enormous protest march through the streets of Brussels in May 2005 (COM40:74, COM70:97) were strongly associated with precisely this issue (cf. AE, July 9, 2008) and created a substantially altered political context. Inside the Commission, this nurtured the wish for an act that would "put citizens at the heart of the market" (COM73:168). Given that "everyone can become a patient eventually" (COM24:84)—an argument later actively strengthened by a requested Flash Eurobarometer (No. 210 "Cross-border Health services in the EU," 2007)—a new act on cross-border healthcare provision seemed the ideal solution. However, following years of negotiations revising the coordination of social security regimes, DG EMPL did not want to open up the issue (COM73:72), while Internal Market Commissioner McCreevy considered cross-border healthcare a "hot potato and was happy to pass it on" (COM35:32; also AE March 22, 2006). In this context, President Barroso sought to give cross-border healthcare a more "social air" (COM35:58) and thus assigned the lead to DG SANCO, an "ambitious" DG keen to enhance its "visibility" (COM73:96; also COM23:134).

In January 2005, preparation started in DG SANCO's unit for Health Strategy and Health Systems in parallel with DG EMPL's closely related Implementing Regulation on the Coordination of Social Security Systems (COM24:12; Chapter 5.4.3). In DG SANCO's case, the political level was involved throughout, including during active drafting (COM73:33, COM24:60) and regular meetings up through the hierarchy (COM24:116). Putting its health system approach to work, DG SANCO attached much importance to differing from existing approaches in the areas of social or common market policies (COM24:250). In this, broad "preliminary consultations" (COM24:74) with a wide range of external interests of different national representatives and organized interests such as health professionals' organizations, public health NGOs, patient groups, and public and private service providers and funders (COM24:58; also SEC[2006] 1195/4) provided vital input.

At the same time, opening up drafting to a wider range of often strikingly different external interests limited DG SANCO's ideal position on a number of initially more market-liberal provisions. A set of minimum criteria for what constituted cross-border health services, established earlier in a High-Level Process of Reflection on Patient Mobility and Healthcare Developments (AE, December 9, 2003) now pushed the proposal towards more re-regulation. The proposal also strengthens the role of the state by committing member states to provide information on cross-border healthcare. However, where external interests were split between further strengthening complaint procedures, liability insurance, or guarantees to individuals, on the one hand, and applying a more liberal principle of caveat emptor ("let the buyer beware"), on the other (AE, April 20, 2007; UK Healthcare Commission 2007), DG SANCO abstained from adopting a clear re-regulatory stance and instead took the middle ground between liberalization and re-regulation (SEC[2006]1195/4: 13–14). Likewise, proposing reference networks and pooling resources among service providers for rare diseases and innovations is neither re-regulating nor fully liberalizing. In reality, it simply copies economically successful practices in bordering regions in France, Luxembourg, and Belgium, as well as in Scandinavia (COM24:44, AE, April 20, 2007) "to create something which looks like a health proposal and not just either a little [re-regulatory, author] social security scheme, or a new [market-liberalizing] civil services proposal" (COM73:72). In a similar vein, and in response to a demand from the European Parliament (AE, May 24, 2007), DG SANCO followed the consumer organization BEUC (EurActiv 2008) in its push to strengthen administrative cooperation in health services at specific points of single contact.

DG SANCO ambitiously announced the proposal and formal interaction started at the beginning of 2007 with the first of four inter-service group meetings held that year (SEC[2008]2163: 2). The ISC followed suit in September 2007 (COM24:122), after which "a bunch of problems" arose (COM20:80). Many cabinets and Commissioners questioned the political viability of the act: "[t]his may be a perfectly good technical solution, but actually is this a good idea? Politically?" (COM73:138). Some officials involved remembered the interaction as "ferocious" (COM73:117), employing war-time images of "officials on the barricades with knifes between the tooth" (COM107:138). There were clear dividing lines, with DGs EMPL, MARKT, INFSO, and TRADE fundamentally opposing DG SANCO (see below, AE, December 19, 2007). Consequently, DG SANCO very often felt "isolated among those three, four DGs," and DGs EMPL and MARKT in particular actively forged an alliance (COM20:40, COM35:110). In turn, DG SANCO received support from DG ENTR (COM24:214).

In this conflict-laden context, the Secretariat-General headed by Commission President Barroso, aware of the public's scrutiny of its political advances, intervened and stopped the process, basically advising the other services to "not rock the boat" (COM73:72). It withdrew the act from the Commission's internal agenda "just days before it was supposed to be discussed by the College" (Kurpas et al. 2008: 21; AE, December 19, 2007).[25] Bowing to political sensibilities, the incoming Cypriot Health Commissioner Vassiliou, arriving in the Commission in April 2008, later pledged to submit the proposal to College only after the Irish referendum on the Constitution had been held in June 2008, but still in time for Barroso to harvest support from the left in the European Parliament in the run-up to his re-election (COM73:72; AE, April 1, 2008).

What followed was a very unusual revision and redrafting process. "With the blessing of the President" (COM73:141) and the agreement of the Secretariat-General and SJ, DG SANCO shepherded the second proposal through the political process in the Commission "not quite as a *fait accompli*, but as a sort of take it or leave it" (COM73:141). ISC was abridged to "really just a couple of days with one big meeting" (COM24:250; also COM73:126) and a final decision was taken in July 2008. As one DG SANCO official remembered:

> What was decisive was the President's Cabinet and the Legal Service acting together.... If they had not allowed us to do this then we would have never got it through [the College of Commissioners]. And they basically—once the President's Cabinet says "yes, we think this is a good text which should be approved"—then other people tend to calm down a bit! (COM73:150)

Far from being masters of this process, DG SANCO certainly did "not end up where we thought we might have ended up many years ago" (COM73:186). Influential member-states' interests and internal interactions brought out a new regime "[c]ouched in a language which is—a lot of it is—very rights based language. Patients have the right to: information, quality of care and so [on]. All that was very much developed beyond anything much that was in the previous text" (COM73:54). Along this line, throughout the text the term "health services" was replaced by "healthcare," alluding more directly to patients, while healthcare *service* is used to refer to healthcare providers and professionals (COM73:60). As advocated particularly strongly by the European Parliament (COM73:54, COM107:124), the health Art. 152 was added as a treaty reference to stress the difference with respect to liberalization of other services based solely on the internal market Art. 95. Moreover, the new Health Commissioner Vassiliou proved to be "quite interested in listening" (COM19:117) to related policy developments in DG EMPL (Chapter 5.2.4). As a result, she turned the non-discrimination clauses typically associated with nationality into a broader principle that would also cover race, gender, and other discrimination grounds (COM24:44, COM73:63).

However, by far the most controversial issue was how to regulate authorization and reimbursement. Repeating arguments along the above-established lines of conflict, DG MARKT protested that such interventions were unnecessary in a liberalized European market, were detrimental to patients (who would be deprived of free movement and choice) and contradicted extant *acquis* on the professional qualifications directive and on the e-commerce directive (2000/31/EC, COM35:25). DG SANCO agreed that prior authorization to receive full reimbursement was a hindrance to market freedoms (AE, February 28, 2007), but acknowledged that consumer interests in health at times warranted re-regulation and that in any case it was due time for "legal clarity" (COM24:44). During a period when its internal standing was waning, DG EMPL worried that the directive would be "somehow duplicating" or "even taking away, undermining" the existing coordination regulation (COM73:186; also COM35:41). Furthermore, in the light of DG EMPL's hierarchy arguing that the "directive is completely senseless. If the only reason is for Kyprianoú to have his own act the game is not worth the candle" (COM107:136, authors' translation), DG SANCO willingly accepted wording "vetted by" DG EMPL (COM73:159) that ensured that social policy *acquis* would remain untouched (COM24:222, COM107:144).

The social democratic take on state-financed social service provision was vigorously defended by Communications Commissioner Wallström, supported by Trade Commissioner Mandelson (AE, December 19, 2007, *FT*, December 20, 2007). Wallström (cited in Europolitics 2007) ferociously opposed DG SANCO's stance and declared "fundamental reservation" about the text for haplessly addressing its connection to "Regulation 1408/71 [on the coordination of social security], fairness and subsidiarity."[26] However, responding to member-state concerns, DG SANCO quickly realized that resistance against "unpredictable" financial consequences (COM73:39) could endanger the proposal and re-introduced prior authorization at the country level upon evidence that the outflow of patients undermines the financial balance or planning of the hospital sector—something it had initially rejected. Thus, DG MARKT "were the people who lost out" (COM73:147), while other DGs secured their interests. DG SANCO accepted the input of "Vice-President Wallström's people who . . . wanted something which they thought they could sell on the basis of helping citizens and giving citizens rights and information" (COM73:147). Thus, the final proposal combines the re-introduction of prior authorization with the request to treat authorization demands without delay, and to be objective, non-discriminatory, and transparent.

In contrast to the other proposals in this sub-chapter, this process was inherently political and shows a picture of a Commission motivated by ideological positions. The position-formation process was characterized by very open and broad consultations as well as substantial intervention from the political level. While the proposal underwent substantial changes throughout the process, the decisive power resource for DG SANCO to ascertain its position in the end was support from the political level and particularly the Secretariat-General, as well as supranational and public legitimacy for more social EU initiatives (as a result of difficulties with the service directive).

In this last sub-field, the tension between internal-market policies and social policy goals is certainly extremely evident. What is more, the conflicts are often ideologically motivated. In three out of four cases, DG MARKT held a pre-fixed and consciously liberal position on a hitherto more interventionist regime. In the earlier cases, it sufficed for DG MARKT to keep interaction at the administrative level and to argue that other DGs' *acquis* would remain untouched to see this position adopted in College. Only in the last case, led by DG SANCO, was the liberal position substantially challenged by other DGs—pointing to the relevance of general public attention on the EU and the resulting political sensitivity as an important explanatory factor for more interventionist policies. At the same time, the combination of strong member-state interests that were difficult to circumvent and internal conflict between portfolios brought to the fore different strategies of the respective lead in addressing this tension. The strategies ranged from narrow, sectoral problem-solving approaches (coordination of social security and to a lesser degree recognition of professional qualifications) across strategic subterfuge (services in the internal market) to incremental muddling through (cross-border healthcare) so as to achieve adoption in College.

Each strategy demonstrated the relevance of specific factors in position formation. Following the image of the Commission as technocratic actor, implementation experiences with extant *acquis* and sectoral expert community mattered for problem solving. Partisan ideology and individual's influence on positions is visible where officials acted much more politically and tried to strategically secure their interests or muddled through a policy minefield in an attempt to do so. Moreover, the above strategies translated into different interaction dynamics where the lines of conflict between DGs EMPL, MARKT, and SANCO were most significant, as well as being remarkably stable. And yet they played out differently, depending on the match or validity with ECJ case law, anticipated member-state reactions and inter-Commission alliances.

NOTES

1. The most important acts concerned are Directives 76/207/EEC on the implementation of the principle of equal treatment for men and women as regards access to employment, vocational training and promotion, and working conditions; 79/7/EEC on the progressive implementation of the principle of equal treatment for men and women in matters of social security; and 86/613/EEC on the application of the principle of equal treatment between men and women engaged in an activity, including agriculture, in a self-employed capacity, and on the protection of self-employed women during pregnancy and motherhood.
2. This refers to the ability of a party to demonstrate that the connection to and the harm suffered from the action challenged is sufficient to support that party's participation in a court case.
3. The *Starting Line Group* is a UK-based network of national and European NGOs and organizations from the area of anti-discrimination that pursue their interests explicitly through a strategy of informing policy debates and pursuing concrete legal measures (Chopin 1999).
4. The Belgian Research Commissioner, for example, appeared to be quite supportive because his home country was putting in place national equal-treatment legislation at the same time.
5. Traditionally, in publicly provided social security, the principle of mutualization had prevailed, where risks were allocated through a large basket and could therefore be spread across persons with different characteristics, which enabled equal conditions for all clients.
6. The veto may have been issued by DG ELARG, headed by Commissioner Verheugen from Germany—the only country that later abstained from a vote in the inter-institutional process (AE, October 13, 2004).
7. In June 2007, 14 infringement procedures for non-implementation of the race equality directive had reached the stage of a reasoned opinion (AE, June 28, 2007).
8. Most importantly, the AGE Platform Europe, representing senior citizens; ILGA, promoting equality for lesbian, gay, bisexual, trans-sexual, and intersex people; the European Women's Lobby; and the European Network against Racism (ENAR).
9. This DG was particularly interested in the potential effect of the discrimination directive on mortgage credit, which had, inter alia, explicitly been excluded from a directive on consumer protection in financial services (COM42:90; cf. Chapter 7.3).

10. The expression alludes to the typical example given: the elderly landlady letting a room in an apartment with a shared kitchen and bathroom and not wanting a male, a lesbian, or a black tenant.
11. In April 2005, an MG Rover plant at Longbridge in the West Midlands closed down, laying off between 3,000 and 4,000 workers. France experienced large redundancy figures through the actions of Hewlett Packard (COM44:70, COM43:30, COM74:44, *FT*, October 20, 2005).
12. Here, interviewees alluded to the national experiences of drafting officials who were all of Italian origin, and a culturally grounded skepticism against provisions giving way to clientelism (COM63:1).
13. Goods had been classified according to the Statistical Classification of Products by Activity (CPA), works contracts according to the General Industrial Classification of Economic Activities (using NACE Rev. 1) and services had followed the UN classification used in the GATT (Provisional Central Product Classification, CPC Prov.). In addition, since 1996 a non-binding version of the CPV nomenclature had been used by DG MARKT when publishing notices in the Official Journal of the European Union (Recommendation 96/527/EC).
14. The most important are directives on the supplementary supervision of insurance undertakings in an insurance group (98/78/EC), life and non-life insurance (79/267/EEC and 73/239/EEC, amended to 92/96/EEC and 92/49/EEC), credit institutions (2000/12/EC) and investment services in the securities field (93/22/EC).
15. This expert came from a member state with a particularly high concentration of financial conglomerates and advanced regulation in place (Belgium). He was subsequently replaced by a national expert again recruited from a country with advanced legislation in the area (the Netherlands).
16. Solvency I and Solvency II combined 14 existing insurance and reinsurance directives in one ruling so as to establish a comprehensive solvency system.
17. In parallel with the drafting process, the OECD had proposed a recommendation on the assessment of reinsurance companies (1998), while the IAIS had published principles regarding minimum requirements for the supervision of reinsurers (2002) and standards for best practices in the supervision of reinsurers (2003).
18. These infringement procedures sensitized member states to the implementation difficulties related to minimum harmonization requirements and the acceptance of foreign training evidence for health professionals (in early 2001, against Spain, Portugal, France, the Netherlands, and Ireland [IP/00/11]; in February 2001, against Italy, France, and Germany [IP/01/186]; and in July 2001, against Austria, Greece, France, Spain, and Italy [IP/01/1129]).
19. Interestingly, going public to calm down the opposition was a strategy repeated right before the adoption in the College, this time by Commission President Prodi (*FT*, February 15, 2002).
20. Services are defined as any self-employed economic activity normally performed for remuneration. Examples are legal or tax consultancy, and recruitment, property, construction, architectural, or tourist services.
21. Note that during the inter-institutional process, the lack of control was lamented even by employers. They asked the Commission to give the host country responsibility for control and/or requiring service providers to register there (UNICE position paper of 5 October 2004: 5; UEAPME position paper of November 2004: 13).
22. The Regulation on the Coordination of Social Security Systems (1408/71/EC, today 883/2004/EC) and the accompanying Implementing Regulation (574/72/EC). The Commission proposal for the 2004 Regulation had already been adopted in the College in 1998 and is therefore not covered here.

23. This concerns sickness, maternity, accidents at work, occupational illnesses, invalidity benefits, unemployment benefits, family benefits, retirement and pre-retirement benefits, and death allowances.
24. In fact, member states had already called for modernization of the coordination of social security in 1992 (Edinburgh Council) and this demand was underlined by DG EMPL in its 1997 Action Plan for Free Movement of Workers (COM[97]586). In particular, the Spanish Presidency in 2002 had put the issue on the agenda, concerned about aging northern European pensioners in this country (Hervey and Vanhercke 2010: 116).
25. Note that the move to postpone was also influenced by the intervention of socialist MEPs (COM73:165, also cf. Martinsen 2009: 802).
26. Interestingly, this stands in sharp contrast to a supportive conservative Swedish government (e.g., AE, December 4, 2006), underlying the party-political influence on the matter.

6

Research and Innovation Policy

6.1 INTRODUCING THE POLICY AREA

This second case study chapter focuses on the sampled position formation processes in the area of research and innovation policy. This area comprises all measures aimed at the production of knowledge and new products and processes, thereby seeking to enhance the competitiveness of a specific sector or of an entire economy. Research and innovation activities can be seen as two different aspects of knowledge-production policy that have developed asymmetrically at EU level. On the one hand, we find sophisticated and long-established traditions of transnational cooperation in research policy, which accounts for a sizable share of the Community budget and—since the Lisbon Treaty—can also rely on a new treaty base for regulatory measures (Art. 182(2) TFEU). On the other, innovation policy is still struggling to find a solid footing in the EU's regulatory framework.

Since the founding days of the European Community, supranational *research policy* measures have been legitimized on the basis of their contribution to economic growth and industrial development (Guzzetti 1995). Although Jean Monnet's vision of a "European Technological Community" did not find expression in the Treaties of Rome, research in nuclear energy did become a cornerstone of the Euratom Treaty in 1957. However, because of member states' reluctance to confer powers to the supranational level, cooperation in research and technology remained largely intergovernmental until the 1980s (Héritier 1999). The role of research policy at EU level was strengthened by Commission President Jacques Delors' identification of research and technology as a central device in his strategy for the creation of a Single Market (Grande and Häusler 1994; Ross 1994). The first Research Framework Programme (FP), which focused on industrial energy and information technology research, was established in 1984, although it still lacked a proper legal basis. With the ratification of the Single European Act (SEA) in 1987, research policy became a Community responsibility. The Community was charged with promoting "all the research activities deemed necessary by virtue of other Chapters in this Treaty" which encourage European industry to "become more competitive at international level" (Art. 130f(1) TEC/179(1) TFEU). Building on this basis, the Maastricht Treaty of 1993 introduced Qualified Majority Voting (QMV) in the field. The next landmark was set in 2000, when Research Commissioner Busquin launched the European Research Area (ERA), which has since represented the framework for all EU research policy (COM [2000]6). The basic idea of the European Research Area is to create an internal market for research or, as Busquin's successor Potočnik put it in 2007, to make the movement of knowledge across Europe the EU's "fifth freedom".[1] Since then the EU Commission has increasingly proposed regulatory measures in the area of research and innovation, culminating in the inclusion of a new legal base in the Lisbon Treaty for measures that support the construction of an ERA (Art. 182(2) TFEU).

Innovation policy activities explicitly supporting the transformation of research results into marketable products only appeared on the EU policy agenda in the early 1990s as part of the Research Framework Programmes: the fourth Framework Programme (1994–8) had a pillar that financed activities in the innovation-related areas of technology transfer, innovation diffusion, and results dissemination. Thus, innovation activities were initially conducted in the context of research policy and were therefore based on the research articles of the Treaty. Today, innovation policy activities are based on the Industry Article 173 TFEU, which invites the EU and member states to guarantee the necessary conditions for the EU's competitiveness by "fostering better exploitation of the industrial potential of policies of innovation, research and technological development." In addition, innovation activities in Europe can receive financial support from the EU Structural Funds and the European Investment Bank.

Although research and innovation activities have historically been funded under a common legal instrument—the Framework Programme—they have been managed within the EU Commission by separate DGs: A directorate in DG XIII ("Information Society, Telecommunication, Markets, Technologies, Innovation and Enhancement of Research"), which was merged into DG ENTR in 1999, was responsible for innovation policy, while DG XII (today DG RTD) oversaw the EU's research policy (Chapter 4). Since the early 2000s, the EU has taken a new, holistic approach to innovation to signal its entry into the "knowledge-based economy" in the context of the Lisbon strategy (Borrás 2003). Nonetheless, administrative responsibilities have remained divided in the Commission and continue to raise "coordination issues among different policies" (Rossi 2005: 3). Whereas research activities predominantly fall under the responsibility of DG Research and Technological Development (DG RTD) and innovation policy is part of DG Enterprise and Industry's (DG ENTR) broad portfolio, sector-specific DGs are responsible for research and innovation measures within their own domains.[2] Examples are the DG for Information Society (DG INFSO), which manages information technology policy, DG Transport and Energy's (DG TREN) responsibility for some energy activities, and DG ENTR's responsibility for space and security. This can be observed in the drafting, management, and implementation of Framework Programmes, which is shared between the lead department DG RTD[3] and a number of other "research DGs." "Research DGs" manage the specific thematic components of the FPs, they "have a research budget and 'own' their parts" (Andrée 2008: 10). While DG RTD has always been the lead DG, the selection of additional research DGs has changed over time, with DG RTD's responsibility expanding to embrace more and more parts of the program and the other DGs struggling to retain their autonomy (see Section 6.2).

The political and administrative leadership of the two focal DGs in research and innovation policy, DG RTD and DG ENTR, displays a rather heterogeneous composition, with particularly frequently changing Directors-General in DG ENTR during our investigation period. Furthermore, a slight bias towards small and southern member states can be identified in the Research portfolio, and towards Social Democrats, Germans, and other larger member states in the Enterprise portfolio. DG RTD was headed politically by Commissioners Busquin (1999–2004, Belgium, Social Democrat) and Potočnik (2004–10, Slovenia, Independent), and administratively by Directors-General Mitsos (2000–5, Greece) and Silva Rodríguez (2006–10, Spain). DG ENTR was headed by Commissioners Liikanen (1999–2004, Finland, Social Democrat) and Verheugen (2004–10, Germany, Social Democrat) and by Directors-General Colasanti (2000–2, Italy), Mingasson (2002–4, France), Reichenbach (2004–5, Germany), and Zourek (2005–10, Austria).

In reflection of the dispersed administrative responsibilities in the Commission, our study's 14 research and innovation proposals also vary in their administrative leadership (Table 6.1). While five were under the responsibility of DG RTD, three were managed by DG EAC, two each by DG INFSO and DG ENTR, and one each by DG AGRI and DG SANCO. The initiatives can further be grouped into three categories: (1) Research Framework Programmes (four cases); (2) innovation support programs (six cases); and (3) research policy regulations and directives (four cases). The former two sub-groups are distributive measures exclusively composed of Decisions and mostly based on either the research articles Art. 166(1) TEU (Art. 182 TFEU) and Art. 7 Euratom or on the industry article of the Treaty 157(3) TEU (Art. 173 TFEU). The latter sub-group consists of regulations and directives, which are predominantly more recent initiatives. This in part reflects the Commission's move towards proposing regulatory research measures. However, as discussed in more detail in Section 6.3, the two proposals drafted by DG AGRI and DG SANCO lie somewhat apart for reasons of policy substance.

Over our period of investigation, the proposals are fairly evenly distributed across the Prodi and Barroso I terms (eight and six cases, respectively). In terms of their adoption procedure in the College of Commissioners, ten proposals were adopted in oral procedure, while four were adopted in written procedure. This is primarily because legal acts with substantial budgetary implications are usually put to oral discussion in the College (COM60:119).

6.2 RESEARCH FRAMEWORK PROGRAMMES

The Framework Programmes for Research and Technological Development (FPs) are the EU's main research policy instrument. The first Framework Programme was launched in 1984 and since then FPs have been set up consecutively roughly every four years. Their priorities have broadened constantly, from an initial focus on energy and information technology research to the introduction of social sciences in FP4 (1994–8) and of space and security research in FP7. Moreover, the FP budget has shown a tremendous increase from €25 million per year in FP1 to €7,767 billion per year in FP7 (Guzzetti 1995; Andrée 2009). As EU funding to nuclear research must be based on the Euratom Treaty, the Commission always proposes two acts in parallel: an EC program, which provides support to a broad variety of research sectors (based on Art. 166(1) TEU), and a Euratom program, which is exclusively devoted to nuclear energy research (based on Art. 37

Table 6.1. Sample of cases in research and innovation policy

Proposal number	Contents	Lead DG	Type of instrument	Treaty base (TEU/Euratom)	Commission adoption date	Commission adoption procedure	Council procedure	Sub-group
COM[1999]658-2	MEDIA—Training Programme (2001–2005)	EAC	Decision	Art. 150	Dec. 14, 1999	Oral	QMV	Innovation support
COM[1999]658-3	MEDIA Plus—Development Programme (2001–2005)	EAC	Decision	Art. 157(3)	Dec. 14, 1999	Oral	Unanimity	Innovation support
COM[2000]256-2	Multiannual Programme for Enterprise and Entrepreneurship (2001–2005)	ENTR	Decision	Art. 157(3)	Apr. 26, 2000	Oral	Unanimity	Innovation support
COM[2000]323	eContent Programme (2001–2005)	INFSO	Decision	Art. 157(3)	May 24, 2000	Oral	Unanimity	Innovation support
COM[2001]617-1	Programme on the conservation, characterization, collection and utilization of genetic resources in agriculture	AGRI	Regulation	Art. 37	Oct. 31, 2001	Written	QMV	Regulations & directives
COM[2001]94-1	6th Framework Programme (2002–2006)	RTD	Decision	Art. 166(1)	Feb. 21, 2001	Oral	QMV	Framework Programmes
COM[2001]94-2	6th Framework Programme (Euratom) (2002–2006)	RTD	Decision	Art. 7 Euratom	Feb. 21, 2001	Oral	Unanimity	Framework Programmes

Table 6.1. Continued

Proposal number	Contents	Lead DG	Type of instrument	Treaty base (TEU/Euratom)	Commission adoption date	Commission adoption procedure	Council procedure	Sub-group
COM[2004]96	eContentplus Programme (2005–2008)	INFSO	Decision	Art. 157(3)	Feb. 13, 2004	Written	QMV	Innovation support
COM[2005]119-1	7th Framework Programme (2007–2013)	RTD	Decision	Art. 166(1)	Apr. 6, 2005	Oral	QMV	Framework Programmes
COM[2005]119-2	7th Framework Programme (Euratom) (2007–2011)	RTD	Decision	Art. 7 Euratom	Apr. 6, 2005	Oral	Unanimity	Framework Programmes
COM[2005]121	Competitiveness and Innovation Framework Programme (2007–2013)	ENTR	Decision	Art. 156, Art. 157(3), Art. 175(1)	Apr. 6, 2005	Oral	QMV	Innovation support
COM[2006]604	European Institute of Innovation and Technology	EAC	Regulation	Art. 157(3)	Oct. 18, 2006	Oral	QMV	Regulations & directives
COM[2008]467	European Research Infrastructures	RTD	Regulation	Art. 171, Art. 172(2)	Jul. 15, 2008	Written	QMV	Regulations & directives
COM[2008]818	Quality and safety of human organs intended for transplantation	SANCO	Directive	Art. 152(4)	Dec. 8, 2008	Written	QMV	Regulations & directives

Euratom). Primary law thus obliges the Commission to propose such programs (Art. 7 Euratom, Art. 166(1) TEU). A distinct characteristic of research activities undertaken under the Euratom Treaty today is that decisions require the unanimous vote of member states in Council and only the consultation of the European Parliament. Both framework proposals define the programs' broad outlines, the total budget, its distribution across various thematic priorities and the funding instruments.[4] Tables 6.2 and 6.3 detail proposal and process characteristics relating to position formation and interaction on research framework programs.

6.2.1 6th EC Framework Programme

The 6th EC Framework Programme (FP6, COM[2001]94-1, 2002–2006) was prepared by the lead DG RTD with the assistance of the "research DGs" INFSO, TREN, ENTR, and FISH. The guiding theme for the development of FP6 was the creation of a European Research Area (ERA), as announced by Research Commissioner Busquin in 2000. However, DG RTD had already started to draw up a new program in 1999, knowing that FP5 was coming to an end in 2002. Preparatory documents were drafted by DG RTD's thematic directorates and the research DGs, who were granted a large amount of autonomy. Due to their specific expertise in individual research areas, this was considered "very logical, very inevitable" (COM100:107). The single thematic drafts were collected by DG RTD's coordination unit which had to ensure that they were structured coherently and were in line with DG RTD's overall program orientation (COM100:107). Mirroring this at political level, DG RTD's deputy Chef de Cabinet traditionally acted as a liaison between political vision and administrative drafting and was "the person who really coordinates and steers the drafting" (COM102:27).

Drafting involved a broad consultation process, which DG RTD had launched in 1999 (COM100:103). In addition to the lead DG's comprehensive external consultation, the other research DGs also engaged in parallel consultations with their individual research sectors (Andrée 2009). All the DGs drew on a dense network of expert groups associated with the Framework Programmes. The network included 21 "External Advisory Groups" created in 1998 to assist the Commission with implementing FP5. These groups were structured along thematic research lines and were composed of specialists in each respective research sector. Accordingly, they provided advice on the content of the individual thematic areas (COM100:48). For example, the Information Society Technology Advisory Group (ISTAG) advised DG INFSO on information technology research. Its main advice for FP6 was to structure the information technology aspect according to the long-term vision of creating an "ambient intelligence landscape" in Europe—an electronic environment designed to be sensitive and responsive to individual demands.[5] And, indeed, the information technology objectives set out in FP6 are largely consistent with the advisory group's ambient intelligence vision (see COM[2001]94-1: Annex 1, para. 1.1.2). This illustrates the very specific and sectoral focus of these advisory groups, which implied, however, that they were less able to address broader, cross-cutting aspects of the program (COM122:31). Such issues were discussed instead by the Scientific and Technical

Table 6.2. Position formation on research framework programs

Proposal number	Contents	No. of key provisions	Main line of proposal (content)	Uncertainty	Salience	Origin (hierarchical level)	Process duration (months)	External consultation	Main position-formation factors
COM[2001]94-1	6th Framework Programme (2002–2006)	6	Transformation of a funding instrument into an auxiliary instrument helping to establish a European Research Area	No	No	Political	12	Public	- Extant *acquis* - Individuals' influence - Organized interests
COM[2001]94-2	6th Framework Programme (Euratom) (2002–2006)	4	Budget increase, continuation of activities, working towards international project ITER	No	No	Administrative	12	Specific	- Extant *acquis* - Anticipation of Council majority - Experts - Partisan ideology
COM[2005]119-1	7th Framework Programme (2007–2013)	7	Budget increase, introduction of basic research funding at EU level, simplification	No	Yes	Administrative	18	Public	- Extant *acquis* - Organized interests
COM[2005]119-2	7th Framework Programme (Euratom) (2007–2011)	4	Realization of international project ITER in Europe, budget increase	No	Yes	Administrative	18	Public	- Extant *acquis* - Anticipation of Council majority - Experts

Table 6.3. Interaction on research framework programs

Proposal number	Contents	Deviating DGs	Informal interaction	Position-based conflict	Process-based conflict	Main line of conflict	Most powerful DG	Main power resources
COM[2001]94-1	6th Framework Programme (2002–2006)	INFSO	Intense	2	1	Budget distribution, instruments, DGs' management autonomy	RTD	- Lead DG - Entrepreneurship
COM[2001]94-2	6th Framework Programme (Euratom) (2002–2006)	BUDG	Little	2	0	Budget	BUDG	- Entrepreneurship - Horizontal services - Meta game
COM[2005]119-1	7th Framework Programme (2007–2013)	INFSO ENTR TREN FISH	Intense	2	1	Budget distribution, externalization	RTD	- Organized interests - Lead DG - Entrepreneurship
COM[2005]119-2	7th Framework Programme (Euratom) (2007–2011)	—	Little	—	—	—	—	—

Research Committee (CREST), which had been created in 1974 and included member state representatives. In addition, a public consultation was launched in the context of a Communication in October 2000 "to extract some major trends about what the stakeholders wanted" (COM100:130). Despite such extensive external consultation, officials from both the administrative and the political levels stated frankly that "the real public, the man in the street doesn't know what the Framework Programme is" (COM100:126) and that "the public doesn't really care that much" about the Framework Programme (COM102:293).

Based on these preparatory actions, DG RTD's administration had already prepared a draft proposal for the 6th Framework Programme when the new Research Commissioner Busquin came into office in September 1999. However, Busquin considered his DG's draft to be "too conservative, too much status quo" and "blew it from the table" (COM102:176). Instead, he wanted "something completely new" (COM102:176) and consequently managed the drafting of a new text from the top down himself. With the help of his deputy Chef de Cabinet and his DG's administrative hierarchy, the new proposal "was more or less imposed on the services" (COM102:70). For Busquin, the development of a European Research Area was the central project. Therefore, the Framework Programme designed under his aegis was intended to become a structuring device in the future creation of a European Research Area—Busquin sought "to transform the FP from a mere funding programme into something that helps to implement research policy" (COM102:37). It should be noted that the idea of a European Research Area had already existed within the Commission for several decades. The very first Research Commissioner, Spinelli (1970–2), had already formulated this vision in the 1960s (for an overview of the history of the European Research Area, see Andrée 2009). From then on, "the idea stayed in the Commission services, in the way the fire is staying in a forest. You do not see it, but it is there" (COM52:28). Thus, after DG RTD's hierarchy had not been able to convince Busquin's predecessor Cresson of the idea, "Busquin [finally] understood" (COM52:28). One Cabinet member confirmed that "it was a concept that was in his [Busquin's] briefing from DG RTD" (COM102:41). Busquin then "picked up on that and built his own story" (COM102:41). The Research Commissioner wanted to carry out "real politics" rather than merely distribute money, and the European Research Area project presented him with an opportunity to transform the research portfolio from a managerial, distributing service into a "real" policy-making one. It was a chance to "bring European research policy onto the agenda, and also to bring himself onto the agenda" (COM11:45, authors' translation).

Contacts between the responsible DGs were continuous but somewhat unstructured, despite them having managed the Framework Programmes jointly for years (COM11). They became more intense when DG RTD merged the individual thematic research sections from the thematic directorates and DGs in spring 2000, about a year before the final proposal was adopted (COM100:26). As one DG RTD official recollected, exchanges took place "through the institutional channel, through the informal channel . . . there was a lot of constant information flow on what we were doing" (COM100:76), including "a little internal bulletin called 'FP update' just to inform the people" (COM100:76). Individual conflicts were sorted out bilaterally or in ad-hoc meetings at the service level (COM11:173) and between cabinets at the political level (COM102:245). Throughout the process, the lead DG was on "friendly terms with [its] counterparts in the other DGs, more particularly DG INFSO, which was the main interlocutor" (COM55:139) because it was the DG holding the second largest budget share in the Framework Programme. There were few "very significant moments of tension with these other DGs, except in the phase on the negotiation on the budget" (COM100:88). In addition, two innovations introduced by DG RTD stirred up disagreement between the lead DG and DG INFSO.

First, and most importantly, the Research Commissioner proposed redesigning the funding instruments in FP6, which were considered the most important tool in creating a European Research Area (COM52:39). In order to have a structuring effect on the research landscape, transnational research cooperation would have to take place on a larger scale and "to shift from small projects to large projects" (COM52:41). Important new instruments proposed by DG RTD's hierarchy were Networks of Excellence (NoE), Integrated Projects (IP), and "Article 169 projects," as well as coordinated actions, such as "ERA-NETS." The latter were envisioned as replacing a number of small- and medium-scale shared-cost actions that had existed under FP5. This issue was especially contentious within the lead DG—between the hierarchy favoring the innovation and the administration expressing concerns—and among stakeholders (COM52:64, COM100:60). But it also led to conflicts with other DGs, most decisively with DG INFSO, which "just wanted to continue doing what they were always doing and were not very fond of changing the instruments" (COM102:53, also COM100:50, COM11:78). DG INFSO, "being much closer to industry than DG RTD" (COM11:78, authors' translation), defended its stakeholders' position. The position assumed by this DG, therefore, was that "what is good for the European IT industry is the right thing to do" (COM11:78, authors' translation). As the new, larger instruments proposed by the lead DG "were, of course, not that suitable for industry" (COM11:78, authors' translation), the result was "a battle with INFSO, because INFSO said 'no, we also need to keep small projects'" (COM102:114, also COM52:71, COM102:53). At the end of the day, both DGs succeeded in asserting their respective positions. The solution found was to provide a toolbox of many different instruments from which each research DG could choose. This meant that new, large-scale instruments proposed by DG RTD co-existed in the proposal with the old, smaller-scale instruments preferred by DG INFSO. The framework document was designed to be sufficiently flexible to allow adequate leeway in its actual implementation (COM11:75). Thus, while DG RTD was successful in introducing new instruments, DG INFSO succeeded in ensuring that it could continue to use the old instruments.

Second, DG RTD proposed a change in the program structure. Whereas up until then the Framework Programmes had always been structured along thematic areas, FP6 was now to be organized along the three European Research Area objectives: (1) Integrating the ERA, (2) Strengthening the ERA, and (3) Structuring the ERA. This met with opposition from DG INFSO because the new structure implied that it would no longer have its own "information technology Programme," and instead would only manage a "Theme" *within* the "Integrating the ERA" objective led by DG RTD. Due to DG INFSO's "reluctance" (COM100:178) to move away from the old FP structure according to thematic areas, an interviewee from DG INFSO remembered that "[a]t the beginning we were of course not pleased about that" (COM49:89, also COM59:227). Given the "political" aspect of this issue, it was resolved at political level where the lead DG could forcefully avail itself of the European Research Area vision (COM55:125). One DG RTD official admitted that the new structure "was decided here [in DG RTD], and in a way it was imposed [on] the other DGs" (COM100:178). Thus, acting as a gatekeeper and proactively structuring the negotiation process, while keeping the core decisions to the political level, gave DG RTD a "certain power" (COM11:210, authors' translation) in its position as the lead DG.

Lastly, in the budget discussions, too, the lead DG skillfully used its power to structure internal debates and left the crucial negotiations to the end. In order to prevent the services from getting lost in quibbles about their exact budget allocation across research areas, and by exploiting the agenda-setting power conferred on him as head of the lead DG, the Research Director-General Mitsos chose not to include any budget figures in the internal draft proposal that went into inter-service consultation. Only after the draft proposal had successfully passed the formal inter-service consultation, did Director-General Mitsos go to the other services' Directors-General and present the figures (COM102:77, also COM100:88 and DG RTD's CIS-Net cover note no. D/501291). Subsequently, the budgetary distribution was discussed and approved at political level (COM11:140).

Evidence of a strategically acting Commission is visible throughout the entire process described above. The lead department's approach to the legal text was significantly influenced by its Commissioner's personal ambition to establish a political prestige project, and also strongly influenced by existing Framework Programmes and by the research community. Supported by an experienced hierarchy in the DG, actors in favor of a program restructuring, brought together "huge experience and a very vast knowledge" (COM100:86). The DG used this to strategically exploit its agenda-setting role by orchestrating the negotiation sequence and offering workable compromises.

6.2.2 7th EC Framework Programme

The 7th Framework Programme (FP7, COM[2005]119-1), which lasted from 2007 to 2013, was the first research program brought in line with the EU's seven-yearly budget and financing cycle (the Financial Perspectives). In contrast to FP6, which marked a break with the preceding programs, FP7 systematically built on FP6 with its European Research Area mission. Apart from pursuing continuity, the lead DG RTD pursued two major political priorities: achieving a doubling of the annual research budget (as compared to the previous program) and the establishment of a European Research Council (ERC). The ground for these two innovations had been prepared by Research Commissioner Busquin, who was replaced by Research Commissioner Potočnik in September 2004. While still in office, Busquin had already drawn up several papers for FP7. Similar to the drafting of the FP6 legal text, these papers had been prepared by Busquin together with a small circle of people in his DG's hierarchy (COM2:41). Most important was a Communication issued in June 2004 that had led to a large public consultation (COM[2004]353). It was "the last paper from Busquin and had six main axes for the future" (COM102:39). Given the publication date close to the Commission's Communication on the new Financial Perspectives in July 2004 (COM [2004]487), "it was quite heavily debated, because people saw it as very important for the budget discussion" (COM61:29). In addition, it had proposed the creation of a European Research Council and the introduction of two new research themes, Space and Security. This Communication had gone through inter-service consultation in spring 2004, so that the other research DGs had already been heavily involved at that point in time.[6]

The beginning of the lead DG's concrete preparations for FP7 was marked by the recruitment of a seconded national expert from Sweden to DG RTD's drafting unit in autumn 2003 who would work full time on the preparation of FP7. This was one year after FP6 had been launched and 18 months prior to the adoption of the FP7 proposal in April 2005. Again, the external consultation on this act was extensive. DG RTD organized two substantial public consultations and several specific ones in thematic areas. The substantial consultations, on the Communication (June 2004) and on the selection of research themes (November 2004), each generated around 1,800 responses from universities, research institutes, industry, governments, and individuals. However, a DG RTD official drily concluded that the consultations did "not give much in substance" (COM2:41) because respondents were only interested in receiving more funding: "normally researchers, they want their own areas, and member states they want areas where they are strong" (COM2:41). In this light the main message received from the consultation responses was a request for simplification and for continuity—"the buzzword at the time" (COM61:54, also COM[353]2004). Taking up this request, Commissioner Potočnik discussed intensively with his Cabinet and his DG's hierarchy how to simplify the program management and its application rules (COM10:29, COM7:143). One result was the structuring of FP7 in four blocks, which "came very late, just 3 or 4 months before the proposal [was tabled]" (COM2:32).

As we observed during the discussion of the drafting of FP6, DG RTD's thematic directorates and the other research DGs consulted 17 Advisory Groups that assisted in the implementation of FP6 (COM2:59, COM59:36). In addition, stakeholders participating in European Technology Platforms (ETPs) also gave their input. These research platforms had been established during FP6 and were composed of industry and academia. Their position was especially valued by the Commission, as it gave "much more structured input, input which is already elaborated between the players" (COM59:47, also COM61:90). The drafting process was further accompanied by media debates on stem cell research (COM102:293)—a carry-over from the FP6 inter-institutional process. Here, sensitive ethical and cultural concerns had clashed on the question of whether the EU should fund research on super-numerary embryos or whether this should be limited to banked or isolated human embryonic stem cells in culture (see *FT*, August 12, 2004; *FT*, October 28, 2004).

In the preparation of FP7, coordination between services was far more formalized than for the previous program. A DG RTD coordination official emphasized that his DG had learned from the drafting of FP6 that the dismissal of the administration's proposal by its hierarchy as well as the centrally steered drafting process and the imposition of political decisions had upset all the services. DG RTD's coordination unit therefore aimed to include all actors at service level and have "a lot of discussions" (COM61:92). The lead department established a comprehensive inter-service group, as demanded by the new impact assessment rules (COM59:118), and also several sub-groups on the program's horizontal aspects and thematic priorities (COM7:92, 174, COM59:141). A formalized involvement was described as "psychologically important" in that it gave the others "the feeling that things are more transparent and that they are involved" (COM102:222). In addition, the coordination unit established a formal regular meeting of the Directors-General of all research DGs.[7] Thus, officials from the lead department "were at all times in contact with the different interlocutors from the different DGs at various levels" (COM7:92).[8]

To understand the position formation process in this case, it is important to note that because of the alignment with the Financial Perspectives and its corresponding parallel schedule, DG RTD "had to have it [the FP7 proposal] ready, in principle" when the new Commission came into office in September 2004 (COM2:32). Thus, incoming Commissioner Potočnik's timeframe between coming into office in September 2004 and having to present FP7 in April 2005 was extremely tight, only about half a year. This implied that much of the FP7 substance had been pre-formed by the hand of the outgoing Commissioner Busquin. Commissioner Potočnik decided "to build the proposal in continuity of what Busquin had prepared" (COM102:39), while putting "his own kind of touch to it" (COM2:32) and focusing on two aspects. First, he made the doubling of the annual program budget his priority. Responding to this, other research DGs, such as DG INFSO and DG TREN, demanded a doubling of the budget shares for their respective thematic areas as well (COM61:29). DG RTD, however, considered this "unrealistic" (COM2:101), given that new activities were introduced in FP7, most importantly the European Research Council and the research areas Space and Security, which also demanded a share. Copying negotiation tactics that had proven successful when preparing FP6, budget figures were again left blank until the text was approved in the formal CIS-Net consultation. Only then did DG RTD's Director-General Mitsos go to the other Directors-General to arrange a pre-agreement on budget calculations (COM2:105, COM102:91, also DG RTD's cover note to CIS-Net consultation no. RTD/3267). This was then negotiated at Cabinet level (COM2:73) and the final decision followed in College (COM10:68), since setting the final budget "goes beyond the power of the Directors-General" (COM10:75, authors' translation). The budget deal finally struck was considered fair by all services (COM2:101): Once the new elements in FP7 had been subtracted, all the other parts got a "more or less proportional" increase (COM59:104), making it difficult to argue for larger shares as everybody had been treated equally (COM59:104, COM2:101).

Closely connected to DG RTD's success on the internal budget negotiations is the introduction of a European Research Council (ERC), which the research community had strongly lobbied for in advance (COM8:78, COM59). The ERC represented a substantial novelty in that it introduced funding to basic, "investigator-driven" research at European level. The idea of an encompassing European basic research funding agency modelled on the American National Science Foundation (NSF) had already existed in the European scientific community for a while (Gronbaek 2003). In particular, advice from the Commission's science-dominated European Research Advisory Board (EURAB), from a European Research Council

Expert Group (ERCEG), and from a High Level Expert Group (HLEG) was decisive for designing the European Research Council.[9] In the run-up to FP7, external pressure from the scientific world became so strong that the Commission and member states could no longer ignore it (COM8:78). Thus, although many DGs had feared the European Research Council "more as a taxation—the more the ERC got, the less [budget] they would get" (COM2:123), given the external pressure from stakeholders the introduction of the European Research Council in FP7 was perceived as a "fait accompli" (COM2:123) or "inevitable[ness]" (COM8:91). The political leadership of the lead department, in turn, saw the European Research Council as promising for the development of European research policy and took advantage of the strong stakeholder support on this issue: "from the very first moment Commissioner Potočnik took a very clear ownership of . . . the ERC. He really believed from the very first minute in the necessity to have this kind of new instrument" (COM7:62). In addition, the lead department internally skillfully linked the "bitter pill" (for the other services) of creating an European Research Council to an overall budget increase and could therefore secure general internal support for the European Research Council.

Once this had been accepted, a debate within the Commission still arose on externalization and allocation to agencies as DG RTD sought to externalize large parts of the program management, including the ERC's, to an external agency (COM52:41). As in the case of the Competitiveness and Innovation Framework Programme drafted in parallel (see Section 6.3), this was hotly debated within the Commission. The "big discussion" was primarily between DG INFSO (opposing externalization) and the lead service (in favor of externalization, COM102:139). Moreover, it was also debated whether there should be none (DG INFSO's position), one (DG BUDG's position), or two executive agencies (DG RTD's position), how they would be managed and how many staff would be needed (COM10:107, COM102:139). Whereas Research Commissioner Potočnik "had strong support from his Enterprise colleague Verheugen on this" (COM102:139) and succeeded in introducing two executive agencies in the final proposal, DG INFSO managed to exempt its ICT activities from outsourcing (mirroring the parallel Competitiveness and Innovation Framework Programme outcome, see Section 6.3). DG RTD officials emphasized DG INFSO's strong bargaining position given that it held the second-largest program share and remarked that "they are very good at what they are doing" and that "the Commissioner, Madame Reding, is quite strong" (COM2:61). The latter point is supported by the minutes of the respective College meeting, which document the discussion of the issue among Commissioners and show that Commissioner Reding succeeded in ensuring that "the agency's activities did not concern research in the field of information and communication technologies" (PV[2005]1696: para. 22).

Although the drafting process of the 7th Research Framework Programme was managed more openly and inclusively within the Commission than that of FP6, it was nonetheless once more dominated by DGs' strategic interests in retaining or expanding their competences. Moreover, DG RTD did not propose the establishment of a European Research Council because it deemed it functionally useful, but in response to effective stakeholder lobbying. Again, DG RTD's position as lead department and gatekeeper rendered it powerful because it was able to employ a strategy that was difficult for others to oppose and that could successfully secure a doubling of the budget and the introduction of a European Research Council.

6.2.3 Euratom Framework Programmes

The two Euratom Framework Programmes in our sample built on a long-standing history in EU nuclear research, which had been one of the very first areas of European research funding (Guzzetti 1995). The Euratom Framework Programme is organized into three main areas—research into nuclear fission, nuclear fusion, and direct nuclear research activities conducted by the Commission's Joint Research Centre (JRC)—which are managed in distinct ways. Nuclear fission research covers various areas, including improving the quality, efficiency, and safety of power plants, the management of nuclear waste and/or radiation protection. Fusion research is focused on one ongoing project: the development of a prototype for the first fusion reactor to generate electrical power in Europe—the International Thermonuclear Experimental Reactor (ITER). First agreed in 1985, this experimental fusion reactor is co-financed by the EU (through Euratom) together with the Soviet Union, the United States, and Japan. The preparations of the FP6- and FP7-Euratom proposals were both strongly influenced by the international ITER negotiations. Most importantly, the US initially withdrew from the project in 1999, which made it highly uncertain whether the participating states would reach agreement on further development in the course of FP6-Euratom, but the US re-joined in 2003, giving the project fresh impetus for the FP7-Euratom.

The drafting process was further influenced by the drafting of the respective EC Framework Programme proposals because the two parts of the program were to be presented in parallel (COM54:62). However, whereas the drafting of the EC program proposals involved extensive consultation, the preparation of the Euratom programs was more like to the routine-driven bureaucratic behavior observed in our innovation support cases (see Section 6.3). The drafting authority for the Euratom program lay with DG RTD's Euratom directorate, with a central coordinating unit managing the process (similar to the process observed for the EC program drafting). The content itself was prepared by the individual Fusion and Fission units in the Euratom directorate. The directorate's final Euratom proposal was delivered to DG RTD's central coordination unit, which checked its consistency with the EC program (COM54:102). Subsequently, at DG RTD's political level, it was usual for only Euratom's budget to be discussed and not its content (COM121:89). Neither were other DGs substantially involved "because it is only a small group of people who are interested" (COM102:97). The stakeholders with whom the Euratom officials closely interacted were a small community of nuclear researchers, assembling in various expert groups.[10] This was especially the case for fusion research, where almost all research in Europe is transnational and receives funding from FP-Euratom (COM121). The tightly interwoven community extended into DG RTD, where officials working on Euratom had previously been employed in nuclear research facilities and had been educated and socialized in a similar way to their stakeholders (COM54, COM96, COM121). It is possible that a resulting common ground of reasoning, both internal and external to the Commission, reinforced the program's status-quo bias even more (Banchoff 2002).

DG RTD's preparation of the *6th Euratom Framework Programme* (FP6-Euratom, (COM[2001]94-2) was colored by the DG's concern that the Euratom budget be cut further, as had been the case for the last few Framework Programmes. Given the unanimity requirement in Council, this meant that member states' attitudes towards nuclear power had to be carefully regarded when formulating budget requests. As member states displayed "more fundamental differences of opinion on... very emotive issues" such as nuclear energy, the Commission's room for maneuver was limited (COM54:98). Austria, which has no nuclear power plants on its territory, was the most reserved towards committing the EU budget to nuclear research (COM2:45, COM54:98). For the Euratom officials "certainly this was in our minds when we drafted the programme" (COM54:98, COM121:53). Moreover, at the time when FP6-Euratom was being drawn up, public acceptance of nuclear energy was low, still suffering from the consequences of the Chernobyl accident in 1986, which had triggered an anti-nuclear movement. Thus, in 1999 and 2000 nuclear energy was "perceived by society presently as being on the downtrend" (External Advisory Group—Fission 2001: 3), which clearly made the drafting process more difficult for the Euratom officials because it further limited their room for maneuver (COM 121:34).

The funding of nuclear research also gave rise to value-laden discussions inside the Commission. Although no other service was involved into the drafting process, at the political level the FP6-Euratom proposal prompted disagreements between the Commissioner for Research, Busquin, and the Commissioner for Budget, Schreyer. Schreyer, a German Green Party member, objected ideologically and fundamentally to the public financing of nuclear research in general.[11] She emphasized that notwithstanding her formal role as Budget Commissioner (COM82:34) she did not merely have a position on FP6-Euratom's budgetary amount, but also on its content. She took advantage of the fact that Commissioners—unlike their services—also have the task of setting the Commission's broad policy guidelines, for example in this case whether Europe should invest in the future in nuclear or in renewable energy (COM82:38, 130). Thus, when the FP6-Euratom proposal was debated in College, Commissioner Schreyer revealed herself to be "really adamantly opposed to nuclear energy" (COM102:97). This battle on the funding of nuclear energy research was recalled as the fiercest debate in College at the meeting when the two FP6 proposals were discussed (COM102:99). Presumably, the Budget Commissioner took advantage of the critical public climate towards nuclear energy at the time (which supported her position) and her service's formal veto power in legal acts with its financial implications to downsize the FP6-Euratom budget (COM121:76). Schreyer's efforts paid off as she succeeded, in particular, in reducing the share allocated to fusion, that is, the share devoted to the international ITER project. A DG RTD official remembered that "in the internal proposals €850 million was the number, and in the dealings between us, the Commissioner and DG BUDG, it went down to €700 million" (COM121:79, also AE, February 21, 2001). This was a substantial defeat for the lead department, given that it meant a decrease when compared to the fusion budget in FP5-Euratom (€788 million) and the DG's strong intention to prevent further budget cuts. However, DG RTD's position was weakened given that the

ITER at the time relied on a shaky international collaboration due to the United States' withdrawal in 1999. Thus, DG BUDG benefited from the parallel international negotiations, which did not render investment in this project very appealing, as well as from its formal veto power for legal acts with financial implications (COM11:127) and its Commissioner's personal commitment.

The drafting of the *7th Euratom Framework Programme* (FP7-Euratom, COM [2005]119-2) resembled that of the FP6-Euratom document in many regards.[12] It was described as "a multi-faceted approach which then iterates around the key actors, the programme committee, the national stakeholders and research stakeholders" (COM54:34) and strongly involved a number of expert groups on nuclear research. However, the preparations differed in that recent developments in the international negotiations on ITER had garnered considerable public attention (e.g. *FT*, November 17, 2004). In 2003, the US decided to re-join the international agreement, which gave the project new drive and a new justification for the Commission to dedicate increased diplomatic and financial resources to what became a more certain and promising collaboration. Thus, in 2004 and 2005, Research Commissioner Potočnik and Director-General Mitsos were both personally involved in the ITER negotiations (COM61:94). Moreover, the political context was rendered "more favorable" (COM54:98) in 2004 and 2005 by greater debate about climate change and energy supply (COM54:98). It was perhaps as a result of this context, unlike that surrounding the drafting of the FP6-Euratom, that no value-laden conflicts about the necessity or appropriateness of nuclear research funding arose (COM102:138). In addition, unlike under the Prodi Commission, the Barroso I College did not contain any Green party members (see Chapter 4).

Both Euratom cases illustrate how political considerations, most importantly the requirement for unanimity in the Council, shape the internal preparations and considerably limit the lead DG's room for maneuver. Likewise, the embeddedness of the Euratom program in an international context had an impact on position formation. The drafting of FP6-Euratom further reveals how the sensitive issue of nuclear research evoked ideological positions among Commission members, most notably at the political level, where they exercised power in support of their own ideological commitment.

Overall, our case studies of the Commission's Research Framework Programme proposals show how the distributive aspect and the consecutive order of these programs strongly influenced position formation. While the services sought bureaucratic competences and were interested in maintaining established stakeholder relationships by defending or expanding their budget, their political levels were further interested in personal enrichment and pushing forward political projects during their terms in office. Taking another point of view, innovations often demanded an entrepreneurial role on the part of individuals in the lead department's administrative and/or political hierarchy. In particular, the close cooperation between DG RTD's Director-General with "huge experience and a very vast knowledge" (COM100:86) and a Commissioner who was a "political animal" (COM11:45, authors' translation) and seized the gains from new policies from a political point of view, rendered DG RTD very powerful in the process of developing the 6th Framework Programme. This entrepreneurship on the part of certain of individuals, in turn, was transformed into a source of power in interaction with other services. In addition, DGs predominantly anticipated member state votes strategically in Council in those cases that demanded unanimity in the Council (the Euratom programs).

6.3 INNOVATION SUPPORT PROGRAMMES

The six innovation support programs analyzed in our sample consist of five comparably small consecutive funding programs proposed between 1999 and 2004, and one comprehensive Competitiveness and Innovation Framework Programme (CIP) proposed in 2005. Although they came under the responsibility of different DGs, namely EAC, INFSO, and ENTR, all of the drafting processes were strongly influenced by the fact that they were follow-up editions in a series of consecutive funding programs. In all cases, the lead department based its draft, to a significant extent, on the predecessor program when designing the new proposal, thus, the Commission's fall-back option was always defined by the extant *acquis*. In all cases, the responsible DG based its preparations for a new program on two major sources of input: the previous program's compulsory mid-term assessment and the input of its comitology committee—the so-called "programme committee" composed of member state representatives (COM51:50, COM96:97). One context condition that influenced the drafting of funding programs proposed in 1999/2000 was the Commission's fraud scandal and the subsequent resignation of the Santer Commission in 1999. The subsequent Kinnock reforms included an external evaluation of financial mismanagement in the Commission, which revealed "evidence of poor management" in a number of Commission funding programs (see Kassim 2008: 655). In response, the Commission's horizontal services DGs ADMIN and BUDG were mandated to oversee the policy DGs' management of funding programs more closely—which clearly constrained the DGs concerned with distributive innovation policy. Tables 6.4 and 6.5 detail position formation and interaction on innovation support programs.

6.3.1 MEDIA Training and MEDIA Plus

The MEDIA Plus programs were prepared by DG EAC—which was at that time called DG X for "Information, communication, culture, audiovisual" (Chapter 4)—and consisted of two proposals: MEDIA Training (COM[1999] 658-2) and MEDIA Plus—Development, Distribution and Promotion (COM [1999]658-3). As in the case of the Framework Programmes (see Section 6.2), the Commission proposed two different acts with distinct legal bases that required different inter-institutional procedures. The Training part was based on Art. 150 (Education), which required qualified majority voting in Council and a co-decision by the Parliament. The Development part, by contrast, was based on Art. 157 (Industry), which required a unanimity vote in Council and only the consultation of the Parliament. However, unlike the drafting of the EC- and Euratom-Framework Programme, the two MEDIA programs were treated as one coherent package within the Commission: they were structured similarly and drafted by

Table 6.4. Position formation on innovation support programs

Proposal number	Contents	No. of key provisions	Main line of proposal (content)	Uncertainty	Salience	Origin (hierarchical level)	Process duration (months)	External consultation	Main position-formation factors
COM[1999]658-2	MEDIA—Training Programme (2001–2005)	7	Simplification, increased industrial focus, budget increase	No	No	Administrative	12	Specific	- Extant *acquis* - Experts
COM[1999]658-3	MEDIA Plus—Development Programme (2001–2005)	6	Simplification, budget increase	No	No	Administrative	12	Specific	- Extant *acquis* - Experts - International policy transfer
COM[2000]256-2	Multiannual Programme for Enterprise and Entrepreneurship (2001–2005)	6	Rationalization, budget increase	No	No	Administrative	15	Specific	- Extant *acquis* - Individuals' influence - Anticipation of EP majority
COM[2000]323	eContent Programme (2001–2005)	5	Merging of two smaller programs, emphasis on private industry, budget increase	No	No	Administrative	20	Specific	- Extant *acquis* - Organized interests - International policy transfer
COM[2004]96	eContentplus Programme (2005–2008)	5	Shift of emphasis from private to public sector, budget increase	No	No	Administrative	12	Specific	- Extant *acquis* - Individuals' influence - Experts
COM[2005]121	Competitiveness and Innovation Framework Programme (2007–2013)	11	Merging of several small innovation-funding programs, budget increase	No	No	Political	8	Public	- Extant *acquis* - Anticipation of Council majorities - Organized interests

Table 6.5. Interaction on innovation support programs

Proposal number	Contents	Deviating DGs	Informal interaction	Position-based conflict	Process-based conflict	Main line of conflict	Most powerful DG	Main power resources
COM[1999]658-2	MEDIA—Training Programme (2001–2005)	INFSO BUDG	Low	3	0	Demarcation line with DG INFSO's eContent program	EAC	- Bureaucratic legitimacy - Lead DG
COM[1999]658-3	MEDIA Plus—Development Programme (2001–2005)	INFSO BUDG	Low	3	0	Demarcation line with DG INFSO's eContent program	EAC	- Bureaucratic legitimacy - Lead DG
COM[2000]256-2	Multiannual Programme for Enterprise and Entrepreneurship (2001–2005)	BUDG	Low	1	0	Budgetary request	ENTR	- n.a.
COM[2000]323	eContent Programme (2001–2005)	EAC BUDG	Intense	3	1	Budgetary request	INFSO	- Proximity to EP majority - Lead DG
COM[2004]96	eContentplus Programme (2005–2008)	BUDG	Medium	2	0	Budgetary request	INFSO	- Proximity to EP majority - Supranational competence
COM[2005]121	Competitiveness and Innovation Framework Programme (2007–2013)	INFSO TREN	Intense	3	0	Degree of integration, degree of externalization	ENTR	- Meta game - Initiative's origin - Lead DG

the same unit for "Audiovisual Support" in DG EAC. The two proposals were DG EAC's third series in this area, succeeding MEDIA (1991–1995) and MEDIA II (1996–2000). The MEDIA Training proposal addressed audiovisual professionals, trainers, and firms operating in the audiovisual sector and proposed a budget of €50 million. Its aim was to encourage networking, improve continuous vocational training for professionals in the sector, create jobs, and make the European audiovisual industry more competitive. The MEDIA Development proposal addressed audiovisual enterprises and suggested a budget of €350 million. More specifically, it supported the development (design and conceptual phase) of audiovisual products, their distribution (via cinema, TV, or video retailing) and their promotion (e.g. via festivals). Given the context of the "digital revolution" and growing competition, in particular from the US, the aim of the programs was to strengthen the competitiveness of the European audiovisual sector, thereby ensuring that linguistic and cultural diversity was respected.

The drafting processes of both programs began in late 1998—"knowing that MEDIA II was coming to an end in 2001" (COM98:30)—and was steered by the Head of Unit who had already been involved in the management of MEDIA II. Although DG EAC's Commissioner Reding (Luxembourg, Conservative) was supportive and "liked" the program, she was not substantially involved (COM60:87). The responsible officials drafted the program "on the basis in particular of the results of the midterm evaluation of MEDIA II" (COM98:30), which had been carried out by the external consultancy *BIPE Conseil*. They followed the consultancy's main recommendation for "continuity with MEDIA II, but changes in the implementation of the programme, because MEDIA II was a little bit artisanal" (COM60:72). This referred to the MEDIA program's dual cultural and industrial focus (COM98:147). In the new proposal, DG EAC therefore aimed to strengthen the industrial angle by devoting a larger budget share to market instruments, such as a so-called "automatic" scheme that supported and rewarded commercially successful films and thus followed the rationale of "success brings success" (COM98:43). Moreover, as this automatic support to successful films (in cinema) had been effective in the MEDIA II program, DG EAC proposed extending this scheme to video distribution. A further novelty proposed by DG EAC in MEDIA Development was support for the promotion of audiovisual products, such as through festivals, to "increase the visibility of European creations" (Agence Europe 1999). Here, practices from the successful American film industry, which invested heavily and successfully in film promotion, served as a template (AE, November 20, 1999).

The drafting of the MEDIA programs involved little interaction among services (COM60:107). The responsible Head of Unit in DG EAC proactively went to "meet whatever DG on an informal basis just to see whether the text" (COM98:117) was acceptable to them. In this process "INFSO, the Legal Service and DG BUDG were . . . [the] main interlocutors" (COM98:117). DG INFSO had a strong position on the MEDIA proposals because it was drafting its closely related eContent program in the same period (COM[2000]323, see Section 6.3.2). Conflicts emerged due to a blurring of portfolio demarcation lines caused by technical advances on the audiovisual market. This had led to "an ideological debate about the so-called convergence" (COM60:52), namely, "as the technologies were converging, a part of the most liberal views in Europe considered that audiovisual regulation should be aligned to the telecom" (COM60:52). DG INFSO held the same liberal position and argued that support for audiovisual policy should be integrated into its own support for information technology (i.e. the eContent program). Actors within and outside of the European Commission were split on this issue, forming coalitions in support of either DG EAC's or DG INFSO's point of view. The latter's position was advocated by large media companies and the governments of Germany and the UK, while DG EAC had the alliance of "all the ministers of culture" (COM60:52), France in particular, and of the European Parliament (Brochhagen 2010: 140–5). DG EAC, however, could evoke the position of the former Commission President Delors, who had clearly distinguished the two sectors, arguing that "the audiovisual is not a merchandise like others, so it requires a specific regulation" (COM60:32). This historically rooted argument effectively helped DG EAC in defending its position against DG INFSO and in retaining responsibility over its MEDIA programs.[13]

A second line of conflict evolved around the amount of Community budget dedicated to the program (COM60:81, COM98:81). DG EAC's hierarchy aimed at achieving a "critical mass" (COM60:100) and "of course our first request, or our first discussions with DG BUDG were even more ambitious" (COM98:58) than what appeared in the written inter-service consultation, which was €50 million (Training) plus €400 million (Development). However, revealing a bargaining style of interactions, a DG EAC official added "that is a negotiation game, as often: you ask for 100 when you want 60" (COM98:58). DG BUDG, in turn, argued that "the amounts are too high, . . . there is a financial framework and everybody has to respect it" (COM98:58). During the written consultation, DG EAC's budget proposals were further reduced to €50 million plus €350 million from DG BUDG. Because the budget service drew all budget lines evenly, it seems as if the aim was to achieve a certain total amount that conformed better to the Community's financial framework, rather than removing specific funding actions because of their content (unlike the FP6-Euratom case, see Section 6.2.3). Despite the budget cut, the lead department was satisfied with the outcome because even the reduced amount meant an increase of 30 percent compared to the preceding MEDIA II (COM98:58). As a senior DG EAC official stated, "DG EAC made . . . progress in terms of budget. That was important" (COM60:81). A desk-level official stressed that DG BUDG was convinced by the technical quality of the draft proposal (COM98:58), which had depended on the legislative skills available in the DG, including the responsible Head of Unit's being "a very good lawyer" (COM98:109). The draft proposal's high technical quality was considered valuable throughout the internal preparations: "There seemed to be a good agreement and understanding on the way we structured it, which was quite systematic and not so political" (COM98:85).

To sum up, the MEDIA drafting processes were characterized by a strong role played by the extant *acquis* and experts coupled with the drafting skills of the responsible Head of Unit. The lead department's position largely relied on the previous programs and the corresponding mid-term evaluation, as well as on policy templates from the US. When confronted with opposition from other DGs, DG EAC benefited from its acquired expertise, which the responsible Head of Unit skillfully applied when defending his DG's position against DG BUDG and DG INFSO, as well as from its acknowledged claim to the area of audiovisual support.

6.3.2 eContent and eContentplus

In parallel with DG EAC's MEDIA support programs, DG INFSO also regulated the closely related area of digital content publishing. During our period of investigation, it prepared the eContent program (COM[2000]323) and the eContentplus program (COM[2004]96), two market-oriented programs aimed at increasing the accessibility and usability of digital content to end-users and re-users. The programs offered support for the production, use, and distribution of European digital content, and promoted linguistic and cultural diversity on global networks such as the Internet. The preparation of these two programs differed to some extent as a result of personnel shifts and changing context conditions. On the one hand, and similar to DG EAC's drafting of its MEDIA programs, in both cases DG INFSO started preparing a new program as soon as the mid-term evaluation of the previous program had been prepared, which meant about one year before the new proposals were adopted by the College of Commissioners (COM96:52; COM130:10). On both occasions, the lead department also consulted with member states via the program committees of the previous programs. However, there was a difference regarding the relevance of the expert information received: experts were an important source of information for the eContentplus drafting, whereas for the earlier eContent proposal, exchanges with other stakeholders had been more relevant.

The eContent program proposed in 2000 was a merger of two former programs, INFO2000 (1996–1999, Council Decision 96/339/EC) and the Multilingual Information Society Programme (MLIS, 1996–1999, Council Decision 96/664/EC). The former program had already focused on support for electronic content, the latter on digital developers, encouraging them to design multi-language and multi-cultural products (COM96:39). The new eContent program built on these predecessors and aimed to improve the global position and competitiveness of Europe's content industries. It addressed content producers, distributers and users, which included publishers, online providers and public institutions producing information used by others, with a focus on small and medium-sized enterprises (SMEs).

The proposal was designed by the DG INFSO unit responsible for digital content "together with the publishing industry" (COM55:41). In DG INFSO's view, these actors were better equipped to indicate the "real needs" (COM96:188) of the market than expert reports. The DG engaged in an extensive "pre-consultation process" with industrialists, including a tour through the major publishing houses in Europe and the United States (COM96:188). Although the industry stakeholders essentially requested a continuation of the support actions of the previous programs and a budget increase, the tour also led to the introduction of something new. Based on what the drafting official had observed on his tour through the US, he suggested that the eContent program should introduce support for risk-capital funding (COM96:181). However, this scheme did not find its way into the final proposal because the Information Society Commissioner Liikanen was "completely against" it (COM96:84). The reason was that some member states, such as Germany—which wanted to retain support for venture capital at its regional *Länder* level (COM96:84, AE, December 23, 2000)—had signaled their disagreement, and the Commissioner feared opposition in Council. Given the unanimity requirement in Council, Commissioner Liikanen decided the best option was: "Do not mingle with it!" (COM96:181). Accordingly, the risk-capital scheme was removed from the draft even before the lead DG had engaged in consultation with other DGs. This shows that whereas the administrative level in this case had engaged in learning (from the United States) and sought to introduce a seemingly appropriate problem solution, the Commissioner was more closely attuned to the likely mood of future inter-institutional negotiations.

Inter-service consultation with other services was intense, involving close interactions across different hierarchical levels throughout the process. In correspondence with the MEDIA case study described above, interactions with DG EAC also took place. DG INFSO bilaterally contacted DG EAC early on to assess whether the MEDIA activities could be integrated into its eContent program. DG INFSO suggested having "a big programme that would bring together the MEDIA programme and eContent and to have a container" (COM96:55; also COM60:107). This discussion was passed on to the level of the Directors-General (COM96:67). As illustrated in the MEDIA case above, we assume that DG EAC was ultimately able to build on its historically legitimated claim to this policy area and prevent DG INFSO taking over its MEDIA parts. Accordingly, DG INFSO was advised to emphasize the demarcation lines between the two areas in its final proposal.

Moreover, disagreements with DG BUDG occurred on the overall program budget. Whereas DG INFSO requested the "critical mass" of €200 million (COM96:54), DG BUDG proposed the "symbolic figure of 100 million euro" (DG BUDG's response to CIS-net consultation no. 16022). Referring to an insufficient *ex ante* evaluation, DG BUDG submitted a pending opinion (*avis suspendu*). Services managed to settle this conflict at the administrative level and eventually agreed on €150 million, which represented a significant increase of 50 percent compared to the previous programs. The lead DG was very satisfied with this outcome (COM96:54), given the budget service's firm hand in that period following the Kinnock reforms, which demanded that "all the Community's instruments should be evaluated against strict criteria by September 2000" (DG BUDG's response to CIS-net consultation no. 16022). Written documents from the inter-service consultation suggest that in order to obtain a higher budget, the lead DG had exploited its agenda-setting position: in its draft proposal it strategically (re-)introduced a higher budget than it had initially agreed on with the budget service.[14] Moreover, DG INFSO stressed that it had further benefited from the position of the European Parliament, which had shown itself to be supportive of the eContent program: "DG BUDG became a little bit less worried, seeing what kind of strong support we had from the Parliament" (COM96:65).

Overall, the lead department seemed strategically motivated, both when formulating its positions (aiming to expand its area of competence) and when defending its position against other services (exploiting its support from the European Parliament). Although the opposing DGs were successful in defending their positions on individual issues, in the final analysis, DG INFSO was more powerful in asserting its position on the overall act and in substantially increasing the funding volume.

DG INFSO's approach to its proposal for an eContentplus program seemed less strategic. The substantial change introduced with this program was its overall focus. Whereas the eContent program focused on the private publishing industry, the new proposal addressed public content owners of educational, cultural, and geographic information. This time DG INFSO did not rely on organized interests as the main source of input (see the eContent program), but on the mid-term assessment of the foregoing eContent program prepared by external experts. The analysis, upon which the drafting officials based the new program (COM130:22), revealed the preceding program's "impact" as well as "some of its shortcomings." The change in the main information source was related to two factors. On the one hand, the *dot.com bubble crash* in 2000 had led to bankruptcy for some of the former stakeholder community, which the DG could therefore no longer consult (COM97:77). On the other hand, a new Director responsible for electronic content issues had arrived, who proposed a change in the program's target audience. The Director's professional background in public research induced him to shift the program's focus to the public sector instead of private industry (COM96:171), based on the view that "society as a whole would benefit, and not just specific industries" (COM130:30). This approach is clearly visible not only with respect to specific provisions such as the target audience, but also in the overall thrust of the proposal, which suggested that funding target "areas where the market failed" (COM97:31). Accordingly, the final proposal reads that the eContentplus program aimed "to maximize the impact on a group of actors beyond the participants of the programme" (COM[2004]96: 9). Thus, the personal beliefs of the responsible Director at the time substantially influenced DG INFSO's approach.

Looking at the interactions with other DGs, it is noteworthy that in the run-up to the eContentplus program, DG INFSO no longer stated a claim on DG EAC's MEDIA activities. The internal conflicts were therefore limited to those with DG BUDG, with the discussions resembling those carried out five years previously. Once again, the lead department proposed a substantial budget increase—from €100 million to €163 million for the four-year period. And once again, the budget service reduced this amount and submitted a pending opinion in CIS-net (*avis suspendu*) based on an insufficient impact assessment. Once more, the DGs managed to reach agreement at administrative level: DG INFSO accepted a reduction to its initial budget request and prepared a more comprehensive *ex ante* evaluation "in a hurry" (COM130:54). Here, again, the European Parliament was supportive of DG INFSO's higher budgetary request, which was carried through to the inter-institutional process (COM97:107). The lead DG was able to further defend its position by referring to the success of its earlier programs, which created the general understanding within the Commission that "this [programme] was a good thing to do" (COM96:171).

In sum, the lead department's program approach was mainly influenced by knowledge-based factors, such as the previous program, the corresponding expert evaluation, and the responsible Director's personal beliefs. However, the lead DG was also rendered powerful in its interactions with DG BUDG by strategic support from the European Parliament and supranational competences acquired through earlier policy-making.

6.3.3 Multiannual Programme for Enterprise and Entrepreneurship and the Competitiveness and Innovation Framework Programme

The two remaining innovation support programs in our sample were managed by DG ENTR. In 2000, the Commission tabled a proposal for the Multiannual Programme for Enterprise and Entrepreneurship (MAP, COM[2000]256–2), which was the fourth in a series of Community funding programs in support of European enterprises, in particular small and medium-sized enterprises (SMEs), which had started in 1983. As had been the case in the earlier programs, the MAP aimed to help small enterprises throughout Europe to overcome the numerous financial and administrative obstacles they encountered. However, in its new program the Commission proposed a new emphasis on enterprises and entrepreneurship in general, rather than only SMEs and micro-enterprises. Most support was devoted to an SME support network of "Euro Info Centres" and to seed capital. Moreover, a number of soft measures received support (benchmarking, studies, and conferences). The budget proposed was €230 million, which doubled that of the previous program.

Similar to the processes described so far in the area of innovation support measures, the lead DG started with its preparations after it had received the mid-term evaluation of the predecessor program in early 1999 (COM51:35). Although the drafting was largely perceived as a "bottom-up exercise" (COM56:67), it was disrupted by the Commission's administrative re-organization in the context of the Kinnock reforms. In January 2000, the DG that had been responsible for the previous MAP programs, DG XXIII (Enterprise Policy, Distributive Trades, Tourism and Cooperatives), was merged with the much larger DG III (Industry) and with parts of DG XIII (Information Society, Telecommunication, Markets, Technologies, Innovation and Enhancement of Research) to become DG ENTR (Chapter 4). Following the arrival of a new Director-General and an expanded mandate for the newly created DG ENTR, DG XXIII's draft was revised in the space of a few weeks, given that the proposal was due to be adopted in May 2000 (COM51:40). Whereas the first draft had largely presented continuity with the previous program, the incoming Director-General Colasanti, who had previously headed DG BUDG, sought to simplify and streamline the new program by cutting some small pilot projects for micro-enterprises. This was opposed by his Commissioner Liikanen, who—similar to what we observed in the eContent case above—was much closer to the political arena. In this case, the Commissioner had been receiving letters of complaint from Members of the European Parliament, who promised their support for the Commission's budget request for the program only if the Commission abstained from cutting back small pilot projects for micro-enterprises (COM51:61, COM103:24).[15] Responding to the European Parliament's demands, the Commissioner managed to retain some projects for small and micro-enterprises in the MAP proposal. With respect to interactions with other DGs, DG ENTR's administrative level drafted its proposal very much "in isolation" (COM56:49), without much exchange with other services. The interactions among DGs centered on a "major difficulty" with the budget service about the program's "expenditure implications" (COM56:86). This led DG BUDG to issue a negative opinion in CIS-net. Again, DG BUDG's position was related to the strict management demands emanating from the Kinnock reforms (COM51:90). The lead DG had to insert the "modifications [DG BUDG] wanted to the financial statement in order to make them happy," which involved a lot of "to-ing and fro-ing in order to get [DG BUDG's] agreement to a text which [DG BUDG] gave in at the end" (COM56:86). Although these interview quotes from a DG ENTR official suggest that his DG had to substantially modify its initial draft, lacking further empirical evidence it is difficult to assess the substantial scope of modifications. What we do know is that the budgetary amount proposed in the final proposal doubled that of the previous program, which is remarkable.[16] Without being able to draw on further empirical evidence, DG ENTR as lead department must have been successful in defending substantial aspects of its budgetary demands, presumably on the basis of its experience in and legitimacy for making industrial policy. Perhaps it also benefited from the support the European Parliament had promised and from the fact that its Director-General had previously headed DG BUDG and therefore possessed substantial skills in negotiating with the budget service.

While the battle with DG BUDG resembled a strategic bargain, the lead DG's individual position-formation process can be described as mainly expertise-based drafting, which, however, was also influenced by political demands from the European Parliament, by the rationalization efforts of the Director-General and by the political concerns of the Commissioner.

Following up on the MAP, which ended in 2005, DG ENTR presented the Competitiveness and Innovation Framework Programme (CIP, COM[2005]121). The aim of this program was to support innovative projects bringing together private and public actors, and to set the right framework conditions for innovation to prosper in the EU. Its activities predominantly targeted SMEs and public authorities and involved a total budget of €4.2 billion. The program not only covered the activities previously managed under DG ENTR's MAP, but also several other Community innovation funding streams. In total, seven funding streams were merged into the CIP. Although these initiatives were all related to the area of innovation, they had a sectoral focus and were therefore dispersed across several DGs. DG ENTR had responsibilities in the field of entrepreneurship, SMEs, industrial competitiveness and innovation; DG INFSO for information and communication technology (ICT) activities; DG ENV for environmental technologies actions; and DG TREN for a program on intelligent energy.

In contrast to the MAP drafting, which had followed a strong bottom-up rationale, the new program was a clear top-down proposal initiated by the Commission's Secretariat General in July 2004 in the context of the upcoming Financial Perspectives (2007–2013, COM[2004]487) and the re-launch of the Lisbon strategy, which aimed at making the EU "the most dynamic and competitive knowledge-based economy in the world" by 2010 (Commission of the European Communities 2005b). The Commission realized that in order to request a significant budgetary increase from member states for the area of competitiveness under the new Financial Perspectives, it would need to demonstrate efficient resource management. This required the rationalization of existing policy instruments (COM49:235), according to the principle of "one instrument per policy area, one fund per programme" (Commission of the European

Communities 2004: par. III.B). For the policy DGs concerned—DGs ENTR, INFSO, ENV, and TREN—merging a number of small innovation funding streams gave these programs a chance to "survive" (COM5:34). Thus, when the lead DG ENTR started drafting a concrete idea for a CIP in July 2004, the other DGs had already prepared their own drafts for the follow-up editions for phasing-out programs, including public consultations and fully fledged *ex ante* evaluations (COM68:41), which in part were ready for adoption in the College (COM51:125). These processes were now suspended and the mandate was to merge the individual programs into one single CIP, which was to be adopted rather swiftly together with other Lisbon Strategy initiatives on April 6, 2005. Given the challenge to present a coherent proposal under time pressure, DG ENTR concentrated on a fast-track integration of the different parts of the program.

Consequently the drafting demanded intense cooperation between a number of portfolios, which took place in a rather unusual manner. While interactions in the Commission typically work their way upwards from the service to the political level (see Chapters 2 and 10), in this case the direction was top- down. First, discussions took place at the political level among the responsible Commissioners. After the political level had come to agreement on which funding streams were to be integrated, the dossier was first handed to the Directors-General, who defined the broad guidelines, and then to their administrations, which worked out the details (COM51:174). This involved the four DGs responsible for the program—DGs ENTR, INFSO, TREN, and ENV (COM13:84)—and DG ECFIN, which was responsible for some of the financial schemes. Moreover, the horizontal services, particularly DG BUDG, the SJ, and the SG, were strongly involved in finalizing this new initiative (COM5:106, COM13:84, COM13:100).

The main debates evolved around two points. First, as it held overall responsibility for the new initiative, DG ENTR would have liked the new program to be as integrated and as centrally managed as possible (COM51:149). The lead DG was supported in this respect by the SG and by DGs ENV and BUDG. This desire was opposed, in turn, by DGs INFSO and TREN, which feared that DG ENTR wanted to "eat" them (COM49:253). Reflecting and defending their stakeholder views, they wished to retain as much responsibility for their areas as possible. They argued that "from the point of view of the beneficiaries it is of little value" (COM51:150, authors' translation) to integrate well-established funding streams into a common frame that would obscure the accessibility of EU funding (COM51:124, COM56:111, COM59:162). Whereas the lead department had to recognize that the DGs, unsurprisingly, forcefully defended their constituencies, the respective Commissioners were less reluctant about this merger, given that they were "not concerned about the content but only about money" (COM3:60, authors' translation). The political level hoped that a large and comprehensive innovation program would strengthen their position in the financial discussions with member states and would lead to a budgetary increase, so that they were willing to "fight jointly for the budget" (COM82:76, authors' translation, also COM5:59). Thus, while the administrative level was concerned about retaining bureaucratic autonomy and defending the interests of established stakeholder communities, the political level had its eye on political negotiations with member states. Nonetheless, what united them was the interest in producing a proposal that would be accepted in Council. Following on from this, seemingly contrasting visions could be integrated in a solution that proposed a single act with a sub-structure that allocated substantial bureaucratic autonomy to the portfolios involved. The evidence presented above suggests that DG ENTR benefited from the political decision on a CIP taken in advance, nesting it in the discussions on the Financial Perspectives, as well as from its brokerage power as lead DG. Nonetheless, DG ENTR had to make compromises towards the other DGs by structuring the CIP into three sub-programs—one for Enterprise and Innovation (including eco-innovation) managed by DG ENTR and DG ENV, one ICT Policy Support Programme managed by DG INFSO, and one Intelligent Energy Europe Programme managed by DG TREN. By retaining the management of their own sectoral sub-programs, DGs INFSO and TREN could satisfy their stakeholders' demands (COM3:101).[17]

Second, and closely related, the three-pillar structure allowed the individual DGs to manage their respective actions differently. Whereas DGs ENTR and TREN both externalized a number of management activities to an executive agency (the Executive Agency for Competitiveness and Innovation, EACI), DG INFSO succeeded in retaining management responsibility over its own activities. The lead department accorded DG INFSO "power to decide this," which was also "completely respected by all the other DGs" (COM68:82). This last quote illustrates that while interactions were described as "excellent" and "very intensive" and as an example of "a very good mutual respect" (COM68:95), they were also characterized by DGs defending their own "turf." This sums up a drafting process that was defined from the outset by strong interests, both at the political level (envisaging a larger budget in support of the Lisbon Strategy) and at the administrative level (defending stakeholder benefits and bureaucratic autonomy). These factors, which had influenced individual DG positions, served as sources of power later on, with DG ENTR being able to build on the CIP already decision taken by the political level, its framing in the Financial Perspectives, and its brokerage position as lead DG.

In sum, the position-formation processes of the innovation support programs discussed in this section offer four main insights. First, the drafting officials largely based their proposals on the previous programs, including their mid-term evaluations. While one major aim was to achieve a budget increase, services often also aimed for simplification or rationalization in accordance with the Commission's then highly topical simplification agenda. Second, the political level, while also prioritizing the budget, often kept a close eye on the subsequent inter-institutional negotiations and therefore advised the services to take these political concerns into consideration. Third, although the CIP as a top-down initiative initially looks like an outlier, it features the same two patterns. Thus, in these cases the patterns are consistent over time.

Fourth, in their interactions with other services, DGs that had based their own positions on functional motivations often appeared to be concerned first and foremost about protecting their own "turf" or their budget demands against the budget service—and they were quite successful at this given their longstanding experience in their respective areas.

6.4 RESEARCH POLICY REGULATIONS AND DIRECTIVES

Before delving into the case studies in this section, it is worthwhile mentioning that among this sub-group, two acts do not fully comply with the definition of research and innovation policy established in this chapter's introduction. This concerns the "Programme on the conservation, characterization, collection and utilization of genetic resources in agriculture" (COM[2001]617-1) and the proposal for a directive on "Quality and safety of human organs intended for transplantation" (COM[2008]818). However, as the former was labeled in Eur-Lex as "agricultural research" (directory code 3305000) and the latter as "industrial policy research sectors" (directory code 13103020), they have been included in our sample (see Chapter 3). The case studies provide indications of their links with research and innovation policy. Moreover, whereas the legal acts for the Programme on Genetic Resources in Agriculture (COM[2001]617-1) and for the European Institute of Technology (COM[2006]604) are "Regulations," the case studies reveal that their objectives include distributive measures (Tables 6.6 and 6.7).

6.4.1 Programme on Genetic Resources in Agriculture

The proposal for a "Programme on the conservation, characterization, collection and utilization of genetic resources in agriculture" (COM[2001]617-1) offered support and coordination for the preservation of genetic resources in agriculture that were threatened by extinction. It mainly addressed farmers, private companie, and NGOs, with gene banks and scientific institutes as marginal beneficiaries. The program is an unusual case in the sense that the lead DG AGRI prepared it against its will and only in response to external pressure. Moreover, during drafting, DG AGRI ignored substantive requests made by member states and the European Parliament, which led to strong opposition in the inter-institutional process, and the Commission had to finally withdraw its proposal. A new proposal was tabled in 2003, which took account of member states' concerns and was thus adopted in Council (Council Regulation No. 870/2004 of 24 April 2004). DG AGRI's 2001 proposal was a follow-up program to a regulation from 1994 that had run until 1999 (Council Regulation [EC] No. 1467/94) and proposed funding over five years of up to €10 million per year (COM[2001]617-1: Explanatory Memorandum, para. 3). While the earlier program of 1994 had been financed through the Community budget for internal policies, DG AGRI proposed that the new program be financed through the European Agricultural Guidance and Guarantee Fund (EAGGF) section of the European Common Agricultural Policy (CAP) budget.

Here drafting started in early 2000 under the auspices of the DG AGRI unit that was responsible for managing agricultural research at the time. The program was prepared in response to increasing pressures from the European Parliament, Green parties, and NGOs demanding that the Commission comply with the United Nations Convention on Biological Diversity (CBD) it had signed in 1992, thus committing itself to preserving diversity among plants and animals.

Table 6.6. Position formation on research policy regulations and directives

Proposal number	Contents	No. of key provisions	Main line of proposal (content)	Uncertainty	Salience	Origin (hierarchal level)	Process duration (months)	External consultation	Main position-formation factors
COM[2001]617-1	Programme on genetic resources in agriculture	6	Abandoning the program, cost and management efficiency	No	No	Administrative	20	Specific	- Anticipation of Council majority - Anticipation of EP majority - Individuals' influence - Experts - International policy transfer
COM[2006]604	European Institute of Innovation and Technology	8	Establishment of a European MIT as a symbol of Barroso's potency	No	Yes	Political	20	Public	- Individuals' influence - International policy transfer - Anticipation of Council majority
COM[2008]467	European Research Infrastructures	7	Introducing a legal framework for transnational research infrastructures, granting them VAT exemption	No	No	Administrative	14	Public	- Anticipation of Council majority - Experts
COM[2008]818	Quality and safety of human organs intended for transplantation	11	Cross-border coordination of organ donation, increase of donor pool	Yes	No	Administrative	24	Public	- Extant *acquis* - Anticipation of Council majority - Experts

Table 6.7. Interaction on research policy regulations and directives

Proposal number	Contents	Deviating DGs	Informal interaction	Position-based conflict	Process-based conflict	Main line of conflict	Most powerful DG	Main power resources
COM[2001]617-1	Programme on genetic resources in agriculture	—	Medium	—	—	Delineation of portfolio responsibilities	—	—
COM[2006]604	European Institute of Innovation and Technology	RTD	Intense	3	1	Budget volume	EAC	- Initiative's origin - Support from horizontal services
COM[2008]467	European Research Infrastructures	TAXUD	Intense	2	1	Delineation of portfolio responsibilities	RTD	- Support from horizontal services - Lead DG - Meta game
COM[2008]818	Quality and safety of human organs intended for transplantation	SJ JLS	Intense	2	0	Degree of supranational intervention	SANCO	- Proximity to EP majority - Supranational competence

The Commission finally agreed to propose a program, which "landed on the shoulders of the agricultural research service" (Lorenzen and Kölling 2008). From the very start, DG AGRI considered the conservation of genetic resources misplaced in its portfolio and its own tradition of managing the CAP (Lorenzen and Kölling 2008). Unlike research or innovation DGs, DG AGRI had little experience with *direct* research management requiring the management of calls for proposals and the selection, supervision, and evaluation of programs. On the contrary, because of the way the CAP was managed, DG AGRI actually had a long tradition of *indirect* management: EAGGF funds are transferred to member states, which are then fairly autonomous in managing their projects. In particular DG AGRI's Deputy Director-General Demarty (France) was opposed to direct management because of the huge personnel costs this implied and because of the inherent risk of fraud he would then have to deal with (COM53). While he would have preferred not proposing such a program at all, his Commissioner and Director-General did not consider this a viable option, given the external pressure from member states and the European Parliament (COM53). Thus, Demarty succeeded in at least introducing indirect funding, which, however, met major opposition from member states which demanded a stronger managerial role by the Commission (COM53). To this was added member states' concern that including support for the conservation of genetic resources in the scope of the CAP would imply a decrease in funding to other activities traditionally covered under the CAP.

DG AGRI organized the drafting process in strong cooperation with a small group of independent experts (COM53; COM[2001]617-2). Interactions with other DGs on this proposal were smooth and not extraordinary, taking place informally and formally, but without meeting fundamental opposition. The lead DG willingly accepted DG RTD's demand to respect "clear boundaries" (DG RTD's response to CIS-net consultation no. AGR 15032) regarding agricultural research managed under the 6th Research Framework Programme. The SJ objected that the lead DG had not prepared a proper impact assessment, but could be convinced that a report prepared by the group of independent experts sufficed as a substitute (COM53:48).

In conclusion, position formation reveals how a DG may be constrained by its traditional portfolio role and tasks and by the aim of combining bureaucratic prosperity with external demands, and therefore reject adapting to and learning from international developments in the policy field.

6.4.2 European Institute of Technology

The proposal for a European Institute of Technology[18] (EIT, COM[2006]604) was aimed at establishing a European supranational research university modeled on the successful Massachusetts Institute of Technology (MIT) in the US. The EIT proposal emerged on the European agenda in response to Commission President Barroso's political will to leave a mark of his Presidency (COM58:161). When he took office in November 2004, the EU was four years into the Lisbon Strategy, which, however, received a disappointing review in the "Kok Report" of its performance in the transition into a "knowledge economy." Responding to this three months later, in February 2005, Barroso announced his idea of a European university modeled on MIT. The EIT would be designed to integrate the three points of the Lisbon Strategy's "knowledge triangle"—research, innovation, and education—and would bring together academic, scientific, and industrial stakeholders. While some national-level universities existed that took such an integrated approach—such as Cambridge University, the Swiss Federal Institute of Technology Zürich (ETH), and the Karolinska Institute in Stockholm, at supranational level, EU activities had so far mainly focused on only one or two elements of the "knowledge triangle." By attracting the best researchers in Europe, the EIT was supposed to become Europe's "new flagship for excellence in higher education, research and innovation" (Commission of the European Communities 2006).

To Barroso's dismay, the idea of a "European MIT" did not attract much sympathy, either among the policy community or within the Commission. The external resistance concerned the functional necessity of establishing a supranational university. Member states referred to subsidiarity and emphasized that education and vocational training systems came under national responsibility (COM101). Instead of establishing another university "top down," Europe should invest instead in those world-class universities that already existed, such as Cambridge, Oxford, and the ETH Zürich (*FT*, February 8, 2005). Consequently, the EIT's drafting process was accompanied by significant public attention, in particular "among the *FT* readers" (COM101:176), as the British newspaper had been "extremely critical" (COM101:176). One DG EAC official even perceived a "hate campaign" run by the *Financial Times*, which was "publishing exactly the days before we [the Commission] were coming out with some proposal" (COM99:145, *FT*, February 14, 2006).

Internal resistance, in turn, primarily concerned the question of funding, because the EIT required a budget, but the Financial Perspectives for the impending years (2007–2013, COM[2004]487) did not include a funding stream for this initiative. Given that the total budget had already been set, this implied that research and innovation initiatives funded under the relevant "Competitiveness" heading 1A, such as research and innovation programs, would have to be downsized so as to free up money for the new EIT. The relevant DGs and their stakeholders therefore feared cutbacks regarding existing initiatives. In particular, "DG RTD saw the EIT as a threat to FP7" (COM99:18) currently under negotiation in the inter-institutional process, fearing that parts of the 7th Framework Programme (such as the European Research Council), could be sacrificed to fund the President's initiative. A point emphasized by interview partners was that "to some extent RTD was also representing the views of the stakeholders community" (COM101:91; also COM99:58, COM12:202), who were concerned about "their" funding (in the 7th Framework Programme). Despite this strong opposition, the EIT remained on the political agenda and was even further promoted and modified to meet all concerns because it was "the pet of the President" (COM99:23). All in all, it was deemed that the EIT being the President's initiative made its preparatory process "very special" (COM101:30).

Administratively, the President tasked DG EAC (led by Commissioner Figel', Slovakia) with drafting an EIT proposal. Under the premise that the President's initial idea would not be completely dismissed and that ultimately there would be a legislative proposal, DG EAC's main task was to adjust and to promote the design of the EIT in such a way that it was agreeable for important veto players whose consent would be needed in the subsequent inter-institutional decision-making process (COM99). In addition, given that within the Commission "there was a spirit of strong polemic around the EIT concept" (COM99:10), the President's SG "did not want to have internal people" and therefore recruited three "contractual agents" (COM101:26) into DG EAC's unit on "School, education and higher education policies" (COM99:10). These three officials formed "a specific team" responsible for the EIT in DG EAC, led by the responsible Director, who was, again, considered "the most important person" in preparing the proposal (COM101:148; also COM99:10, COM124:82). This small team drafted two Communications further elaborating the EIT structure, and both initiated an open consultation, which generated a high level of response (COM[2006]77 and COM [2006]276). Moreover, an impact assessment was prepared, which was, however, referred to as a "kind of reverse engineering approach" by one DG EAC official, as it was not prepared "in order to take the decision" (COM101:189) but *after* Barroso had decided to establish an EIT and in parallel to drafting the regulation.[19]

Because the aim of the EIT was to integrate education, research, and innovation, drafting required the cooperation of the three DGs responsible for these "knowledge policies": Next to the lead DG EAC (higher education), this included DG RTD (research) and DG ENTR (innovation). Not only because of the question of EIT funding, but also because of historically rooted sectoral differentiation, there was reluctance among these DGs to work together across organizational boundaries. DG ENTR "thought innovation is their business, they do innovation; they thought this [the EIT] will never fly" (COM99:23), and perceived the EIT as "yet another kind of research driven instrument, and not as an innovation instrument" (COM101:76). DG RTD, in turn, "was very much focused at that time with the creation of the European Research Council; so they didn't want any element of disturbance" (COM99:23)—not only in terms of budget, but also in terms of defending new supranational research instruments against member states (COM12:201). Nonetheless, despite their initial reluctance, DGs RTD and ENTR interacted closely, given that they admitted that the President's initiative was "an important file" (COM124:84). In the course of the preparations, the EIT draft actually developed into something that a DG EAC official described as "a joint proposal from EAC, ENTR and RTD, led by EAC" (COM101:57). When the Commission finally tabled an EIT proposal on October 18, 2006, the lead DG had clearly benefited from the file's political origin. The political weight of the President's initiative provided DG EAC with sufficient power to overcome severe resistance. At a more practical level, the lead DG was supported by the SG and the SJ throughout the process. A DG EAC official emphasized the "good cooperation with the legal service that offered support from the very beginning" (COM101:80).[20] The SG played a particularly significant role in brokering a solution to the problem of EIT funding (COM101:80, see the next paragraph).

Nonetheless, Barroso's initial idea was modified to such an extent in response to internal and external opposition that the final proposal only became a weak reflection of the original idea. First and foremost, Barroso's vision of a single-site European university built of brick and mortar—a truly "European MIT"—had been abandoned. Instead, a networked structure of collaborations among existing institutes, so-called "Knowledge and Innovation Communities" (KICs) was proposed. The resulting defense by member states such as Germany, the Netherlands, Sweden, and the UK, of their national competence for higher education strongly impacted on the internal process. The member states used various channels to express their opposition, such as bilateral exchanges with Barroso himself (COM101:80) or responses to the Commission's two Communications. For instance, one DG EAC official noted disdainfully: "On one of the Communications Germany returned the document with detailed changes, going through line by line, checking word for word" (COM99:142). DG EAC further substantially adjusted the handling of human resources devoted to the EIT and particular EIT degrees and diplomas of a "supranational standard of excellence"—two further issues that were highly contested among universities and member states. Both actor groups feared losing their best researchers to a supranational competitor and that existing national standards would be diluted (COM99). In the final proposal, EIT personnel no longer had to be seconded by national universities and research institutes and the participating universities could choose between joint degrees with other EIT participants or their own individual degrees. Lastly, DG RTD and the scientific community succeeded in defending the 7th Framework Programme's budgetary resources: the final proposal only refers to initial start-up costs of €308.7 million, which would be covered by "unallocated margins beneath the ceilings of sub-heading 1A" (Commission of the European Communities 2006: 8). Notably, DG BUDG also had to be convinced, for whom it was a "political difficulty to insert this within the existing financial perspectives" (COM101:82). Here, DG EAC was supported by "the SG [which] took a rather important role on liaising with the budget people, and trying to combine the political and legislative part of the proposal with the financial one" (COM101:80). Concluding, despite the substantial compromises that had been made on the design of the EIT, the lead DG proved to be most powerful, as it nonetheless managed to overcome substantial resistance and formally table an EIT proposal.

Position formation on the EIT resembles a competence-seeking process throughout. President Barroso, although addressing a functional problem in the European research landscape, was primarily determined to set a symbol of his personal influence. However, DGs opposed, driven by lobbying of their stakeholder constituencies and their own desire to defend their own "turf" and budgets. The lead DG was able to overcome the opposition by benefiting from the initiative's top-down drive, including the President's readiness to adjust his initial idea to accommodate internal and external opponents, as well as from strategic support from the Commission's key horizontal services at administrative level.

6.4.3 European Research Infrastructures

The legislative proposal for a Regulation on European Research Infrastructures (ERI, COM[2008]467)[21] prepared by DG RTD was aimed at establishing a legal framework for pan-European research infrastructures. Research infrastructures are "facilities, resources and related services that are used by the scientific community to conduct top-level research in their respective fields.... [which] may be 'single-sited' or 'distributed'" (Commission of the European Communities 2008c: recital 6). Examples of existing European research infrastructures are the European Organization for Nuclear Research (CERN) or the European Molecular Biology Laboratory (EMBL). Pan-European research consortia had hitherto been established on a case-by-case basis and an individual legal framework had to be designed for every new infrastructure based on a variety of existing national and intergovernmental legal bases, such as the German GmbH, the British Ltd., the European Cooperative Society (ECS), or an international agreement. In the mid-2000s, the Commission and the research community began to argue that future European research infrastructures would be so large and their installation so costly that they would increasingly require involving several member states across Europe to pool their expertise and resources (COM1:35). This would inevitably result in battles over the appropriate legal tool and their compatibility with various national legal frameworks.

DG RTD therefore started to develop a standard legal framework, the "European Research Infrastructure" (ERI) in early 2007, with the work being carried out by its unit on research infrastructures. In this process, the officials in charge emphasized the high demands on specialized knowledge of EU and member state law to draft such a regulation (COM1:111). This included expertise on taxation legislation, which—apart from its complexity—was very controversial (COM57:198). Therefore, early on in the drafting process—and foreseeing the contentiousness of its proposal—the lead DG consulted legal experts engaged in the management of existing research infrastructures, as well as those with expertise on the relationship between national and supranational law. Together with these experts, DG RTD prepared different studies in order to support its position against prospective opponents (COM9:42).

More specifically, DG RTD's position clashed with DG TAXUD on two (interrelated) issues: first, DG RTD's aim to grant ERIs value-added tax (VAT) exemption at national level; second, to nonetheless base its proposal on research Art. 171 TEU (Art. 187 TFEU) instead of using an article from the Taxation Chapter of the Treaty (e.g. Art. 93 TEU, upon which the VAT Directive is based, COM9:73). An important detail was that the choice of legal base had significant implications for the inter-institutional decision-making process. An initiative based on a taxation article would be discussed by the Economic and Financial Affairs Council (Ecofin) and require unanimity in Council (COM9:36). An initiative based on a research article, by contrast, would be discussed by the Research Ministers and only required the consent of a qualified majority of member states in Council (COM9:73). Thus, DG TAXUD, in line with the national finance ministers, complained that DG RTD had purposefully designed the ERI proposal in a "financially attractive" way (COM57:198). They alleged that the lead DG had created a free-riding situation for its stakeholders by exempting future ERIs from paying value-added taxes at national level and stressed that any regulation allowing tax exemptions would have to be based on a taxation article. DG TAXUD, "having frequent contacts with finance ministries warning about this" (COM5:180), agreed that "taking a decision from the unanimity area indirectly into the qualified majority area ... is politically an extremely delicate matter" (COM9:38, authors' translation). Thus, the shadow of the inter-institutional process was clearly cast over position formation within the Commission. More specifically a Research Cabinet member described the situation at the time as follows:

> So you get the extent where the Commission—which is of course a single unified body with its own single position—in its relations with the Council—which is also a single body [laughs]—[exposes itself as] TAXUD obviously dealing with the Ecofin Finance Ministries and the Research and Competitiveness Council with DG Research and [Commissioner] Potočnik. (COM5:180)

The delicateness of the issue was further amplified by the fact that basing a legal act that covered taxation issues *not* on a Taxation Article had never been done before. Thus, DG TAXUD was "fearing precedence" (COM1:190; also COM9:73). If DG RTD regulated taxation issues on a research legal basis it would enter DG TAXUD's area of responsibilty, something the latter DG opposed as "a matter of principle" (COM1:149, COM9:36, COM57:198). In order to prevent precedence, "TAXUD had a very clear, dogmatic position, which is: Everything related to fiscal policy cannot be based on a chapter in the Treaty which is called Research" (COM1:90).

In the internal conflict, DG RTD could draw on the expertise gathered in advance and on support from the horizontal services. Most importantly, lawyers working in the Commission's SJ found drafting the ERI legal basis very stimulating (COM01:110): as it was a case of precedence, it implied "the further development of European law" (COM9:42, authors' translation). Thus, the SJ had created ownership by being involved closely in the drafting of a technically appealing solution. What is more, DG RTD also had the active support of the President's SG. The SG defended "very explicitly" (COM9:41, authors' translation) the same opinion as DG RTD and the SJ. It likewise preferred the act to be based on a research article requiring a qualified majority in the Council, as it wanted a smooth decision-making process (COM9:41). More specifically, after DG TAXUD had issued a negative opinion in the inter-service consultation, the SG summoned this internal troublemaker for a serious discussion (COM9:38). This even reached the top of the administration, involving DG TAXUD's Director-General Verrue and the Commission's Secretary General Day (COM57:213). DG RTD officials admitted that in this conflict they "needed to have the arbitrage of the Secretariat General" (COM1:95). However, as DG TAXUD was still not willing to give up its negative opinion, the quarrel reached the political level. Lastly, the responsible Research and Taxation Cabinet members—again, with a member from the President's Cabinet as arbitrator—brokered a compromise, which included minor adjustments to DG RTD's text (COM1:153).

The actors in favor of a Research treaty base and qualified majority voting emphasized that from a general Commission view it was "ridiculous to stand on [the] vanity of insisting on unanimity, when it meant shooting Europe in the foot in terms of being able to innovate and build research infrastructures quickly" (COM5:178). Therefore, the implications of the choice of a legal base for European integration were decisive for why the political units in the Commission supported the lead DG's position. The ERI legislative proposal had wider implications for the process of European integration beyond presenting an institutional framework for research infrastructures: it proposed tax exemption under a non-taxation legal basis, which allowed the Commission to "circumvent" national taxation competences by using other Treaty articles which did not demand unanimity (COM9:36, 147).

As we observed for the case for the European Institute of Technology above, the ERI proposal also presents a functional solution to an existing supranational problem. Again, the position-formation process, however, displays a great deal of strategic action. Actors formed their position in anticipation of future decision-making and with an eye to extending or defending their own "turf." Internal reconciliation demanded the intervention of the President's horizontal services, which successfully evoked the legal act's wider implications for European integration.

6.4.4 Quality and Safety of Human Organs for Transplantation

The "Proposal for a Directive of the European Parliament and of the Council on standards of quality and safety of human organs intended for transplantation" (COM[2008]818) prepared by DG SANCO aimed at increasing organ donation rates across Europe by ensuring that "human organs used for transplantation in the EU comply with the same quality and safety requirements" (COM[2008]818: 4).[22] The Human Organs proposal formed the "third plank of a triptych" of directives based on Art. 152(4) of the Treaty, succeeding a directive on blood and blood derivates (2002/98/EC) and on tissues and cells (2004/23/EC). In particular, the latter directive's approach and its implementation strongly impacted on DG SANCO's approach to the proposal discussed here (COM6:25).

The Human Organs initiative can be seen as a spill-over policy of the internal market, given that the need for coordinating regulation in the area had risen with the free movement of people within the EU.[23] Given a broad heterogeneity of national consent systems and standards of quality and safety—substantially increased by Eastern enlargement—the Human Organs proposal was aimed at introducing preliminary harmonizing measures. DG SANCO proposed standards on the collection, provision, and exchange of information in the process of organ donation, obliging member states to establish individual "national quality programmes" and "standard operating procedures" that complied with the standards laid out in the proposal. Taking a minimum harmonization approach, the proposal also had a market-making effect, as common quality and safety standards would be expected to facilitate the exchange of human organs across member states (COM[2008]818: 4).

DG SANCO began to work on the initiative with a strong tailwind from the European Parliament to take action on this issue (COM6:29). As a first noticeable step, the DG launched a public consultation on "Organ Donation and Transplantation Policy Options at EU Level" in June 2006. During the two years of drafting, the lead DG consulted broadly and thoroughly in order to establish the problem definition and an appropriate and consensual solution. It relied extensively on external experts, most notably on two human organs expert groups—one composed of member state authorities and one with "stakeholders, including industry" (COM6). These expert groups were described as "*the* important groups for us [DG SANCO] in drafting everything" (COM6). Most relevant was the information provided on two areas of expertise: the implementation process of the Tissues and Cells Directive and the organ donation system in Spain, which drafting officials considered to be "*the* perfect system" (COM6).

Initially, the lead DG had "modelled the Directive a lot like the Tissues and Cells Directive" (COM6:55). However, some member states that were experiencing problems in the implementation of this directive (such as Germany) expressed "huge concerns" (COM6:131) and therefore urged DG SANCO to make the Human Organs proposal more flexible in the sense of entailing less supranational harmonization. DG SANCO, interested in taking an approach that would allow it to achieve its aim of improving the European organ donation situation, took this concern on board, as it was alerted by the negative effects of the Tissues and Cells Directive and did not want to risk a decline in the number of organ donations. However, the concerns voiced by member states also alerted the SG. The President's service, playing out its role as the "Commission's watchdog" (Cini 1996) was worried because "[w]e have been attacked quite a lot as a Commission that we are interfering with member state competence" (COM6:97) and consequently cautioned DG SANCO to be sensitive to member states' interests and "make sure that you do your job right" (COM6:97).

More specifically, the SG considered the proposal for a Human Organs Directive as "an important initiative" (COM6:97) because it had been selected as a test case for national parliaments' subsidiarity check of EU legislation.[24] Following the introduction of an "early warning mechanism" in the Lisbon Treaty, the Conference of Community and European Affairs Committees of Parliaments of the European Union (COSAC), consisting of Members of the European and national Parliaments, wanted to test how coordination among national parliaments would work within the envisaged timeframe of eight weeks. The Human Organs proposal was the sixth test case. Now the SG wanted to make sure that DG SANCO's proposal passed the subsidiarity check for political reasons because otherwise the new instrument might easily prove damaging to the Commission. Consequently, the SG was "quite tough" (COM6:171) on the lead DG, ensuring that it did not overstretch its legal basis and kept the Directive flexible (SG's response to CIS-Net consultation no. D/360334).

In opposition to the SG's position, the Legal Service, however, "thought that we [DG SANCO] were *very* flexible; they wanted us to put some more obligations on the member states [and] a more stringent oversight concept of some sort of chain within the member states, to actually make sure that these activities are coming out" (COM6:51). Thus, the lead DG had to negotiate between these two powerful horizontal services and develop a compromising final position. Apart from these issues, a further DG strongly involved in the drafting process was DG JLS, which had many concerns about data protection for organ donors and recipients. As the Human Organs proposal introduced measures on the treatment of donors' and recipients' personal data, it touched on DG JLS' Data Protection Directive (95/46/EC). Therefore, DG JLS demanded "a lot of cross references to data protection in the text" (COM6:117; also DG JLS' response to CIS-Net consultation no. D/360334).

All in all, the interaction process was described as intense, making use of several communication channels, such as bilateral contacts to individual DGs, regular meetings in an inter-service steering group and discussions at Cabinet level (COM6:80, 125). Throughout the process, the lead DG had "really good relations with everyone [which] has facilitated a lot the process" (COM6:125). In the end, the final proposal reveals a number of compromises, in which, however, the lead DG was able to secure its middle position between the SG's and the SJ's demands. The empirical evidence suggests that the lead DG certainly benefited from the European Parliament's support and from its supranational competence in the area established by its experience on the closely related Tissues and Cells Directive.

In sum, the Commission's position formation process on the Human Organs Directive exemplifies how the lead department may be functionally motivated to find the best solution to a prevalent problem and willingly rely on external advice. A strategic rationale only appeared when the Commission's SG advised the lead DG to pay attention to the proposal's placement in the broader political context, which in this case involved national interests and the European Parliament.

Concluding our insights on position formation on research and innovation regulations and directives we find both similarities and differences to the two other sub-fields in this policy area. The differences most likely stemmed from diverging policy instruments across sub-fields, that is, the first two comprising consecutive funding programs and the latter one singular regulatory measures. As a result of this distinction, the lead DG's position when preparing regulations and directives was far less influenced by extant legislation. Instead, the strategic anticipation of member state positions played a far more important role. Likewise, across our cases, horizontal services appeared as important actors in the interaction process. However, the cases with financial implications mostly involved DG BUDG, whereas in the latter sub-field the SG and the SJ often played an important role as arbitrators or by offering their political weight to a specific position. A major similarity across all three sub-fields is the DGs' strong reliance on internal and/or external experts when forming their positions. However, independently of how actors initially had formed their position, when interacting with other services, DGs were often concerned about defending their own areas of responsiblity and/or budget. Also, in a number of cases, individual actors who exerted entrepreneurial pressure were more motivated by personal or organizational enrichment than by content. In general, when forming their own positions, Commission actors appear to be far more open to external ideas than when pushing through an established position against other actors internally. In the latter case we observe a lot of competence-seeking.

NOTES

1. See Commission Press Release SPEECH/07/257. Note, however, that, formally speaking, "knowledge" is not one of the EU's freedoms.
2. On January 1, 2011, DG Research officially became "DG for Research and Innovation." This change in name reflects the increased emphasis the Barroso II Commission placed on innovation (see also Chapter 4).

3. This includes the DG for the Joint Research Centre (DG JRC), which is closely affiliated to DG RTD. DG JRC manages the Community's JRC institutes located throughout Europe and therefore operates slightly differently to most policy DGs in the Commission.
4. Following the two framework proposals and after a few months delay, the Commission submitted several "Specific Programmes" and the "Rules for Participation." The Specific Programmes elaborate the objectives defined in the initial framework proposals in more detail.
5. See European Commission/Directorate-General for Information Society (2000) *ISTAG Recommendations for FP6*. Brussels, December 2000, available at <ftp://ftp.cordis.europa.eu/pub/ist/docs/istagfp6a.pdf>, last accessed March 26, 2013.
6. Next to the lead DG RTD, the "research DGs" holding budget shares and management responsibilities in FP7 were DG INFSO, DG TREN, and DG ENTR. During the preparation of FP7, DG FISH had to give up its position as a "research DG" since maritime research had been transferred to DG RTD (COM10:68).
7. Because the Research Director-General had to skip these meetings quite often on grounds of other obligations (such as negotiating an international nuclear research project, see discussion Section 6.2.3), the effectiveness of these meetings was called into question (COM61:92).
8. In parallel to drafting the legal text, a separate unit in DG RTD's Directorate A prepared an impact assessment. This was done with "a lot of external experts" (COM61:86) and "was a slightly parallel world to the development of the legislation" (COM61:86). Thus, other than the initial purpose of an *ex ante* impact assessment, it was done *in parallel to* as opposed to *in advance of* the policy legal drafting and therefore did not necessarily influence the legal text. Indeed, DG RTD officials openly stated that instead of using the document as an expert basis for their legal draft, they used it strategically to support their position in the inter-institutional negotiations against member states (COM7:156).
9. See European Research Council Expert Group (ERCEG) report from 15 December 2003, <http://erc.europa.eu/sites/default/files/document/file/expert_group_final_report.pdf>, last accessed December 5, 2012.
   See High-Level Expert Group Report from February 2005, <http://ec.europa.eu/research/future/pdf/hleg_fullreport_frontier_research_april2005.pdf>, last accessed December 5, 2012.
10. The most important were the Scientific and Technical Committee on Euratom (STC), two Consultative Committees on Energy Fusion and Fission (CCE-Fusion and CCE-Fission), and the Advisory Group on Energy (AGE), including sub-working groups such as the Strategic Working Group (SWOG) and the European Energy Research Area Working Group (ERAWOG). The consultation of the STC in preparation of the Euratom-FP is obligatory, though not binding (Art. 7 and Art. 134, Euratom Treaty, also COM54:22).
11. Schreyer's fundamental opposition to nuclear energy had also evidenced itself in her choice of policy portfolio when taking office in 1999 under Commission President Prodi. The President had also offered her the Research portfolio, but she declined it due to potential conflicts with her ideological Green beliefs (COM82:20).
12. While the FP7 EC-part lasted from 2007 to 2013 (see Section 6.2.2), FP7-Euratom lasted from 2007 to 2011, in accordance with the stipulation laid down in the Treaties that the Euratom program cannot be longer than five years (Art. 7(2) Euratom).
13. However, it should be noted that five years later, when Commissioner Reding moved from DG EAC to DG INFSO in autumn 2004, she took the MEDIA programs with her (COM60:52).
14. In its written response, DG BUDG argued that it had been "surprised to see that this demand also includes an amount of €40 million for 2001, although in the meeting we

had on the 11th of February, we agreed on a maximum of 20 million, which was confirmed by the Commission during the Orientation debate" (DG BUDG's response in CIS-net consultation no. 16022).

15. Although the European Parliament was only consulted on the MAP decision, it was able to exert influence on the program through to its budgetary competences (COM51:61).
16. This judgment is based on a comparison with the other innovation support programs prepared in parallel: the MEDIA proposals suggested an increase of 30 percent and eContent an increase of 50 percent compared to their predecessors.
17. In particular, the need to satisfy DG TREN's constituency is also mentioned in an unpublished briefing on the CIP prepared by DG ENTR for its Commissioner Verheugen on December 8, 2004.
18. During the inter-institutional negotiations in 2007, the EIT was renamed from "European Institute of Technology" to "European Institute of Innovation and Technology" at the request of the European Parliament.
19. This resembles what we also observed regarding the FP7 impact assessment (see Section 6.2.2).
20. This is also visible from the SJ's CIS-Net response, which emphasizes "l'excellente coopération entre nos services" (CIS-Net response No. JUR[2006]60489). Moreover, it should be noted that—unlike many of our other cases—the SJ's response does not include detailed changes to the legal text, which supports the assessment that this horizontal service had been closely involved from early on.
21. During the inter-institutional negotiations, the initiative was renamed the "European Research Infrastructure Consortium," abbreviated as ERIC.
22. The proposal belongs to the area of public health and not to research and innovation policy, but was classified as "research policy" because it touches on human organs intended for research purposes; however, it explicitly *ex*cludes them from regulation (COM[2008]818: 4).
23. For example, a national system of "presumed consent" (such as in Spain) also applies to non-nationals: if you are a tourist and die in an accident, your organs are automatically put up for donation unless your relatives explicitly protest.
24. Prior to the adoption of the Lisbon Treaty, eight "subsidiarity checks" had been launched, twice yearly from 2006 onward, as test runs for the early warning mechanism, see Minutes of the meeting of the XL COSAC, Paris, November 3–4, 2008: <http://www.cosac.eu/42france2008/ordinary-meeting-of-the-xl-cosac-2-4-november-2008/j3-ordinary.pdf>, last accessed December 26, 2012.

7

Consumer policy

7.1 INTRODUCING THE POLICY AREA

This third and final case study chapter addresses Commission position formation in consumer policy, a field comprising all policy measures aimed at protecting the end user of products and services against risks or disadvantages in economic life. While this definition suggests active regulatory protection of consumers, much of Brussels' early regulation in the area had amounted to consumer policy of the "hidden type" (Weatherill 2005: 5). European market integration was mainly justified by broader choice, lower prices, and higher quality for consumers, so that consumer interests were simply equated with competition policy during the early stages (Cseres 2005: 153, 194). Any efforts to develop more specific consumer protection competences were initially rejected by the member states (Weatherill 2005: 6–9). However, there were significant differences between national regimes, which created various trade barriers, so that supranational market-making invariably affected consumer protection rather directly (Pollack 1997c).

Accordingly, the Commission soon based its consumer-policy efforts on internal-market competences, most notably on Art. 95 TEC (114 TFEU), which required qualified Council majorities only (Cseres 2005: 196–8). Paralleling its early legal ventures, the Commission also ensured that stakeholder calls for supranational consumer protection were clearly audible in Brussels (Pollack 1997c). As early as 1961, it advised national consumer associations that "the general interest of consumers in the common market are not represented to the same extent as those of producers" (Commissioner Mansholt, cited in Young 1997b: 158). The *Bureau Européen des Unions de Consommateurs* (BEUC)—a European umbrella association—was founded only two months later and the Commission still provides one-third of its operational budget today.

The Maastricht and Amsterdam Treaties made the health, safety, and economic interests of consumers explicit purposes of Community policy and a separate consumer protection title required a high level of protection in all Community initiatives (Cseres 2005: 198–200; Weatherill 2005: 15–18). Some observers considered these revisions a "breakthrough" for European consumer policy, but most still fear a "triumph of market freedom over market regulation" (Micklitz et al. 2004: 375; see also Micklitz and Weatherill 1993). The consumer policy title is, in fact, limited to supplementary actions only and requires Council unanimity. As a result, Commission officials still prefer to base their initiative on trade barriers and internal-market competences (COM112:105 and 141).[1]

Nevertheless, the institutional differentiation of consumer-policy competences within the Commission reflected a gradual emancipation from purely competition-based approaches (Rischkowsky 2007: 30; Weatherill 2005: 17–18). Consumer policy was initially covered only by a minor unit in the DG that preceded DG COMP (DG IV) and was pooled with environmental affairs between 1981 and 1989 (DG XI). Consumer responsibilities were then outsourced to a single-standing service that became DG XXIV only in 1995. This new Directorate-General significantly promoted the involvement of consumer associations, but lacked its own legislative capacity. Today's strength was reached only when it became DG SANCO in 1999 and was reinforced with substantial manpower from DG ENTR and DG AGRI in the wake of the BSE crisis (Guigner 2004; Chapter 4).

DG SANCO's policy output has grown robustly over the last two decades (cf. Kurpas et al. 2008), but the history of European consumer policy shows frequent cross-cutting responsibilities within the Commission. Given their proximity to internal-market policy and cross-border producer interests, consumer-policy issues often meet the concerns of DG MARKT and DG ENTR. Moreover, DGs with a more sectoral orientation—like DG AGRI (agriculture), DG TREN (transport and energy), and DG INFSO (information society and media)—may hold stakes as well. The diversity of policy preferences and the scattered formal responsibilities thus make consumer policy a particularly fruitful area in which to study position formation within the European Commission.

The sampling procedure described in Chapter 3 resulted in 18 consumer-policy initiatives summarized in Table 7.1. The set includes proposals for Directives (8) and Regulations (8), and also for two Decisions. The cases are equally distributed over the Prodi (9) and Barroso I (9) Commissions, with a slight weighting towards initiatives adopted during 2008 (6). In addition, the sample is quite evenly split as regards internal Commission procedures (8 oral vs. 10 written cases). In institutional terms, the sample neatly reflects the historical evolution of consumer policy competences in the Commission. The majority of 14 cases was based on the Treaty provision for the internal market (Art. 95 TEC/114 TFEU), three depended on specific titles on transport policy, and only one was justified by the separate consumer protection title (Art. 153 TEC/169 TFEU).

In terms of the internal distribution of internal competences, half of the cases were prepared under the lead of DG SANCO, which was politically headed by Commissioners Byrne (1999–2004, Ireland, independent) and Kyprianoú (2004–2006, Cyprus, ALDE). After the 2007 enlargement, political responsibility for DG SANCO's competences was split into health and consumer issues and Commissioner Kuneva (2007–2008, Bulgaria, ALDE) became solely responsible for the latter. Administratively, DG SANCO was headed by Directors-General Coleman (1999–2003, UK) and Madelin (2004–2008, UK) during our investigation period.

The enterprise and industry department (DG ENTR) prepared three of the sampled proposals under its own auspices but was also involved in several others. During our investigation period, Commissioners Liikanen (1999–2004, Finland, PES) and Verheugen (2004–2010, Germany, PES) held political responsibility for this DG, while the Directors-General Colasanti (2000–2002, Italy), Mingasson (2002–2004, France), Reichenbach (2004–2005, Germany) and Zourek (2005–2010, Austria) provided administrative leadership.

Table 7.1. Sample of cases in consumer policy

Proposal number	Contents	Lead DG	Type of instrument	Treaty base	Commission adoption date	Commission adoption procedure	Council procedure	Sub-group
COM[2000]139	General product safety	SANCO	Directive	Art. 95	Mar. 29, 2000	Oral	QMV	Product
COM[2000]222	Food supplements	SANCO	Directive	Art. 95	May 8, 2000	Written	QMV	Food
COM[2000]392	Universal service/users' rights in electronic communications	INFSO	Directive	Art. 95	Jul. 12, 2000	Oral	QMV	Contract
COM[2001]546	Sales promotions	MARKT	Regulation	Art. 95	Oct. 2, 2001	Oral	QMV	Contract
COM[2001]784	Air-passenger rights	TREN	Regulation	Art. 80 (2)	Dec. 21, 2001	Written	QMV	Contract
COM[2002]443	Consumer credit	SANCO	Directive	Art. 95	Sep. 11, 2002	Written	QMV	Contract
COM[2003]356	Unfair business-to-consumer commercial practices	SANCO	Directive	Art. 95	Jun. 18, 2003	Oral	QMV	Contract
COM[2003]424	Nutrition and health claims made on foods	SANCO	Regulation	Art. 95	Jul. 16, 2003	Oral	QMV	Food
COM[2003]671	Addition of vitamins and minerals and of certain other substances to foods	SANCO	Regulation	Art. 95	Nov. 10, 2003	Written	QMV	Food
COM[2005]457	Placing on the market of pyrotechnic articles	ENTR	Directive	Art. 95	Oct. 11, 2005	Written	QMV	Product
COM[2006]428	Food additives	SANCO	Regulation	Art. 95	Jul. 28, 2006	Written	QMV	Food
COM[2007]53	Common framework for the marketing of products	ENTR	Decision	Art. 95	Feb. 15, 2007	Written	QMV	Product
COM[2008]9	Safety of toys	ENTR	Directive	Art. 95	Jan. 25, 2008	Written	QMV	Product
COM[2008]40	Provision of food information to consumers	SANCO	Regulation	Art. 95	Jan. 30, 2008	Oral	QMV	Food
COM[2008]106	Protecting children using the Internet	INFSO	Decision	Art. 153	Feb. 27, 2008	Oral	QMV	Product
COM[2008]614	Consumer rights	SANCO	Directive	Art. 95	Oct. 8, 2008	Oral	QMV	Contract
COM[2008]816	Passenger rights in water transport	TREN	Regulation	Art. 71(1)	Dec. 4, 2008	Written	QMV	Contract
COM[2008]817	Passenger rights in bus and coach transport	TREN	Regulation	Art. 71(1)	Dec. 4, 2008	Written	QMV	Contract

We also find proposals by more sectorally oriented DGs in the sample. On the one hand, this concerns the transport DG TREN, which was directed by Commissioners De Palacio (1999–2004, Spain, EPP), Barrot (2004–2008, France, EPP), and Tajani (2008, Italy, EPP), as well as Directors-General Lamoureux (1999–2005, France) and Ruete (2006–2008, Germany). On the other hand, it concerns the information society DG INFSO, which was politically led by Commissioners Liikanen (1999–2004, Finland, PES), Rehn (2004, Finland, ALDE), and Reding (2004–2008, Luxembourg, EPP) and was administratively guided by Directors-General Verrue (1999–2002, France) and Colasanti (2002–2008, Italy). Finally, we find just one case drafted in the internal market DG, which was, however, relevant for the interaction on a number of the other consumer policy cases. During the investigation period, DG MARKT was under the political responsibility of Commissioners Bolkestein (1999–2004, Netherlands, ALDE) and McCreevy (2004–2008, Ireland, AEN).

Turning to the substance of the Commission proposals under analysis, different types of possible consumer risks and disadvantages are covered. The first and largest group are proposals addressing the risk of economic disadvantage in either general or more specific contractual transactions (Contract). The initiatives concerned propose furnishing the consumer with various rights in the preparation or conclusion of a contract. Second, a group of five Commission proposals cover particular safety risks associated with retail products or services (Product). The proposals in this group deal with the distribution of safety risks between producers and consumers. Third, a set of five acts concern health risks associated with the consumption of foodstuffs (Food), where the proposals are once again aimed at re-distributing risk-bearing between consumers and food producers. Given that these sub-fields may be subject to different external pressures and may be handled by different Commission DGs, the chapter will devote a separate section to each of them.

7.2 CONTRACTUAL CONSUMER RIGHTS

The first subset of Commission proposals in this chapter covers supranational rules and regulations on the preparation, conclusion, and execution of contracts between businesses and the final consumers of products or services. In this field, functional pressures from market creation in Europe towards the supranational regulation of contractual consumer rights are most obvious: as soon as a business-to-consumer transaction crosses national borders, the question arises which rules to apply. Differing national conceptions of contractual consumer protection may particularly conflict in previously densely regulated sectors such as transport or communication, but even in simple sales contracts rather different private law traditions may clash.

Producers and service providers as well as consumers need answers to this question in order to engage in cross-border transactions. In fact, reliable rules on contractual relationships and the trust they generate can be seen as the lifeblood of a functioning business-to-consumer market in Europe. Yet, this does not prescribe which regulatory options the Commission and its services choose. Internal actors may resort to mutual recognition principles, partial harmonization of relevant rules, or opt for a total harmonization with regard to certain products or sectors. These various options will invariably meet or oppose different interests within but also beyond the European Commission. To study the resulting dynamics, this subsection covers proposals that deal with contractual consumer rights with varying breadth and depth and from different sectoral angles. Tables 7.2 and 7.3 detail proposal and process characteristics.

7.2.1 Universal Service

The first case focuses on the telecoms sector, which had originally been dominated by state-owned companies or regulatory monopolies but was formally liberalized across Europe in 1998. In this setting, the proposed directive on universal service and users' rights in electronic communications (COM[2000]392) specifies that basic communication services should be available to all users, sets rules on how member states may oblige service providers in this regard and defines consumer rights in service contracts on electronic communication. Prior to the proposal, universal-service obligations varied across the member states, but some basic supranational rules existed. Against this background, the proposal enhances consumer service access, on the one hand, and extends existing liberalization efforts, on the other. While the scope is widened from fixed telephony to all electronic communications and the proposal contains some additional contractual consumer rights, the initiative explicitly requires member states to distort markets as little as possible and to avoid undue provider burden.

This rather liberal Commission position was unsurprising given that the proposal came as part of a broader telecoms package geared towards more liberalization and a lighter common framework (COM127:61). Drafting began in early 1999 (COM127:33) and involved two officials in constant exchange with the entire unit (COM127:15). Although the administrative level of DG INFSO initiated the process, the DG's hierarchy exerted significant time pressure (COM127:281). DG INFSO's leadership saw the package as "a corner stone in ensuring Europe's transition to a new knowledge based economy" under the Lisbon strategy (IP/00/749). Stakeholders were extensively consulted through a public consultation in November 1999 and a working document in April 2000 (COM[2000]392: 40-8). Besides industry associations, companies and consumer organizations, national ministries in particular responded (COM127:269). DG INFSO's declared aim was to highlight "a new political importance for user's rights" (COM127:151; likewise COM128:33), which were seen as "the other side of liberalization" (COM128:43). However, a closer look shows that the liberal thrust of telecom regulation in Europe was not to be changed substantially. The proposal extends the scope to all electronic communications which was meant to make the regulation technology neutral (COM114:41). This intention also informed the obligation for member states to explicitly ensure access to data communication at rates sufficient for Internet access. Consumer associations would have preferred including broadband access as well (BEUC 2000a: 3), but because the technical pre-conditions varied sharply across European regions, the drafting officials considered a market intervention of this kind to be too strong

Table 7.2. Position formation on contractual consumer rights

Proposal number	Contents	No. of key provisions	Main line of proposal (content)	Uncertainty	Salience	Origin (hierarchical level)	Process duration (months)	External consultation	Main position-formation factors
COM[2000]392	Universal service/users' rights in electronic communications	7	Clarification and adaptation of user rights in the liberalized communication market	No	Yes	Administrative	19	Public	– Extant *acquis* – National positions – Organized interests
COM[2000]546	Sales promotions	5	Removal of trade barriers for cross-border sales promotions	No	No	Administrative	41	Public	– ECJ jurisprudence – Experts – Organized interests
COM[2001]784	Air-passenger rights	6	Extend contractual air-passenger rights	No	Yes	Administrative	36	Specific	– Anticipation of Council and EP majorities – Extant *acquis*
COM[2002]443	Consumer credit	16	Protect weak consumers and hold creditors responsible	Yes	Yes	Administrative	27	Specific	– Experts – Organized interests – National positions
COM[2003]356	Unfair business-to-consumer commercial practices	6	Consolidate and target existing national and supranational regulation	No	No	Administrative	30	Public	– Anticipation of Council majority – Experts – ECJ jurisprudence – Organized interests
COM[2008]614	Consumer rights	11	Consolidate and target existing national and supranational regulation	Yes	Yes	Administrative	58	Public	– Experts – Anticipation of Council majority – Organized interests
COM[2008]816	Passenger rights in water transport	5	Extend contractual water-passenger rights	No	No	Administrative	35	Public	– Extant *acquis* – Experts – Anticipation of Council majority
COM[2008]817	Passenger rights in bus and coach transport	6	Extend contractual road-passenger rights	No	No	Administrative	35	Public	– Extant *acquis* – Experts – Anticipation of Council majority

Table 7.3. Interaction on contractual consumer rights

Proposal number	Contents	Deviating DGs	Informal interaction	Position-based conflict	Process-based conflict	Main line of conflict	Most powerful DG	Main power resources
COM[2000]392	Universal service/ users' rights in electronic communications	COMP SANCO	Medium	3	2	Internal responsibility for competition issues	INFSO	- Support from horizontal service
COM[2000]546	Sales promotions	SANCO SJ	Little	3	2	Approach to and internal responsibility for supranational consumer protection	MARKT	- Lead department - Bureaucratic legitimacy
COM[2001]784	Air-passenger rights	—	—	0	0	—	—	—
COM[2002]443	Consumer credit	MARKT	Intense	3	0	Market creation vs. consumer protection	SANCO	- Lead department - DG alliances - Public legitimacy
COM[2003]356	Unfair business-to-consumer commercial practices	MARKT	Medium	3	2	Internal competence for business-to-consumer law	SANCO	- Supranational competence - Lead DG
COM[2008]614	Consumer rights	MARKT JLS SJ ENTR	Medium	3	1	Approach to harmonization of national consumer-protection laws	SANCO	- Proximity to Council majority - Public legitimacy - DG alliances
COM[2008]816	Passenger rights in water transport	—	Intense	0	0	—	—	—
COM[2008]817	Passenger rights in bus and coach transport	—	Intense	0	0	—	—	—

(COM127:51). The contractual consumer rights in the proposal were merely transferred from other European directives (COM[2000]392: 13), and the only innovation—a requirement for service providers to offer number portability—was publicly emphasized as one of the key new consumer gains (IP/00/749). This was welcomed by consumer associations and national regulators and opposed, especially, by mobile operators (BEUC 2000a: 9, COM[2000]239). DG INFSO positioned itself right in the middle of these demands by implicitly allowing charges for portability, which, in addition, was made subject to consumer requests. The key question, however, regarded how far national regulatory agencies were allowed to intervene in markets in order to guarantee universal service provision. In its ideal position, DG INFSO considered such interventions to be completely unnecessary in a liberalized European market, but "some member states" were of a different opinion and DG INFSO grudgingly accepted this constraint (COM[2000] 239: 25). Given that it was facing a parallel infringement procedure, it is highly likely that it was France that exerted pressure in this respect (*FT*, April 28, 2000).

The internal interaction on the universal service case was unusually short and took place only during the formal inter-service consultation three months before proposal adoption (COM127:65). DG INFSO officials maintained that only the formal frame permitted meaningful interaction for individual negotiations with the interested DGs (COM127:93, 219). This rested on the assumption that other DGs would accept DG INFSO's competence in the policy area and only verify whether the lead DG had "stepped over the border" (COM127:71). In this sense, the negotiations were seen as a means of administrative interaction that avoided formal rejections and political interventions (COM127:79). However, this approach did not work with DG COMP, not least because the personal interactions had been rather conflictual (COM127:97). Given that DG INFSO's proposal still allowed governmental intervention to achieve universal service provision, DG COMP argued that it should come under Art. 86 TEC (Art. 106 TFEU) on regulatory monopolies which, as a side effect, would have turned DG COMP into the lead DG (COM127:125). DG COMP clearly would have preferred this option because it had just started to revise a directive of its own under Art. 86 TEC on telecommunication terminal equipment (Commission Directive 88/301/EEC). This directive had been a major liberalization breakthrough but DG INFSO now considered it essentially unnecessary. In the end, DG INFSO succeeded in holding on to "its" treaty base, but only after the Secretariat-General had brokered a compromise that allowed DG COMP to table its own directive after the DG INFSO package was officially adopted by Council and the European Parliament (COM127:137). On a much lower scale, another controversial issue concerned disabled persons. DG SANCO in particular sided with consumer associations and argued that universal services should be enjoyed by disabled people to the same extent as by non-disabled people (COM127:85–93). For DG INFSO, however, this "guarantee of result" would have involved too much market intervention, but offered a compromise ensuring an equivalent level of access (COM127:103).

In sum, the overall process has a technocratic bent blending with some competence-seeking elements. The DGs involved formed their positions in line with the extant *acquis*, national positions, the demands of organized interests and internal turf considerations. Where the resulting positions clashed, the active support of the Secretariat General was crucial for securing the positions of the lead DG INFSO.

7.2.2 Passenger Rights in Air, Water, Bus, and Coach Transport

Like the DG INFSO case, the three DG TREN proposals in our sample concern regulations for recently liberalized and growing sectors. However, in these cases, the Commission introduced strong market interventions to the benefit of passengers. Compared to its predecessor regulation, the proposal on air-passenger rights (COM[2001]784) not only covers passengers beginning travel within the EU, but also protects all passengers using a European airline on flights into EU territory. For passengers denied boarding, the proposal more than quadruples the existing compensation rates to €750 for flights shorter than 3,500 kilometers and to €1,500 for all longer flights, and also increases airlines' assistance obligations. Moreover, the proposal prescribes compensation and assistance in the case of flight cancellations or delays, both of which had previously been unregulated.

The other two DG TREN proposals on seaway and maritime (COM[2008]816), and on bus and coach transport (COM[2008]817) fit the same pattern. They prescribe a set of consumer rights for which either no or only very rudimentary rules previously existed (European Commission 2006a: 24, COM[2008]817: 3). In addition, they establish the liability of bus and coach operators in the event of accidents and surpass the most encompassing national rules in this regard (European Commission 2006a: 8 and 30–1). Similar to the air-transport proposal, passengers should also enjoy privileges in the event of cancellation or delay. Furthermore, both proposals establish a regime for persons with reduced mobility that also exceeds national rules (European Commission 2006a: 15). So how did this rather consumer-friendly position in the transport sector come about?

DG TREN prepared its regulatory plans by starting an information campaign on existing air-passenger rights (COM[2000]365: 6), complemented by a 2001 White Paper aiming to "refocus Europe's transport policy on the demands and needs of its citizens" (COM33:140, BEUC 2002a: 2–3). At this time, denied boarding, especially, was a common form of yield management in the airline business, where overbooking occurred for technical, but also for economic reasons (COM(2001)784: 3–4). The DG TREN officials realized that this issue had a high salience and "was all the time in the media" (COM33:136).[2] Drafting was described as a feedback process in which the officials matched possible regulatory initiatives with the "'political momentum" sensed from stakeholder contacts and media reception (COM33:164, 176). Thanks to an early consultation in January 2000 that elicited ample responses from all affected stakeholders (SEC [2000]535: 2, COM[2000]365: 8–9 & Annex II), DG TREN was already able to identify most of the issues that became part of the proposal (COM[2000]365: 9, COM33:136, 146). On this basis, the unit prepared an official Communication in late June 2000 that was presented publicly and jointly by DG TREN's Commissioner De Palacio and DG SANCO's Commissioner Byrne. The document claimed that "it is time for the Community to respond and to strengthen the protection of passengers" (IP/00/639). This triggered a formal Council resolution as well as a report by the European Parliament.

The DG strategically chose air transport as the first area of passenger rights regulation to tackle because it represented the most advanced European transport market (COM[2000]365: 8). The liberalization process had been "about advantages for the industry," and the drafting officials now recognized "the consumer's right to benefit" (COM33:124)—a position also backed by the Lisbon idea of "putting citizens at the heart of the internal market" (COM33:176). The airlines opposed the move fiercely, but DG TREN confronted them with an ultimatum backed by the Council (2000/C293/01): if no voluntary agreement was drawn up by April 2001, DG TREN would push for a legislative proposal. Although the European airline associations managed to put together and submit an agreement with a delay of one month, this did not go far enough for DG TREN (COM33:302, COM[2001]784: 2) and the European Parliament report in mid-2001, roughly six months before proposal adoption, agreed with this hardline position (European Parliament 2001: 7). By that time, DG TREN already had a legislative text in the drawer and the official inter-service consultation was launched only two months later. Consumer associations strongly welcomed the proposal (BEUC 2002a: 8), while the air-transport operators withdrew their cooperation entirely (COM[2001]784: 5).

Seven years later, the very same DG TREN unit published the proposals on passenger rights in water and road transport. Once air transport had created a precedent, DG TREN kept its new emphasis on passenger rights cooking in a series of communications, white papers, and review documents. Legislative drafting for the two specific proposals began in 2006 (COM33:226), with one official assigned to each transport mode, while all proposals were also discussed by those officials who had previously worked on air-passenger rights (COM33:376). However, progress was thwarted by political obstacles. While "everything was ready by the end of 2007 . . . there was not the political will to go through at that time . . . and [it] came only six months later" (COM33:616). This change of "political momentum" coincides with the coming into office of Commissioner Tajani, who arrived from the European Parliament and was thus said to have a focus on citizen-friendly regulation (COM33:482). While their internal hierarchy was decisive, the officials also tested the waters amongst external stakeholders (COM33:434) and commissioned several studies covering passenger rights, obstacles faced by disabled passengers, and the related industry costs. Highlighting a lack of uniform rules, missing solutions for cancellations and delays, and a dearth of passenger information, these studies provided the basic justification to go forward (COM[2008]816: 6, COM[2008]817: 6–7). But even before this, a formal communication in February 2005 "identified which rights should be strengthened by Community action irrespective of the means of transport" (COM[2008]816: 2). On this basis, specific policy papers were issued in 2005 and 2006 and were followed by stakeholder meetings (COM[2008]816: 6, COM [2008]817: 5). All of these documents took the air-transport law as the benchmark, thereby advocating a comparatively high level of protection from the outset. National representatives signaled no opposition (COM33:362), but the drafting officials faced a clear divergence of demands between carriers and consumer associations (COM33:320).

The reasoning behind the choice to mainly benefit the latter group followed the same logic as the air-transport case: After "market opening for international services" in both transport modes, "passenger rights should be put in place to make the passengers benefit, not only the industry side or the operators" (COM33:140). Even more strongly, DG TREN argued that a common passenger-rights regime at a high level of protection could be directly derived from the principle of free movement of persons in the internal market. And since "there are no passengers' associations at the European level for any type of transport which could defend the interests of users of all modes of transport," DG TREN saw the need to step in (COM[2005]46: 3). Drafting merely amounted to adapting existing laws to the peculiarities of the respective transport modes (COM33:141). The consumer associations applauded (European Commission 2006a: 7), while the transport operators objected and highlighted a range of voluntary commitments that, in their view, made regulation unnecessary (UITP 2005, 2006; European Commission 2006b: 6; EPTO 2009). Regarding the liability rules, DG TREN simply argued again that the existence of such rules in other sectors made their application necessary for bus transport as well (COM[2008]817: 3)—a position supported by the member states but fiercely opposed by the industry (European Commission 2006a: 8–9; ECTAA 2009; EPTO 2009). The industry also opposed the proposed regime on delays and cancellations, but here, particularly, the air-passenger rights law served as an archetype (COM33:434, European Commission 2005a: 9–10). Finally, the rules on persons with reduced mobility were also derived from other laws on air or rail transport (European Commission 2005a: 5). These did not elicit opposition from member states, despite creating enormous costs in both sectors (European Commission 2006a: 14–17, 2006b: 7).

These three passenger rights cases involved little or no conflict within the Commission. While DG TREN's strong and intentional focus on "consumers" in the initial air-transport case is close to the policy mandate of DG SANCO, the drafting officials recalled nothing but "synergies" (COM33:230). Some information was exchanged informally, but DG SANCO did not press for specific issues (COM33:234), especially after DG SANCO Commissioner Byrne helped in publicly defending an early DG TREN communication on the issue (IP/00/639). In the same vein, the formal ISC went smoothly and the proposal was adopted in December 2001 (COM33:242). Likewise, the preparation of the later proposals on bus and water transport involved informal exchanges and formal meetings on the impact assessments (COM33:104, 218, 390), but neither DG SANCO, DG EMPL, nor DG MARKT held substantially diverging views (COM33:201, 264–8). In any case, the outcome simply mirrors DG TREN's original positions already expressed in the air-passenger rights directive.

In sum, in all three cases, DG TREN took a consciously consumer-focused perspective on an otherwise liberalized market. In the first case, this position was shaped by the public attention on the regulated issues and by the anticipated political support granted by Council and the European Parliament; in the later cases it sufficed to refer to the extant *acquis* DG TREN had created itself and to the abundance of data the consultations and DG TREN's experience had produced. This allowed DG TREN to push through its rather interventionist ideas within the leeway granted by the Council.

7.2.3 Consumer Credit

A similarly consumer-friendly position was taken by DG SANCO in its 2002 proposal on consumer credit (COM[2002]443). The existing directive contained only a minimum clause, so that a variety of consumer-credit regulations flourished in the member states. By contrast, the new proposal prescribed total harmonization, but did so at a very high level of consumer protection. It extends the scope of the existing directive, for example by covering surety agreements, advances on current accounts, and overdraft facilities. Piecing together rules from the more restrictive European member states, the proposal includes detailed creditor obligations in consultations and communications with the consumer (COM[2002]443: 11–13). Moreover, the proposal establishes the principle of responsible lending which was not known in most national regimes and which makes the creditor fully liable for the lender's abilities to fulfill the contract (COM [2002]443: 15). Similarly, the legal text proposes joint and several liability where sellers act as a credit intermediary, as in most car sales, for example. Previously, such advantageous consumer rights existed only in the UK. Additional and wide-ranging rules on contract terms as well as the creation of redress systems reinforce the view that DG SANCO proposed a sort of highest-common-denominator solution in protecting European consumers.

This revision was made possible by a review clause in the existing directive (COM119:113, COM89:31). DG SANCO's predecessor had produced some technical reports, studies, and amendments, but the principal overhaul did not start before the summer of 1999 (COM119:17, 111, COM89:44). Before involving their political masters, the drafting unit in the freshly reinforced DG SANCO invested heavily in what they considered to be a complicated draft, given that it touched upon so many and such widely differing regulatory traditions (COM89:37). "Making a single European rule" was seen as "hideously difficult" (COM89:44) both for "political and for technical reasons" (COM111:194). Issues concerning consumer credit had huge public appeal (COM119:197). During the 1990s, new instruments such as product-related credits, credit cards, and account overdrafts pushed private consumption upwards and became the "lubricant of economic life" (COM89:31). At the time of drafting, consumer credit amounted to a growing share of 7 percent of the EU-15 GDP—in other words, this was a salient issue that, unsurprisingly, attracted heavy media attention (COM89:31, COM119:197, COM[2002]443: 3).[3] Within this context of high uncertainty and high salience, the preparations were well advanced when the officials presented the first draft to the cabinet (COM111:149, COM89:44). When the cabinet presented "the political points" to Commissioner Byrne, he assessed the draft as "one of the major consumer proposals" at the time (COM111:149, 198).

Accordingly, the drafting unit issued a discussion paper in June 2001 on all major ideas contained in the later proposal (COM89:70). Subsequent meetings with member state representatives, business associations, and consumer bodies (COM119:88, COM[2002]443: 3–5) indicated a "clear desire" from the consumer side (COM111:80) and unanimous industry opposition, especially with respect to the principle of responsible lending. In response, DG SANCO entirely avoided further contacts with the banking sector (COM119:88, ESBG 2003: 2–3). The drafting officials were convinced that the consumer was unable to fully understand credit agreements and thus needed to be protected against exploitation of that very fact by the banking industry (COM89:86). Rather than the "average," they had the "weak consumer" in mind, a position that was strongly informed by the contemporaneous academic discourse on behavioral economics

(COM89:82). Thus, they intended "to create a very comprehensive, very exhaustive consumer credit regulation which would be burdensome for industry" and which was modeled around the more restrictive national regimes (COM89:46). Besides industry, DG MARKT, in particular, was opposed, especially since this DG had its own regulatory plans for the sector (COM119:43). These were more responsive to the banking sector (COM111:96, ESBG 2003: 7–9), which turned to lobbying DG MARKT after DG SANCO denied further consultation (COM119:88). DG MARKT especially fought the responsible lending principle as "too much interventionist" (COM119:100, also COM89:80). And where DG SANCO and the consumer representatives pushed for the inclusion of mortgage credits (COM89:86, BEUC 2002b: 3–4), the industry side and DG MARKT were very eager to leave this sector untouched (COM119:119). More generally, the banking sector frowned on DG SANCO's approach of "selecting the most stringent provisions on consumer credit in force in each Member State" (ESBG 2003: 2–3, 10), in line with DG MARKT's general preference to continue to rely on mutual recognition in financial-service regulation (COM119:59). Disregarding this opposition and despite knowing that some highly consumer-friendly rules were considered to be "totally outlandish" in other European member states, DG SANCO officials transferred, for example, the liability rules from Section 75 of the UK Consumer Credit Act (COM89:41). A clash within the Commission was inevitable.

Historically, financial services had come under the primary responsibility of DG MARKT (COM89:90). Some jointly developed green papers and legislative proposals created a regular structure of meetings and working relationships between the two DGs (COM119:15, 84). However, DG MARKT had not accepted DG SANCO's responsibility and actually assigned the area of consumer financial services to a policy officer who worked almost full time on the file (COM119:175). Tension was already foreshadowed when the responsible Directors-General exchanged letters in 2001 (COM119:127) and particularly when DG SANCO published the 2001 discussion paper—because DG MARKT "didn't feel that was the text we had actually seen" (COM119:123). The DGs had just jointly published a recommendation on home loans—the predominant model of mortgage credits. In the context of this joint recommendation, DG SANCO's unilateral and public attempt to include mortgage credits in its own remit appears to have been a very strategic choice (COM89:31). It took DG MARKT by surprise and also explains the blockade during the ISC (COM119:119, 123), where the SJ was another critic of DG SANCO's approach (COM111:124). In the face of DG MARKT's and the SJ's formal vetoes, DG SANCO's cabinet opted for bilateral negotiations. They identified opponents and allies before the decisive special chefs meeting and prepared themselves for this meeting by engaging in bilateral coalition-building against DG MARKT (COM111:142). In the end, the SJ remarks and the softer comments of other DGs were taken on board, while there were also "political choices" for which cabinet members "had to arbitrate" (COM111:154)—not only with DG MARKT, but also with other dissenting cabinets (COM111:124). This allowed DG SANCO to achieve a written procedure that facilitated overcoming the opposition of Commissioners who feared losing their face in public. The President's cabinet strongly supported this approach (COM111:154, 162).

Yet, three issues were left to the political leadership of the DGs involved. First, the inclusion of mortgage credits had to be sacrificed by DG SANCO. As "banks have a huge power in the member states," DG MARKT was assertive on this provision based on the support of other Commissioners who complied with national pressures (COM111:70). Second and more relevant for the proposal as a whole, DG SANCO asserted its position on the principle of responsible lending. DG SANCO officials explained this success by substantiating their arguments with data on rising over-indebtedness and numerous press reports on individuals trapped in the credit-card carousel (COM89:70–118, COM119:197). Nevertheless, the issue had to be individually negotiated by the cabinets of Commissioners Byrne and Bolkestein, where the Commissioner of the formally responsible lead DG was said to have the right to "maintain" the original position after everybody was properly informed and consulted (COM89:118–19)—a rather unusual case in light of the typically consensual decision-making in the College. And third, the joint and several liability rules transferred from the UK were negotiated. Despite earlier opposition, DG MARKT's political leadership relented because it was difficult to legitimize a position going against "something very popular in the UK" so that "no self-respecting politician was going to come around and change that" (COM119:62). The prospect of a politically detrimental reception for the proposal thus appears to explain DG SANCO's success. In the end, these political negotiations led to a legislative text that contained almost all of DG SANCO's original ideas (COM111:132).

To sum up, position formation on consumer credit has entailed some technocratic, some competence-seeking but also quite some policy-seeking elements. DG SANCO adopted the view of a very specific academic discourse on behavioral economics, which led drafting officials to be responsive to consumer associations and to emulate the most consumer-friendly national positions it could find among the member states. At the other end, DG MARKT pro-actively served the interests of the banks, with whom it had developed strong ties in earlier legislative exercises. When these positions clashed, the interaction processes were driven by turf considerations and political bargaining. DG SANCO, especially, engaged in alliance-building and made use of its formal advantages as lead DG and of the public legitimacy of some of the chosen positions. Its internal opponent, by contrast, was only successful on positions that were backed by national interests in anticipation of Council negotiations.

7.2.4 Sales Promotions

DG MARKT also had to defend its liberal stance on European market-making in other areas of consumer rights. In 2001, it tabled a proposal on cross-border sales promotions such as price reductions, free gifts, coupons and vouchers, and promotional contests (COM[2001]546). A myriad of different national rules existed that restricted sales promotions in one way or another (European Commission 2001a: esp. Section 1). The DG MARKT proposal, by contrast, bans all national rules that either generally prohibit sales promotions, set limitations on their value, proscribe them outside seasonal sales or stipulate prior authorization procedures. This set of prohibitions undermines national powers in consumer protection. Only partly cushioning this highly liberalizing approach, the proposal harmonizes information obligations for sellers and promoters. The rules are too numerous to be listed here, but a comparison with the legal status quo (European Commission 2001a: Section 1) reveals that they extend some information requirements contained only in some national regimes. Likewise, the proposal harmonizes some rules on protecting children and adolescents. While some of these rules appear to be consumer friendly, the overall thrust of the Commission clearly favors market liberalization over the consumer protection provided for in the national regimes.

Interestingly, DG MARKT was originally not even striving for a European regulation, rather only wanted to enforce the general mutual-recognition principle. However, complaints from individual companies pushed the unit into publishing a green paper in 1996 (COM79:29, COM133:33). The paper proposes an assessment methodology for classifying national laws on commercial communications as either non-proportionate and trade-inhibiting, justified, and proportionate in the national context, or justified and proportionate for the European level (COM[96]192). Sellers and commercial communication providers such as advertising agencies supported this approach (COM[98]121: 3), and the DG MARKT unit asked all 15 member states to delegate one or two officials from the national ministry of economics to an expert group that began work in May 1998 (COM133:54, European Commission 2001a: section 5). This group concentrated first on sales promotions, because in the context of a related infringement procedure, DG MARKT officials hoped to create a "fourteen governments against Germany" situation that would make this single member state accept mutual recognition, thereby avoiding actual legislation (COM133:29).[4] However, the group identified restrictions on sales promotions in almost all member states, which made a more encompassing approach necessary (COM133:57). DG MARKT officials decided to maintain the classification in the earlier Green Book as the basis for prescribing whether the national rules should be prohibited, should fall under mutual recognition or should be harmonized.

However, the group of national experts was not just a conveyor belt for national interests. In reality, the detailed assessment methodology it applied rested on the ECJ's proportionality test (e.g. in C-288/89: para. 15, or C-384/93: para. 45) and thus ensured that the process was targeted at DG MARKT's initial aim of market creation. In fact, the final report contained quite a few signs of sustained member state opposition (see European Commission 2001a: section 2). Nonetheless, DG MARKT held its ground and "regular feedback" during these stages of drafting yielded "an enormous, a very, very positive response from the industry" (COM133:156), whereas consumers regretted the consideration of only economic consumer rights and complained about the lack of access to the actual proposal formulation (BEUC 2002c: esp. 5–6).

This biased responsiveness of DG MARKT also mirrored the internal battle with DG SANCO, which was preparing its own proposal on unfair commercial practices (see Section 7.2.5). Since sales promotions were only one of these practices, the consumer-policy DG claimed that DG MARKT's long-standing approach was now on their "turf" (COM79:55). While DG SANCO's policy line focused on business-to-consumer relationships, DG MARKT's proposal was at least equally motivated by efforts to battle unfair cross-border competition among producers (COM79:51). While DG SANCO worked to achieve "harmonization," DG MARKT worked "on the basis of mutual recognition" (COM91:143–51). And while DG MARKT officials considered their assessment procedure to be a superior problem solution and defied DG SANCO's inroad as an attempt to extend competences (COM79:72), DG SANCO officials viewed mutual recognition as being "too liberal" (COM79:35).

Given such differences of principle, it is surprising that the interaction process intensified only during the final stages of position formation. Despite invitations to the expert-group meetings, no DG SANCO input was recalled (COM79:47, 37, COM113:92). Only when the formal inter-service consultation was launched in early 2001, did DG SANCO suddenly provide extensive comments and thereby put the brakes on the formal process (COM133:92). Because "they were not ready with their Green Paper . . . they kept this proposal hostage so that it was proposed at the same time" (COM113:96). And DG SANCO's strategy worked: both DG MARKT's sales-promotions proposal and DG SANCO's Green Paper on EU Consumer Protection were adopted in the same meeting of the College of Commissioners (PV[2001]1538: 12). Thus, the world could see that there were two options on how to supranationally regulate consumer rights.[5] However, with respect to the substance of the proposal, DG MARKT's ideal position was not changed. Likewise, DG MARKT defied the SJ's request to draft a directive instead of a regulation by arguing that a single regulation would create much less red tape for the industry. This position had significant legitimacy at the time because in the wake of the Lisbon strategy's emphasis on competitiveness, the high-level Mandelkern group was developing a related "better regulation" strategy for the Commission (COM79:58).

Overall, DG MARKT's position on the sales-promotions proposal can be explained by a market-making motivation driven by existing ECJ jurisprudence, the results of the expert group's assessment and the outright support of the most strongly affected interests. DG MARKT was able to defy opposing demands by resorting to its rights as a lead DG vis-à-vis DG SANCO and on bureaucratic legitimacy vis-à-vis the SJ.

7.2.5 Unfair Commercial Practices

This success was short-lived, however. DG SANCO's proposal on unfair commercial practices (COM[2003]356) was aimed at establishing a "framework directive" for all pre-contractual business-to-consumer transactions and thus revived the battle over areas of responsibility. But this time DG SANCO's own proposal also had a liberalizing bent. It touched on a range of areas that had previously been covered by supranational law, but because these acts had set minimum standards only, more protective national rules existed. The proposal, however, entails a country-of-origin principle for traders and prohibits member states from enacting any further regulation of commercial practices. It bans unfair commercial practices, which must be judged by standards of professional diligence and the practice's potential to materially distort decisions of a reasonably well-informed and circumspect (i.e. a rational) consumer. By contrast, some national laws and jurisprudences, most notably those of Belgium and Germany, based their fairness assessment on the assumption of much less attentive consumers (SEC[2003] 724: 8), so that the Commission position is also much more liberal in this regard.[6] The proposed text applies a similar logic to misleading and aggressive commercial practices. In contrast to these liberalizing steps, a codified list of generally unfair and thus banned practices—including pyramid schemes, inertia selling and liquidation sales that give purchasers a wrong impression—extends specific national consumer-protection measures to the EU-15 and somewhat strengthens consumer protection (Schmedes 2007: 288, SEC[2003]724: 7). So how did this DG SANCO position come about?

Despite DG MARKT's earlier attempt to enter the field, DG SANCO remained formally responsible for managing most of the existing supranational laws in the area (COM91:97, 110). With the onset of the Prodi Commission, moreover, a specific DG SANCO unit was assigned to this *acquis* and exposed differences and contradictions in the existing directives (COM91:111). An initial "scoping paper" on the idea of a unifying framework directive generated "political drive" because Commissioner Byrne was very interested in a highly visible consumer-policy proposal that would underline his competences (COM79:62, COM91:114, 179, COM111:98). However, the earlier battle on sales promotions had made industry aware of DG SANCO's regulatory ambitions (COM91:103) and in spring 2001 an alliance of 14 business lobbying groups approached Commission President Prodi arguing that a restrictive initiative could seriously undermine European competitiveness (Hargreaves 2001).

Against the background of this political pressure, the DG SANCO officials wanted to have "as much facts and basic data on the table as possible" (COM91:103). They therefore commissioned a broad study on national regulations and a Flash Eurobarometer report; they issued a broad public consultation in parallel with DG MARKT's sales promotions proposal; and they conducted a voluntary impact assessment (COM91:97, COM112:165, SEC[2003]724: 2; Schulze and Schulte-Nölke 2003). Following this intense external consultation, it became clear that a majority of member states supported a framework directive (COM[2003]356: 2, SEC[2003]724: 22).

With turf disputes and early industry opposition in the background, the drafting unit faced the challenge of producing a strong proposal for their hierarchy without stirring up further "ideological battles" among external interests (COM112:285). They thus re-framed consumer policy as one dimension of the internal market in which "the fragmented regulation of unfair commercial practices causes cost, complexity and uncertainty for firms *and* a lack of consumer confidence in cross-border transactions" (SEC[2003]724: 3–4, emphasis added). Rather than a high level of protection, an equal level of protection throughout Europe became the most important concern (also see Byrne in AE, June 19, 2003, or SEC[2003]724: 8). Consumer associations, however, feared net losses of protection, while industry cheered (AE, May 15, 2004; UNICE 2003; BEUC 2004b: esp. 5–6 & 8–10).

Similarly, the rationalist conception of the benchmark consumer was strongly contested. When DG SANCO suggested simply applying ECJ case law, thus removing "legal uncertainty and complexity" (SEC[2003]724: 8), the consumer associations were shocked (EURO COOP 2003; BEUC 2004b: 7–8). Knowing quite well that this choice was the "most important trade-off in the proposal," DG SANCO officials maintained this position as "a balance... struck between the need to protect the most vulnerable consumers and the freedom of business" (Commission of the European Communities 2003: 26).

But interaction with DG MARKT was nevertheless "painful" and "very complicated" (COM91:123, 127). With the issue of sales promotions in the background, the DG SANCO officials anticipated this difficulty and informed their political hierarchy early on (COM91:290). Meetings at desk-officer level occurred during the early stages (COM133:90, COM91:123), but parts of the proposal had to be negotiated directly between the Byrne and the Bolkestein cabinets (COM91:130–4). Given that DG MARKT had preferred to keep regulatory competences under its mutual-recognition approach, DG SANCO was more successful in fully harmonizing consumer policy under its own management. Nevertheless, this was not a full-blown victory. The proposal is less protection oriented than one would expect, and one may speculate that this was also due to DG MARKT's internal opposition. But DG SANCO's primary interest was to push through the directive above all, so that the early industry opposition rendered some compromise with the traditional regulatory actor likely (COM91:296).

In sum, early interventions by organized interests, legal and economic expertise from studies, and the impact assessment, the anticipation of member state interests and existing ECJ jurisprudence together explain the position taken by DG SANCO. It successfully defended these positions in the turf battle with DG MARKT by resorting to its fresh supranational competences and by structuring the negotiations along the formal advantages granted to the lead department. DG SANCO thus cemented its competence claim on supranational consumer-protection law.

7.2.6 Consumer Rights

It is unsurprising that DG SANCO tried to replicate this role model for the 2008 consumer-rights proposal (COM[2008]614). Whereas the first framework directive had targeted pre-contractual consumer protection, this next step directly addressed business-to-consumer contracts. Again, this area was covered by European directives with minimum harmonization clauses, resulting in partially more protective national rules (COM[2008]614: 3). The proposal for an exhaustive directive meant replacing all existing laws in the area and fully harmonizing existing rules on an average level of regulatory protection, while achieving only some minor consumer benefits. The scope of supranational law is widened with regard to off-premise and distance contracts, as used in online trade, for example. The respective rules on pre-contractual information requirements go slightly beyond existing law, particularly with regard to hidden charges, and now free the consumer of his overall obligation to pay. Some stringency is also added through the 14-day cooling-off period, which surpasses existing European and most national laws. Finally, some enhanced protection can be found in the regulation of contract terms, most notably in the explicit requirement of "expressed consumer consent" before contract conclusion. However the act also undermines higher existing national standards on traders' after-sales obligations, for example, and thus takes only a middle ground with respect to existing regulatory options.

Using the former success on unfair commercial practices as a stepping stone (COM93:164), drafting was again justified by inconsistencies in the existing *acquis* (COM93:74). The officials followed the earlier role model and started by building a "knowledge base" (COM120:117) in the form of a huge comparative legal analysis and the involvement of a range of consumer focus groups (COM28:5, COM93:184). Stakeholders were consulted in February 2007 on the basis of five specific discussion papers and a Green Paper, which elicited responses from a broad audience (COM120:59, COM118:81, Commission of the European Communities 2008a: 1). This was complemented with a stakeholder conference, a set of written questionnaires and a series of workshops (COM28:5, COM[2008] 614: 4). Lastly, a specific Eurobarometer and an "extremely huge number of bilateral meetings" (COM120:49) complete the picture of an extraordinary consultation process aimed at including all stakeholders (COM120:109). At the political level, the issue only prompted interest when Commissioner Kuneva entered office in 2007. She was solely responsible for European consumer policy and the proposal was the only major legislative initiative under her responsibility. She thus claimed political ownership (COM120:49) and "was able to devote much time and media attention" (COM120:129), which resulted in a rushed and highly visible finalization of the proposal in 2008 (COM120:53, COM93:224, 216).

In substantial terms, the "twinned objectives" of reducing business reluctance to trade across borders *and* of enhancing consumer confidence in buying across borders figured prominently once again (COM93:46, COM120:37, COM[2006] 744: 7–8). Both objectives could be achieved through the horizontal consolidation of extant EU law (COM80:47), which translated into the idea of a "full harmonization" of consumer rights (COM120:41). This was the most contested provision both within and beyond the Commission. Unsurprisingly, DG MARKT pushed once again for the inclusion of a mutual-recognition clause (COM93:100, COM118:103, COM28:28), seeing it as a kind of liberalization insurance even if the Council were to water down other proposal provisions (COM118:113). DG JLS, in contrast, argued that the Council had included a sort of "country-of-destination" principle in the DG JLS-led Rome I regulation, meaning that the law of the consumer's place of residence should matter for this proposal as well (Commission of the European Communities 2008a: 6). The DG JLS officials urged consistency in this regard so as not to endanger the ongoing development of European contract law (COM93:108), a position that was strongly supported by the SJ (COM80:83, COM118:99).

DG SANCO ultimately opted for the middle ground. DG MARKT's position was challenged as being disadvantageous for consumers (COM93:120) and politically unfeasible after anti-liberalization protests in the wake of the services directive and the failed 2005 referenda had revealed public opposition to blunt liberalization attempts (COM118:103). It was "more a question of politics rather than policy" (COM93:108). However, DG SANCO also did not fully buy into the DG JLS position because a country-of-destination rule would have contradicted the principle of enhanced market access for traders and was also not seen as a safe bet in the Council (COM93:50, 108). Indeed, DG SANCO officials "came to the conclusion that the only way [they] can create a common set of rules and a uniform feeling of [consumer] confidence was targeted maximum harmonization" (COM93:58) and neither consumer nor business interests were happy with this compromise outcome (COM80:69, BEUC 2009; DG Health and Consumer Protection 2007: 10).

Solutions involving compromises that would be acceptable to the Council informed DG SANCO's position on most other key provisions as well. While business opposed the extended cooling-off periods, both consumer associations and national governments favored the solution contained in the final proposal (DG Health and Consumer Protection 2007: 13–14). By contrast, where the majority of member states aligned with business interests as in the case of individually negotiated contract terms (DG Health and Consumer Protection 2007: 12), the proposal contains the position most preferred by the business side. In the same vein, setting the length of guarantee periods was said to have been "a question of pitching" the varying national approaches (COM93:228). DG SANCO would have preferred more than the finally agreed two-year period, but these plans were surrendered in the final political negotiations within the Commission where DG ENTR, in particular, led by the German Commissioner Verheugen, voiced opposition (COM71:37).

Internally, DG SANCO had not been secretive about its plans and DGs MARKT, JLS, ENTR, and the SJ had all known about the proposal since 2003 (COM120:59, COM28:36, COM80:35). Nevertheless, the interested DGs started to meet in the steering committee for the impact assessment only (COM120:67, COM118:85), with DG MARKT actually delegating four or five officials (COM118:91). During the formal inter-service consultation roughly three months before final adoption, the document underwent considerable modification (COM93:132), in particular in response to DG MARKT comments (COM118:95). Through parallel informal negotiations, DG SANCO resolved most of the issues (COM120:51, 89), but failed in settling the more general principles (COM118:95). The approach to harmonization, especially, was known to be a political choice (COM80:89), and the proposal was scheduled as an oral procedure from the start (COM93:144). This put the political cabinets upfront (COM93:128, 136) and they managed to generate "unanimous support in the College" (AE, October 8, 2008). The discussion revolved very much around political feasibility in the Council, while DG SANCO's compromise solution also received the explicit support of DG ENTR (COM71:33–9).

In sum, DG SANCO relied on the basic structure of its earlier unfair commercial practices directive and generated broad expertise on the regulatory status quo in the field, which enabled the officials to take those policy positions that stirred the least conflict with external interests, most importantly the national governments in the Council. Internally, DG SANCO came out on top by relying on the proposal's proximity to the Council position, on the lack of public acceptance for the liberalizing option and on alliances with other Commissioners.

Summarizing the findings in the first sub-field of consumer policy, the policy positions were indeed largely driven by an emancipation from a perspective that takes only cross-border competition of producers into account. With the exception of DG MARKT's sales promotions proposal, the policy-formulation processes indicate a view of the consumer as a specific market participant with particular needs and interests. This was particularly evident in the cases drafted in the sectorally specialized DGs. Both DG INFSO in the universal service case and DG TREN in the passenger-rights cases had largely fulfilled their mandates of liberalizing the respective sectors and they needed new justifications for further competence development. Likewise, emancipation from mere negative integration was mirrored in the intense "turf" conflicts between DGs SANCO and MARKT. Upholding the consumer's interests was vital in DG SANCO's large-scale initiatives because it represented the only way to delineate and to justify its own competences against the traditionally responsible DG.

Besides their political plans, all the lead DGs invested heavily in identifying national preferences that constrained them to varying degrees. Depending on their original objectives, adopting policy solutions from existing supranational law, from national policy regimes and from the positions of specific organized interests was a repeatedly observable strategy. In some cases, ECJ jurisprudence provided a convenient backdrop, while in most cases broad fact-finding endeavors defined the range of available options from which drafting officials could choose. Once such choices were made, interactions across DG borders became intense, especially between DGs SANCO and MARKT, where the public legitimacy of a specific position was often relevant for settling conflicts. Other power resources varied, but it is interesting that the more sectorally oriented DGs caused much less conflict despite their sometimes strongly interventionist positions.

7.3 CONSUMER PRODUCT SAFETY

Product-safety regulation mirrors the overall development of European consumer policy quite neatly. During the early stages of the internal market, the main considerations were trade obstacles emerging from complex national product-safety regimes and inertia in the Council due to the requirement of unanimity voting (Vos 1999b: ch. 2). With the Single European Act, the Commission thus developed the "new approach" of product regulation. Following a Commission proposal, a qualified Council majority now only agrees on essential safety requirements for a product group, while detailed standardization is delegated to private bodies (Vos 1999b: 56–8; Chapter 5).[7] Markets flourished on this basis, but so did the spread of product risks and—with the Maastricht emphasis on consumers—the focus shifted towards safety concerns. The General Product Safety Directive of 1992 established a very basic safety criterion for non-standardized products and a European market-surveillance system. The one DG SANCO case on general product safety and the three DG ENTR cases on pyrotechnic articles, the revised new approach framework, and the issue of toy safety reflect the differing foci of European product regulation quite well. The case on safe Internet use by children, however, stands separate to this pattern because it is a funding program developed in the sectorally specialized DG INFSO. Tables 7.4 and 7.5 detail the respective proposal and process characteristics of position formation and interaction on consumer product safety.

Table 7.4. Position formation on consumer product safety

Proposal number	Contents	No. of key provisions	Main line of proposal (content)	Uncertainty	Salience	Origin (hierarchical level)	Process duration (months)	External consultation	Main position-formation factors
COM[2000]139	General product safety	8	Establish consumer "safety net" in European product regulation	Yes	Yes	Administrative	27	Specific	– Organizational restructuring – Experts – Extant *acquis* – Individuals' beliefs
COM[2005]457	Pyrotechnic articles	7	Harmonize trade and safety in Europe	No	No	Administrative	46	Specific	– Extant *acquis* – Anticipation of Council majority – Experts – Organized interests
COM[2007]53	Common framework for the marketing of products	7	Reinforce "new approach" to product legislation	No	No	Administrative	38	Public	– Extant *acquis* – Experts – Organized interests
COM[2008]9	Toy safety	9	Update "new approach" to toy safety	No	Yes	Administrative	70	Public	– Extant *acquis* – Experts
COM[2008]106	Protecting children using the internet	5	Maintain and widen the scope of projects on child online safety	No	No	Administrative	14	Public	– Extant *acquis* – Experts

Table 7.5. Interaction on consumer product safety

Proposal number	Contents	Deviating DGs	Informal interaction	Position-based conflict	Process-based conflict	Main line of conflict	Most powerful DG	Main power resources
COM[2000]139	General product safety	ENTR	Intense	3	1	Character of and competences in European product regulation	SANCO	– Lead department – Bureaucratic legitimacy – Public legitimacy
COM[2005]457	Pyrotechnic articles	SJ	Medium	2	0	Instrument type and implementation structures	ENTR	– Proximity to Council majority – Bureaucratic legitimacy
COM[2007]53	Common framework for the marketing of products	SANCO	Medium	2	1	Character of and competences in European product regulation	ENTR	– Lead department – Supranational competence
COM[2008]9	Toy safety	SANCO	Medium	2	0	Character of and competences in European product regulation	SANCO	– Public legitimacy – Supranational competence
COM[2008]106	Protecting children using the internet	—	Intense	0	0	—	INFSO	—

7.3.1 General Product Safety

Compared to its precursor directive, the 2001 proposal for a new General Product Safety Directive (GPSD, COM[2000]139) drafted by DG SANCO clearly promotes a safety focus in European product regulation. It extends the scope to all goods used by consumers or in consumer services. Whereas the old regime excluded specifically regulated product groups, the proposal now addresses all safety-related aspects left unregulated by the specific legislation. The general producer obligation to market only safe products remains, but it is enhanced by more explicit obligations regarding warnings, recalls, and cooperation with authorities. Furthermore, the proposal enhances the obligations and powers of national and supranational authorities and extends the European Rapid Exchange of Information System (RAPEX) on unsafe products and consumer protection.

This clear emphasis on protection coincided with DG SANCO's internal empowerment. The responsibility for managing the existing GPSD had only shifted from the predecessor DG ENTR in 1998 and DG SANCO started drafting shortly afterwards (COM87:46, COM 117:41, COM[2000]139: 19). The process was steered from the administrative level, where one of the three officials involved had previously implemented the existing directive at the national level. DG SANCO's political hierarchy was, however, absorbed by the BSE crisis (COM117:99, COM87:63). Contact with individual companies was avoided (COM87:151) and DG SANCO consulted European umbrella organizations of consumers, trade unions, retailers, employers, and SMEs, as well as networks of standardization bodies and market-surveillance authorities that took part in the existing implementation committee (COM87:127, 87:149, COM[2000]139: 18). Mixing factual and strategic information, stakeholder contacts served as a "basis for identifying the issues that needed to be looked after" while "assuming that the positions given by the experts would then also determine political positions in the end" (COM87:51, 163). Furthermore, DG SANCO commissioned a comparative legal study of the national laws transposing the extant directive (Centre de Droit de la Consommation 2000), which also provides factual and strategic information on national positions.

Alongside this activity, the officials started with a clear baseline position: while "the bulk of legislation was more internal market," their proposal should provide "the regulatory side more oriented toward protection" (COM117:49). This suited the degree of public salience enjoyed by consumer safety at the time. Apart from BSE, the Commission was also under fire after a 1998 scandal on illegal softeners in plastic toys had prompted a ban under the existing GPSD framework but only allowed slow and inadequate supranational responses (COM87:63, 165, also see Buckley 1999). Exploiting this attention, DG SANCO officials even wanted to include consumer services in the framework. This intention had to be discarded, however, because the opposition of industry stakeholders and DG ENTR was backed by large member states (COM87:147, COM117:19, BEUC 2000b). At any rate, the more important issue was extending the GPSD to all regulatory loopholes in existing product regulation, most notably those of the "new approach" type (COM117:53). This position met with strong misgivings in DG ENTR, but DG SANCO officials conceptualized the revision as a catch-all "safety net," an aim that was explained out of their own national experiences and that was further supported by academic expertise highlighting legal uncertainty in the relationship between specific legislation and the GPSD (COM 87:71, Centre de Droit de la Consommation 2000). The study also recommended the enhanced information and recall obligations for distributors and producers, a position that met with a predictable pattern of consumer support and industry opposition but was additionally justified by similar provisions in the US and Australia (cf. COM[2000] 139: 9, 17, BEUC 2000b; UEAPME 2000). Regarding enhanced market surveillance, DG SANCO officials started from the outright assumption that the "surprisingly low number of notifications... did not really reflect the reality of dangerous products in the market" and thus decided that "more regulation" was needed for the RAPEX system (COM87:59, 127).[8] Using scare tactics, DG SANCO argued internally that only the preferred simplification of decision-making procedures could avoid future scandals for the Commissions (COM 87:179).

This protection focus led to conflicts with DG ENTR particularly as a result of overlaps with the "new approach" directives managed by this DG. DG SANCO had to set itself apart from DG ENTR's focus on the free circulation of goods (COM117:47–9, COM25:82, COM72:118). Because they represented the "consumer protection DG," the drafting officials actually saw their role in "challenging" what was happening at DG ENTR (COM87:111). But while conflict potential was high, the interaction process itself went rather smoothly (COM87:103). Two of the DG SANCO officials involved had previously worked in DG ENTR and informal working relationships were very intense throughout the whole process (COM117:67–83, COM87:79). Despite the substantial rifts, everything was resolved at the administrative level and no political coordination was necessary during or after the ISC (COM87:87–99).

DG SANCO achieved success on this proposal by exploiting its agenda-setting role as the lead DG and setting a "more balanced internal market" as a goal early on (COM87:123). Consultation and expertise generation was organized around this aim, which kept alternative policy considerations out of the process. The new division of labor within the Commission further underlined the high legitimacy of consumer protection and encapsulated the political will to produce legislation beyond the existing approaches (Guigner 2004). DG ENTR asserted its view only with regard to DG SANCO's original plea to centralize standardization because this would have fundamentally altered the approach that had defined EU product regulation since 1985.

In sum, the position of DG SANCO can best be explained on the basis of organizational changes in the Commission and the convictions of individual officials backed by academic expertise and gaps in the extant *acquis*. In internal interactions, the combination of formal powers, the new bureaucratic mandate and the high public legitimacy of consumer protection at the time made DG SANCO the most powerful DG.

7.3.2 Pyrotechnic Articles

The next case was actually drafted by DG ENTR and covered pyrotechnic articles, which includes fireworks and also products used in airbags, seat-belt pretensioners, and stage effects, for example (COM[2005]457). The proposal, which covers a product group regulated only at the national level and follows the "new approach", removes all national restrictions, defines only basic requirements and delegates everything else to the market. The essential safety requirements state that pyrotechnic articles should be physically and chemically stable, must resist handling and transportation as well as water and extreme temperatures, must be protected against untimely or inadvertent ignition, and must not deteriorate over time, all of which essentially mirrors existing national rules (European Commission 2005d: 9). However, the manufacturer must now provide only one product for conformity assessment, while guaranteeing that all other products conform to this type, whereas some member states had required that one product from each batch had to be tested before marketing. This stipulation further reduces governmental control of the pyrotechnic market. However, the proposal also sets age limits for using these articles that previously did not exist in all member states (European Commission 2005d: 12). Unlike other "new approach" laws, it explicitly allows national upward deviations and trade limitations for certain fireworks. The remainder of the text, however, resembles the usual "new approach" pattern of including rules on information exchange and safeguard procedures, as well as the usual mandate to standardization bodies and a final provision on an implementation committee.

Despite the possible dangers of fireworks, drafting did not meet with contemporaneous public interest. Although the 2000 fireworks explosion in Enschede increased Dutch governmental pressure (COM32:204), drafting was essentially driven by a requirement of the 10-year-old explosives directive, which excluded pyrotechnics and promised separate legislation (COM[2005]457: 2). The increasingly embarrassing delay, repeated national requests, the parallel overhaul of the "new approach" and a dynamic head of unit had prompted drafting (COM32:42), but DG ENTR did not have specific aims beyond gaining a Council majority for the proposal's contents (COM32:144). Thus, the implementation committee on the explosives directive and the later consultation were used to anticipate member state positions (COM32:64, 124). Initiated by a questionnaire, consultation took place through meetings with national authorities and the stakeholders they had named (COM[2005]457: 2–5). This group had several chances to comment on working drafts, but the major consumer association showed "little interest" (COM32:64, European Commission 2005d: 11). In order to add technical expertise, DG ENTR involved CEN, the European standardization body, and also practitioners notified under the EU's explosives regime (COM32:200).

The drafting officials quickly realized that they had to cover two vastly differing markets: the accident-prone consumer fireworks accounted for a market of only €700 million of yearly volume, which was mainly based on Chinese imports, while the automotive components accounted for more than €5.5 billion generated by a European trade surplus which, however, faced rising competition from the Far East (COM[2005]457: 6; CEPS 2006: 9–10). They thus pursued a reduction in industry costs based on the "new approach" idea of "tested once accepted everywhere," on the one hand, and the reduction of accidents and faulty products, on the other (COM32:44, European Commission 2005d: 6–8). The inclusion of airbags and other pyrotechnic car safety equipment was explicitly demanded by the respective manufacturers, and DG ENTR "adapted its proposal" accordingly

(European Commission 2005d: 11). Likewise, aerospace parts were excluded on request and the remaining scope exemptions were carefully delineated in line with existing laws. All of the rules on product characterization and essential safety requirements represent an attentive mix of existing national approaches, closely resemble the compromise solution that had previously been developed as a voluntary solution in CEN and were already fixed during the first stakeholder meetings (COM[2005]457: 5, European Commission 2005d: 9). The remaining producer obligations, the national market surveillance requirements and the provisions on standardization followed the "new approach" discussed in Section 7.3 (CEPS 2006; European Commission 2005d: 7). Only for age limits and further restrictions on particular fireworks was full harmonization not possible because many member states were anxious to maintain their national rules and Council agreement was unlikely (European Commission 2005d: 10), a fact that DG ENTR learned through the early public consultation (COM32:192).

Finally, DG ENTR sought to sustain good working relations with national experts and planned a specific committee. The SJ expressed opposition during the ISC in arguing that the existing explosives committee was sufficient. The SJ also objected to DG ENTR's original plan of proposing a regulation rather than a directive (COM32:112). Because DG ENTR initially declined both requests, the issue went to cabinet level. With regard to the type of legal instrument to be used, DG ENTR yielded because a directive was more consistent with the "new approach," made it easier to implement national exemptions and therefore it "was . . . easier to sell it to the member states" (COM32:124). Regarding a separate comitology committee, DG ENTR's cabinet could demonstrate to the SJ that the national experts on explosives differed from those on pyrotechnic articles. Faced with this knowledge on the relevant policy context, the SJ gave in to the "more plausible argument" (COM32:120). And although DG SANCO officials had participated since the initial stakeholder meetings in 2003 (COM32:178), they did not voice particular demands (COM32:66, 166). Interaction on this case was a "typical process with very little controversy" (COM32:260).

In sum, the process followed an ideal type of technocratic decision-making: DG ENTR had no political aims, merely followed legal requirements based on extant law, was eager to be consistent with other acts and was decidedly open to demands from affected stakeholders, while the only major constraint was the acceptability of the technical issues in the Council.

7.3.3 Common Framework for the Marketing of Products

One and a half years later, the subsequent case drafted by DG ENTR was more encompassing in its scope and ambition. The proposal does not regulate a specific product group, rather is a horizontal framework decision providing a toolbox for the future regulation of individual products (COM[2007]53). It thus represents an overhaul of the "new approach" itself established in the famous 1985 Internal Market White Paper (COM[85]310: esp. 17–23), a set of implementing directives, and not the least in the 25 product specific "new approach" directives that have been concluded since then. The proposal is clearly meant to enshrine this liberal model for the future. It explicitly defines itself as a blueprint for all Community legislation on product harmonization. Community intervention should remain restricted to essential requirements to be expressed only in terms of the results to be achieved, rendering a product tradable if it complies with the technical standards derived from there. The proposal establishes different modules for product supervision and stipulates that the choice of module for a particular product group should be the least burdensome method for the producer. This was effectively the status quo in DG ENTR's product regulation; the novelty is that these principles have now been promoted to legal status. Likewise, the detailed rules on CE mark, on conformity assessment procedures, and on the "notified bodies" performing them reflect existing regulations. Member state rights and obligations as well as the safeguard clauses regulating how national authorities can intervene under the supervision of the Commission also closely resemble the principles of individual "new approach" directives. Only the detailed obligations for economic operators look like DG SANCO's 2001 General Product Safety Directive and were only partly present in individual "new approach" directives. In sum, the overall thrust of the proposal is a consolidation and expansion of the rather liberal "new approach" to product regulation.

The abstract legal concepts "not everybody in the street has heard of" made officials quite confident that the issue would remain off the public radar (COM72:282). The initiative emerged instead from the implementation of existing "new approach" directives and corresponding discussions among DG ENTR officials, national civil servants, and enterprises that were affected (COM27:175, COM72:108). In 2003, stakeholder demands were distilled into a formal Communication to the Council, which then formally determined that Community action was necessary (COM27:157, COM[2007]53). With this political backing, five people started to work on the legislative package and institutionalized a weekly meeting with all DG ENTR units implementing individual "new approach" directives in order to identify those issues that were truly horizontal in nature (COM27:41). Consultation efforts were stepped up sharply (COM27:349), initially by 20 working documents that were widely circulated among external stakeholders in 2005. This was complemented by an online consultation and "fact finding questionnaires" for different stakeholder groups, including the consumer umbrella organization BEUC, but also 800 face-to-face interviews with SMEs (COM[2007]53: 3). DG ENTR also discussed working drafts in the Senior Official's Group on Standardization and Conformity Assessment Policy (SOGS), which was comprised of national standardization officials. They were seen as the "pivotal" stakeholders as they had hands-on experience with legal simplification (COM27:273, COM72:302). Strategic anticipation was less of an issue as the 2003 Council resolution indicated that there was adequate room for maneuver and political interference in technical details was not feared (COM27:229, COM72:260).

Although much of this happened on the initiative of the administrative level, DG ENTR's German Commissioner Verheugen became involved during the endgame. On the one hand, he pushed for the proposal because it was listed in the Community work program during the German Council presidency and his home country strongly desired a revised framework for intra-European trade (COM27:219, AE, February 12, 2007). On the other hand, Verheugen had seized political ownership of the EU's better regulation strategy, which stylized the reduction of "red tape" as a central instrument in the effort to achieve the growth targets of the Lisbon agenda.

This all nicely suited the drafting officials' aims of "simplification" and "congruence" (COM72:78, COM[2007]53: 5) and was very much welcomed by the trade businesses (e.g. EuroCommerce 2007: 2). Drafting was an exercise of "deepening" the existing provisions, while the "new approach" emphasis on trade rather than safety was not questioned (COM27:69). This was clearly inconsistent with the legal position DG SANCO had developed in the meantime (COM94:35), but DG ENTR considered safety to be an issue of enforcement and market surveillance rather than of general legal principle (COM27:257–71, COM72:108). Unsurprisingly, consumer representatives were quite unhappy. Besides the possible extension to more sensitive product groups, also criticized by DG SANCO (COM26:180), they feared the "industry majority" in private standardization bodies and argued for a more systematic inclusion of "public interests" in the technical decisions (ANEC 2006: 1–2). This demand ran counter to the "new approach," however, which was aimed at removing all technical specifications from the political sphere—a "basic principle" that DG ENTR never intended to change (COM27:77, COM72:110). The CE mark—the symbol of the "new approach"—was also a source of conflict. Non-industry groups and DG SANCO (COM26:112) objected that the different safety requirements and the varying testing rules for specific products underlying the sign might wrongly lead the consumer to assume that they were purchasing a safe product (COM27:106; ANEC 2006: 6). DG ENTR officials, by contrast, did not consider the CE mark to be relevant for consumers (COM27:106, COM26:112, SEC[2007)174: 6), rather first and foremost to be a symbol that had become "a real asset in international trade" and a "symbol of business-friendly legislation" (Enterprise and Industry Directorate-General 2005: 2).

Anticipating conflictual positions, the DG ENTR officials invited DG SANCO officials to the weekly internal meetings (COM27:177, COM72:290) and the latter achieved the exclusion of food and feed legislation mainly based on the argument that they had successfully established their competence with an encompassing and working European *acquis* (COM26:180). However, DG SANCO's product-safety unit, in particular, developed "a great interest" (COM27:54) and even assigned human resources to monitor what DG ENTR was doing (COM26:174). Besides their criticism of the CE mark, the main issue was the relationship between DG ENTR's "new approach" revision and the General Product Safety Directive (COM94:99). Much of this centered on DG ENTR's parallel proposal on market surveillance not sampled here, but also affected negotiations on the overall package that was formally coordinated as a whole. In addition to technical inconsistencies in market surveillance, DG SANCO basically criticized the fact that DG ENTR disregarded "the whole new structure of the consumer policy" (COM94:37). DG SANCO officials arranged four or five meetings of the Verheugen and Kuneva cabinets and the proposals were kept cooking for about five months after the formal ISC (COM94:123). They subsequently went through negotiations at the *special chefs* meeting, which was then followed by the *Hebdo* and, ultimately, the College (COM72:210). The different cabinet meetings were joined by drafting officials themselves and also included the SJ officials who helped in resolving the legal inconsistencies between the GPSD and the DG

ENTR proposals (COM72:214). Whereas each of the administrative levels had clung tightly to its own pet measure and navigated the conflict into stalemate, negotiations at the cabinet level were more solution oriented (COM72:164, 394, COM94:85–99). DG SANCO was only partially successful regarding the particular proposal under analysis. Besides the fact that the "new approach" was revived, the CE mark was not abolished as it was the image of the "new approach" and enjoyed high legitimacy and support among industry stakeholders. However, DG SANCO managed to insert at least some of the GPSD principles on information obligations and safeguard procedures into the decision. Thus, while the judgment may differ on the overall package, DG ENTR was still more powerful, especially since they refused substantial changes from the outset, structured the whole position-formation process around this aim and garnered unanimous support from the affected major stakeholders.[9]

In sum, the responsiveness to external stakeholders reflects the rank order provided by the "new approach": first come the officials implementing it, then comes the trade business as the most directly affected stakeholder and integral supporter of the system, and only then come consumer interests. This principle provided the basis for the lead DG to structure interaction in the necessary way to maintain the fundamentals of existing market-making legislation.

7.3.4 Safety of Toys

DG ENTR's will to consolidate the "new approach" was initially also the motivation behind the toy-safety proposal (COM[2008]9). The existing toy-safety directive had been the first "new approach" regulation of mass consumer products in 1988 (COM[2008]9: 2). Nevertheless, some enhanced emphasis of safety aspects is evident in the new legal text. The proposal includes products that are not exclusively intended for use by children and comes without prejudice to the GPSD (see Section 7.3.1). It is more restrictive on toy usage and toys in foods, and extends regulations on choking and suffocation risks. Rules on the chemical properties of toys now take up twice as much room in the text and ban a range of additional substances. However, labeling requirements and the provisions on the obligations of economic operators, conformity assessment, member state duties, safeguard procedures, and Commission competences follow the word-by-word pattern established in the parallel "new approach" framework decision. Two issues are remarkable, however. First, member states are now expected to organize and perform market surveillance explicitly along the lines of DG SANCO's product-safety directive. Second, the Commission may now change detailed safety requirements via a comitology procedure, which deviates from the original "new approach" spirit precluding governmental involvement in product specification. So, to sum up, the proposal mostly defends the classical pattern but is geared more towards consumer protection in scope and product properties and makes some concessions to DG SANCO's safety law.

The original impulse for the proposal came from technical difficulties implementing the old directive in the light of a rapidly changing market (COM25:60). This was voiced especially by member state representatives in the old directive's implementation committee (COM25:206). Already in 2002 a draft proposal had been distributed to national representatives, while the Commission publicly announced the revision as one priority in the 2003 simplification program (COM25:52, COM[2003]71: 25). Thus, toy safety became part of DG ENTR's broader strategy and the responsible desk official was at least in weekly exchange with the unit drawing up the more general "new approach" framework (COM25:158). In addition, the most formative exchange occurred in the committee of national representatives. Rather than "strategic planning," the drafting officials sought "scientific knowledge" in this forum because they considered their sectoral legislation to be much less politically sensitive than the broader "new approach" revision (COM25:216–22). The group discussed seven consecutive draft proposals (COM25:296) and only afterwards a public consultation was held online, which mainly elicited responses from industry (COM[2008]9: 3). In addition, DG ENTR devised specific studies on chemicals in toys so as to have the latest scientific knowledge available (COM25:200).

But this technocratic focus was strongly challenged in August 2007 when huge and repeated recalls of Chinese toys hit the European market roughly half a year before actual proposal adoption. These recalls were revealed and disseminated through the RAPEX system managed by DG SANCO under the GPSD and they immediately raised the public salience of the issue (COM25:82). The drafting officials saw press reports on "consumers losing faith in toys" turn into internal pressure by Commissioner Verheugen, who wanted "immediate results" (COM25:224, 340, COM26:216).[10] Comparing the seven earlier draft proposals with the final one, it is apparent that quite a few changes occurred due to this late-stage public pressure for more intervention. Examples are the reference to DG SANCO's GPSD, the producer duty to consider any foreseeable use of toys by children and the tighter rules on toys in foods, all of which entered the proposal texts only after summer 2007.

The really "'big issue," however, were chemical toy properties, which had already caused several consumer scares long before summer 2007 (COM25:200). The outstanding political importance of these rules kept the cabinet involved throughout the process (COM25:102), and more stringent chemical safety rules were sold as the major improvement on publication of the proposal (e.g. IP/08/91). In practical terms, however, the drafting officials transferred many of the details from existing laws such as the REACH regulation, the cosmetics directive, and several harmonized standards, while DG SANCO's product-safety unit provided relevant expertise as well (COM26:60, 82, COM[2008]9: 4–5).

On other provisions, the industry-friendly line of the "new approach" pattern prevailed, however. Consumer associations continued to criticize the CE mark (COM[2008]9: 6) and in-house testing of toy compliance (BEUC and ANEC 2008: 11–12). The drafting officials asked for a "political decision" on these points from the DG ENTR cabinet, which obviously argued for the industry-friendly solution. This was supported by earlier stakeholder responses and the impact assessment also qualified third-party testing of toys as "proportionate" (COM25:82 and 102). However, with regard to the comitology involvement in changing the chemical regulations, DG ENTR was unable to stick to the "new approach" spirit of limiting governmental intervention as far as possible when the European Parliament published a resolution calling for more flexible political reactions to newly emerging consumer risks (BEUC and ANEC 2008: 6).

The administrative interaction with DG SANCO was quite cooperative during the early process (COM26:62, 206), where DG ENTR could profit from toy-related recall information in the RAPEX database as well as from in-house expertise on chemical issues that the DG SANCO unit controlled (COM25:74, 258, COM26:198–206). However, the initial cooperation was gradually overshadowed by the parallel negotiations on the broader "new approach" framework and particularly by the massive toy recalls in summer 2007. DG SANCO Commissioner Kuneva jumped on the issue and established the so-called Consumer Product Safety Review—a working group that was to report on the lessons learned from the toy scandals. In addition, she started negotiating voluntary agreements with the toy industry (COM26:222, COM25:244), travelled to China to hold bilateral talks on the safety of imported goods (Dickie 2007) and held a speech on the general "new approach" framework in the European Parliament warning that it could weaken consumer protection (IP/07/1318). These inroads into a sector that DG ENTR was about to re-regulate signaled that the broader battle on product safety was far from over and led to reservations among DG ENTR's political leadership (COM25:244). When the formal inter-service consultation began in December 2007, DG SANCO made its agreement subject to comments. The provisions on scope and national market surveillance, especially, directly impinged on the relationship between the "new approach" and the GPSD. And although information on the subsequent negotiations is scarce, the late concessions to DG SANCO in the form of cross-references to the GPSD indicate that public political pressure mattered quite a lot. The toy scandals put DG ENTR under significant time pressure, while the conflict on internal Commission competences also figured publicly in the parallel European Parliament negotiations on the general "new approach" framework (COM26:13). The two facts together allowed DG SANCO's political leadership to credibly threaten to undermine the process—either by blocking its adoption or by publicly arguing that the DG ENTR proposal disregarded the up-and-running consumer-information and recall system. Although DG ENTR had pushed through all other issues reinforcing the "new approach" tradition, its role as the most influential player on this particular proposal was somewhat undermined by the fact that DG SANCO had created a valuable precedent on the relationship between the "new approach" and its own general product-safety directive.

Summing up the case, the drafting initially followed a technocratic model for more than four years and relied on expertise and parallel laws. But some of the most decisive provisions were affected by public and political pressures during the last year of proposal finalization and internal interaction.

7.3.5 Protecting Children Using the Internet

The final safety case stands at some distance from these lines of conflict. It was drafted by the sectorally oriented DG INFSO and presents a decision on a funding program to foster the safety of children using online technologies (COM[2008] 106). More specifically, it presents a continuation of the preceding "Safer Internet Plus 2004–2008" program and entails only minor changes. The scope of eligible participants is widened by rendering international organizations or third-country entities eligible. The proposal removes a former priority on unwanted content such as spam but includes two new priorities on harmful conduct—targeted especially at online grooming (befriending children in chat rooms for sexual purposes) and bullying—and on establishing a knowledge base. All other rules on the possible project forms, the distribution of the budget over time and priorities, tendering, Commission competences, and comitology remain unchanged.

While the preceding programs had been partly driven by highly publicized actions against child pornography during the early century (COM132:212), the proposal was actually accompanied by little contemporaneous public salience. Nevertheless, the rising usage of new media by children and young people and the parallel increase in harmful online content or conduct provided enough reason and made it "quite obvious to continue" (COM132:41). What is more, the previous program had already foreseen an evaluation with a view to a possible successor program and was expiring in 2008. The drafting of the new program thus began in January 2007 and was handled mainly by one desk official who discussed basic decisions with his unit and was further supported by an internal expert drawing up the financial annex (COM132:66, 72, 178). Though it was almost exclusively dealt with at the administrative level, the basic direction of the program, the evaluation report prior to publication and the extension of scope to international beneficiaries were agreed with DG INFSO's cabinet (COM132:140, 222). External stakeholders were consulted through a public online consultation combined with targeted consultations via a mailing list of former program beneficiaries, the yearly "Safer Internet Forum," and day-to-day contacts with various practitioners in the field (COM132:62–4, 208). This was further backed by a range of Eurobarometer results on media usage by children from the years 2003 to 2005, a specific qualitative survey of children in early 2007, and a secondary analysis of relevant national studies—whereby the drafting official explicitly bemoaned the lacking comparability of national data (COM132:51, 222). Internally, the drafting unit already consulted DGs JLS and BUDG and the SJ when developing the very initial consultation documents because "it makes sense that those Directorates-General controlling relevant expertise have a say" (COM132:76, 198). DGs EAC and JLS assisted in developing risk scenarios and their involvement was also helpful because the program targeted networks that included their stakeholders, such as teachers and police authorities (COM132:72, 80). However, no substantially deviating positions were reported and—given the mere continuation of the program and the common insight that child protection was necessary—were also never very likely (COM132:118).

Besides mere continuation, DG INFSO mainly sought to maintain high public awareness of the issues covered (COM132:216), while the Commission was seen particularly as a necessary lead given that national reactions to the truly transnational nature of online issues varied strongly (COM132:45). This conviction also inspired the scope extensions to international stakeholders, which was the most sensitive innovation of the proposal (COM132:130). Especially during the consultation, the drafting officials understood that the program deals with global media and thus global problems (cf. COM[2008]106: 4) and relevant paralleling initiatives were handled by international organizations such as UNICEF, UNESCO, and the Council of Europe. In this light, DG INFSO intended to foster international promotion of successful European policy approaches such as contact points and help lines (COM132:134 and 136). But financing projects outside the EU had no precedents within DG INFSO and member state opposition was feared. While the drafting official initially intended to include internationalization openly and frankly in the proposal, the internal legal units, the DG INFSO cabinet, and the SJ apparently changed the legal phrasing into a less offensive option for the Council, while the drafting official also qualified these adaptations as "co-operative" (COM132:154, 140, 146).[11]

The earlier priority on spam, in contrast, was dropped completely because it was not targeted at children and had since been covered by other DG INFSO law (COM[2008]106: 7). The focus on harmful online conduct followed a range of stakeholder interventions on cyber-bullying and grooming, which had become increasingly virulent with the spread of social networks (COM132:208). And as the evaluation of the former program had revealed a lack of systematic data, the drafting official decided that financing systematic research under the new priority "knowledge base" was warranted (COM132:220, 51). The necessary budget was merely transferred from the existing program and provides an extrapolation of the projects running under the old program, many of which were intended to be continued (COM132:186). This also entailed the agreement of DG BUDG because officials "had practiced that for years" (COM132:243). Likewise, the implementation and comitology rules follow the old program and met with no internal resistance, so that the principal factors explaining the positions are the existing program and the input and expertise of practitioners in the field. Given that the political aim was clear among all participants, the process itself followed a purely technocratic logic.

In conclusion, our cases in the sub-field of European product safety regulation show that the issue of emancipation of consumer protection from the original market-making thrust of existing European law is far from settled. The regulatory field is heatedly contested between powerful producer interests and calls for more consumer protection. This is mirrored by an equally heated battle for competences within the Commission. As the old bull in the field, DG ENTR was able to build on the economic success of a long-standing *acquis*, historical relationships with cross-nationally operating producers and day-to-day expertise in implementing "new approach" directives. Nonetheless, the precedent for a more consumer-focused approach created by the GPSD allowed DG SANCO to increasingly step into DG ENTR's turf, in particular where publicly visible scandals supported its claims, as in the toy-safety case. Only the DG INFSO case stands out, partly because it comes as a supporting funding program, but partly also because the clearly defined competences of this DG have not been questioned by other Commission players.

7.4 FOOD SAFETY

The EU is one of the largest food producers in the world and the food industry is the largest manufacturing sector in Europe (MacMaoláin 2007: 5–6; CIAA 2011). At the same time, food directly affects the well-being of each and every citizen (Ansell and Vogel 2006: 4). Tensions between producer and consumer interests are thus particularly likely in the regulation of the food sector, but in European rule-making, trade considerations initially prevailed over public safety and health concerns (Alemanno 2006: 239). The Commission tackled trade obstacles by harmonizing the composition of specific foods, while leaving the health and safety implications to the member states. Furthermore, two fundamental decisions of the ECJ—*Dassonville* (C-8-74) and *Cassis de Dijon* (C-120-78)—revolved around foodstuffs and emphasized the importance of the internal market (MacMaoláin 2007: 20–2). However, market creation decelerated as subsequent case law increasingly accepted national safety concerns and Council unanimity hampered further harmonization (Clergeau 2005: 115). After 1985, European food regulation was thus also subsumed under the "new approach" (Alemanno 2006: 240–1). This set-up was shattered when the BSE crisis broke in 1996. Following immense public outrage, the Santer Commission moved the risk-assessment competences from DGs ENTR and AGRI to DG SANCO (Vos 2000), but subsequent scandals on dioxin in eggs and swine fever added further to public pressure. Only a few days after entering office, President Prodi and DG SANCO Commissioner Byrne thus announced a legislative food-safety strategy, the creation of an autonomous food-safety agency (EFSA), and the centralization of Commission competences. A white paper on food safety was published in January 2000 (COM[1999]719) and during the spring all food-related units were moved from DGs AGRI and ENTR to DG SANCO (Clergeau 2005: 129–33). This set the stage for our investigation period and explains why DG SANCO is assigned formal responsibility for all five food safety proposals in the sample detailed in Tables 7.6 and 7.7.

7.4.1 Food Supplements and Addition of Vitamins, Minerals, and other Substances

The first of these proposals is a directive on food supplements (COM[2000]139), that is, concentrated sources of vitamins and minerals sold in dose form, such as soluble tablets of Vitamin C. This proposed directive is limited to vitamins and minerals, leaving other nutrients unregulated, and, although a range of countries such as Germany and Austria had treated them as medicines subject to pre-market licensing, defines supplements as foodstuffs (COM88:26; Europe Information Service 1999). In conjunction with a general ban on further national trade restrictions, this accounts for the strongly liberalizing thrust of the Commission position in line with the most liberal existing national regimes. But some more restrictive elements are also contained, such as a European-wide safeguard procedure (COM[2000]222: 2), quite restrictive labeling rules and, especially, a conclusive list of permitted vitamins and minerals that renders some products previously marketed in the UK now illegal (Eberhardie 2007). Any future changes on permitted nutrients and their levels have been transferred to a comitology procedure.

The proposal on the artificial addition of vitamins, minerals, and other substances to foods (COM[2003]671) came three years later, but is strongly related to the initial one. This later proposal largely mirrors the first one with regard to

Table 7.6. Position formation on food safety

Proposal number	Contents	No. of key provisions	Main line of proposal (content)	Uncertainty	Salience	Origin (hierarchical level)	Process duration (months)	External consultation	Main position-formation factors
COM[2000]222	Food supplements	7	Harmonize safety-relevant rules on food supplements	Yes	No	Administrative	113	Specific	– Organized interests – Anticipation of Council majority – Experts – Extant *acquis*
COM[2003]671	Addition of vitamins, minerals, and other substances to foods	11	Harmonize safety-relevant rules on food enrichment	Yes	No	Administrative	155	Specific	– Organized interests – Anticipation of Council majority – Experts – Extant *acquis*
COM[2006]428	Food additives	5	Streamline future additive authorization without changing underlying principles	No	No	Administrative	24	Specific	– Organized interests – Extant *acquis*
COM[2003]424	Nutrition and health claims made on foods	8	Build a regime on nutrition- and health-claims approval in line with increased consumer protection	No	No	Administrative	24	Specific	– National positions – International policy transfer – Extant *acquis* – Organized interests – Anticipation of Council and EP majorities
COM[2008]40	Provision of food information to consumers	10	Equip consumer with easily understandable and health-related food information	No	Yes	Administrative	36	Public	– Organized interests – Anticipation of Council majority

Table 7.7. Interaction on food safety

Proposal Number	Contents	Deviating DGs	Informal interaction	Position-based conflict	Process-based conflict	Main line of conflict	Most powerful DG	Main power resources
COM[2000]222	Food supplements	ENTR	Medium	3	1	Harmonization in line with trade or consumer-protection focus	SANCO	- Supranational competence
COM[2003]671	Addition of vitamins, minerals, and other substances to foods	ENTR AGRI	Medium	2	0	Limiting enrichment only to foods with favorable nutritional profiles	ENTR	- Proximity to Council and EP majorities - Bureaucratic legitimacy
COM[2006]428	Food additives	ENTR AGRI	Intense	2	0	Stakeholder interests and financing line	ENTR	- Organized interests - Horizontal services - DG alliances
COM[2004]524	Nutrition and health claims	ENTR AGRI	Little	2	0	Producer burdens induced by DG SANCO's consumer focus	SANCO	- Horizontal services - Public legitimacy
COM[2008]40	Provision of food information to consumers	ENTR AGRI	Medium	3	2	Consumer health vs. internal market concerns	SANCO	- Lead department - Public legitimacy - Proximity to Council majority

permitted minerals and vitamins, the pre-market control of labels, the comitology and safeguard procedures, and a ban on any further national restrictions. It entails additional liberalizing effects in that it allows any purpose for the addition of nutrients that was legal in any of the member states before. It also allows the addition of certain other substances that were legal in only some states. It is more interventionist, by contrast, where it requires a full nutritional profile on the labels of fortified foods. In sum, the first two food cases move regulatory powers to the supranational level by harmonizing some more restrictive national rules and by liberalizing a broad range of others.

The two cases had been drafted together in the very same DG III unit (COM88:22), which only became part of DG SANCO in October 1999 (COM88:42, COM115:31). However, although European food policy was in the spotlight at the time, the specific contents of the two proposals were hardly salient in public, but for the growing industry they were. When artificial and enriched foods emerged in 1990, DG III's service level received manufacturer complaints and started to tackle related trade restrictions (COM88:30, 86, 106, 154). Originally, the products entered Europe as US imports to the UK, from where they were distributed in line with the mutual-recognition principle. However, their treatment as medicines, especially in France, Germany, Austria, Spain, and Italy, hampered trade and also protected local producers (COM88:30). In this context, pharmaceutical companies and their governments pushed DG III's political leadership to shelve its early harmonization attempts in 1993 (COM88:112, 194). The unit kept the issue cooking, however, and the 1996 single-market review as well as a 1997 Green Paper bemoan the remaining trade barriers (SEC[96]2378: 27, COM[97]176). Shortly afterwards, the unit enacted infringement procedures against Germany and Austria and issued a public discussion paper which started the drafting process of a proposal covering both areas (COM88:116; Europe Information Service 1999, 2000). The industry concerned remained the most active external stakeholder and two purposely founded industry groups were the first to respond positively to the 1997 discussion paper (Europe Information Service 1997a, 1997b). However, the drafting officials also contacted the Consumers' Consultative Council and its successors, a forum of the major European umbrellas and national consumer organizations (COM88:178). Given that scientific evidence on health risks was inconsistent, of dubious quality, and only scantily available (DG III of the European Commission 1997: 6–7; Eberhardie 2007), the unit also involved the Scientific Committee on Food (SCF), which was comprised of university-level experts (COM30:33, COM88:186), while the officials were in permanent contact with member state representatives (COM88:30). The resulting positions were "more or less a continuation" of what had been developed in DG III. The major aim was still "to facilitate trade in these products" (COM88:22–6), but since national restrictions rested on public health concerns, some harmonization was considered necessary.

In the face of early member state opposition, the drafting officials decided to separate the two proposals because an encompassing harmonization was assumed to be unfeasible in the Council (COM88:90). For two reasons, food supplements were tackled first (COM88:98, 30). The first reason was the faster growing market, the second was the fact that food producer complaints had initiated the process in the first place. The complaints also explain the basic decision to treat supplements as foods rather than medicines: filing them with the food unit allowed this new product group to be aligned with an existing broader framework, which is also why the proposal addresses vitamins and minerals only (COM88:34). Other substances such as herbal extracts could simply not be as easily defined as foods in legal terms. By contrast, the rather restrictive decision to enact a positive rather than a negative list of permitted nutrients was not fixed during the early drafting stages (Europe Information Service 1992) but was included only when European food policy came under fire for mismanaging health risks during the final stages of internal drafting. This approach was seen as a means to deal with the scientific uncertainty that persisted on artificially enriched diets and the list's contents and other technical details directly result from the expertise provided by the Scientific Committee on Food (COM88:186, COM[2002]222: 2). The comparatively extensive labeling rules also follow from such risk-avoidance concerns and are partly transferred from the general framework on nutrition labeling and the misleading-advertising directive (COM88:38, COM30:51).

The uncoupled food-fortification proposal shows mostly the same position formation pattern. The act was re-announced in the 2000 White Paper, was paralleled by infringement procedures,[12] and a draft proposal was distributed to external stakeholders (COM[2003]671: 11). The policy formation also addressed both trade creation and harmonization of safety rules. Thus, the provisions on scope, the removal of further national intervention possibilities and allowed purposes for nutrient addition follow a liberalizing line of reasoning. The latter provisions, in particular, were contested from the consumer side as they basically allow food fortification for any thinkable purpose (BEUC 2003b: 4). The drafting officials transferred these rules from the *Codex Alimentarius*—a collection of food-safety standards managed by the World Health Organisation (WHO)—but freed the voluntary addition of nutrients from almost any restrictions, arguing that a change in dietary habits can be expected (COM88:70–4). In other words, the producer choice to enrich foods was left to the pure logic of supply and demand.

Other safety-relevant rules were geared more towards consumer protection. The permitted nutrients and their levels again followed from scientific advice (COM88:186–90), while other provisions on labelling rules or future EFSA involvement are transferred from existing European law (COM[2003]671: 31). Only the inclusion of other substances apart from vitamins and minerals stands in stark contrast with the earlier food supplements proposal, which had excluded them explicitly. However, the industry had managed in the meantime to persuade the Council to introduce such substances to the earlier food supplements proposal and, anticipating that this Council position would hold, the drafting officials included them in the food fortification proposal as well, despite strong consumer concerns (COM88:194, BEUC 2004a).

Given the unit's relocation during drafting, which was clearly meant to underline a change of emphasis from industry policy to health and consumer protection (COM88:42, COM115:31), analyzing the interaction is a complex endeavor. Previously, the Commission's small consumer policy service had occasionally challenged the process due to its "more restrictive attitude" (COM88:54). But when actual responsibility moved to DG SANCO, the draft proposals were signed by both sides and not much was left open for negotiation. Now as colleagues of their former "opposite numbers," the drafting officials still had "to explain and to describe all the issues and the potential interests," but they managed this without procedural conflicts (COM88:54).

However, tensions between industry and consumer interests stirred up more internal conflict when it came to the food fortification proposal three years later. While the DG SANCO unit stayed true to its original trade focus, DG ENTR jumped on one specific issue. The DG SANCO unit had originally intended to limit enrichment to foods with particular nutritional profiles (see the health claims proposal below), a position that would have strongly reduced the marketing potential of enriched foods. Since the health claims proposal and particularly the issue of nutritional profile had triggered intense conflict among external stakeholders, as well as in the Council and in the European Parliament (e.g. AE, January 14, 2004), DG SANCO gave in to ensure the political feasibility of the act. A more minor but also controversial issue occurred with DG AGRI, which demanded that enrichment should also be allowed in certain oenological practices covered by a DG AGRI-led regulation on the wine sector. DG SANCO took this demand on board by excluding the respective products through the scope provisions.

Positions on food supplements and food fortification can be mainly explained by the demands of organized industry interests and by the anticipation of member state opposition, but also follow from scientific advice and significant transfers from existing European law. It was possible to maintain the early emphasis on trade on the basis of the long-standing supranational competence in the policy area, which provided regulatory blueprints, and the personnel's expertise in day-to-day food policy-making (COM88:38). In the latter case, the initial member state opposition also opened latitude for consumer protection concerns, yet some of the more restrictive rules may have simply come from the "impetus" of having a new DG, which signaled that the Commission intended to "put the consumer to the forefront" (COM88:142).

7.4.2 Food Additives

Another food safety case in our sample regulates food additives (COM[2006]428), meaning substances that are usually not consumed as foods. This includes sweeteners, colorants, thickeners, anti-foaming and glazing agents, and packaging gases, which are most commonly known by their E-numbers and for which liberalization had already been achieved through four European directives. With regard to scope, approved food additives, general usage rules and labeling requirements, the proposal merely consolidates what existed in this *acquis*. The only meaningful innovation in the proposal concerns its future implementation with new notification requirements for producers, monitoring tasks, and, most importantly, rendering any future changes to the list of allowed food additives subject to an authorization procedure that was proposed in parallel to the proposal at hand. In essence, this makes such decisions subject to EFSA risk assessment followed by a comitology-like procedure. Previously, changes had to be made through a co-decision procedure involving the European Parliament. Thus, the food additives proposal leaves the existing liberal regime intact but moves any future decisions out of the political realm into tertiary decision-making.

The proposal was listed in the 2000 White Book on Food Safety and was thus on the to-do list of DG SANCO's chemicals unit (COM29:74). However, in contrast to the huge political upheavals that had stimulated the White Book in the first place, the basic impulse that set off drafting in early 2003 emerged from the "regulatory community," meaning "colleagues up to Head of Unit, their opposite numbers of the member states officials and the middle-ranking regulatory affairs coordinators for the food associations" (COM80:55, COM29:161). From the very beginning, the drafting officials went for a mere "simplification" with "very little changes". Streamlining implementation and authorization was warranted under the new general principles of European food legislation (COM29:58, COM80:51). In this light, the drafting process could have been briefer, but officials had to wait for the proposals on the details of the authorization procedure and on enzymes and flavorings, which were meant to be published as a package (COM29:126). They used the resulting three-year delay for testing their proposal among the major stakeholders. Consumer associations and member states were surprisingly uninterested, leaving the drafting officials with little to build on (COM29:50, 180), while much more input came from a large number of specialized food-industry associations (COM29:54, COM[2006]248: 3).

Two important conflicts were nevertheless revealed this way. The first concerns processing aids—additives that have no technological effect on the final food but may be contained nevertheless. Consumer associations considered the distinction between additives and processing aids as potentially detrimental for consumer health. Initially, DG SANCO favored removal of processing aids before the foodstuff is sold (Directorate-General Health and Consumer Protection 2005: 15), but given the huge economic impact, both the industry and DG ENTR resisted and DG SANCO finally gave in (COM115:15, COM[2006]428: 4; BEUC 2006: 4).[13] Second, the future management of food additives was surrounded by controversy. Officials had originally planned that producers would need to re-apply for authorization of specific additives every ten years (Directorate-General Health and Consumer Protection 2005).[14] However, despite supporting positions from consumer associations and national governments, DG SANCO gave in to the industry fear that the additional controls would stifle innovation. Only a duty to disclose information upon request survived (COM[2006]428: 4; Hagenmeyer 2006: 296–7). Still following a producer-friendly line, DG SANCO was even more uncompromising when it came to the essential aim and the most "fundamental change" of the overall act. Moving decisions about the future authorization of additives to a comitology procedure under the participation of the EFSA was meant to increase efficiency, while MEPs and consumer associations feared that this would effectively sideline societal interests in the future (COM29:31, 58; BEUC 2006: 2; Hagenmeyer 2006: 297; AE, July 12, 2007). Surprisingly, this demand to increase the independence of DG SANCO was internally supported by DG ENTR, a rather unusual ally. DG ENTR welcomed lower costs for producers in line with its approach in its own chemicals regulations (COM115:137). And this support was not least a *quid pro quo* for the industry-friendly line on processing aids and DG ENTR's early inclusion in the drafting process (COM29:86).

DG ENTR's support was also precious in an internal quarrel with DG AGRI based on the fact that some financing should come from a specific funding line in the European Agricultural Guarantee Fund negotiated with the Council in parallel. With the help of DG BUDG, an administrative solution was hammered out without excessive controversies (COM155:165, COM80:67, COM29:161).

Summing up, the main positions can be explained on the basis of support from organized interests that were in favor of DG SANCO's overall aim to ease their regulatory burden, while everything beyond procedural questions was transferred from the existing supranational law. Where minor conflicts occurred, they were either solved through support from organized interests or from a horizontal service (DG BUDG) and allied DGs (DG ENTR).

7.4.3 Nutrition and Health Claims

The next food safety case is characterized by a much more interventionist thrust (COM[2003]424). It regulates nutrition and health claims, such as "low fat" or "calcium aids in the development of strong teeth," in labeling, presenting, and advertising foods. Besides a few scattered supranational rules, some member states had enacted specific laws that restricted or even banned health-related claims (BEUC 2000c). The proposal covers all claims, including pictorial, graphic, or symbolic representations, and establishes general principles according to which claims must not be false or misleading, depreciate other foods, or imply that a balanced diet cannot supply adequate nutrients. Health claims must be accompanied by statements on the importance of a balanced diet and a healthy lifestyle, must describe the food quantity and the pattern of consumption required to achieve the claimed effect, and must warn potential risk groups about detrimental nutrient dosages. The proposed provisions are immensely detailed and encompassing compared to the freedoms producers previously enjoyed, so that we can speak of a highly interventionist position here.

In this regard, it is surprising that the proposal was drafted by the very same DG SANCO unit that had been assigned responsibility for the rather liberal supplements and fortification proposals (discussed in Sections 7.4.1 and 7.4.2). Having worked in food legislation for more than 20 years, the officials had considerable strategic abilities and felt that stakeholder interests had converged on a European claims regulation (COM30:51). Similar to other proposals, the basic idea emerged in early discussions with member state representatives and multinational companies which were concerned about trade issues (COM30:55). However, the context of European food policy changed after the BSE crisis and the proposal at hand was clearly affected by this. It was first announced in the 2000 White Paper on Food Safety, which outlined the Commission's change of emphasis towards more consumer protection. Jumping on this bandwagon, the main European consumer group immediately published a policy paper on claims, which seems to foreclose the later DG SANCO position by proposing general principles, restricted usage in the case of unhealthy nutritional profiles and premarket approval (BEUC 2000c). The producer side, by contrast, tried to avoid an interventionist regulation and agreed on a voluntary code of practice in January 2001 instead (CIAA 2003).

In this setting, the drafting officials acquired the hierarchy's agreement through an internal "scoping paper" in early 2001 (COM30:127, 271). In contrast to the food safety proposals analyzed so far, the drafting officials ranked consumer interests first, while a level playing field for food producers was only a secondary concern (COM30:47). A consultative consumer committee and the Scientific Committee on Foodstuffs were heard, but the real information-gathering came about through bilateral contacts with individual companies and interest associations (COM30:33, 149, COM88:21–5). The unit published a discussion paper in summer 2001 and a preliminary legal text in 2002, and leaked a draft proposal in June 2003 (COM33:187–93; Directorate General Health and Consumer Protection 2001, 2002; BEUC 2003a).

During a time when the public salience of European food policy was still rather high,[15] the first paper tested the most interventionist regulatory ideas, such as the general restriction regarding claims on alcoholic beverages, the need to substantiate claims with generally accepted scientific data (with the burden of proof resting on producers), the pre-market authorization of claims, and the regulation on limiting claims only to specific nutritional profiles—that is, only healthy combinations of fat, fatty acids, sugars, and salt (Directorate General Health and Consumer Protection 2001: 4, 9–10). This latter idea was dropped from the 2002 draft proposal (Directorate General Health and Consumer Protection 2002), but re-entered the text following consumer protests. The provision led to strong concerns on the part of food producers and retailers (CIAA 2003; EuroCommerce 2003), who argued that DG SANCO had unlawfully entered the field of public health and exceeded the market-making justification of the proposal indicated by its treaty basis (Art. 95 TEC; AE, January 14, 2004; Hauer 2006).

But DG SANCO also underlined its pro-consumer bent in a likewise contested provision on the regulatory approval of health claims. Apart from a small list of generally accepted claims on widely recognized substances such as Vitamin C, for example, all health claims have to undergo a complex pre-market authorization procedure involving the provision of scientific data by producers, an EFSA evaluation, a subsequent public consultation and a comitology procedure before the Commission ultimately decides on approval of the claim. This provision intentionally draws on the existing Swedish regime, the only one in Europe that includes a requirement of this nature (Directorate General Health and Consumer Protection 2002: 10).

The general principles were partly derived from ECJ case law and taken over from the WHO *Codex Alimentarius* so as "to avoid confusion and limit potential trade disputes" (COM[2003]424: 3–5, Directorate General Health and Consumer Protection 2001: 9). Nevertheless, by also covering graphic claims and by shifting the burden of proof onto producers, DG SANCO exceeded these internationally agreed rules and was again supported by consumer representatives (BEUC 2003a).

Likewise, the prohibition of implied health claims, which includes references to overall health and well-being, to psychological or behavioral functions, to slimming or weight control, as well as claims involving health professionals such as doctors, went beyond national and international rules, thereby brandishing another red rag at the European industry that generated consumer applause (BEUC 2003a: 4; EuroCommerce 2003, AE, January 14, 2004). Unmistakably abandoning the realm of balanced decision-making, the drafting officials used their regular interactions with member state representatives to find out whether these positions would find a qualified majority (COM30:163–5). In this regard, a 2001 European Parliament resolution also signaled support for a regulation that would make approval of claims subject to prior scientific assessment (COM[2003]424: 7–8).[16] Information on the actual coordination process is scarce. Despite their long-standing contacts in the field, the drafting officials mentioned only formal interactions (COM30:87). Internally, "questions often came from DG ENTR where, of course, the interests of the producers and manufacturers have been sort of represented" (COM30:73). Likewise, internal coordination documents highlight that DG AGRI voiced the producer fears of smaller companies that cannot afford the envisaged authorization procedure. Beyond this, they pointed out inconsistencies with their own regulations on fruits and wines and also opposed the prohibition of claims for alcoholic beverages, a position that also ranked highly on the wish list of the food industry (CIAA 2003). Internal documents indicate that two rounds of formal ISC were necessary. However, even in the second round, both DG ENTR and DG AGRI withheld their agreement. Thus, the final decision had to be negotiated among the political leaderships of the DGs involved and it was apparently taken only in the Commissioner's meeting of July 16 (PV [2003]1621).

Nonetheless, almost all of DG SANCO's original ideas from the first discussion paper figure in the final Commission proposal, so that the political context apparently made a markedly consumer-friendly proposal very welcome. In fact, the Secretariat General had supported DG SANCO during the ISC and added that "the revised proposal constitutes a strong signal about the intention of the Commission to respond to the challenge of promoting public health through different actions such as labelling of foods" (SG response CIS-Net consultation 440018).

In sum, position formation was a result of transfers from existing regulatory solutions at the national, European, and international levels, while most positions followed the demands of organized interests and were adopted with a view to inter-institutional actors. In the interactions, support from horizontal services seems to have been decisive in helping to assert DG SANCO's position.

7.4.4 Provision of Food Information to Consumers

The final food safety case addresses food labeling and nutrition declarations more generally (COM[2008]40). The area was covered by two existing acts, but the proposal enhances the emphasis on consumer empowerment in several respects.[17] It introduces new principles whereby labeling should address a high level of consumer protection and enable informed consumer choices regarding health, economic, environmental, societal, and ethical considerations. Beyond this, the proposal entails detailed rules on mandatory information and labeling, while it also explicitly allows the development of non-binding national schemes for nutrition declarations—which may also involve graphical representations such as nutrition "traffic lights." In particular, the rules on the nutrition declaration with their front-of-pack requirement and a clarification of per-serving labeling shift the status quo towards a more restrictive European law. Finally, the proposal transfers a range of important future decisions into the realm of comitology. So, as for the health claims, we see a proposal moving significant competences towards tertiary decision-making, while the actual regulatory decisions underline a Commission position that restricts producer behavior to the benefit of consumers.

The proposal was drafted in the same unit as the claims proposal, which was negotiated in Parliament and Council at the time of drafting. It also came in parallel with a range of soft law initiatives as DG SANCO (especially upon the initiative of its Director-General Madelin) began to tackle the problem of people being overweight in cooperation with a very inclusive stakeholder network engaged in the development of voluntary approaches. A 2007 White Paper on nutrition, obesity, and health issues stressed the need for consumer information and the proposal was framed along these lines (COM[2008]40: 2; Bounds et al. 2008). Legislative drafting began in early 2005 (COM30:131) and was revealed to external stakeholders through a discussion paper in February 2006 (Directorate-General for Health and Consumer Protection 2006). Like the other food proposals, it dates back to the 2000 White Book on Food Safety (AE, February 4, 2003).[18] However, the decision to make nutrition labeling an obligation was taken in early 2005 only after some early talks with member states did not reveal fundamental opposition and obesity became a topic in public debates, particularly in the UK. Accordingly, it was decided that a single directive should be drawn up by two desk officers supported by their head of unit, the Director-General, and the legal and horizontal units (COM30:131, COM80:109). Again, this involved some officials who had already been responsible for virtually all previous European food laws, so that the administrative level had a strong take on drafting. However, owing to the public debates on obesity, this proposal was "much more politicized" than other food initiatives (COM80:59), which increased the interaction with the political level (COM30:269). Here, Director-General Madelin and DG SANCO's management board, including all directors as well as the Commissioner's cabinet, were important channels. This group mapped possible constituency reactions to different policy options and asked Commissioner Kyprianoú for decisions (COM80:152). In fact, the Commissioner committed himself publicly to a restrictive route on obesity in a front-page interview in the *Financial Times* that threatened the industry with legislation and was followed by a number of DG SANCO-led press reports on the Commission's strategy (e.g. Mason and Parker 2005).

Having set the political compass, the drafting officials were prepared for a heated debate when conducting a broad-scale public consultation (COM80:150, COM [2008]40: 5, cf. Directorate-General Health and Consumer Protection 2006). The document was also explicitly sent to national governments and was discussed in several existing stakeholder groups. This activity was flanked by direct contacts with umbrella organizations, individual companies, and member state representatives.

Their own experience in DG ENTR's predecessor DG made the drafting officials aware that their position would raise problems and they thus sought factual and strategic information as well as informal internal contacts early on (COM30:307, 351, COM80:85). However, significant parts of the internal coordination took place on a formal basis. The steering committee for the impact assessment was very important because it was the only channel that could uncover the extent of DG ENTR's opposition, which—given the advanced drafting process—indicated the need for political coordination (COM30:255, COM115:66). In the ISC, DG ENTR claimed that it had deliberately been improperly consulted and blocked

DG SANCO's proposal with five pages of comments, immediately involving its own cabinet as well (COM115:55, 66). At this stage, the process had become "quite controversial" (COM80:71) and the conflict between DG ENTR—backed by industry—and the lead DG SANCO—backed by consumer associations—was particularly visible on three core issues.

First, DG ENTR questioned DG SANCO's approach on principle, demanding that the internal market rather than consumer health should be the primary focus given the chosen legal basis of Art. 95 TEC (now Article 114 TFEU, COM115:63, 95). The retail industry argued that the approach violated the better regulation strategy of the Commission (EuroCommerce, 2008, likewise UEAPME 2008), which was politically mastered by DG ENTR Commissioner Verheugen (COM115:63).

Second, the manifold provisions on mandatory food information were even more controversial. In line with consumer representatives that saw them as a means to avoid misleading practices (BEUC 2008), DG SANCO pushed for all-encompassing ingredient information, references to allergenic substances, and, most importantly, a nutrition declaration to be provided mandatorily.[19] They only failed to include a mandatory ingredient list for alcoholic beverages, which was declined due to a lack of political feasibility in an evenly split Council (COM30:77; Directorate-General Health and Consumer Protection 2006: 11; Bounds et al. 2008). Beyond this, DG SANCO wanted to make origin labeling mandatory for all included ingredients. In line with the industry, however, DG ENTR countered that this would result in unsustainable costs and would violate the basic principles of the internal market (COM115:31; CIAA 2008). With regard to the presentation of information, DG SANCO succeed in achieving that this had to be done in a conspicuous place and in an easily visible, clearly legible, and indelible way, including a minimum font size of 3mm. The minimum font size, in particular, provoked industry outrage (AE, February 6, 2008; EuroCommerce 2008: 3–4; UEAPME 2008), but DG SANCO's position was backed by the 2006 consultation revealing that NGOs and member states identified readability as a major issue (Directorate-General Health and Consumer Protection 2006: 11–12). A similar pattern emerged on mandatory nutrition declarations, which had to be on the front of the pack and communicated per 100g/ml. The decision that nutritional values must also be provided as a percentage value of particular reference-population intakes was taken very early on, intentionally disregarding voluntary producer agreements (COM30:65). The 2006 consultation showed that "Member States on the whole tend to favor a mandatory system" (Directorate-General Health and Consumer Protection 2006: 15) and anticipation of Council preferences seems to have taken place on this issue as well.

Third, all these debates were trumped by the conflict on the presentation of the nutrition declaration. DG SANCO justified its position on the basis of the results of the impact assessment, which had attested that front-of-pack declarations have "the greatest potential impact on consumer decisions" (MEMO/08/64: 3). Here, the industry's voluntary "guideline daily amount" (GDA) system, although clearly meant to avoid a mandatory scheme (EuroCommerce 2008), left some imprints on the proposal. With its obligatory "per portion" reference value and the front-of-pack rule, the DG SANCO version was much more strict and consumer friendly (cf. also BEUC 2008: 3; CIAA 2006, 2008). However, it did not go so far as introducing "interpretative elements," such as the traffic-light system enacted in the UK (Bounds et al. 2008). Such elements allow consumers to compare the nutritional value of foods at a glance and thus create competition between healthy and unhealthy foods, which was desired by consumer associations and feared by the industry (AE, February 6, 2008; CIAA 2006; BEUC 2008). Still, DG SANCO took the middle road by allowing national deviations without making such presentations obligatory at the European level, again indicating the influence of split Council preferences on this matter (Directorate-General Health and Consumer Protection 2006: 17).[20] Anticipating reactions in the inter-institutional process also appears to be the driving factor behind the rules on future implementation of labeling rules. The wide usage of comitology procedures covers possibly highly contested issues, for instance the rules on color-coded nutrition declarations or future changes to the list of mandatory information and its presentation (BEUC 2008: 3). As for the additives and the claims proposals, DG SANCO moved these issues into the realm of administrative decision-making so as to help the proposal pass more easily in the Council.

In all of these fundamental conflicts, DG ENTR especially had to concede a series of net losses. Most of these were finally negotiated among the cabinets of Commissioners Verheugen (DG ENTR) and Kyprianoú (DG SANCO; COM115:66), and DG ENTR's political heads were said to have backed down in the expectation of a future return (COM115:72). Commissioner Verheugen, moreover, was much more compliant than his administrators as regards the nutrition declaration because he wanted to avoid a negative political signal to the European public (COM71:53). Likewise, DG AGRI was only partly successful in defending its area of responsibility with regard to wine regulation. DG SANCO only excluded a mandatory ingredient list for alcoholic beverages because of a lack of member state support, but the proposal also stipulates a five-year review clause for this exemption so that the conflict had only been postponed.[21]

Summing up, DG SANCO formed its position along the lines of the proactively shaped agenda to fight obesity, which granted the leeway to go for an interventionist labeling regime. This position was, however, was constrained by the preferences of the member states. The possibility of starting internal coordination only during the later stages and of setting the agenda in line with a publicly backed consumer health focus early on bolstered the assertiveness of DG SANCO. Minor victories by other DGs happened only where they were supported by member state governments.

Taken together, the food-policy initiatives also highlight the process whereby European consumer policy set itself apart from purely market- or competition-based approaches. More than in the other two sub-fields, the public legitimacy for a more consumer-focused line and the concentration of respective competences in one Commission department following the BSE crisis enabled DG SANCO to build stable relationships with external interests on the consumer side, to generate comprehensive internal and external expertise, and to develop an encompassing and principle-based *acquis*. On this basis, DG SANCO was able to exploit its advantages as the lead department to actually expand its own competences where internal opposition needed to be overcome. In the end, turf conflicts with DG ENTR and DG AGRI were much less pronounced compared to the initiatives on consumer rights or product safety, and the only consistently limiting factor were the particular interests of the Council.

NOTES

1. The ECJ judgment on Case C-376/98 *Germany v. Parliament and Council* on tobacco advertising in 1998 also strongly sustained this market-based interpretation of the Commission's consumer-policy competences (Micklitz et al. 2004: 375).
2. Searches for flight "overbooking," "cancellation," and "delays" indeed resulted in 227 hits in the *Financial Times* between 1998 and 2001, of which 13 hits addressed EU competences and five mentioned the specific proposal. Compared to other cases in the sample, this is an enormous media reception.
3. An *FT* search for "consumer credit" covering the drafting period from 1999 to 2002 resulted in 371 hits. Fourteen articles explicitly mention EU activities, while none of the articles makes explicit reference to the upcoming proposal. One prominent topic during the drafting phase (12 of 371 articles) was the implications of the EU's e-commerce directive—developed by DG MARKT and adopted by the Council in May 2000—on the market for online credit cards and related lender restrictions for the purposes of consumer protection.
4. A Dutch CD club tried to enter the German market with a "3 for the price of 1" offer that was prohibited by the German *Rabattgesetz*. In 1998, a reasoned opinion was sent to Germany and, having failed to react, Germany was referred to the ECJ in 1999 (IP/98/653, IP/99/440).
5. With the benefit of hindsight, this strategy paid off: The sales-promotion proposal and DG SANCO's later proposal on unfair commercial practices were both handled in the same parliamentary committee. MEPs preferred SANCO's proposal, adopted it and simply did not discuss the sales promotions any further. MARKT's proposal then fell victim to the 2005 drive for simplification of European legislation (COM79:64, European Commission 2005b). DG MARKT's strategy on commercial communications ended with this single, failed proposal.
6. The liberalizing effect of this decision easily becomes evident if we assume that consumers are distributed along a dimension of rationality in purchase decisions. If the legislator takes the least rational individual in this distribution as the benchmark, then all consumers receive legal protection. If the consumer of average attention is chosen, then it is willingly accepted that the lower half of the distribution of consumers may make inappropriate decisions.
7. For a full list of extant "new approach" directives, including the links to the original legal texts, see <http://www.newapproach.org/Directives/DirectiveList.asp>, last accessed: September 23, 2011).
8. While initial industry opposition on enhanced market surveillance was hardly surprising, DG SANCO fought for the view that strict but common market surveillance rules in Europe eased cross-border market access while protecting the "good guys in the market" against "free-riders." This perspective spilled over to the European industry umbrellas which then united with the consumer side on this issue, which, in turn, supported later negotiations in the Council (COM87:127–35, COM117:19).
9. The judgment may change if the parallel proposal on market surveillance (COM[2007] 37) is taken into account. This aspect states that market surveillance for consumer goods and their health and safety aspects is covered by DG SANCO's GPSD framework. In addition, it clarifies that all information requirements under DG ENTR's new market-surveillance regime should employ the RAPEX infrastructure also handled by DG SANCO (COM27:207). This issue was surrendered at the political level of DG ENTR because "the pressure to bring something out is more important than finding the factually correct solution" and SANCO's cabinet capitalized on this by signaling sustained resistance (COM27:207, COM72:194).

10. Over the period between 2002 and January 2008, an *FT* search on "toys," "safety," and "consumer" (excluding Toyota) resulted in 72 hits, with the bulk of results concentrated in the last half-year.
11. Drafting officials were surprised at how easily the issue went through the Council and suspected that it was simply hidden well. With the benefit of hindsight, this paid off because the EU engaged in close cooperation with Russia, one of the main sources of harmful online content (COM132:172–4). Note that an anticipation of member state positions on all other issues was disqualified as too difficult and irrelevant (COM132:168–72).
12. The complaint in the case of the Netherlands was lodged by Kellogg's, a company selling a range of fortified cereals (C-41/02). In the case of Denmark, the stumbling block was "Ocean Spray Cranberry," a fruit drink enriched with Vitamin C (C-192/01).
13. This would have affected some very commonly used enzymes that cannot be removed for technical reasons. Making them subject to the additives regime would have sharply increased industry costs (Hagenmeyer 2006: 297).
14. Note that this idea would have been consistent with the lessons drawn from the BSE crisis and can be traced back to the 2000 White Book and the 2002 food-safety regulation, which required food regulation to be supported by the most recent scientific data (Hagenmeyer 2006: 301).
15. The *FT* search for "health claims," "functional food," "food marketing," and "food labelling" resulted in 28 hits, of which two explicitly dealt with the Commission's legislative drafting.
16. However, this anticipation of support by external political actors was far from perfect, as the subsequent debates on the proposal in Council and Parliament glaringly revealed (e.g. AE, January 14, 2004).
17. Directive 2000/13/EC on labelling, presentation, and advertising of foodstuffs, and Council Directive 90/496/EEC on nutrition labeling for foodstuffs.
18. Labeling was first mentioned as a consumer policy by Commissioner Byrne in 2003, who, however, explicitly excluded nutrition labeling because both areas were covered by separate directives with varying levels of obligation (AE, February 4, 2003, The European Evaluation Consortium 2003).
19. Following detailed calculation rules, producers must provide the energy value as well as the amounts of fat, saturates, and carbohydrates (the latter with specific reference to sugar and salt), while they are free to present details on fibre, proteins, and certain vitamins and minerals.
20. As their GDA system spread quickly, producers were outraged at this solution, which was again taken up internally by the administrative level of DG ENTR (COM115:39, CIAA 2008; EuroCommerce 2008).
21. DG AGRI had prepared an initiative of its own on wine labeling and did not want to share responsibilities in this sector (COM30:113; Vaqué and Melchor Romero 2008). DG SANCO invested much effort in letting this concession not appear as a weakness. Most notably, it was emphasized that so-called alcopops, a heatedly discussed product group at the time, were covered by DG SANCO's law (cf. MEMO/08/64: 7). In addition, the exclusion of alcoholic beverages came with a revision clause which Commissioner Kyprianoú euphemized by claiming that "[w]e will need to examine this in greater depth in order to define the notion of the obligatory information and determine whether they should be provided under specific legislation applicable to wine or via this new horizontal regulation" (AE, January 31, 2008), while claiming in the *Financial Times* that "alcohol is not a privileged product" (Bounds et al. 2008).

8

Expert Groups in the Commission

Knowledge Providers or Political Device?

Zooming out from the individual case studies, this and the following two chapters focus on specific aspects of internal position formation that help us elucidate the different types of Commission agency at play. Besides the role of public sentiment (Chapter 9) and internal coordination structures (Chapter 10), the Commission's reliance on external expertise is particularly enlightening in this regard.

The use of external expertise is an inherent part of policy-making across both jurisdictions and levels of government (Craft and Howlett 2013). This is particularly true for the EU policy process with the European Commission at its center, which is often depicted as a technocratic body founded on the rule of expertise (Radaelli 1999a). This view is largely a result of the Commission's original design as a non-majoritarian institution legitimized by its problem-solving capacity. Its predecessor, the High Authority, had been initiated by Jean Monnet in the early 1950s as a highly technocratic entity that operated largely on the basis of expertise. Seen from this perspective, the Commission's main mission is to promote supranational policies by providing expert advice untainted by external pressures.

As a rather small institution, however, the Commission has never been self-sufficient. The constant expansion of supranational competences increases the workloads of the individual DGs, and insufficient personnel resources intensify the need for external knowledge (Spence and Stevens 2006). This truth is reflected by the quantity and the diversity of the channels activated by the Commission's DGs in order to acquire external knowledge, as best evidenced by the roughly 1,000 expert groups that assist the Commission in the policy process. Such extensive use of external expertise by the Commission is not necessarily evidence only of independent technocracy at work, however. In fact, the Commission and its DGs are sometimes also availing themselves of political resources when they grant access to external experts. In order to support this claim, this chapter asks the following two questions: To what extent does the Commission use expert groups when drafting European legislation? And in which ways does it actually use these expert groups?

The chapter first defines expert groups and their formal role in the EU policy process. It then provides an overview of the expert group system by exploring its quantitative development over time and its distribution across DGs (Section 8.2). The figures suggest that expert groups are valued beyond their mere provision of factual expertise: we can observe a rise of expert groups over time, but the variation across DG portfolios cannot be fully explained by a functional demand for expertise. Thus, based on the different perceptions of Commission agency between more technocratic and more political rationales (cf. Chapter 2), Section 8.3 develops expectations with regard to the use of expert groups in the process of legislative drafting. In the first case, DGs may involve external experts so as to acquire specialized knowledge they do not have in house. Following a more political rationale, by contrast, expert groups may be used strategically and in anticipation of the inter-institutional decision-making process. Thus, DGs may seek out external expertise in order to legitimize a pre-defined position, or to build a consensus around their proposed policies. This view is confirmed by insights from our case studies and by a comparative overview of the use of expert groups in our 48 cases of legislative drafting. The case studies reveal a strong presence of and a substantial influence exerted by external expertise in the Commission internal drafting process. Although expert groups are most often used for the provision of knowledge, they are also often used strategically with an eye to political considerations. Thus, the analysis of expertise usage in position formation inside the Commission suggests co-existing technocratic and more political types of agency.

8.1 EXPERTS AND THE EU COMMISSION: WHO ARE THE EXPERTS AND WHAT DO WE KNOW ABOUT THEM?

Who are the experts advising the EU Commission? The Commission itself specifies that "[e]xpertise may take many forms, including both scientific knowledge and that derived from practical experience. It may also relate to specific national or regional situations. Expertise may be brought to bear at any stage in the policy-making cycle, although different forms of expertise may be needed at different stages" (Commission of the European Communities 2002b: 6). Because all of these different forms of expertise are vital for policy work, the Commission turns to a broad variety of actors considered "experts" (Radaelli 1999a; Boswell 2008). Individual academics may be best able to provide scientific, research-based knowledge; representatives from industry or other stakeholders may be more able to supply practical knowledge; while officials from national or regional authorities can offer information on specific national or regional situations (also see C[2010]7649).

Our knowledge about the Commission's experts is based on contributions from different strands of literature. Research on the role of expertise and "epistocracy" in the EU administration is a fairly recent, though there is increasing activity (Radaelli 1999a; Moodie and Holst 2013). Studies in the field are rooted in a variety of approaches, ranging from science and technology research (Weiss 1979) to public policy (Sabatier 1978) and international relation studies (Haas 1992). They all highlight the ubiquity and relevance of expertise in the European policy-making process and most specifically regarding the Commission, given its original vocation as a technocratic body and its focus on drafting regulatory as opposed to spending policies. Beyond the Commission's technocratic function, these studies also show that experts and expertise fulfill various roles in the policy process, some of which may be highly political. Those studies that go beyond a mere descriptive classification indicate that the type of usage of experts depends on the characteristics of the policy-making organization and the nature of the policy area. Boswell (2009), for example, shows that politically acting organizations and controversial policy issues are characterized by a strategic, rather than a merely problem-solving or "instrumental" use of expertise.

The literature on EU interest groups emphasizes practitioners, such as economic and societal actors, as providers of expertise to the Commission. Studies on lobbying in the EU describe the Commission as being particularly affected by severe lobbying at the early stages of the policy process (for a literature overview, see Eising 2008). Thus, a large pool of "experts" exists, all ready to offer the Commission their specialized policy advice and all hoping to influence European legislation. The EU interest intermediation system in which these experts operate has been described as pluralist, given the low degree of institutionalized consultation structures (Streeck and Schmitter 1991), or as elite-pluralist and driven by big industry (Coen 1997). Thus, we would expect powerful economic interests to be important providers of expertise to the Commission. Other studies have articulated the difficulty of describing the macro pattern of the EU interest intermediation system per se. Instead, they emphasize differences across policy sectors (Falkner 2000) and Commission DGs (Coen and Katsaitis 2013), and describe EU interest intermediation as being defined by sectoral policy networks (Kohler-Koch 1999), suggesting the existence of a sectoral logic for the experts' involvement. At the micro level, the relationship between EU institutions and interest groups has been described as being based on resource dependencies (Bouwen 2002): when stakeholders lobby for influence, access is granted depending on whether the type of information they can provide is simultaneously required by the EU institutions. Consequently, a broad variety of economic and societal actors participate in expert committees that advise the EU institutions and, in turn, are granted access to policy-making (Broscheid and Coen 2007). In sum, the lobbying literature suggests that the Commission's relationship with providers of expertise is determined by resource dependencies and is either elite-driven or varies across policy domains.

Lastly, a growing body of literature explicitly investigates EU expert committees. A vast variety and number of so-called "committees" exists. First, there are the formal "grand" committees, such as the Social and Economic Committee or the Committee of the Regions. These institutionalized consultative bodies are tasked with interest representation and are formally consulted by the Council and the Parliament. Second, the working groups of the Council and the Parliamentary committees are sectorally organized bodies responsible for the preparatory work of the formal legislators. Finally, about 300 comitology committees advise the Commission and the Council in the policy-implementation phase, while about 1,000 expert groups assist the Commission in policy-making. While comitology committees have a formal say at the stage of policy implementation, expert groups provide non-binding advice to the Commission throughout the policy process, from policy initiation to the monitoring of implementation. So far comitology committees have received far more attention from scholars than Commission expert groups (e.g. Joerges and Vos 1999). This seems surprising, given their abundance and the fact that they are involved in the crucial phase of legislative drafting—the stage at which positions are formed inside the Commission. For our endeavor to study power and conflict within the Commission, these expert groups are of utmost importance.

8.2 A QUANTITATIVE OVERVIEW OF COMMISSION EXPERT GROUPS

European Commission expert groups are "consultative entities set up by the Commission or its services, comprising at least six public and/or private-sector members, which are foreseen to meet more than once" (European Commission 2010a: 3). In line with the Commission's general definition of expertise provided in the previous paragraphs, expert groups comprise a broad variety of actors, ranging from representatives of an institution such as a public authority (national, regional, or local), to civil society or industry, and to independent individuals. As Robert (2012: 430) notes, this "makes it possible for anyone whose skills can be used for the building of public action to be considered as an expert." In the Commission, expert groups are created and managed at the level of the Commission's DGs and are therefore organized along the lines of the DGs' sectoral portfolios. Most often they are created de-centrally—by the DGs or by the respective units themselves with the managerial assistance of the Secretariat-General ("informal groups"). However, they may also be created "formally" by means of a legal act, such as a Commission decision. Expert groups may further be created for a limited time period or as permanent groups. The shape, size, and composition of Commission expert groups vary considerably. Notwithstanding their diversity, an important common characteristic of these groups is that they only give advice to the Commission and do not have any formal veto powers in the policy-making process.

Since 2005, the Secretariat-General monitors an online "expert group register," which provides information to the public on current expert groups.[1] Based on this data, the following two sections discuss the distribution of Commission expert groups over time and policy portfolios. This reveals the strong quantitative presence of these committees in EU policy-making, both in general and in the three policy areas that lie at the focus of our book.

8.2.1 Development over Time

Commission expert groups have existed since the founding days of the European Community. As one Commission official commented: "Expert groups existed from day one; I think God created Eva and Adam, and then an expert group" (COM136:166). The vast number of Commission expert groups is a remarkable characteristic of this consultation system, as shown by Figure 8.1, which portrays the evolution of the number of expert groups over the past 25 years.

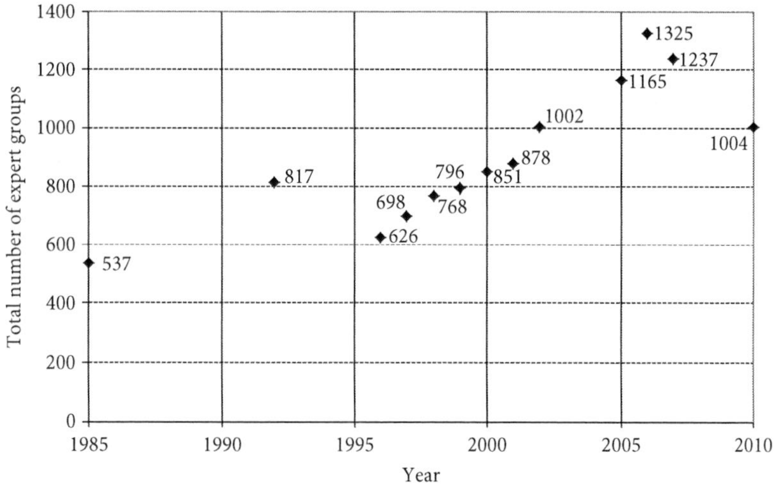

Fig. 8.1. Total number of expert groups over time (1985–2010)

Source: Years 1985, 1992, 1996–99 and 2000–02 based on Brochhagen (2010: 30); 2005 from Broscheid and Coen (2007); 2007 from Gornitzka and Sverdrup (2008); 2010 from authors' data based on the Commission register of expert groups, compiled in February 2010.

Apart from an outlier in 1992, the data reveals a continuous increase in the number of expert groups over time, with a peak in 2006 and a subsequent decline. Data reliability limitations indicate a need for caution when comparing the numbers over time, however. Most importantly, the definition of an "expert group" has changed over the years. It was only in 2005, together with the establishment of the expert group register, that new horizontal guidelines finally laid down a proper definition for Commission expert groups (a definition that was changed again in 2011, C[2010]7649). Earlier estimates therefore largely rely on the DGs' individual assessments and the European Commission's annual budgetary reports.[2] Nonetheless, Figure 8.1 shows that the introduction of the new reporting system in 2005 did not cause a sudden break in the data line, suggesting a certain degree of comparability over time.

The strong decrease of 23 percent in the number of expert groups from 2006 onward is also most likely related to internal reforms. In 2007, the Commission's Secretariat-General launched an internal evaluation with the aim of increasing data reliability and transparency. This included cleaning the register of non-active groups that had existed only on paper.[3] The report suggests that the SG had a sincere interest in trimming down the total number of groups with a view to reducing the "organizational slack" (March and Olsen 1989) that had accumulated over time.

Nonetheless, even taking these changes into account, the number of expert groups almost doubled between 1985 and 2010. The rise in expert groups over time can be explained by assuming that the Commission operates along a technocratic type of agency and has used the groups for problem-solving purposes. Expanding supranational competences and EU regulatory output (Kurpas et al. 2008), which have also increased the Commission's workload, should indeed have resulted in an increased demand for external knowledge and, thus, a need for the Commission to establish more expert groups.

If this assumption holds true, however, we should also be able to observe more expert groups in those policy areas where the EU has an exclusive supranational competence to legislate. And yet the existing studies show that most expert groups can be found in policy areas with mixed competences, thus refuting the hypothesis that more EU-level competences leads to more EU-level expert groups (Gornitzka and Sverdrup 2008).

In contrast, a rise in expert groups over time could also be explained from the viewpoint of a politically acting Commission demanding legitimacy and consensus. As EU competences have expanded, the public has become more aware of the practical consequences of decisions taken at supranational level and therefore increasingly contests them (Tsakatika 2005; see also Chapter 9). Increased controversy around EU decisions renders the policy process more political as the Commission is no longer able to fly under the radar as a technocratic actor, but instead must appropriately justify its proposals and actively build consensus among stakeholders. Therefore, the increase in expert groups over time could also be explained by their use by the Commission to substantiate policy choices and build consensus.

It should further be noted that the internal evaluation already mentioned was a response to an increased politicization of policy advice as the EU itself and its institutions became increasingly politicized (Tsakatika 2005). This trend has also concerned the more than 1,000 expert groups operating "in the dark" and has forced the Commission to adopt regulatory measures that enhance transparency, with regard to its own internal evaluation asd well (ALTER-EU 2009).

Overall, the quantitative development of expert groups over time is indicative of an externalization of policy advice in the Commission, which may be evidence both of an increased demand for technical and political resources provided by expert groups and of the accumulation of some organizational slack over time. The recent decrease, in turn, seems to be a response to a rising contestation of policy advice in the EU, underlining the political aspects of the advisory work by expert groups.

8.2.2 Distribution across DGs

A further distinct characteristic of the Commission's expert-group system observed so far is its sectoral differentiation across the Commission's DGs, as can be seen in Figure 8.2, which displays the distribution of expert groups across DGs for the 1,014 listed in the Commission's registry in February 2010.

Figure 8.2 reveals a strong variation in the extent to which the DGs make use of expert groups. The number of expert groups per DG ranges from 139 groups associated with the DG for taxation and customs (DG TAXUD) to two groups managed by the DG for translation (DG DGT). While 24 committees is the average number per DG, there is no majority of DGs clustered around this value: around half of the DGs have 30 groups or more, while half of them have less than 20 groups (the average is based on all the Commission's 42 services and DGs, of which ten DGs had zero committees and five had one group).

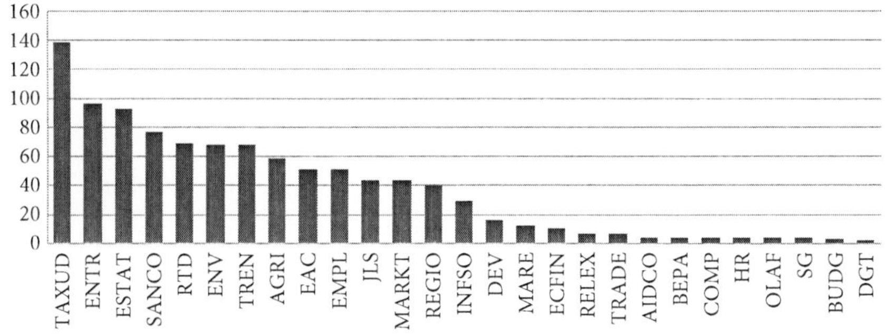

Fig. 8.2. Distribution of expert groups across DGs

Source: Data compiled in February 2010 from the Commission register of expert groups. *N*=1,014 experts groups; only DGs with more than one expert group displayed.

In particular, we observe a difference between public-policy DGs and the Commission's internal administrative services. All the DGs with more than ten committees are public-policy DGs. Only EUROSTAT stands out with 93 groups, which mostly serve to coordinate the development and application of statistical indicators across member states. The overall high concentration of expert groups on public policies suggests that the Commission predominantly uses expert groups for policy-making and not for administrative or procedural tasks (also see Gornitzka and Sverdrup 2008). As regards the main DGs of concern to our analysis, we can see that they are all assembled in the top and middle of Figure 8.2: DG ENTR has 97 expert groups, followed by 77 for DG SANCO, 69 for DG RTD, 51 for DG EMPL, 43 for DG MARKT, and 29 for DG INFSO.

If the Commission is perceived as a technocratic actor that uses its expert groups in a problem-solving way, both regulatory policy-making and insufficient administrative capacities can be expected to increase the demand for external expertise. However, existing research has shown that the nature of a DG's policy portfolio—regulatory versus distributive—does not significantly influence its number of expert groups. To a certain extent, this may be related to the methodological difficulties of coding DG portfolios as either "regulatory" or "distributive" (Gornitzka and Sverdrup 2008). It may also indicate that the hypothesis does not hold true, supporting our argument that expert groups are not only used for the provision of regulatory expertise but also for political reasons, or that distributive measures also demand some form of external expertise (such as "political information," see Coen and Katsaitis 2013). Likewise, a DG's personnel numbers impact in a different way on the number of expert groups than one might have expected—DGs with high staff numbers actually retain more expert groups than those with few personnel. This may be explained by the fact that a DG needs sufficient internal "absorption" capacity to manage its committees: the more personnel, the more expert groups can be handled (similarly for increased capacity to absorb information, see Gornitzka and Sverdrup 2008; Coen and Katsaitis 2013).

Summing up, the distribution across DGs cannot tell us whether the European Commission uses expert groups as a technocratic or a political resource. These mixed findings are consistent with the more grounded, aggregate insights from our case studies (see Chapters 11–12 and the following discussion). Apart from the formal characteristics of DGs, their different policy goals and their traditions of using advice both impact on the extent to which expert groups are used, and these are clearly difficult variables to measure quantitatively (also see Ban 2013).

8.3 THE EU COMMISSION'S USE OF EXPERT GROUPS IN POSITION FORMATION

8.3.1 What to Expect?

So far, a dominant pattern in the literature on interest groups and expertise has been the analysts' focus on the "supply side" of lobbying or advice (Mahoney 2004). Research on EU Commission expert groups has concentrated on processes within committees, largely neglecting to analyze the involvement of Commission expert groups in the policy-making process. The interest of the policy-makers—the demand side—has received far less attention. Hence, knowledge of the Commission's motivation to involve and use external expertise remains limited (however, for the involvement of lobbyists, see Bouwen 2002). This research bias further reinforces this volume's aim to focus on the Commission's needs and its internal dynamics of position formation that lead to certain actors being heard or not heard in European legislation. To understand the Commission's use of expert groups, resource-dependency theory, a strand of organization theory, is applied (Pfeffer and Salancik [1978] 2003). This approach emphasizes that "[t]o understand organizational behavior, one must understand how the organization relates to other social actors in its environment" (Pfeffer and Salancik [1978] 2003: 257). It closely links an organization's internal perspective with external actors and influences and thus examines the interface at which expert groups are located. Organizations need resources to survive and when they are not internally self-sufficient, they obtain these resources from their environment. They need to interact with those parts of their environment that control the resources required, which leads to interdependencies with the actors concerned. In their "struggle for autonomy and discretion" (Pfeffer and Salancik [1978] 2003: 257), organizations actively try to manipulate their interactions and their environment in order to minimize their dependence and achieve autonomy.

One strategy used by organizations to manage environmental interdependence is to establish collective links with elements of their environment and to use these structures to access resources and avert environmental control: "the practice of interlocking boards provides opportunity to evolve a stable collective structure of coordinated action through which interdependence is managed" (Pfeffer and Salancik [1978] 2003: 161). Thus, expert groups can be viewed as a Commission strategy to manage its dependencies and acquire the resources needed to survive. We combine the demand for specific resources with a view to drafting a concrete piece of legislation with insights from knowledge utilization literature. This line of research distinguishes between various sorts and functions of information and scientific knowledge (Weiss 1979). Most importantly, beyond the "classical" problem-solving usage of knowledge to broaden a policy-maker's own information base, expertise may also be used symbolically or strategically (also see Feldman and March 1981). Thus, policy-makers do not only use external advisers to form their own positions, but also to demonstrate support for or the legitimacy of their positions. Assembling experts in institutionalized frameworks such as committees may also serve the purpose of providing negotiation arenas for consensus-building among relevant players (e.g. Siefken 2007).

The different assumptions about the type of Commission agency introduced in Chapter 2 suggest various resources that the Commission and its internal actors may require and that accordingly lead to different uses of expert groups in legislative drafting. Following a technocratic type of agency, Commission DGs may use experts in a *problem-solving* way to acquire the necessary technical expertise to fulfill their bureaucratic drafting tasks. In addition, motivated by more political considerations in the competence- or policy-seeking models of Commission agency, DGs may find two other types of resources essential. First, Commission DGs may desire to generate consensual positions for their legislative proposals and therefore use expert groups for *political consensus-building*, particularly in anticipating a potentially difficult inter-institutional decision-making process. Second, external support for a DG's position may be deemed a necessary resource, which then results in a *politically substantiating* usage. In all three cases, the resource that external experts receive in exchange is access to the policy-making process with the prospect of exerting influence.

Problem-solving usage: The use of experts for the acquisition of technical expertise and information is particularly highlighted by the Commission itself (COM[2002]71). Social-science studies also emphasize the importance of experts in addressing the "functional demands of an ever-expanding European Community for technical information and expertise" (Vos 1999a: 19). This assumption is based on a functional view of actors guided by a problem-solving rationale. If actors are oriented towards the aim of solving problems by maximizing efficiency in the sense of Pareto optimality, this brings to the fore the command of expertise on the problem to be solved (Mitrany 1941/1975).

In line with the distinction drawn in Chapter 2, this type of usage is consistent with the Commission's history and mandate as a highly technocratic body and is stressed by scholars who emphasize the Commission's regulatory approach to public policy intervention. As most prominently asserted by Majone (1996), the EU can be described as a prototype of a "regulatory state." Compared to national governments, whose traditional instruments of intervention are financial measures, the EU has hardly any budgetary competences and its core areas of activity are regulatory measures. Thus, economic and social regulation is the primary instrument of policy intervention in the EU regulatory system. In the words of Radaelli (1999a: 37), "knowledge, rather than budget, is the critical resource in regulatory policy making, and the Commission uses this resource extensively."

However, the Commission's internal capacities are not sufficient to fulfill these tasks. Today's world has become ever more complex, which increases the demands on knowledge to find appropriate answers to problems. This is particularly true for EU policy, which has to find solutions to complex predicaments of trans- or supranational scope. The geographic scope of EU regulation is also challenging for the Commission as an initiator of legislation from another perspective: as a supranational institution, it is too distant from the domestic settings and from the actual impacts of its policy interventions to be sufficiently informed about the practical needs and situations in its 27 member states. This is amplified, moreover, by the organization of the European governance system. Unlike many federal governance systems, the European executive does not have "dependencies" at sub-federal or regional level that implement European law directly. Instead, the Commission has to rely on national administrations to implement EU law, and therefore depends on external information (Scharpf 1988).

These context conditions have produced a serious task overload for the Commission, which disposes of relatively little manpower compared to its far-reaching legal responsibilities (Spence and Stevens 2006). Staffed with less than 23,000 employees in 2010,[4] the institution's personnel resources stand in stark contrast to a pronounced reliance on specialist knowledge to fulfill its tasks properly. Commission officials thus have to depend on external sources of technical and scientific knowledge and of practical and legal information. The problem-solving usage of expert groups by the Commission for legislative drafting is therefore a relevant factor when it is assumed that Commission DGs follow a technocratic type of agency. Expert groups represent a relatively costless source of information and can be seen as an instrument that compensates for the Commission's internal lack of expertise when addressing policy problems.

Political consensus-building usage: In between technocratic and more political models of Commission position formation, convening experts in institutional settings—such as in expert groups—may also represent a valuable means to build consensus among relevant actors in EU decision-making (Joerges and Neyer 1997a; Christiansen and Kirchner 2000: 9). In this sense, expert groups are not seen as arenas for expertise, but as arenas for representation, "transforming experts into agents of compromise" (Robert 2012: 433).

The usage of expert groups for political consensus-building is particularly relevant for the European Commission in its role as an "honest broker" in inter-institutional decision-making, which is located "at the heart" of the European multi-level setting (Nugent 2000b). Given the EU's complex institutional structure of shared power among the decision-making institutions, the Commission has to constantly engage in consensus-building among a diversity of views and interests.

Moreover, the DGs' rate of success is often assessed in terms of how "smoothly" their initiatives go through the complex policy process, from agenda-setting to implementation. Accordingly, the favored policy solutions tend to be those that have a strong chance of being adopted by member states and stakeholders.[5] The Commission therefore aims in its expert groups to coordinate the views of the participants in the policy process. Although expert groups have no formal decision-making powers and their agreements are non-binding, they can foster compromises and work out consensual positions among a diversity of views within a specific policy community. In the EU, in particular, comitology committees have been described as arenas for "supranational deliberation" (Joerges and Neyer 1997a) or as inter- or trans-governmental negotiation forums acting under the 'shadow of hierarchy' of formal decision-makers (Scharpf 1997).

Engaging multiple stakeholders in committees can thus contribute to arriving at politically feasible and consensual decisions. Game theory suggests that expert committees are a way for Europe to overcome its "joint-decision trap" and to pursue "positive action" by allowing for side payments or package deals within these groups (Scharpf 1999: 74–5). They do so by reducing transaction costs and by allowing for repeated interaction, facilitating cooperative behavior. Organization theory also highlights the institutional framework of expert forums, which allow relevant actors of a policy community to meet, exchange (potentially contradicting) views, and reach agreements (March and Olsen 1995: 30). By establishing arenas for interaction, policy-makers can foster "consensus, compromise and cooperation" (Zegart 2004: 376). Such an institutional context facilitates negotiations based on communication and trust, and helps to accommodate diverging interests and to "intentionally produce collective outcomes *despite* diverging interests of their members" (Börzel 1997: 5).

Politically substantiating usage: However, when we consider the Commission to be a politically motivated actor that strives for either increased competences or specific normative goals, the DGs may not only use expert groups to design efficient legislative proposals, but also to substantiate and politically defend their positions against other actors. This consideration draws on the view that organizations not only use information and expertise for problem-solving purposes, but also to substantiate pre-defined positions: expertise "becomes ammunition for the side that finds its conclusions congenial and supportive" (Weiss 1979: 429). Such a strategic usage refers to instances in which the Commission involves expert groups to signal expert support for preferred policy solutions (Boswell 2009).[6]

The EU's institutional structure provides good grounds for the Commission to draw on expert groups for a substantiating usage. The main reason is its fragile basis of legitimacy. Unlike national governments, the European Commission is not headed by elected representatives and cannot justify its legislative initiatives as being linked to the electorate's will; neither are its actions part of a democratically mandated program. The Commission therefore needs to defend its positions and their external validity on alternative grounds. One possible option for the Commission to lend credibility to its positions is to present them as "rational" by demonstrating that they are supported by the "neutral and unbiased" view of distinguished experts (Boswell 2009). In contrast to the problem-solving usage, expert groups are not used by the Commission in this case to form a policy solution, but to substantiate its otherwise defined preferred position vis-à-vis other political actors. Accordingly, expert groups are assumed to have less impact on the content of the Commission's position and final policy proposal. A politically substantiating usage therefore denotes a situation in which the Commission makes reference to expert groups in a policy proposal for strategic purposes. It uses experts to signal the legitimacy of a proposal by, for example, mentioning the consultation and position of high-ranking experts in a proposal's explanatory memorandum.

While a problem-solving usage implies that DGs do not have a pre-defined position and are open to information coming from the outside, a politically substantiating usage assumes that DGs have a pre-defined position that they seek to substantiate with the views of experts. A consensus-building usage, in turn, is located between these two extreme poles—it may imply that a DG imposes its own position on other actors or, alternatively, take place in an open negotiation process. In cases where a DG is uncertain about its preferred policy solution, consensus-building may also be conducted as a more open-ended process of mutual learning. Whether the act of consensus-building is defined by bargaining over pre-defined positions or by open arguing (Elgström and Jönsson 2000) depends on whether a DG is following its own, competence- or policy-seeking agenda or whether it approaches policies more open-mindedly along a technocratic type of agency.

8.3.2 Case Study Insights

For each of our 48 cases, we coded whether expert groups were involved and how they were used—that is, whether the responsible DG used the group for problem-solving (acquiring specialist knowledge), in a politically substantiating way (demonstrating expert approval), or to build consensual positions among the affected parties. As for the other factors in this book, the influence of the expert groups was ascertained via counterfactual reasoning and inter-subjective review (cf. Chapter 3). Note that we did not treat the three analytical types of expert group usage as being exclusive in each empirical case of legislative drafting. This is because a DG could acquire several resources from the same expert group when preparing one piece of legislation; alternatively, a DG might have chosen to involve several expert groups in one drafting process and use them in distinct ways, which also amounts to several different usages in a single case.

A *problem-solving* usage was identified where a DG's legislative position could be directly traced to the suggestions of an expert group in the empirical material (either interview partners explicitly stated so or it was reflected in documents, such as expert-group reports, CIS-Net documents or internal drafts).[7] A *substantiating* usage was coded where an expert group's position was mentioned as being supportive of that of the DG, for instance in the proposal's explanatory memorandum or by interview partners. For example, one member of DG Research's European Research Advisory Board (EURAB), which was involved in the preparation of the 7th Framework Programme (COM[2005] 119–1), mentioned the group as important for DG Research "always only to be able to refer to it, to be able to cite it" (EXP7:31), such as to "defend its position in Parliament" (EXP7:51). A *consensus-building* usage refers to instances in which a DG used an expert group to build a consensus among its participants—either to soften up resistance towards a pre-defined policy goal or to find a common ground among the variety of existing views. The empirical identification relied mainly on interview information. One example of a quote indicating a consensus-building usage is given by an Commission official who qualified an involved expert group as having been a valuable instrument for "bringing the member states together onto a common way of operating" (COM17:99).

Along these lines, our cases have shown that expert groups were used most often for *problem-solving* when a DG had to elaborate the technical details of a proposal and did not have sufficient in-house expertise. One example is the proposal for a directive on food supplements prepared by the at that time newly created DG SANCO (Chapter 7.4.1). Following a precautionary stance on this particular aspect of the proposal, the DG had decided to allow only a positive, exclusive list of vitamins and minerals rather than drafting a negative list of prohibited substances. However, DG SANCO did not have sufficient technical in-house expertise to develop such a positive list. Given this context of technical uncertainty, DG SANCO consulted its Scientific Committee on Food (SCF), a prestigious expert group composed of distinguished independent scientific experts from diverse fields, ranging from nutrition to food technology to bio-technology (COM30:33, COM88:186), and ultimately wrote their suggestions directly into the final proposal (COM88:186, COM[2002]222: 2).[8]

Political consensus-building in expert groups was observed particularly in policy-making at the intersection of social and internal market policies. A strong heterogeneity of welfare systems across the EU member states made regulation in this domain highly conflict-laden and dominated by the legacies of contrasting national paradigms. One example is DG MARKT's proposal for a directive on the recognition of professional qualifications (Chapter 5.4.1), which aims at facilitating the free movement of (mostly self-employed) workers by granting professionals from other member states access and the same rights as nationally qualified professionals. In this proposal, the bulk of professions is regulated by the so-called General System approach, where professionals have to apply for recognition in the host country on an individual basis. The drafting of this act was strongly influenced by the implementation difficulties of the General System, as reflected by non-transparent, unpredictable, and idiosyncratic assessments. The resulting uncertainty with regard to the current legal situation rendered some member states, such as France, supportive of DG MARKT's push for a simplified new legal framework, while others, such as Germany, were "strongly opposed to any change" (COM17:105). In this context of uncertainty and conflict, the lead DG consulted an expert group composed of member state specialists who were assisting in the implementation of the existing General System directives. However, for the drafting of the new proposal, they not only presented DG MARKT with the positions of the relevant actors from these member states and provided knowledge and expertise, but also served as a consensus-building arena. As one official involved remembered, DG MARKT was "trying" to build a consensus among the member state representatives in the expert group and saw this as valuable in "bringing the member states together onto a common way of operating the system" (COM17:99). This example shows how the Commission used an expert group as a consensus-building forum "to find a kind of a common playground" (COM76:36) for a new piece of legislation. This case illustrates the way an expert group can be used politically in a conflict-laden policy context, though without the DG pursuing a pre-defined position.

A *politically substantiating usage* occurred disproportionally in research and innovation policy, a predominantly distributive policy area. Accordingly, policy-making here was frequently dominated by political bargaining about the distribution of the Community budget. The DGs involved often required external support for their budget requests in anticipation of controversial discussions with the EU Council and Parliament (Metz forthcoming). However, expert groups were also used politically for regulatory acts. One example is DG RTD's proposal for a Regulation on European Research Infrastructures (ERI, Chapter 6.4.3), aimed at establishing a European legal framework for pan-European research infrastructures. This proposal was both technically complex and controversial in that it required finding ways to develop a new European legal framework that would not interfere with member state law. One of the main items of controversy was DG RTD's aim to grant ERIs a value-added tax (VAT) exemption at national level, based on a research article of the Treaty. In the lengthy process of developing this proposal, the lead DG involved several expert groups, both to obtain legal expertise and to substantiate its preferred solution internally against DG TAXUD and externally against national finance ministers (see Chapter 6.4.3, COM1:60, 86). One expert group used to substantiate the DG's position was a small "sounding board" composed of seven independent experts from national ministries, national research institutes, and lawyers, which was set up towards the very end of the drafting process (COM1:60). Although formally tasked with advising the Commission "on the general objectives of the intended framework regulation and its content, on the preparation of a stakeholder workshop and on the Impact Assessment" (Commission of the European Communities 2008c: para. 2.4), for DG RTD this body was in practice far more important for political purposes. The expert group was needed to show that "it was not the Commission, who just did it [i.e. the ERI proposal]" (COM1:60), but that it "'was done by lawyers who do not work at the Commission . . . , that these were independent people" (COM1:67). This case clearly shows that in a context of conflicting interests, the Commission may also use expert groups to substantiate a preferred political position.

8.3.3 The Aggregate View: A Multi-model Usage of Expert Groups

Turning to the aggregate results, Figure 8.3 presents the frequency of the three expert group usages in our sample of 48 legislative drafting processes. All in all, expert groups were involved in 33 of the 48 cases of legislative drafting. In many of

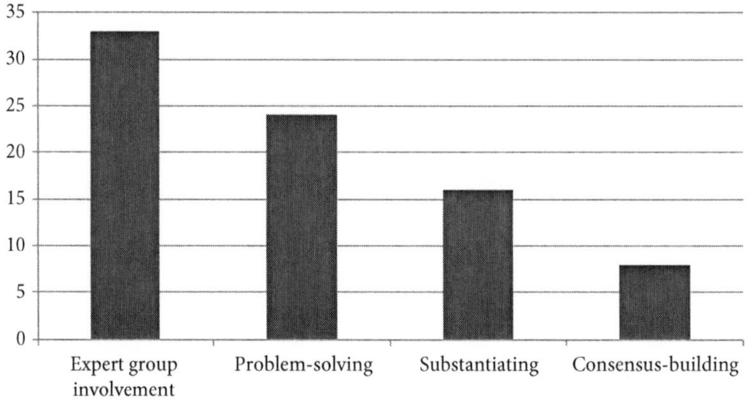

Fig. 8.3. Types of expert-group usage in the European Commission. Absolute number of cases with expert-group involvement and particular usages in our sample of 48 drafting processes

these cases, not just one, but several groups were consulted for the particular legislative proposal—we can, in fact, observe a "multi-model use" of expert groups in the Commission.

The problem-solving usage occurred most often (in 24 cases), followed by a substantiating usage in 16 cases. A consensus-building usage occurred in only 8 cases, in other words, in 25 percent of the cases of expert group involvement. This may seem surprising when we consider that the most important addressees for consensus-building in anticipation of inter-institutional decision-making should be member state representatives, who largely dominate expert groups (Gornitzka and Sverdrup 2008). However, our case studies show that consensus-building is equally provided by other instruments, such as by comitology committees.

The case studies did not reveal any clear patterns regarding the types of usage that most often go hand in hand, such as a substantiating and consensus-building, which both assume a more political agency on the part of the respective DG. This was partly related to the fact that a single legislative proposal could contain both technical details demanding specialists' knowledge and controversial or salient issues requiring external support and the consensual position of member states, whose consent is needed in the inter-institutional process. Thus, the way that expert groups were used was often related to the context of the issue in question.

For example, during the preparation of two salient and controversial, but also technical directives on public procurement proposed in 2000 (see Chapter 5.3.1), DG MARKT involved two expert groups on public contracts and public procurement (COM16:176, 57). The advisory committee on public contracts was composed of member state representatives, while the advisory committee on the opening of public procurement was a mixed stakeholder group including academics and professional associations. In both groups, the emphasis lay on including bureaucrats and stakeholders with long-standing expertise in public procurement at national level. For both directives, DG MARKT used these two groups for the development of technical indicators, as well as to build a consensus and to substantiate its position on controversial points:

> We had discussions in the expert groups, how can we develop indicators, in order to have some statistics, how can we deal with it.... There was of course some overlap, using this expert group to help our position in the Council. So it was not isolated, you could obviously not isolate the text in the expert groups. (COM22:136)

This insight supports the expectation raised in the analytical framework, where we suggested that the nature of the position-formation process depends on policy uncertainty and salience (Chapter 2.3). We had expected issue uncertainty (defined as ambiguous cause–effect relationships that would make it difficult for actors to anticipate or predict the policy outcomes of certain choices) to lead to more technocratically oriented policy-making based on expertise. Accordingly, this would resonate well with a problem-solving usage of expert groups. Issue salience (understood as the contemporaneous public attention or public visibility attached to a proposal), in turn, should evoke a more politically oriented drafting process which would also make a politically substantiating and consensus-building usage of expert groups more likely.

Indeed, with regard to the usage of expert groups, an aggregate view of the latter factor supports this expectation: a substantiating usage was found significantly more often whenever proposals were highly salient, which led to politicized policy-making dominated by power struggles between opposing actors.[9] In such situations, DGs appeared to require the supportive opinion of an expert group more often. A consensus-building usage, in turn, did not appear more often in salient cases or in politicized policy processes. As suspected above, this indicates that using expert groups for consensus-building may be a valuable strategy for those DGs operating along a more technocratic type of agency as well as for those pursuing more political motivations.

With regard to issue uncertainty, our case studies indicate that a distinct, though related issue characteristic was more relevant in explaining the Commission's use of expert groups for technical problem-solving: the technical complexity of a policy issue. This characteristic refers to the extent to which a policy problem is difficult to analyze, to understand, or to resolve. A technically complex issue "raises factual questions that cannot be answered by generalists or laypersons . . . [and therefore] specialized knowledge and training are needed if certain factual questions are to be satisfactorily addressed" (Gormley 1986: 598). Technical complexity differs from issue uncertainty in that in the former case the involvement of specialized experts should always help to find a policy solution. In the case of high uncertainty, by contrast, even specialized experts are not able to indicate the appropriate solution within a short period of time. The relevance of technical complexity rather than uncertainty to explain the Commission's use of expertise in a problem-solving mode can also be observed at the aggregate level of drafting processes. Whereas DGs faced with highly uncertain dossiers did not use expert groups for problem-solving purposes significantly more often, this was actually the case for technically complex issues.[10] Thus, in cases where a Commission DG is confronted with highly complex policy issues, the demand for external expertise is high. In cases of high uncertainty, however, expertise may not always provide an unambiguous answer to a policy problem and decision-makers may turn to resources other than expertise.

When taking such an aggregate perspective, it is important to re-emphasize, however, that the "multi-model usage" of expert groups we identified within single drafting processes showed that technocratic and political policy-making could occur simultaneously in the Commission. This, again, is related to the fact that legislative proposals often contained both technical details and salient or controversial issues, thus evoking different actor rationales and different expert group usages in parallel within the Commission.

8.4 CONCLUSION

The central message derived from the empirical investigation is that Commission officials draw heavily on expert groups when preparing legislation. As an auxiliary administration surrounding the Commission, expert groups form a stable institutional structure that links the Commission to the "outside world." And as our 48 cases of EU legislative drafting show, the Commission most often uses expert groups to improve its drafts by eliciting external knowledge it does not control itself. In two thirds of our cases (33 of 48), expert groups were involved in the drafting process, and in half of our cases (24 of 48), we could trace the influence of expert groups on the legislative position taken by the responsible Commission DGs. By employing a broad definition of "experts," the Commission's DGs thus provide access and influence to a broad variety of actors—ranging from national administrations to societal interests and individual academics. However, as it is possible for a particular expert group to provide several resources simultaneously, we can observe a multi-model usage of expert groups. This is found in relation to many policy proposals that include both paragraphs based on the input of an expert group and paragraphs that present the Commission's position with the expert group being used to support or to build consensus around it.

In a context of mutual resource dependencies between the Commission and its organizational environment, expert groups therefore help not only to acquire scientific and practical expertise, but also to substantiate political choices or to build consensus in the wider context of EU decision-making. More generally, we can observe that a political usage of expert groups plays a vital part in the policy process by linking legislative drafting inside the Commission to the subsequent inter-institutional negotiations.

NOTES

1. The online register of expert groups can be found at <http://ec.europa.eu/transparency/regexpert> (last accessed July 16, 2013). It has been subject to considerable public debate (e.g. ALTER-EU 2009). Since the adoption of new horizontal guidelines in January 2011 (C[2010]7649), groups that have been created by a legal act other than a Commission decision are classified as "other similar entities." Nonetheless, they are still included in the expert group register.
2. From 1998 to 2002, the indicators for experts in the EU political system were based on figures related to the reimbursement of administrative expenses (Metz forthcoming).
3. See European Commission/Secretariat-General (2009), Note to Directors-General and Heads of Services—Subject: Evaluation report on the horizontal rules within the framework for Commission expert groups, *SEC(2009)486, SG.E.1/AM/ptp D(2009)2644*, Brussels, April 2, 2009.
4. See European Commission/Directorate-General for Personnel and Administration (2010), Statistical Bulletin of Commission Staff 02/2010, Brussels.
5. This is indicated by one Research Cabinet member who, when asked about the role of the anticipation of the inter-institutional process, described the Commission's dilemma as follows: "With everything we do in the Commission, that is how we have to work, because there is a difference between what is politically desirable and what is politically feasible. Every time we adopt a proposal we have to make this judgement: How far do we go beyond the feasibility? Knowing that if you come with proposals that are feasible, they are not very attractive. But when you come with proposals that are too far away from what is feasible but desirable—politically desirable for the Commission—then they are not acceptable. So you always have to find the balance. But very often we anticipate . . . what is feasible and what is likely to be decided in the end by Council and Parliament" (COM102:300).

6. The definition of a politically substantiating use employed here also comprises what is referred to as a "symbolic" (Feldman and March 1981) or "tactical" (Weiss 1979) use of expertise. While the former refers to usages of expertise that bestow the policy *content* with legitimacy, the latter denotes cases where expertise is used to symbolize the legitimacy of decision-making *processes* or *organizations* as such. As our study explicitly links the content of policies to the process dimension and sets the use of expert groups in relation to both aspects, a symbolic use is subsumed under the politically substantiating use.
7. However, a politically acting DG also anticipates the views of other political actors and takes them into account when forming its own position. While DGs following this logic will try to outmaneuver the opposition—by using expert groups, for example—this does not mean that their positions are free of external influence. Nonetheless, the point made here is that direct influence from external experts can only be traced if these are used in a problem-solving way.
8. It should be noted that in 2003 the SCF was transformed into a regulatory agency, the European Food Safety Authority (EFSA), together with a number of other expert groups.
9. An independent group t-test was conducted to assess how much salient and non-salient cases differ with regard to a substantiating usage. The probability that salient cases and a substantiating usage co-occur is at the $p < 0.01$ level.
10. Technical complexity was coded dichotomously and relied on the assessments of interview partners. A legislative initiative was classified as highly complex if it was described as very technical or difficult to resolve. Examples are descriptions of dossiers as "rather technical and rather difficult to approach and to get through, to understand what is in it" (COM87:163), as "a very technical proposal" (COM93:208) or as "a very new area nobody had worked on before" (COM39:152). In turn, if none of these instances are mentioned, or if the proposal was explicitly referred to as having been "not rocket science" (COM133), it was classified as low in technical complexity. Independent group t-tests were conducted to test to what extent a problem-solving use occurs more often in uncertain and in technically complex cases. For the latter, the level of significance is at the level $p < 0.01$.

9

Insulated, Technocratic Decision-making? Commission Position Formation and the Public Acceptability of Policy Options

This chapter focuses on the Commission's responsiveness to the diffuse, disorganized European public during position formation. The mechanisms are much less tangible than those concerning the consultation of experts (Chapter 8) and internal coordination structure (Chapter 10), but they likewise pinpoint the type of Commission agency in the pressurized areas of technocratic and political decision-making (cf. Chapter 2). Despite the far-reaching implications of its decisions, the Commission is widely perceived as a merely elite-driven entity that essentially operates outside the public's main field of vision. Prominent scholarly accounts argue that this insulation is an intended result of a technocratic institutional design in which only the de-politicization of policy choices enables credible and lasting commitments to efficient policy solutions (Moravcsik 1998; Majone 2005). Yet, with the progressive widening and deepening of supranational authority in Europe, serious flaws have been identified in this view. Insulated policy-making challenges "even the 'thinnest' theories of democracy" (Follesdal and Hix 2006) that define the relationship of political authority and the citizenry in the European states (Mair 2005). Such normative criticism has resulted in calls to actively politicize Commission position formation (Hix 2006).

While much of the corresponding debates focus on institutional design, the key concern is much more fundamental. A core problem of elite-driven decision-making is the risk that the rules made in Brussels systematically deviate from the preferences held by the citizens who are governed by those institutions. It is this concern that lies at the heart of a "democratic deficit," because "a key characteristic of democracy is the continued responsiveness of the government to the preferences of the people" (Dahl 1971: 1). Doubts about whether this very basic criterion is fulfilled are warranted, given that "elites and the public want different things from Europe" (Hooghe 2003: 286). While executive elites address economic competiveness, the wider public prefers more interventionist policy that "protects them from the vagaries of capitalist markets" (Hooghe 2003: 296; see also Dehousse and Monceau 2009). In addition, classical regulation theory highlights the fact that a detached decision-maker is prone to bias. In the absence of public control, the structural lobbying advantages of specialized interests lead to regulatory capture, that is, the "control of the regulatory process by those whom it is supposed to regulate . . . with the consequence that regulatory outcomes favor the narrow 'few' at the expense of society as a whole" (Mattli and Woods 2009).

Indeed, the preceding chapters highlight that Commission position formation is often informed by specialized industry interests, external experts with varying degrees of independence, specific national demands and the anticipation of aggregate Council positions. But does that mean that the preferences and positions of the diffuse public do not matter during position formation at all?

If the Commission and its internal actors follow the more political rather than the technocratic types of agency, we can indeed tease out conditions under which the public acceptability of policy options becomes an additional factor of position formation. This chapter specifies a respective theoretical argument which is then underscored by assessments of Commission officials and empirical observations from our case studies of internal position formation. The findings are consistent with the claim that the general politicization of European integration provides incentives to pander to public interests while issue salience and public contestation determine whether and how the Commission accommodates these incentives during position formation.

9.1 COMMISSION POSITION FORMATION AND DIFFUSE PUBLIC SENTIMENTS: EXPECTATIONS

With the rather fixed conceptualizations of the type of Commission agency discussed in Chapter 2, extant theory pays little systematic attention to the role of the public concerning power and conflict in Commission position formation. Nonetheless, some implications as to how much the Commission and its internal actors respond to the diffuse public can be derived. Approaches rooted in intergovernmentalism conceptualize the Commission as a purely technocratic actor with the sole purpose of solving coordination problems among nation states (Moravcsik 1998; Majone 2005). It is expected that "most citizens remain rationally ignorant" on the detached and complex issues of international cooperation so that a consideration of immediate public interests is irrelevant (Moravcsik 2002: 614). Responsiveness to public pressure is seen as a significant peril for political progress as it undermines the Commission's task to propose credible commitments to the long-term policy goal of market creation in Europe (Majone 2002; Bartolini 2006). Against these premises, we would expect the Commission to merely implement the aggregate will of national governments while public sentiments should not exert any direct influence on position formation.

In contrast, neo-functionalist theory allows for much more in the way of direct relationships between supranational elites and the public. Here the Commission is understood as a political entrepreneur for whom societal demands for more integration are a decisive element of the self-containing integration process (Haas 1958/1968b: 16). Political elites and especially bureaucrats seize public demand to extend their competences which implies "a widening of the audience or clientele interested and active in integration" leading "to a mutual re-definition of objectives" among the European citizenry (Schmitter 1969: 165–6). In this set-up, the diffuse public becomes an enabling ally for the Commission whose sentiments are constantly monitored in order to find opportunities for further integrative policies fostering the perceived "common weal" (Mitrany 1971; also Haas 1958/1968b). Inspired by this thinking, the policy-oriented literature has conceptualized individual Commission DGs as entrepreneurs who proactively communicate positive aspects of integrationist steps to the public in order to garner support before formal steps are taken (e.g. Cram 1997). Along these lines, we would expect that individual DGs routinely involve the public in position formation while the public attractiveness of particular positions should be a relevant source of power when internal conflict occurs.

However, neither the claim of the public's irrelevance nor the assumption of an increasingly pro-integrative public fit the contemporaneous context of position formation among the Commission's different internal actors. Recent public opinion research, for example, strikingly contrasts the "permissive consensus" that has marked the European Community's infancy (Lindberg and Scheingold 1970). Contemporary public opinion is neither unified nor generally supportive of European integration but rather reacts systematically to supranational politics (Down and Wilson 2008; Toshkov 2011). In the same vein, the visibility of supranational decision-making in the public media shows a positive trend over time (Sifft et al. 2007; Boomgaarden et al. 2010). It reacts systematically to specific European events (De Vreese et al. 2006), and has increased mainly in those areas where most national competences have been transferred to the supranational level (Koopmans 2007). Moreover, the public is not only watching but also feeds its evaluations of supranational decision-making back into the political process. This is the case for European Parliament elections and ratification referenda which are no longer considered to be just "second-order" (Koepke and Ringe 2006; Lubbers 2008). Such public evaluations even transcend European ballots and enter domestic partisan discussion (Kriesi 2007; Hooghe and Marks 2009). And this public involvement is far from being permissive for elitist decision-making as both the emergence of Eurosceptic parties in almost every EU member state and temporal and cross-sectional variation in "Europrotests" forcefully underline (Taggart and Szczerbiak 2002; Uba and Uggla 2011).

In sum, we can observe an increasing "polarization of opinions, interests or values [that] are publicly advanced towards the process of policy formation within the European Union" (De Wilde 2011: 560). Against this societal politicization of European integration, supranational institutions face new legitimacy demands (Zürn 2006), while the failed Dutch and French referenda in 2005 emphasize the fact that European "decision making has shifted from an insulated elite to mass politics" (Hooghe and Marks 2009: 13). The politicization of European integration challenges the idea of insulated decision-making in the Commission and leads us instead to expect a pattern of Commission responsiveness along three dimensions (Rauh 2012).

First, the mere fact that Europe's public has become both a more interested and a more skeptical stakeholder of European integration creates Commission incentives to pander to public interests. No matter whether the Commission follows the political goals of competence enhancement or the fulfillment of value-oriented policy ideals, its future success depends on the continuation of the integration process. An increasingly hostile public opinion, however, may slow down or even halt integration, which would prevent the Commission DGs from acquiring additional competences or from reaching specific policy goals. Thus, the more the wider public becomes aware of supranational decisions and the more the Commission's exercise of power comes under public scrutiny, the more it is rational for the organization to care about the broad acceptability of the policies it proposes.[1]

Second, politicization will not exhibit this effect in each and every Commission initiative. Whether the Commission immediately serves public interests should depend on the likelihood that a particular policy position will influence the public's general evaluation of supranational decision-making. In this regard, we know that the public hardly follows each and every proceeding on the political agenda. In actual fact, cognitive boundaries and information costs result in a selective public attention that varies over time and across issues—particularly if the latter exceed the domestic domain (Aldrich et al. 1989; Soroka 2003; Oppermann and Viehrig 2011). It follows that some Commission initiatives may fly safely below the public radar, while others may concern issues that the public currently cares about. But the Commission can only win the public's favor with regard to the latter. Thus, the *contemporaneous public salience* of the issues to be regulated—that is, the extent to which people care about political issues or hold opinions about them (Franklin and Wlezien 1997; Chapter 2)—moderates the link between politicization and the policy output of the Commission.

Third, if contemporaneous salience is given, the Commission will decide how it can please the public as an additional stakeholder of position formation. At this stage, the decisive question is whether the Commission faces a unified or a divided public opinion. If the Commission DG in question formulates policies that concern valence issues—in other words, topics where public opinion can be reasonably expected to be unimodal (cf. Stokes 1963)—we can expect that the final Commission position will pander to public interests and spread regulatory benefits widely. In contrast, if the DG regulates on positional issues where European public opinion is split, the Commission's response can be less easily predicted. On the one hand, we may expect blame-avoidance strategies where the Commission tries to avoid or to postpone position-taking until public salience fades away. On the other, the Commission, and particularly individual DGs, may also try to proactively stimulate public debate before formal decisions are taken, if they expect that this furthers their preferred policy choices.

In summary, this discussion suggests that the European Commission and its individual DGs should consider diffuse public interests strategically when forming and negotiating common policy positions. First, the background of a politicized integration process creates incentives to care about the broad acceptability of policy positions. Second, whether this affects the internal choices of policy positions in individual initiatives is determined by the contemporaneous public salience of the issue in question. And, third, *how* the Commission and its internal actors respond depends on the degree of conflict among the European public(s). But does this more flexible picture of handling of public concerns succeed over the comparatively static conceptualizations of the Commission as a purely technocratic actor?

9.2 EMPIRICS: IS THE BROAD ACCEPTABILITY OF POLICY POSITIONS A CONCERN IN COMMISSION POSITION FORMATION?

Contributing to a preferably complete picture of position formation within the Commission, our sample of 48 position-formation processes between 1999 and 2009 offers quite some empirical leverage of the influence of the broader public sentiments along the lines raised in the previous section.[2]

First, the general politicization of European integration varies over the investigation period. Figure 9.1 depicts a standardized politicization index that sums up the EU's media visibility as measured by the share of EU-related reporting in four major European newspapers, the polarization of public opinion towards EU membership as captured by the spread (variance) and peakedness (kurtosis) of the respective Eurobarometer item, and actual mobilization on European politics as gauged by the average number of Europrotests.[3] Along the average values of these data, there are at least four periods during which the European public was particularly attentive to supranational powers. These include the first half of 2001, when a wave of anti-globalization protests coincided with manifestations against the EU's defense, fishery, and transport policies, as well as public criticism regarding the renewed outbreaks of the mad-cow and foot-and-mouth diseases in Europe. They also include the episode between autumn 2003 and summer 2004 marking the run-up to Eastern enlargement and the related European Parliament

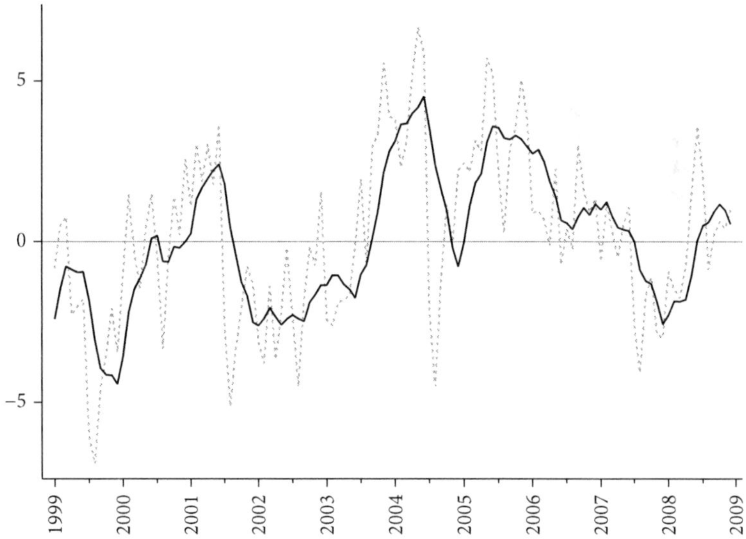

Fig. 9.1. Societal politicization of European integration during the investigation period. The figure presents an additive index combining standardized indicators for the EU's media visibility, the polarization of public opinion, and the average national number of Europrotests. The dashed line indicates monthly values, while the solid line shows the six-month moving average

Source: Rauh (2012: ch. 3).

elections. Politicization was also especially relevant during summer 2005 and the following two years, when the failed French and Dutch referenda and the subsequent discussion on a new treaty basis continuously put the supranational powers in the public spotlight. Finally, following a trough in early 2008, national rallies accompanying national ratifications of the Lisbon treaty, protests on fuel and food prices, and public discussions on the supranational regulation of financial markets pushed the indicator over its average value again. These periods must have created particular incentives for the Commission to care about the broad acceptability of the policies it formulated and/or adopted at the time.

Second, in addition to cross-temporal variation of politicization, the theoretical argument implies some variation over the three selected policy areas. On the one hand, theoretically they should differ in their likelihood of becoming salient among the European public. Whereas social and consumer policy issues are often immediately relevant in citizens' daily live and thus relevant for the overall public evaluation of European integration, this is much more unlikely when it comes to the regulation and funding of research endeavors. On the other hand, there should be differences in the likelihood of a divided public opinion. Decisions at the intersection of social and market policies, especially, touch upon core issues of political economy and social justice that structure political conflict within but also across European member states (cf. Kriesi et al. 2008). Here, the Commission may lack clear signals on *how* best to respond to public demands. In contrast, when consumer issues become salient one would hardly expect public disagreement on whether more protection is warranted or not (cf. Ansell and Vogel 2006: ch. 1). Thus, given a high level of politicization, we would expect that the Commission will be most responsive to public opinion in consumer policy issues, partially responsive in social and market policies, and largely ignorant of public sentiment in research policy.

Third, the systematic process tracing efforts outlined in Chapter 3 allow us to track the theorized mechanism. Apart from showing outcome variation over more and less politicized periods and over salient and non-salient proposals, the theoretical argument implies a range of additional process hypotheses (cf. Chapter 2.3). One implication is that salient and non-salient proposals should differ across the internal actors that dominate the policy-formation process (Wilson 1980: 366; Radaelli 1999b)—the increased relevance of political rather than technical questions should pull the internal hierarchies into the equation, thereby pushing the process more to the political modes of internal position formation. Another implication is that the drafting DG will increase its contact with and responsiveness to public interest groups at the expense of other stakeholders in cases of more salient proposals (Gormley 1986; Pollack 1997c; Klüver 2011). Where the public is watching position formation in the Commission, internal actors will not stubbornly serve member state or industry interest in accordance with their technocratic mandate. Instead, they will additionally consider the interests of widely shared societal segments whose opinion on the Commission is at stake. This leads to yet another implication—our expectation of more conflictual DG interaction in publicly salient cases. When an individual DG starts to pander to public pressure, its internal positions should, on average, considerably deviate from existing policy solutions that were adopted in less politicized periods. According to our argument on the relevance of the legislative status quo in Chapter 2, this should call internal opposition into action. On the other hand, all DGs share a common interest in a positive public evaluation of the Commission overall, which may trump policy differences in the case of extremely salient proposals.[4] In both cases, however, we would expect a stronger involvement of the Secretariat-General on salient issues, either because more mediation is needed or because the administrative and political center is focused on the institution's public image (Kassim 2010).

And, finally, the 137 Commission officials interviewed offer a highly interesting source for strategic considerations on position formation. While all the interviews were case-specific, we asked about the role of the public in drafting, which often prompted rather general statements from Commission officials. Taken together, an aggregate view on these statements offers interesting insights into how policy officials perceive the role of the public during position formation themselves.

9.2.1 Self-perceptions: What Opinions Do the Interviewed Officials Hold?

At first glance, many of the subjective judgments of the policy officials are consistent with the conceptualization of the Commission as a highly technocratic entity that solves coordination problems among nation states without taking public demands into account. Some officials simply claim that "our first clients are the member states. The Commission has to make a proposal for which it gets the qualified majority. Full stop" (COM85:249). This may make decision-making difficult to explain to the public, but it conforms to the duty that Commission officials have in fulfilling the treaty rather than pursuing "only measures that make you popular" (COM34:69). According to these views, interaction with the public often boils down to a communication problem rather than to politics (COM64:129). But even then, in the view of individuals working in the Commission, communication's importance is curbed by the fact that the proposed acts are often perceived as technical and as addressing local authorities rather than citizens (COM4:164).[5]

Consistently, contemporary public sentiments are often seen as irrelevant for position formation. On the contrary, Commission officials are wary not to fall for discursive attention and newspaper headlines and to stick to the task of producing proposals acceptable to the member states (COM58:103). But such statements have to be taken with a pinch of salt because they seem to swing with the salience of an issue. Many of the sampled cases were not immediately salient and officials saw member state dominance where the public was not aware of the particular drafting process, arguing that it "wasn't aware what Europe was doing" (COM60:138), "didn't understand anything of the subject" (COM36:52), or that initiatives were simply "too technical for that" (COM63:230). In contrast, officials stressed in regard to other acts that it "obviously is a bonus if our policies are popular and are perceived by the press and the public" (COM34:61). Though more rare, one does indeed find evaluations that conform to the expectation of a Commission that exploits public demands to further its integrative interests.

Some refer to an indirect relationship where the public largely defines the political climate, which in turn results in proposals being put on the Commission's agenda, but without a clear impact on their substance (COM57:102). Others go further, claiming that the public "should be a constant European concern," meaning that "we don't present a proposal just for the sake or the good will of harmonization or serving specific business interest if we don't see that there is an interest for the consumer or the citizen in general" (COM111:182), and that "people can really see the benefits of European activity" (COM5:149).

Such statements conform to the big political guidelines that characterized the Prodi and Barroso I Commissions we cover in this book. During the first phase of the investigation period in particular, Commission officials faced the Lisbon Goals, including "greater social cohesion." They saw their role as translating this broad political guideline into concrete measures that would put "the citizens at the heart of the internal market" (COM33:176). Further down the line, Barroso's insistence on visible European results placed "a premium on everything which appeared to provide direct advantage to citizens" (COM93:208)—a logic that substantially gained in importance after the Commission officials had seen thousands of people mobilize in the streets of Brussels and other capitals in protest against the liberalization of services (COM93:104). In operational terms, this meant that the lead DGs were required to provide a citizen's summary for each initiative (COM58:42), while a press-clipping service provided them with a summary of public receptions of proposed positions during the drafting processes (COM119:189).

Taken together, neither the conceptualization of a stubbornly technocratic actor nor of an overly responsive organization fully captures the breadth of the general statements on the Commission's interaction with the public. The truth actually lies somewhere in between these extreme views and, in fact, many of the officials' evaluations conform to the strategic handling of public sentiments that the context of a politicized integration process implies. Of course, policy officials acknowledge that such citizen-friendly legislation may not always be possible, which, however, does not prevent them handling such cases strategically, as the following quotes sum up vividly:

> Certainly if we want to continue, probably best would be to improve the people's acceptance of the EU integration process—we should legislate in a way that people can identify with the level at which the decision is taken and with the substance of what we are doing (COM81:40).
>
> [I]t might be a technically sound proposal, it might indeed be necessary, it might be essential to fulfil our treaty obligations or community law, but it is going to make us very unpopular. And in this context it might be very unpopular in Ireland, and they're going to have a referendum on the Lisbon treaty in three weeks time. It is not a really politically opportune moment to present this proposal. So, go on and find an excuse to bury it for three weeks, six weeks, a year, whatever (COM34:109).

Where such strategic considerations occur, public sentiments indeed exert influence on Commission position formation. In formulating their policies, DGs may "run after public opinion" and try to cash in on "the general trend" (COM12:108). The relevance of this factor is clearly related to the specific mandate a DG pursues, with more social files providing an obvious nexus with the public (COM105:309). And besides sensing the general climate of specific policy positions from media coverage or other sources, drafting DGs may also buy specific item batteries in individual Eurobarometer waves (COM8:171).[6] Public support for particular policy positions can also be a bargaining chip in internal interaction with other DGs. In the event of persistent internal conflict, turning to what the citizens want or what can be deduced from Eurobarometer "provides relevant hints" (COM8:167). Seen this way, public sentiments on specific issues can be directly related to internal power swinging up and down conjointly (COM13:190).

Likewise, more public interest is seen to increase the involvement of the Commission's internal hierarchy. Commissioners, particularly, are interested in maintaining their public popularity and in maximizing media coverage (COM34:65). This may create conflicts between political leaders and policy officials at times (COM12:112), but mostly the lower echelons seem freely prepared to adapt their positions to political pressure: "the services, we have a larger view, which allows us to choose at every moment, depending on the political momentum, the kind of proposal we would like to boost at that time" (COM33:164).

Taken together, the general statements of Commission officials support neither a fully insulated nor an overly publicity-oriented Commission. This descriptive overview of insider judgments implies that the preferences of national governments remain the backdrop for position formation, while the Commission seeks the proactive exploitation of public sentiments where it appears to be strategically useful. This final statement demonstrates this view:

> There are two considerations, really. Obviously, the starting point is to say, well, we have looked at an issue and we are trying to move forward in line with the common European interest. But then there are two considerations. One is can we get it through? You know, if you propose something that has no chance of getting through the Parliament or the Council . . . you can do it occasionally, but to do it often is a waste of time and resources. It makes us look politically impotent and it doesn't help Europeans. It doesn't help citizens. So it is just a political exercise. So, that is important. And yes, the other side is that we would hope that everything we do is something that can be explained to the citizens because it is in their interest. But obviously sometimes, the easier it is to make that case, the more we like the dossier (COM113:98).

In line with the results from earlier chapters, these self-evaluations tell a story of a Commission rooted in a technocratic tradition as an agent of member states, but one that is also quite aware of the political implications of its decisions beyond this narrow definition of stakeholders. In their general judgments, the policy officials consider public concerns and prefer policies that are broadly acceptable. But is this preference also mirrored in actual policy responsiveness?

9.2.2 Commission Responsiveness: Does Public Acceptability Affect Policy Choices?

To ascertain whether the public affects the substantial policies proposed for Europe by the EU Commission, we start by looking at press coverage on our individual cases. Following our operationalization of salience in Chapter 3, the concern here is the public attention or public visibility attached to a proposal or to a particular aspect of that proposal (Mahoney 2008). We find relevant contemporaneous press reporting in 18 of the 48 position-formation processes covered. In other words, for 38 percent of our sample, the public could have been aware of regulatory issues even at an early stage of EU policy-making and long before discussions in the Council of Ministers or the European Parliament began. In line with the expectation that public attention may vary with the level of abstraction from immediate citizen concerns, the media coverage differed across the three policy domains covered. With relevant pre-proposal reporting in 50 percent of the cases, the issues at the intersection of social and market policies seem to be most visible, followed by consumer policy (39 percent) and research and innovation policy (21 percent).

Turning to the effect of public salience on the duration of the processes studied, we find that salient proposals take slightly more time in internal preparation (on average 29 months as opposed to 23 for a non-salient proposal), but this difference is not statistically significant. However, publicly visible cases are significantly more likely to be decided at the political level of the Commission (83 percent) when compared to those where no significant press reporting occurred during drafting (48 percent). Relatively independent of contemporaneous news reporting, the public also affected interaction across DGs. In 37 percent of the sampled cases with internal conflict, the drafting officials claimed that anticipated public reception of particular positions was a decisive argument for settling internal conflict. As for public salience, this varied in accordance with the immediate citizen relevance of the scrutinized policy fields: anticipated public legitimacy of contested positions was relevant for half of the cases at the intersection of social and common market policy as well as in consumer policy, but in only one of the research policy cases. These figures highlight the fact that public concerns are far from being relevant for each and every Commission initiative, but that internal drafting becomes sensitive to them if public salience rises.

Our research design allows us to go beyond these descriptive overviews and to trace actual political choices to the public acceptability of the positions the Commission and its DGs finally chose. To this end, we present selected cases where we link the impact of the general level of politicization and the issue-specific salience to power and conflict inside the EU Commission. The Commission proposal for a European Globalization Adjustment Fund (EGF, Chapter 5.2.5), adopted in 2006 during a period of intense politicization (see Figure 9.1) and after only seven months of drafting, provides a rather extreme example. The proposal establishes a European funding instrument to compensate individual workers who have been laid off due to trade adjustments. In a rather unusual drafting process, the idea was promoted by Commission President Barroso himself. The Commission officials involved agreed that this was a rather direct and blunt response to the public criticism the EU faced during the failed ratification of the draft constitution. Realizing that there was widespread opinion that "this European Constitution is the entry gate for the awful globalization" the proposal was a response to the specific political context (COM77:28). In other words, the Commission launched a whole new instrument "just to calm . . . the general opinion in some member states at the time of the adoption of the European Constitution" (COM77:28, equally strong COM67:68, COM43:40, COM74:46). In the words of President Barroso, the Commission considered it "very important to show that we in the EU care" (quoted in Browne 2006). Against this background, the

Commission started to promote its plans way before their official adoption. The EGAF was first announced by Commissioner Spidla in early October 2005 (AE, October 7, 2005) which was flanked by an open letter from Barroso to the Council and the European Parliament as well as by a communication on "European Values in a Globalised World" (COM[2005]525). And not only was the position of having such an instrument influenced by the anticipated public reception, but emerging internal conflict was also settled by the same means. Although DG REGIO opposed the instrument due to budgetary competition and technical inconsistencies with other EU funds, this DG was isolated in the College of Commissioners, which agreed with Barroso's political concerns (COM78:84, also 120).

However, in other cases from the policy field at the intersection of social and market policies, the relevant actors within the Commission could not be so sure about whether the public would receive their preferred policy positions as positively. For example, the 2003 proposal on equal treatment between men and women in services (Chapter 5.2.2) was initiated in a high politicization phase but indicated partly hostile public reactions towards the internal preparations in DG EMPL (see e.g. *FT*, October 31, 2003). One particular point of contention was whether gender could serve as an actuarial factor leading to insurance premiums differentiating between men and women (*FT*, June 24, 2003). Such public discussions mirrored rifts within the Commission where particularly DGs MARKT and ENTR were "strongly opposed to any intervention at all" and ideally "wanted insurance to be completely out" (COM21:75), rendering this one of the "most complicated" proposals from the social policy domain during the Prodi Commission (COM125:115). But although the "hostile reaction from other Commission departments" became publicly visible (*FT*, June 25, 2003) and although the regulation of services stretched the anti-discrimination Treaty base quite far, DG EMPL's Commissioner Diamantopoulou pushed the position through—not least by garnering support in the public domain. On the one hand, the need to tackle discrimination in services was backed by public opinion data—a point repeatedly made by Commissioner Diamantopoulou, as well as in discussions at the political level of the EU Commission (SEC[2003]1213: 5). On the other hand, the Commissioner went on to bolster the "wider public profile of the issue" by proactively feeding her position to the press (COM21:159, COM125:71). When the internal conflict on the inclusion of insurances was sustained until direct negotiations in the College of Commissioners became necessary, these public commitments to the principle of anti-discrimination helped to gain the support of Commission President Prodi. This accounts for the fact that DG EMPL's ideal position is reflected in the final proposal (COM125:55).

As compared to the policies touching on social policy, the public reception of consumer policy is much more easily predictable for the Commission. Raising the level of consumer protection in the internal market usually entails costs for a narrow set of producer interests, while it creates benefits that are widely dispersed over the European public and thus can be easily communicated (cf. Pollack 1997c). So if an initiative of this kind comes in for public scrutiny, the question of how public interest can be pandered to is comparatively clear. Against these premises, Rauh (2012) shows that the Commission adapts its preferred distribution of rights among producers and consumers to swings in both quantitative indices for the overall level of EU politicization (capturing visibility of, as well as polarization and mobilization on EU matters) and the salience of the issue area in question (as measured by the relative frequency of media reports on food safety, product safety, and contractual consumer rights).

To provide a prominent example, position formation on the 2008 Commission proposal for a revised toy safety directive was massively influenced by salience upsurges during drafting (Chapter 7.3.4). Originally, the lead DG for enterprise and industry (ENTR) invested more than five years in drafting the new rules. The particular act was important for the DG in order to defend its so-called "new approach" to product regulation, which was a defining element in liberalizing the single market for goods (cf. Pelkmans 1987). The "new approach" governed market access and was based on the idea of minimizing regulatory intervention by prescribing only essential safety requirements while leaving any technical details and market control to producers and private standardization bodies. However, this liberal approach had come under fire since DG SANCO (health and consumer protection) had successfully proposed the General Product Safety Directive in 2001. This legal act provided for much stricter producer regulation and led to repeated turf wars between the two Commission DGs. While position formation on toy safety appeared for a long time to be a point won for DG ENTR, the picture suddenly changed when huge toy recalls hit the European market in 2007. Although the existing legal framework proved to work quite effectively in uncovering and containing this scandal, the soaring public salience put DG ENTR under pressure because "people wanted to have immediate results" (COM25:234). Asked how this arrived on the drafting desk, an interviewee replied, "it's first of all the press . . . you feel that consumers lose faith in toys so that's one pressure you have" (COM25:242). This clearly has "political aspects because our Commissioner said we are working on it we will give you soon results" so that drafting officials faced demands "from outside but . . . also from above" (COM25:242). Most interestingly, this pressure made DG ENTR change a range of proposal contents within five months after they had gone through five previous years of specific stakeholder consultations (Rauh 2012: ch. 5.5). Against its original plans, DG ENTR gave in to DG SANCO's demands and tightened producer restrictions as regards the essential safety requirements, the regulation of permitted chemicals in toys, and labeling obligations. Though this DG had initially aimed at reinforcing the liberal approach, these final-stage changes enabled DG ENTR's Commissioner Verheugen to finally claim in public that "health and safety of children is non-negotiable and cannot be subject to any compromises" (Commission of the European Communities 2008d).

Another example from consumer policy refers to the 2001 proposal on air passenger rights (Chapter 7.2.2). This defines the rights of air transport passengers and the compensation obligations where air transport operators fail to provide the agreed services. The background was that the lead DG TREN (transport and energy) had been quite successful in liberalizing producer access to the European air transport market and now sought further competences in regulating this market. Arguing that the liberalization process had been "about advantages for the industry," the drafting officials claimed that the Commission therefore had to take the perspective of "the consumer's right to benefit" (COM33:124). At the turn of the century, bad customer treatment by airlines indeed had some salience (e.g. *FT*, January 16, June 11, 1999, *FAZ*, May 17, 2001, *Le Figaro*, May 21, 2001). Public attention was particularly devoted to the issue of overbooked flights, which was "all the time in the media" and provided the "first source of information" for the drafting officials (COM33:136). So in line with the aim to "refocus Europe's transport policy on the demands and needs of its citizens" (COM33:140), the issue was prioritized in DG TREN. Starting with a public communication in June 2000 (COM[2000]365: esp. 15–18), DG TREN threatened airlines into a voluntary commitment, and its strategy found widespread media approval (e.g. *FT*, May 8, 1999, *El País*, October 17, 1999, June 17, 2000, *FAZ*, May 23, 2001). In order to avoid further regulation, airline operators managed to draw up such a commitment in March 2001. But—in a politicized climate of widespread EU protests and heated discussions on the ratification of the Nice Treaty—DG TREN suddenly showed its teeth and also demanded compensation rules for delayed or cancelled flights, thereby widening the scope of the final proposal significantly (COM33:302, COM[2001]784: 2). Although this course of action alienated airline operators greatly, the responsible Commissioner, Loyola de Palacio, could claim upon proposal presentation that "as the European Commission we have strongly promoted passenger protection with this spectacular step ahead" (Commission of the European Communities 2002a).

Several other consumer-policy cases in our sample highlight how the Commission reacts with more interventionist positions when the levels of issue salience and overall EU politicization rise (Chapter 7 and Rauh 2012: chs 4–6). The proposal on consumer credit (COM[2002]443) attracted sustained public interest, as evidenced by the constant media coverage. In this situation, DG SANCO's political leadership opted for a highly interventionist position at a time when the general politicization of European decision-making was set to rise again (COM89:46, COM111:149). And when politicization had reached hitherto unseen heights during mid-2001, DG SANCO publically committed to highly controversial provisions, most notably on the principle of responsible lending, which basically freed consumers of any responsibility in credit agreements (COM119:123, European Commission 2001b). As predicted above, this led to a rather controversial drafting process, particularly between DG SANCO and DG MARKT, which was seeking to maintain existing lender advantages (COM119:71–127). However, during the finalization of the proposal in this strongly politicized period, DG SANCO was able to partly overcome internal opposition by arguing that any less interventionist position would deliver a bad message to consumers (COM119:62). In addition, the internal opposition was defeated with the help of President Barroso and his Cabinet—inside actors who were particularly sensitive to the public image of the institution as a whole (COM111:142–54). In the case of consumer-credit regulation, therefore, the shared Commission interest of sending a positive message to the wider public at least partly overcame conflict between the fiefdoms of the consumer and the internal market.

Likewise, the position-formation process on health claims on foods (Chapter 7.4.3) highlights sensitivity to the public context. During 2001—a period of high EU politicization and high food safety salience due to re-emerging BSE cases—an initial public discussion paper tested the most interventionist and thus most contested regulatory ideas, such as limiting marketing claims only to foods with particularly healthy nutritional profiles (DG Health and Consumer

Protection 2001: 4, 9–10). In 2002, against strong industry opposition and during a period in which both EU politicization and food safety salience had fallen to temporary lows, the respective provisions were dropped from the draft proposal (DG Health and Consumer Protection 2002). However, nutritional profiles re-emerged in the final proposal in 2003. This "late introduction" of the provision into the proposal led to "strong concerns with the food and drink industry" (CIAA 2003, also EuroCommerce 2003), but was very much welcomed by consumers (BEUC 2003a). In line with our expectations, the provisions were reintroduced when issue salience had reached its mean level again and politicization had started to rise as well.

Similarly, the more general proposal on food information (Chapter 7.4.4) entailed strongly interventionist positions as compared to the legal status quo, most of which were already locked-in during the highly politicized phase of 2005 (COM30:131, COM80:109). Most notably, the proposal rendered nutrition declarations mandatory. This provision was hotly contested in the food industry. During early drafting, officials assured themselves of the backing of their political leadership (COM30:269, COM80:152) and proactively ensured that food labeling was publicly visible at the time of drafting. First, a range of DG SANCO-driven soft-law initiatives on obesity found their way into a range of news reports (e.g. *El País*, December 9, 2005, *Le Figaro*, April 21, 2007). Second, DG SANCO's Commissioner Kyprianoú discussed voluntary producer agreements on labeling practices in interviews and threatened that "if this doesn't produce satisfactory results, we will proceed to legislation" (cited in Mason and Parker 2005). Third, one year later, the DG SANCO spokesman publicly announced that new legislation would make labeling easier to understand for European consumers (*FT*, January 27, 2006), while later press reports kept the internal drafting in the public eye (e.g. *FAZ*, November 19, 2007, *FT*, January 31, 2008). In other words, DG SANCO officials themselves made sure that their proposal would be publicly visible once adopted (COM80:59, 138). They thereby managed to overcome external opposition from the food industry, but also internal resistance from DG ENTR (COM80:71, COM115:63), which could only be resolved in direct negotiations between Commissioners Kyprianoú and Verheugen (COM115:66).

In sum, public salience and public sentiments do indeed matter for internal position formation within the European Commission—a finding that particularly holds true in the field of consumer policy and to a lesser extent also in social and market policies. Contrasting this picture, the 14 cases sampled from the area of research and innovation policy indicated little relevance of anticipated public reception. Even in the three research policy cases that received some press attention before proposal adoption, none of the positions finally negotiated among the DGs involved could be explained on the basis of concerns about their possible public reception. Asked directly for the relevance of the public in drawing up the Union's research programs, officials argue that interest only comes from "the scientific disciplines" and "certain industrial sectors," while "the public doesn't really care that much" (COM102:293). Given that "the man in the street doesn't know what the Framework Programme is" (COM100:126), our results imply that the policy area's baseline salience is insufficient for triggering the strategic calculations theorized above.

9.3 CONCLUSION

In sum, the different pieces of evidence in this chapter are consistent with the view that the societal politicization of European integration makes the broad acceptability of specific policy positions an additional constraint on position formation within the Commission. Depending on the baseline salience of the three policy fields in the public eye as well as on the actual salience of individual initiatives, our sample provides examples of a complete strategic repertoire of Commission responses to heightened public interest in European position formation. During both of the office terms we cover in this book, the Commission did care about the public acceptability of its policies and either postponed unpopular decisions, proactively tried to garner public support during position formation, or even amended its original positions by choosing the policy options that spread regulatory benefits more widely across the European public.

This strategic handling of the public acceptability of specific policy positions adds to the picture of a Commission that operates along political, rather than only along technocratic types of agency. This can be judged as good news, particularly because the salience of policy initiatives can be manipulated by societal actors. While elitist and insulated decision-making makes only direct access to decision-makers a successful lobbying strategy, the politicized context makes *voice* a promising strategy for less resourceful interest groups as well (cf. Beyers 2004; Klüver 2011). NGOs representing diffuse societal interests, unions, political parties, or even grassroots movements can gain influence by raising the salience of their requests and by publicly identifying the supranational level as the relevant locus of power. Where strategic position adjustments follow the lines presented here, the politicization of European integration may help to align European policy with widely shared public preferences.

However, one should not overstate the relevance of these mechanisms for democracy in Europe. On the one hand, responsiveness to public concerns is just one factor of Commission position formation and can play out only in the leeway left by the other factors discussed in this book (see esp. Chapter 11). On the other hand, the present perspective on the Commission's policy responsiveness also shows that the risk of stalemate feared by the critics of politicized supranational decision-making is real (Majone 2002). While an initiative's salience mediates only *whether* the Commission considers the public's reception during position formation, the question of *how* it responds is subject to the actual distribution of public opinion on the subject matter. The results from our cases imply that the positive effects of public salience play out very well on issues that are uncontroversial among the public, which is especially underlined by the subsample of consumer policies.

In contrast, European decision-making can become much more erratic where the European public is divided along national or other cleavages. If the Commission tries to avoid blame and shies away from taking decisions when controversial issues become salient, the aggregate outcome will be a much more selective integration process. If European treaties and their legal interpretation also forestall unilateral national actions on unresolved issues, the Commission's responsiveness to public concerns may paradoxically reinforce the asymmetry of negative and positive integration in Europe (cf. Scharpf 2010). And, similarly, where the Commission takes sides on salient but controversial issues, the resulting policy proposal will entail an obvious political bias, making consensus-finding in the Council and Parliament much harder, again undermining the interventionist capacity of supranational decision-making.

So far, the plausibility probes in this chapter underline the fact that Commission position formation is not as insulated as is often assumed, while the flipside of enhanced responsiveness does not automatically lead to more democratic outcomes. Nonetheless, an encompassing answer to our initial puzzle of why the Commission sometimes proposes far-reaching, sometimes controversial, and sometimes inconsistent policies must take the strategic interactions of Europe's central agenda-setter and the wider European public into account.

NOTES

1. The notion of a European public applied here does not equal the related concept of a European public sphere conceptualized in theories of deliberative democracy (e.g. Koopmans and Erbe 2004; Trenz 2005). Scholars in this area argue that we observe little transnational communication exchange. However our interest lies with the vertical dimension: the fact that supranational competences become contested at all is sufficient even if this is compartmentalized along national lines. In other words, what matters is that European citizens are increasingly aware of the fact that supranational decisions affect their lives.
2. A more conclusive test that conceptualizes the dependent variable—i.e. the distribution of benefits between specialized and diffuse interests—on the basis of in-depth policy knowledge, a time-consistent measure of policy-specific issue salience, as well as continuous public opinion measurement is provided by Rauh (2012).
3. Europrotests are defined as "all incidences of contentious claims making to which the EU or one of its agencies is in some way either the source, the direct target, or the indirect target of protests and the actors come from at least one member state" (Imig and Tarrow 2001: 32).
4. For valence issues, one can thus expect a curvilinear relationship between proposal salience and internal Commission conflict. The level of salience at which the common interest trumps policy differences should then be dependent on the level of overall EU politicization (Rauh 2012: ch. 2).
5. As discussed in greater detail in Chapters 1–3, this perception is hardly generalizable. In fact, the majority of the 48 cases sampled address corporate actors or individual citizens quite directly.
6. As for the Commission's usage of expert groups (Chapter 8), it should be noted that questions in these surveys as well as in public consultations are often posed in a suggestive manner so as to generate public support for a policy position that the drafting DG prefers anyway (*The Economist*, February 21, 2008; Kröger 2008; Höpner and Jurczyk 2012).

10

Structural Biases? The Link between Internal Coordination and the Dynamics of Position Formation

Our case studies have underlined that the internal coordination structures of the European Commission are crucial to understanding the policies it proposes for Europe. These structures determine which internal actors can feed their interests and positions into the preparation of legislative proposals and at what point of the proceedings they can do so. However, the agenda-setting phase is characterized by an increasingly—albeit still only partially—formalized process that runs along both horizontal and vertical coordination lines. Where conflicts emerge between DGs, there may be substantial differences as to how much influence is yielded to one or other DG, and this makes the internal coordination structure a relevant factor when it comes to our second research question on internal assertiveness. Thus, this chapter is devoted to a more systematic overview of coordination structures within the Commission and to their relationship with position formation in Europe's central agenda-setter.

In principle, coordination structures remain the same no matter what policies or interests are concerned. Nonetheless, a more systematic examination of *how* these internal structures can and are being used during the drafting stages provides us with additional leverage in identifying the type of agency underlying Commission action. In a Commission motivated by the drive to produce the best solution to a policy problem in a technocratic and purely functional manner, the central resource used in interactions should be expertise and defense of the better argument. Ideally, then, the internal coordination structures should provide all DGs with a means to exchange information and, on this basis, reach the most efficient policy solution. Coordination rules and structures might at times fail to prevent conflict or may distribute information unevenly, which will result in sub-optimal solutions, but they should not be systematically used to favor some positions over others. By contrast, if internal actors follow a more political rather than a technocratic rationale, for example by pursuing competence-maximizing or policy-seeking goals, DGs will intentionally seize on opportunities and loopholes offered by the internal coordination structures to achieve their aims.

In highlighting the historical development of internal coordination and by analyzing the current formal rules of the drafting process, this chapter shows that certain internal actors are indeed structurally privileged when it comes to influencing the contents of legislative proposals. These actors are first and foremost the lead DG, but also increasingly the Secretariat-General (SG) and other horizontal services, notably the Legal Service (SJ) and DG BUDG. Drawing on material from the archives of the European Union, we show that coordination requirements have increased over time, rendering these structures even more important today. While, in the past, strategic actors were able to circumvent structures to pursue their goals (Kassim et al. 2013: 184), the internal coordination rules are difficult to circumvent today, while they still provide caveats or anchor points that may be used strategically. On the basis of our aggregate case study evidence, we show that such structural advantages are indeed frequently used by purposeful internal actors, pointing again to a political rather than a technocratic type of agency when it comes to position formation inside the European Commission.

10.1 INTERNAL COORDINATION IN HISTORICAL PERSPECTIVE

Ever since the first Commission president, Walter Hallstein, decided in 1958 that each and every Commissioner would be in charge of a policy area and a respective service (Noël 1991: 3), coordination across portfolios has been an issue in the EU Commission (prior to this time members of the High Authority shared co-responsibility for all sectors, Groupe de Personnalités Indépendantes 1979a; CEEA 1959: 12). Edmond Wellenstein, who had served as Secretary-General of the High Authority before becoming the first Director-General for Trade in Brussels in 1958, remembered that in the early days, a DG could freely decide when to contact other DGs and whom to talk to:

> [t]here was a weak attempt to do that [coordinate] but since every Commission[er] had its own freedom, they were happy to organize that one. Whereas in the High Authority they didn't have their own freedom, they were keen on getting in on things, yes they had no monopoly of anything, the only way to get in things was to go through the system in the working group or somewhere else, in Brussels they got the royal present right away.... and there was a feeling that you shouldn't meddle into your colleagues' affairs (Wellenstein 1991: 12–13).

But over time, more and more competences were delegated to the Commission and inter-dependencies across different policy areas increased. The need for coordination grew, but the internal structures only slowly followed suit. Even well into the 1990s, inter-service consultation was "ad hoc in nature rather than systematic and continuing" (Bulmer 1993: 361). This particularly benefited whichever DG held the lead on a particular initiative. DGs that chose to act strategically could keep early policy drafts very much to themselves, closing "the doors of their DGs until a policy [was] more or less finalized" (Schout and Jordan 2008: 979).

Such coordination malpractices were perceived early on as being problematic. Even before the much-cited Spierenburg Report (1979), internal coordination was criticized as being irregular and often limited to procedural and formalistic aspects. Substantial policy conflicts were only subject to coordination at the Commission's political level, which reduced the overall likelihood of successful coordination because controversial issues remained stuck in an overburdened College of Commissioners. The College has held weekly meetings since 1958, and almost from the start this became the only occasion when increasingly busy Commissioners could meet as a group (Noël 1991: 14). In order to reduce the College's workload to some extent, preparatory meetings by the Commissioners' cabinets were inaugurated by the Hallstein Commission in 1965 as an ad hoc format. With the Rey Commission in 1967, meetings between sectorally specialized cabinet members—the so-called *Special Chefs*—and weekly between the Heads of Cabinets—the *Hebdo*—became regular practice. But these forums also only mattered during the later stages of drafting and thus improved the mediation of conflicting positions within the Commission to only a limited degree:

> The fact that each Commissioner was given independent authority for an administrative entity and was at the same time charged with developing policies for his resulting sectoral responsibility often delayed political confrontation until the moment when the specific proposal reached Hebdo or, eventually, the College (A.U.R.A. 1972b: 2, authors' translation).

In addition, it was feared that the lack of formal coordination during the early stages of drafting was fostering unhampered informal coordination, leading to closure and informal networking often along national lines with a view to outsmarting officials from the smaller member states (e.g. A.U.R.A. 1972a: 17).

In this light, it was felt that better preparation and coordination of dossiers in the so-called upstream phase was warranted. In the various internal reports and historical documents we examined, three suggestions for enhanced coordination consistently stand out: Inter-service Groups, Groups of Commissioners, and a Central Coordination Unit (SEC[75]350, COM[75]PV332: 15, COM[78]PV485, 2nd partie: 20; Comité des Trois 1979: 69; Groupe de Personnalités Indépendantes 1979b; cf. A.U.R.A. 1972b).

Inter-service groups were devised as a means to discuss policy choices ahead of and in parallel to the formal inter-service consultation as "a way of overcoming departmentalism" (Kassim 2006: 80). Such groups were first set up in the late 1980s and grew in number from 48 in 1990 to 226 in 2004 (Spence 2006a: 148). Some are permanent, creating an institutionalized mode of regular cross-DG exchange on particular issue areas. Others are ad hoc and convene with regard to a specific legislative proposal. Today, they are set up by the lead DG and formally authorized and supervised by the SG. In 2005, furthermore, the Commission introduced new Impact Assessment guidelines that now formally require "Inter-Service Steering Groups" on all items of a cross-cutting nature (European Commission 2005c: 9).[1]

Groups of Commissioners are the second modification of coordination structures frequently mentioned in historical documents. Such thematic groups are composed of a subset of the College and are set up by the Commission President. Their task is to provide early political coordination in position formation. While their structure and number have changed over time, they go back to the founding days of the EU (63/41/EEC: Article 14). In our investigation period, Prodi set up five working groups. While some portfolios are more prominently represented, membership seems to be open in principle to any Commissioner who is interested. Fields of activities are Growth, Competitiveness, Employment and Sustainable

Development (chaired by Prodi, open to all); Equal Opportunities (chaired by Prodi and Diamantopoulou, open to all, permanent members Kinnock and Reding); Reform (chaired by Kinnock, members: Schreyer, de Palacio, Monti, Fischler, Nielson, Lamy, and Vitorino); Inter-institutional (chaired by de Palacio, members: Kinnock, Patten, Barnier, Schreyer, and Vitorino); and External Relations (chaired by Patten, members: Solbes, Nielson, Verheugen, and Lamy).[2] Information on Commissioners' membership in these groups is not available for the Barroso term, but the thematic layout has remained stable (2005/960/EC: Annex, Art. 18).

A Central Coordination Unit is the third repeatedly voiced suggestion for improving internal coordination. The idea in this case is that administrative as well as political coordination should be organized and supervised by a central actor. To render coordination substantial rather than merely formalistic, this unit should be made up of high-level officials with technical mastery and institutional memory and also be directly subordinate to the Commission President. This suggestion first figured prominently in a report named after Professor Édouard Poullet, chair of a working group on the internal workings of the Commission services, who suggested that "a small group of officials should be empowered to supervise the activities in the different working groups and 'task-forces' and amplify informal contacts between responsible Cabinet members and the SG" (A.U.R.A. 1972b: 4, authors' translation; similarly Spierenburg 1979).

While inter-service groups at the administrative level and Groups of Commissioners at the political level were at least formally implemented during the past decades, this third reform suggestion met with on-going resistance within the Commission. Opponents include the long-serving Secretary-General Emile Noël (1979: 4), who was known to prefer the use of "personal networks" as a means of coordination (Kassim 2006: 80). Similarly, the long-standing Commission president Jacques Delors relied on internal networks for coordination, which, however, were aimed much more at pushing forward favored initiatives than at cutting back those of which he was critical (Ross 1995). As Commission president, Delors had veto power in the College to stop the latter anyway. What is more, resistance to central coordination came from individual Commissioners, but also from the administrative level of policy DGs who feared that it would seriously undermine the discretion they held when acting as a lead DG for particular legislative initiatives. With respect to internal dynamics, the SG could "intervene only after the event, to verify whether the . . . coordination rules had been respected" in the past (A.U.R.A. 1972a: 72, authors' translation) and was described as an "administrative postbox" only (with reference to the 1990s: Jordan and Schout 2006: 214).

Central coordination was also seen as redundant because all Commissioners formally hold voting rights in the College. Proposals that were deemed at risk of not surviving the inter-institutional process or considered undesirable for substantial reasons could be blocked in the existing political coordination structure of Special Chefs, Hebdo, and, finally, the College meetings. Voting in the College was always rare, but still, in principle, an option for blocking a proposal, particularly for the President, but also for coalitions of Commissioners from large member states (COM153).

However, the hostile environment for structurally empowering central coordination changed when the general administrative reform led by Commissioner

Kinnock coincided with the altered political context brought about by the continuing enlargement of the Union. The rising numbers of member states exerted strong pressure to reform the Commission's internal decision-making modes. Higher numbers of Commissioners and more heterogeneous positions—not least since the abolition of the practice of allotting two Commissioners to bigger member states (cf. Chapter 4)—increased the risk of blockages at the Commission's political level. At the same time, an internally divided Commission risked weakening the institution's position in the wider political system of the EU. Hence, Commission president Barroso (2007), in particular, explicitly rejected decision-making by voting in an attempt to avoid the image of an internally split institution that could not consistently defend its proposals in Council and Parliament.

De facto, this limited the possibilities for individual Commissioners to ultimately oppose proposals from other services. Consequently, central coordination has become more attractive and important over time, not only as a means to reduce the workload, but also to ensure that internally opposing interests can be heard without undermining the Commission's common influence in the EU's wider political system. In this context, the SG grew from a small entity with four units in the founding days to 23 units under Prodi and 26 units under Barroso I. As we will see below, the Commission's central service nowadays uses this manpower more and more to enforce coordination at the administrative stage of legislative drafting (*FT*, November 10, 2005; Kassim 2006: 80; Kassim et al. 2013: ch. 6). Paralleling this, the formal inter-service consultation on individual proposals has been administered since April 2001 via the electronic CIS-Net system, also managed by the SG (SEC[2008]2180: 5). The exchange between the administrative policy-drafting staff of different portfolios thus became much more formalized than in the past and should in principle ensure systematic inclusion of all "concerned" DGs (Commission of the European Communities 2008b: 8).

In sum, this historical overview highlights the fact that internal coordination structures have only slowly become formalized within the Commission. The discretion of those DGs holding the lead on particular initiatives was the historical backdrop, and all subsequent efforts towards internal reform tried to curtail this discretion by granting more and earlier access points for other DGs, Commissioners, and central services in the Commission. Nonetheless, despite the increasing formalization, the current structures of internal coordination also offer quite a few loopholes for strategic agency seeking to bias the policy positions of the overall Commission.

10.2 CONTEMPORANEOUS STRUCTURES OF INTERNAL COORDINATION

This section analyzes the current internal coordination process in greater detail and identifies the opportunities it provides for different internal actors. Figure 10.1 shows the administrative and political levels of coordination, as well as the parallel centralized coordination through the SG (see also Chapter 2.4).

Administrative level: In the first, informal stages of policy formulation, it is still one DG that is primarily in charge of a proposal. Being explicitly tasked with

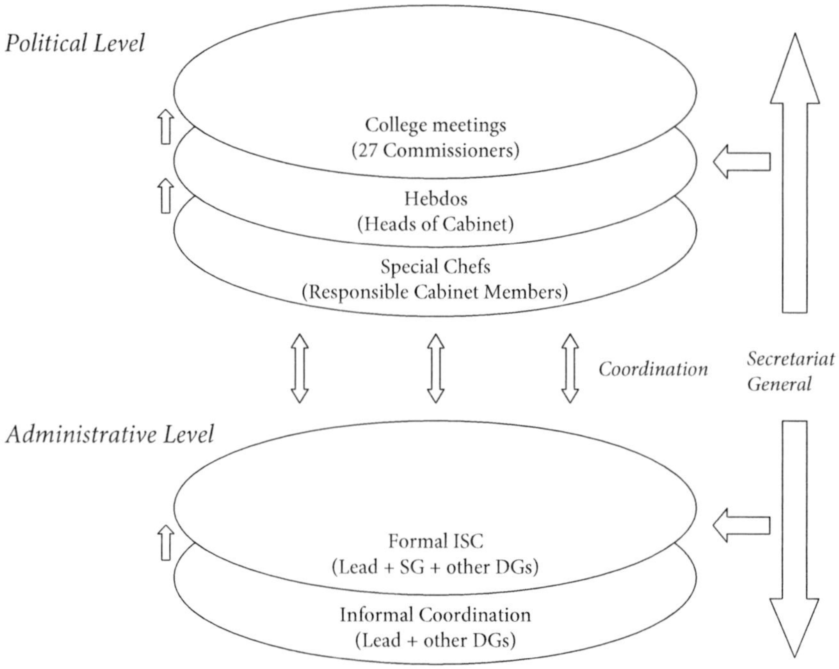

Fig. 10.1. Coordinating steps of position formation in the EU Commission

drafting and thus working full-time on a proposal, this lead DG can establish close relations with external stakeholders. It is therefore able to build up a solid stock of relevant information and/or stakeholder support before the actual upstream coordination with internal actors kicks in. Alongside these informational and strategic advantages, the lead DG writes the first legislative draft, which then represents the foundation for all subsequent negotiations. Besides this general agenda-setting advantage, the administrators in the lead DG are free to decide which other Commission actors are actually involved in drawing up this basic document. While informal contacts to other DGs are possible during this stage, a DG acting strategically can still deliberately shield its initiative from opposing actors until it reaches the stage of an actual legislative text. In other words, it can influence at which stage anticipated internal opposition will be accommodated, depending on what approach is expected to yield a more favorable outcome: either it discusses its own policy ideas in informal bilateral exchanges early on, or it waits until the formal coordination process requires it to contact other parts of the Commission.

Only when there is a firm intention to proceed with a common Commission proposal and the lead DG's initial ideas are actually cast as a legislative text, do other DGs have to be consulted in the more formal stage of administrative coordination. As noted above, this formal inter-service consultation (ISC) now happens through an electronic database that formalizes exchanges between the staff of different portfolios and should, in principle, ensure the systematic enrollment of all "concerned" DGs (Commission of the European Communities 2008b: 8). Nonetheless, besides the obligatory consultation of the horizontal services (SG, SJ, and DG BUDG), as well as DGs ADMIN, COMM, and OLAF in cases that directly touch upon their competences, even today there is some room for interpretation and coalition-building when deciding which policy DGs are actually considered to be "concerned" (COM57:244, 118). Again, this can be an advantage for a strategically acting lead DG that anticipates internal opposition.

Typically, the formal ISC remains open for four weeks. While this is already a short timeframe for preparing a technically sound response, particularly for DGs that were not involved during earlier stages, our sample also revealed even shorter, so-called fast-track ISCs (see also Section 10.3.2). And even if an opposing DG provides critical input to the draft of the lead DG at this stage, these remarks do not have to be systematically incorporated. Formally, negative opinions in CIS-Net that are not accommodated by the administrative levels of the involved DGs are automatically handed upwards to the political coordination levels. This again creates strategic opportunities for the lead DG. It can decide whether it is more favorable to accommodate opposition immediately or hand it over to the political level, which might produce a different outcome (Commission of the European Communities 2008b: 11). Thus, granting other policy DGs with influence on the substance of a proposal will depend very much on whether the lead DG is actually open to other positions and better arguments or whether it wants to exploit the opportunities offered by the coordination process to push a fixed position through. In any case, a strategically acting lead DG can anticipate at which process stages and decision-making levels it could get a possibly controversial proposal through and can use the existing coordination structures accordingly (Hartlapp 2011).

Political level: In terms of political coordination, one can distinguish, first, between different procedures—that is, whether a proposal is adopted in written or in oral procedure—and, second, between different coordinative steps. A *written procedure* is initiated by the SG at the request of one or more members of the Commission. All cabinets receive copies of the agreement and have the opportunity to respond before a given deadline, otherwise their agreement is assumed. Under an *oral procedure*, once a proposal has moved to the political level, coordination takes place in the three consecutive negotiation forums mentioned earlier. A Special Chef meeting comprised of the sectorally responsible members of all Commissioners' cabinets is chaired by the respective member from the Commission President's cabinet. Everything that cannot be cleared at this stage subsequently moves on to the Hebdo, in which the Heads of Cabinet, chaired by the SG, seek to achieve consensus on as many points as possible. In general, these earlier stages of the political coordination process are considered to be an effective clearing-house mechanism, aiming "before the proposal gets to the table of the College, that the major issues are solved" (COM46:86, also COM58:48), while avoiding new issues being raised (C[2010]1100: 3). And, indeed, recent figures indicate that the Prodi Commission discussed only 4 percent of all decisions in College, while the number dropped to 2 percent under Barroso I (Azzi 2009: 45). Even in cases where there is conflict, actual votes are rare (Egeberg 2006a: 8; Barroso 2007). This practice has also been attributed to the

Commission President's more recent efforts to coordinate diverging positions across portfolios before they reach the political apex of the Commission via the SG as his administrative arm (Kassim et al. 2013: 151–80).

But also within this structure of political coordination, the lead DGs' advantages from the administrative phase persist. "[B]y the time the proposal comes to the formalized collective decisional agency, namely the College of Commissioners, and even though the College may have considerable discretion over the action it can take, thinking will already have been conditioned in a fragmented way within the DGs" (Bulmer 1993: 361). What is more, for initiatives typically reflecting the policy problems and solutions proposed by the lead, adjustments made at the political stage will, at best, downscale the proposal to deliver consensus decisions rather than changing the core substance in favor of other DGs' interests (cf. positive versus negative coordination in Mayntz and Scharpf 1975: 147–9; for an application to the Commission: Hartlapp 2011). In any case, coordination structures are such that other services' potential to exert influence is ridden with informational and strategic prerequisites at the political coordination stage, too. Operating through a number of structural conditions, these prerequisites can be very much influenced by the lead DG. Although the power of the primarily responsible DGs has been curtailed somewhat over time, even the contemporaneous coordination structures provide the lead DG in question with significant agenda-setting powers over the policies the Commission as a whole proposes for Europe.

Central coordination by the SG: Even though the strategic opportunities of the lead DG are only partially curbed by internal coordination structures, our historical overview indicates that increasingly a second "circuit of horizontal coordination in the Commission [has taken place] via the Secretariat-General" (Christiansen 1997: 81). As one official stated, "ten years ago they were merely the secretariat" (COM102:322) but today's Working Methods of the Commission stress that the "President provides the final say on all issues of coordination," while the SG—"if necessary—carries out this coordination work directly" (European Commission 2010b: 11–17). The SG plays an increasingly important monitoring role throughout the whole internal coordination, "intrud[ing] into the day-to-day work of the services" (COM127:339). Besides chairing the Hebdo meeting at the political level, it nowadays also aims at early steering and screening of the internal processes in order to prevent later conflicts and facilitate the political coordination. And while critical voices stress that the SG "has neither the time nor the political muscle systematically to pursue better coordination across the entire organization" (Jordan and Schout 2006: 214), today it has various coordination instruments at its disposal. SG officials may attend inter-service group meetings or may step in whenever they deem it necessary to halt a process, steer it in a particular direction, or act as brokers when conflicts occur (COM15:65, COM57:30). In this respect, two new coordination elements that render the SG "not only a kind of secretariat but really a policy maker" (COM69:200) are particularly important: policy coordination officials and long-term planning procedures. Both elements actually address the coordination at the administrative stage before formal mechanisms and political negotiations kick in. And both aspects show that today the SG can decisively influence the policy contents or the political direction of the Commission's legal initiatives.

First, "policy coordination officials"—sectorally responsible SG administrators—monitor the workings of a specified set of DGs. They look "at the preparation of the documents, the quality of the documents and the internal coordination, in other words, that all associated or concerned DGs have been properly consulted" (COM66:51), "so that things do not come jumping on the agenda from one DG which the others do not know about" (COM17:285, also COM46:35), and they also provide input in the form of "political orientation" (COM6:217). Typically, the SG does not proactively exclude DGs from the decision-making process, but it can provide additional internal interests with early access to the drafting table. Consequently, "they are becoming very much involved and they intervene in whatever they see" (COM69:200), wanting "to ensure that the other services of the Commission deliver on the priorities and objectives of his [President] Commission [and] give a stronger steer" (COM56:164). In abstract terms, the SG today essentially decides whether extreme positions with potential for internal conflict can go ahead or whether other inside interests are already taken into account during early preparation. Formerly, such political agency in using the coordination structures rested predominantly with the lead department. Today, the lead department de facto has shared powers with the SG in deciding when to fight its battles with other services.

Second, the SG plays a pivotal role in planning which proposals will be coming forward and, at times, even in assigning the lead DG for a legislative proposal. "Historically . . . the different services of the Commission did develop proposals. And it was only when it was quite a mature proposal that the SG reacted. Now they [i.e. the SG] are actually trying to get another ground floor, and say: sorry, that is not on this year" (COM44:117). Thus, today the SG acts as "gatekeeper" (COM127:355). As one SG official states, it is now the Commission's central service that decides "whether [a particular proposal] is a good idea that deserves to see the light of day. If [the proposal] is not, one of our jobs is to make sure that it does not. So we are on the opposite side from them, and a more powerful opposite side than some of the other DGs" (COM15:113). The assignment of one legal initiative to the Commission's annual work program is part of the long-term Strategic Planning and Programming (SPP) cycle of the Commission managed by the SG and introduced with the "Activity Based Management" of the Kinnock reforms in 1999/2000 (Tholoniat 2009). As part of the SPP, the operational annual Commission's Legislative and Work Programme (CLWP) defines the concrete initiatives to be launched and also which DG is going to be lead on each of them. On the one hand, it is described as "a very bottom-up process" (COM15:41); on the other, and increasingly so over time, it entails a very hierarchical component. After bilateral talks where the SG and the President's Head of Cabinet receive the respective Director-General and discuss the items that the DG proposes, the SG ultimately decides about the timing and, more importantly, about priorities, necessary cooperation and "non"-initiatives (COM66:30).

In sum, today's coordination structures place the SG in a privileged situation to prioritize positions on the Commission's agenda. Planning sequences, timing, and controlling which particular inside interests can bias a specific policy, the SG is clearly empowered by internal coordination structures. At the same time, the SG can limit a lead DG's discretion to bias a legislative proposal. However, more systematic coordination by the SG at an early stage does not necessarily produce more balanced outcomes in a technocratic sense: the central role of the SG in monitoring the coordination process, paired with its recent task to set political priorities, points instead to more centralized political steering, which depends on the President's political preferences rather than on balanced policy-making.

So far the chapter has shown that the coordination structures may favor the lead DG as well as the SG if these actors want to bias the policy agenda of the Commission in one way or another. And, indeed, evidence from our case studies shows that internal actors sometimes *use* these opportunities to pursue their strategic aims.

10.3 DEMONSTRATING STRUCTURAL EFFECTS: LINKING COORDINATION AND POSITION FORMATION

Our case studies and interviews provide a range of evidence about how internal coordination structures actually impinge on the policy choices of the European Commission. In this section, we thus provide an aggregate view of how the different nuances of internal coordination structures we have identified above play out in day-to-day policy making.

Initially, we have to note that in order to understand the Commission's policy choices, the administrative levels of position formation are at least as important as the political levels. First, whereas proposals can, in principle, also be initiated by the political level, our sample identifies the administrative level of the Commission DGs as the main driving force in policy formulation. In only 7 of our 48 cases, process-tracing revealed a Commissioner or the Commission President as prime movers in the drafting process.[3] Particularly in view of the fact that our case-selection procedure is intentionally biased towards larger-scope proposals, this result is at odds with the literature that focuses only on the political relevance of Commissioners. In fact, it fits in with the criticism of administrative dominance over political decisions, which was popularly voiced by Commissioner Verheugen in 2006 (Hagelüken 2006).

Second, the reality of successful agenda-setting by lower-ranking Commission officials is further underlined by the fact that actual conflicts between them and their political masters are a rather uncommon phenomenon in our sample. It was possible to trace positional differences between the administrative and political levels of involved DGs in only 12 of the 48 drafting processes. What is more, 6 of these conflictual 12 cases were from the small set of drafting processes (7) that were driven by the political level. This suggests that the inherent tensions of political and bureaucratic decision-making (e.g. Christiansen 1997) come mainly into play when Commissioners try to decisively influence particular initiatives on their own. When trying to impose particular policy choices upon the administrative level, they will most likely meet opposition from their services. In this light, it is probably not so surprising that our sample suggests that Commissioners have rarely developed positions that were independent of what their services proposed. Overall, the lead DG's administration is the central actor when it comes to initiating legislation and reaping the strategic opportunities offered by the early stages of coordination.

While the political level rarely triggered specific legislative initiatives in the first place, however, it often acted as a broker when internal conflict and the coordination structure pushed an issue onto the agenda of Commissioners and cabinets. As we showed in the case studies, 38 of our 48 cases involved substantial policy conflicts among DGs. In a majority of 26 of these cases, conflicts were ultimately resolved at the political level. Here, either the responsible cabinet members, the Chefs de Cabinet or the Commissioners themselves discussed parts of the proposal. But only in thirteen of these cases did the College itself seal the proposal. Our data, furthermore, do not indicate that the share of legal acts demanding political negotiations decreased under the Barroso I Commission as one might expect, given the increasing early-stage coordination activity by the SG. What we do observe, however, is that almost 88 percent of the acts designed as political decisions (i.e. formally adopted under oral procedure in the College, cf. Chapter 3.2) were indeed decided at the political level. For those cases that were intentionally selected as being adopted under written procedure in the College, the number is much lower. Here, only 32 percent were subject to a decision at the political level. Given the coordination procedures, this indicates that the legal acts included at least one open point that could not be resolved in the ISC and required debates at the political level. The fact that the agenda of most initiatives is set at the administrative level and that most conflicts are resolved prior to reaching the Commissioners at the political level also has implications for the efficiency of thematic groups of Commissioners as a mechanism of internal coordination. Despite their discussion in repeated internal Commission reforms, none of the interviewees mentioned these groups as having played a causal role in the internal position-formation processes studied in this book. Given that we selected proposals that systematically affected the interests of different DGs, while also focusing on initiatives with a large scope, we thus conclude that these groups of Commissioners are not of high relevance for the question as to which policies the Commission as a whole drafts for Europe.

The picture looks only slightly different when we consider the inter-service groups that operate at the administrative level. These unite officials from different services, typically at the desk-officer or Head of Unit level (COM7:103, COM46:50) and "with the correct services on board . . . pre-empt the big issues" (COM54:38). And yet we detected the presence of such inter-service groups in only less than the half of our cases. Here, the obligation to institute "inter-service steering groups" that came with the 2005 guidelines on impact assessments (European Commission 2005c: 9) seems to have been relevant. While inter-service groups were present in only 5 of the 29 cases adopted under Prodi (17 percent), 13 of the 19 cases adopted under Barroso I (68 percent) featured such a group. Nevertheless, we could barely trace a decisive role of such groups for the final Commission position because the way these groups operate in practice "is then very much driven by the DG that has the responsibility" (COM57:68, also COM1:172, COM54:46, COM91:131). Again, this result points to the need to study *how* coordination structures are actually used by internal actors.

It should be recalled that in a Commission motivated by the desire to produce the best solution to a policy problem, coordination structures and processes may impact on internal position formation as a by-product of design deficiencies. While obedient technocrats are expected to follow the formal rules and coordination structures, these structures may fail to prevent conflicts or reach efficient outcomes where they provide actors with differing levels of information. And yet it is under the more political types of Commission agency that we would expect actors to proactively turn coordination into a power resource that is intentionally used to reach a desired outcome in interactions. Our case study evidence shows that the lead DG, particularly, but sometimes also the SG, actually does exploit internal coordination structures to push their preferred positions through.

10.3.1 Lead DG's Power in Factual Interactions

In our case study material, 38 of the 48 cases analyzed involved substantially deviating policy positions across DGs. And in 32 of these conflictual cases, we found the respective lead department to be most powerful.[4] In many of these cases, the lead DG exploited the power accorded to it by the coordination structure to push its preferred position through to the final Commission proposal. The formal asset of being lead DG served as a power resource for the DG in question in two different ways: by providing either a strategic or an informational advantage.

First, DGs benefited from their position of being lead DG due to strategic and gatekeeping advantages in 22 of the 38 conflictual cases. A good example is the proposal on Services in the Internal Market (Chapter 5.4.2). This case shows how the liberal proposal that came out of the Commission and led to a public outcry was not the result of balancing different views that had existed inside the Commission. Quite the contrary: it was caused by the lead DG MARKT's liberal stance and its skilful subterfuge strategy that circumvented internal opposing positions by availing of opportunities offered by the internal coordination rules. While other DGs, such as DGs EMPL, TREN, or SANCO, had indeed voiced opposition, the lead DG exploited its position to keep the proposal under wraps at the services level for as long as possible and then shepherd it through the political level in a moment of low attention. Likewise, it carefully orchestrated the sequence of events and meetings at political level to its own benefit. What is more, the use of strategic advantages allowed DG MARKT to limit potential discussions in the College and led a high-ranking official in the Commission to argue that "if there has been one internal problem with this Directive it is that it went so quickly through the Commission that we did not have time to have inside problems" (COM65:29). Thus, it seems fair to argue that, given that other DGs had already been critical about the approach taken by DG MARKT, without the lead DG's advantage to use coordination structures for its own benefit, the proposal would likely have seen more cut-backs and limits to the far-reaching horizontal liberalization.

Second, in 17 of the 38 cases where there was conflict, the informational advantages associated with the role as lead DG proved to be a means to ascertain a position. If the lead department decides to act strategically, other DGs may encounter difficulties in using their participation rights and in exerting influence on the contents of legislative proposals. This is underlined by a representative survey with Commission staff carried out in 2008. Kassim et al. (2013: 189) find that in the context of coordination, only 50 percent of Commission officials find it easy to obtain information from other DGs. The informational advantage of being in the position of lead DG played out, for example, in a number of consecutive innovation-support programmes (see Chapter 6.3). Here, the respective lead DG often benefited from having commissioned mid-term evaluations of the previous programs. These reports provided the lead DG with the necessary information to argue for maintaining certain funding streams or introducing a budget increase in the subsequent program. Thus, by being the lead DG and having collected data and information, these DGs were clearly in a superior position when compared to other DGs that were merely consulted on the acts.

The respective lead DGs' advantages are inadequately balanced by the requirements for the formal ISC via CIS-Net introduced in 2001 (see Section 10.2). Also within these rules, the lead DG can, for example, influence the timeframe in which other DGs might voice their concerns. While deviations from the usual four weeks nowadays have to be accorded with the SG, this can severely limit the influence of other policy DGs on a particular proposal. The proposal for the directive on Equal Opportunities in Services and for the European Institute of Innovation and Technology (EIT) each passed in two weeks. Even shorter ISCs of just one week took place in the case of the proposal for Nutrition and Health Claims Made on Foods and on the European Globalisation Adjustment Fund (Chapter 5.2.5). As visible from the latter case, a short timeframe can be very problematic for the consulted services who are not working full-time on the initiative in question and possibly face a high workload of their own at the same time (in the example given, DG REGIO, see below, Section 10.3.2). This underlines that coordination empowers some actors more than others and that a strategically acting lead department can deliberately "play" with variability of coordination structures to its own advantage.

Note that playing the internal coordination structures in this way is an option for strategically acting DGs but cannot be treated as automatic for all Commission initiatives. In fact, we observe quite a few cases in which DGs do not solely rely on formal coordination rules when preparing a legislative act. In 23 of our cases, informal interaction across DG boundaries was intense, in 16 it was classified as medium, and in only 9 cases was it low.[5] Comparing across both Commission terms covered by our sample of drafting processes, intense informal interactions are much more likely in the cases that fall under the Barroso I presidency. This supports the argument that, stimulated by the new formal coordination structures under Barroso and pushed by the SG, DGs are also increasingly forced to interact with each other informally. And yet formal coordination structures still leave loopholes that—in prominent cases such as the Services directive and the European Globalisation Adjustment Fund—can hold substantial explanatory power for our original puzzle of why the Commission sometimes proposes far-reaching, highly controversial, or bluntly inconsistent policies for Europe.

10.3.2 The Role of the SG and Other Horizontal Services

While recent studies suggest that the SG increasingly pursues its own political agenda and uses its structurally privileged position to pursue it (prominently Kassim et al. 2013), the aggregate view on our empirical cases reveals a slightly different picture. In fact, substantial policy input by the SG was a rare phenomenon in our sample. In only 7 of our 48 cases (15 percent), did the SG hold a policy position that deviated from the original ideas of the respective lead DG. And in only four of these cases was the SG able to assert its demands in the final Commission proposal. This is hardly evidence for a consistent agenda pushed by the SG. Besides pushing for its own policy goals, the SG's structural role was relevant where conflicts between the lead DG and other policy DGs occurred. In 9 of our 38 conflictual cases (24 percent), support of the SG for one of the contrasting positions explained their assertiveness when it came to the contents of the final common Commission proposal. In our sample, at least, the SG's structural role was not that of a political agenda-setter within the Commission, rather conformed to the view of a powerful broker in quarrels between policy DGs.[6]

Evidence on such power of the SG can be found in the position-formation process for the European Globalisation Adjustment Fund (Chapter 5.2.5). In order to balance trade-adjustment redundancies, governments can claim financial assistance for retraining or job-search allowances to reintegrate these workers into employment. In particular, the instrument's target group was much debated in the Barroso I Commission. DG REGIO, which typically is the home of EU cohesion policy, aimed for a structural recreation of economic activity and therefore wanted the instrument to intervene via two strands, one targeting individual workers and the other one targeting enterprises. DG EMPL, in turn, was eager to target workers only, and to extend its own portfolio by creating a visible ad hoc "instrument that was identifiable, which was part of the identity of DG EMPL" (COM78:96, also 74:156, cf. SEC[2006]274). Although DG REGIO had already been present from the outset at the debates that gave birth to the idea of an EU restructuring fund, the regulation finally proposed in early 2006 is clearly biased towards targeting individual workers. The SG proactively intervened in the position formation process early on to the benefit of DG EMPL and went ahead with a fast-track ISC, in turn limiting DG REGIO's time to come up with opposing arguments.

Beyond the SG, our case studies highlight the role of other horizontal services within the Commission. Recall that the new rules on formal inter-service consultation make the consultation of some actors mandatory (see Section 10.1). In our sample of drafting processes, the Legal Service (SJ) as well as DG BUDG figured prominently besides the SG in the interaction patterns we observed. Both the SJ and DG BUDG held a substantially deviating position in eight of our 48 cases (17 percent of our sample each). DG BUDG was able to assert these demands in four cases, the SJ in five. Like the SG, in addition, these two horizontal services served as a power resource for policy DGs opposing each other. In the 38 cases with internal conflicts, support by DG BUDG was necessary to explain the assertiveness of specific policy DGs in seven cases, compared to support from the SJ in no less than 11 cases. Like the SG, DG BUDG and the SJ appear as internal actors that sometimes push their own agendas, but first and foremost they are important when it comes to brokering internal conflicts.

Spending programs, such as in research and innovation policy, formally required the consent of DG BUDG, which, however, often had a more restrictive view on spending than the policy DGs managing the programs. As our case studies show, this frequently led to conflicts with the budget service, which made it difficult for the lead DG to successfully propose its preferred spending volume, given DG BUDG's formal veto power in the matter (see Chapter 6.3). In the case of regulatory acts, in turn, it was almost exclusively the SG's and SJ's consent or dissent that had an impact on internal power plays. How the Legal Service influenced the power balance between DGs is particularly visible in the preparation of the Implementing Regulation on the Coordination of Social Security Systems (Chapter 5.4.3). DGs MARKT and EMPL opposed each other on the question as to whether non-authorized hospital care would be reimbursed at the level of the treatment country. DG EMPL benefited from the SJ's support when defending its position against DG MARKT, who wanted to stretch existing case law on the basis of a legally shaky interpretation. Thus, the superiority of the SJ in the area of interpreting case law was paired with its veto power derived from coordination structures—which in this case played into the hands of DG EMPL. In sum, it is not so much the technocratic know-how of horizontal services in ensuring the high technical quality of a proposal in terms of language, legal, or financial expertise that explains their relevance for internal interaction. In actual fact, the importance of their consent or dissent for policy DGs is explained by their formal internal veto power during the ISC. Thus, the way in which horizontal services impinge on position formation within the Commission actually speaks more for a political type of agency than for a technocratic exchange in search of the better argument.

To complement this case study evidence with more general insights into how the horizontal services exploit their structural advantages, we turn to the perceptions of our interviewees.[7] Of course, our interviewees do not represent a random sample of all Commission officials and are nested in the specific policy sectors we are covering (cf. Chapter 3.3). However, all of the interviewed Commission officials have considerable experience in legislative drafting and cross-departmental coordination. And a question on powerful internal actors explicitly addressed internal power in general, abstracting from the specific legislative proposals in question. And, indeed, horizontal services are evaluated as powerful by a large number of interviewees. Particularly the Secretariat-General (SG) and the Legal Service (SJ), both at the direct service of the President of the Commission, score highly, but DG BUDG in "charge of the money of the Commission" (COM111:257) also figures prominently again.

Interviewees assign power to the SG on the basis of its political steering function, which is derived from working closely with the Commission President, so it is seen as acting as "primus inter pares" (COM15:133) and considered "even stronger now than it has been historically" (COM44:119), particularly after 2004 (COM51:245). Thus, the SG can "arrange things" while, in contrast, the Legal Service can "object to things" (COM116:385). The characterization of the SJ as a "'make-or-break service" (COM127:355) "of crucial importance"' (COM56:151) is shared by many interviewees up to the highest political level. They explained that "nothing moves if the legal service does not agree" (COM96:212, also COM116:373), that "the Legal Service has the authority to invite all the DGs around the table and say 'you won't go out of this office if you have not agreed on a solution'" (COM83:48, also COM5:155, COM6:217), that "if Legal Service says something . . . we all have to shut up" (COM29:276) and that "you cannot have a conflict with Legal Service because they always win" (COM36:214).

DG BUDG, in turn, completes the circle of the horizontal services perceived as being powerful. Producing few substantial policies, it is a service that largely escapes outside notice. Nonetheless, DG BUDG is hugely important internally because it "effectively sets the whole framework for the operation of the Commission" (COM54:112) and any spending of community money depends on the consent of "the guardian of the Commission's or the Community funds" (COM7:224). Thus, as one interviewee summed up, "it is really difficult for you to get a proposal through, if you have one of those three [horizontal services] against you . . . with a negative opinion which was maintained in special chefs and Hebdo, you would really find it very difficult to get it on the College agenda" (COM104:255).

10.4 CONCLUSION

This chapter demonstrates that different roles and the actors filling them within the Commission have unequal opportunities and face unequal constraints in including preferred positions in a final legislative proposal. Coordination structures first and foremost allow the lead department to influence the amount of information available for others concerned, to control the number and constellation of other DGs involved, and to steer the amount of administrative exchange on positions or political debate before proposal adoption.

The SG, in turn, is not as ubiquitous in policy formulation as analyses of internal reform imply, but it nevertheless systematically intervenes to shape the sequence and timing of coordination and decides about the issues on the agenda. Moreover, it is a significant power broker when other DGs clash over policy choices. And next to the SG, the structures of formal inter-service consultation render the SJ and DG BUDG important actors that decisively use their internal veto power when brokering policy choices that ultimately form the Commission's overall position.

The chapter highlights the fact that such differential empowerment of internal actors matters in political terms. Rather than being only a source of technocratic inefficiencies in cross-departmental coordination, our case studies show clearly that such caveats and anchor points in internal coordination structure are very often used strategically to intentionally push through positions regarding which internal opposition was already voiced or anticipated. Actors within the European Commission often follow a decidedly political type of agency when it comes to internal coordination, which, in turn, substantially affects the agenda for the regulation of European societies.

NOTES

1. Gradually introduced from 2003 onward, today it is compulsory that an Impact Assessment (IA) accompanies all major legislative proposals. IAs have been fully operational since 2006, with an Impact Assessment Board (IAB) controlling the quality of the IA.
2. Information obtained from <http://ec.europa.eu/reform/refdoc/index_en.htm> (last accessed: August 27, 2013).

3. Given the high workload of the cabinets, such early interference must take place selectively, and involvement may depend on a combination of context factors, proposal characteristics, or personal interests (e.g. Radaelli 1999a).
4. The "most powerful DG" per case was the one that was able to move the policy choices closest to its ideal point on the most important key provisions in the proposal under analysis (cf. Chapter 3 for operationalization details).
5. Informal interaction was coded as intense if such interaction occurred often and regularly throughout the process, or at least at various times, and did so right from the beginning, or if informal contacts involved at least three different hierarchy levels. Medium informal interaction means that DGs interacted at least at various times throughout the process or very rarely but before and during the ISC or involved two hierarchy levels. Low informal interaction was coded for cases in which no or only very infrequent informal contacts could be detected.
6. Note, however, that our research design cannot systematically analyze the policy-planning stage where the SG may have exerted influence along the lines outlined in Section 10.2 above.
7. We posed the following question: "We know from national administrations that ministries have different reputations. If you look at the different DGs within the Commission, which DGs would you consider as rather powerful?" And we also asked the mirror question enquiring about the weakest DGs inside the Commission.

11

Many Factors Matter in Position Formation, but Some Matter more Often than Others: Evidence across Cases

The in-depth case studies of 48 drafting processes and the discussion of specific aspects of position formation presented in the preceding chapters indicate that there is no one-size-fits-all blueprint for the formation and negotiation of legislative proposals in Europe's regulatory powerhouse. Our process-tracing efforts demonstrate that a multitude of factors explain which positions and political choices ultimately end up in the legal text passed to the Council and the European Parliament. What is more, *how* these factors are used by actors within the European Commission depends significantly on the nature of the issue, the political context, and the specific goals internal actors pursue with a particular proposal.

However, more systematic commonalities and differences can also be observed across our cases. In a first step of aggregation, this chapter provides a bird's-eye perspective on the prevalence of those sets of factors we expected to constrain or enable policy positions and interaction within the Commission: the legal status quo, existing internal coordination requirements, the inter-institutional decision-making system and optional resources in a system of multi-level governance (cf. Chapter 2). Based on a systematic comparison of our cases, we can now state which factors within these categories play a more systematic role and we also propose tentative arguments as to why we observe these distributions.

Before jumping straight into our descriptive findings, however, two caveats on generalization are in order. The first is a reminder that we are dealing with a purposeful sample (see Chapter 3.2). It should be recalled that the cases are roughly equally distributed across internal decision-making procedures (written or oral), types of legislative instrument (directives, regulations, and decisions), and the Prodi and Barroso I Commissions. However, case selection was intentionally tilted towards legislative acts with a comparatively broad scope and towards issue areas that typically concern more than one Commission DG. Our results may thus not be telling for minor acts that individual DGs can draft without any interference, but they should apply to broad legislative initiatives of a cross-cutting nature.

The second caveat on generalization concerns the interpretation of our quantitative descriptive results. We are looking for patterns of internal position formation and interaction without, however, understanding the factors we have examined as a set of clearly defined, independent variables that explain a single dependent variable. As argued theoretically and as is evident in the preceding policy chapters, a single factor might affect the specific policy choices in a particular policy proposal through various mechanisms (see also Gerring 2008; Hartlapp et al. 2010b). Thus, this chapter mainly answers the question as to how often a specific factor was needed to understand the specific policy choices and outcomes in the individual case histories. The interplay of specific factors and mechanisms will be more closely considered in Chapter 12, where we return to the ideal-type models of position formation in the EU Commission.

With these two constraints in mind, the following presentation is structured in line with the two basic research questions raised in Chapter 2.1: Which factors mattered most often when an individual Commission DG formed its policy position on a particular legislative proposal? And which factors mattered most often for assertiveness when such positions clashed during the drafting of the proposal within the Commission?

11.1 FACTOR PREVALENCE IN INTERNAL POSITION FORMATION: WRESTLING THROUGH PILES OF LEGISLATION, EXPERT OPINIONS, STAKEHOLDER INTERESTS, AND MEMBER STATE OVERSIGHT

On the most descriptive level, we can state that legislative drafting within the European Commission is a rather time-consuming process. On average, drawing up a legislative text required 25.6 months of preparation (median duration: 24 months), where the most extreme outliers were the cases on public procurement vocabulary (Chapter 5.3.2) at 6 months, and on toy safety (Chapter 7.3.1) at 70 months. Duration is unevenly distributed, with the drafting processes in research and innovation policy being significantly shorter than those in consumer policy.[1] Our case studies suggest that policy characteristics might explain this difference. Most of the cases regarding research and innovation policy involve periodical funding programs, such that clear drafting deadlines must be met before the preceding program expires. Furthermore, the previous programs often serve as role models that considerably facilitate drafting in research and innovation policy. By contrast, many of the consumer-policy cases start from a status quo of varying national rules, which makes legislative drafting more complex from both a political and a technical perspective. This partly applies to acts at the intersection of social and common market policies, too, explaining this group's placement between the other two.

It should also be noted that the duration of policy formation within the Commission is positively and statistically significantly related to the duration of the respective inter-institutional negotiations.[2] This implies that decision-making within the Commission already mirrors some of the political complexity that drives the speed of inter-institutional decision-making (Golub 2007). In addition, in 35 of our 48 cases we found evidence that the Council discussed issues that had led to conflict inside the Commission. Against the Commission's formal agenda-setting powers, these findings provide strong evidence for the claim that internal Commission decision-making is quite indicative and at least as important for the political outcomes in European politics as is the inter-institutional process.

So which factors actually mattered for position formation in our 48 cases? What were the sources of specific policy content and what, in turn, constrained Commission policy choices? We discuss the findings on each of our four sets of factors before turning to comparative conclusions.

11.1.1 Factors Grounded in the Legal Status Quo

As expected, the legal status quo impacts strongly on the internal position formation of the EU Commission. In all but three cases, the drafting officials drew on the EU's extant *acquis* to form their position on the legal initiative in question. This can be taken as good news for the credibility of European policy—particularly if it works in favor of consistency and reduces contradictions in the legal status quo. But it can also be understood as a lack of flexibility, significant path dependency, and a status quo bias in Commission position formation. An aggregate perspective on the case studies presented earlier indicates that the truth lies somewhere in between.

In 40 of our analyzed cases, the drafting DG drew on existing law that was managed within its own portfolio, whereas in only 22 cases, laws drafted by other DGs were also taken into account. The latter often happened after internal conflict had highlighted inconsistencies and suggested adaptations. What is more, our cases provide ample evidence that the choice of which existing law and regulatory concepts are taken into account is often a strategic one. We observed this in particular in DG MARKT's recourse to its own existing mutual recognition policies when forming positions on social or consumer policy rather than taking other existing harmonization concepts into account (cf. Chapters 7.2 and 5.4). Likewise we see it in DG ENTR's defense of its own light-touch "new approach" in product safety regulation that strategically disregarded other regulatory solutions developed by DG SANCO in the meantime (Chapter 7.4). We also saw some cases in which a DG created a precedent with one piece of legislation and then built a whole battery of legal acts on this initial act. The various anti-discrimination proposals (Chapter 5.2) and the passenger rights initiatives (Chapter 7.2.2) are compelling cases in point. Here, lead DGs EMPL and TREN explicitly used their home-made precedents to extend their reach in formerly unregulated areas. In the case of consecutive research and innovation funding programs, again, DGs built on the existing funding framework not only to ensure continuity for applicants, but also to justify their (increased) budget demands (Chapter 6). So while the strong prevalence of the extant *acquis* might sometimes be evidence of a technocratic approach ensuring the consistency of EU-level law, it often also has a decidedly political component when it enables DGs to achieve specific policy goals or helps them to expand their "turf."

We also found more strategic Commission agency than expected with regard to *ECJ jurisprudence* as a factor in internal position formation. Existing ECJ adjudication affected policy choices during drafting in 20, that is, roughly 42 percent of the cases in our sample. At the intersection of social and market policy, as well as in consumer policy, existing jurisprudence from Europe's court most often worked as an enabling and only sometimes as a constraining factor for policy goals pursued by the drafting DGs. Good examples are the various anti-discrimination cases where DG EMPL was able to justify its approach on the basis of preliminary rulings by the ECJ and willingly adopted some of the choices taken therein (Chapter 5.2). In consumer policy, DGs MARKT and SANCO often justified the need for supranational regulation or harmonization on the basis of infringement procedures against individual states that had identified inconsistencies in national consumer protection laws.[3] Exemplary cases within this policy area are the processes on sales promotions (Chapter 7.2.4.) and food supplements (Chapter 7.4.1).

Sometimes, however, ECJ jurisprudence may also curtail the ambitions of internal Commission actors. Whereas DG SANCO originally went for high protection standards on unfair commercial practices and nutrition claims on foods, the concept of the "average rational consumer" established by the Court in consecutive preliminary rulings provided a real barrier to rules tailored to less attentive consumers (Chapters 7.2.5 and 7.4.3). Here, ECJ law accounts for Commission proposals that were less interventionist than originally intended by the drafting officials.[4]

Taken together, our findings on this factor are hardly sufficient to claim that the Commission merely executes ECJ jurisprudence without its own "political aims or visions" (Martinsen 2009: 795). Instead, jurisprudence was often used as a springboard or functioned as fertile ground for developing new policy solutions that then served the internal Commission actors' aims. In this view, our findings are consistent with a differentiated view according to which "integration through law" places constraints on "market-restricting" policies but may be enabling for matters of non-discrimination or individual rights (Höpner and Schäfer 2012).

11.1.2 Factors Grounded in Internal Coordination

In Chapter 2, it was expected that the need for internal coordination inside the Commission might impinge on the positions of individual DGs. We thus controlled systematically for a possible effect of actual or anticipated *organizational restructuring* within the Commission's administration. Such reshuffling of and within DGs (also see Chapter 4) was sometimes, though not often (only seven of our 48 cases), a relevant explanatory factor for the Commission's position.

It was most consistently relevant for some consumer policies where, in fact, the empowerment of the fully fledged DG SANCO in 1999 was the result of competences being moved from DGs ENTR, AGRI, and MARKT (Guigner 2004). Particularly in the early cases on food supplements (Chapter 7.4.1), general product safety (Chapter 7.3.1), and unfair commercial practices (Chapter 7.2.5), DG SANCO developed positions that explicitly differed from the existing policies of those other DGs in order to justify the new organizational layout. Alternatively, DGs assumed a position in anticipation of future organizational restructuring, for instance in order to lock in preferred policies. The continuity in the 7th Research Framework Programme, for example, can be partially explained by resistance against reshuffling units in DG RTD (which this DG had experienced in the previous 6th Research Framework Programme, see Chapter 6.2.1). Though rare, these instances highlight the fact that position formation within the Commission may be driven not only by technocratic conduct or the pursuit of ideological goals, but also by simple turf considerations and organizational *raisons d'etre.*

11.1.3 Factors Grounded in the EU's Inter-institutional System

With regard to the EU's inter-institutional system, our results show that Commission DGs heavily anticipate the political feasibility of specific positions in the *Council.* This factor was relevant in more than 80 percent of our cases, held across all policy fields examined, and made a difference irrespective of the Council decision rule. The anticipation of Council votes was taken into account as an unambiguous constraint for proposals requiring Council unanimity (e.g. Euratom Research Framework Programmes, Chapter 6.2.3), but also set limits on internal positions when "only" a qualitative majority of member states was required (e.g. on consumer rights, Chapter 7.2.6). In addition to sounding out the political feasibility of certain pre-set ideas, early contacts with the Council also mattered when a DG was not pursuing a clear agenda in the first place. One example is the regulation of pyrotechnic articles, where DG ENTR welcomed any collective input from the member states with a view to drafting a piece of legislation that would be acceptable to the Council as a whole (Chapter 7.3.2). In these and most other cases, the aggregate interests of member states effectively influenced position formation. Thus, as expected in Chapter 2, the political feasibility in the EU's inter-institutional decision-making system constrains the Commission's internal legislative drafting without determining it fully—actors within the Commission operate under the "shadow of hierarchy" of the formal decision-makers (Scharpf 1997).

We also coded whether particular *national positions* impinged on the policy choices of Commission DGs. Rather than the aggregate Council position, this factor captures bilateral instances where a drafting DG followed individual member state preferences or adopted national policy models. These were either voiced by national governments and internal Commission actors or were picked and chosen by a DG without being actively pursued by national actors. Such an influence could be traced in half of our cases, but we observed much more variation across our three policy areas than we did for anticipating Council votes. National positions were relevant more often at the intersection of social and common market policies than in the other two policy fields. Where EU proposals touch on national social policy, they often meet deeply entrenched national institutions and values, for instance with respect to welfare state arrangements. Dealing with this status quo in areas of shared competences is demanding on position formation in both technical and political terms. Consequently, information from the situation in a specific nation state is welcomed because it might offer a viable solution or template for a given policy problem. This was the case for the financial conglomerates proposal, when a Benelux country with the most advanced national regime was asked to carry its regulatory model into the Commission (Chapter 5.3.4). Another glaring example of strategic picking-and-choosing of national positions is the case on consumer credit. Here, the policy proposed by the lead DG was essentially pieced together from the most stringent and interventionist consumer-protection rules the drafting officials could find among the regimes of European member states (Chapter 7.2.3). Taken together, responsiveness to particular national positions can have political reasons or may be driven by more technocratic considerations with respect to information gains. In summary, position formation in the Commission is thus far from independent of individual or aggregated member state interests as originally intended for a technocratic clearing house (Haas 1958/1968a). And our findings on these two factors exemplify how a national position may enter the Commission's internal legislative preparations via various mechanisms.

Interestingly, however, drafting DGs seemed to be far less concerned about the *European Parliament*'s political preferences, although it has been argued that increasing EP relevance in inter-institutional decision-making diminishes the Commission's agenda-setting powers (Ponzano et al. 2012; but see Crombez 2000; Tsebelis and Garrett 2000). In our sample, the consideration of EP interests made a difference for the proposed Commission positions in only 18 of all 48 processes considered (38 percent). What is more, in our sample, EP anticipation during drafting was equally likely under consultation and co-decision procedures and thus did not vary with the EP's formal role in the inter-institutional process.

Indicating that EP anticipation is at least not exclusively tied to concerns of political feasibility, the anticipation of (specific) interests in Europe's parliamentary assembly, and respective early contacts often followed a logic of garnering external support and legitimacy for pre-defined agendas—very similar to a mechanism we observed for organized interests (see Section 11.1.4). The comparatively strong prevalence of the EP factor in research and innovation policy has to do with the fact that the EP is an important veto player for the Commission when drafting spending programmes. But the case studies show that the EP appeared to be more generous than the Council and that the Commission actors thus contacted MEPs at an early stage in order to ensure their later support in inter-institutional negotiations. Using the EP as a means to overcome reluctance by external and internal actors was also relevant in some of the social policy cases. One example is the public EP hearing that DG EMPL organized during the drafting of the proposal on gender discrimination in services so as to exert pressure on more critical Commissioners (Chapter 5.2.2). Likewise, EP demands on Commission President Barroso regarding the general framework for equal treatment created a very favorable environment for asserting DG EMPL's regulatory plans within the Commission (Chapter 5.2.4).[5]

Partisan ideology is the least prevalent factor in our sample. Our tracing of processes revealed only five instances when party positions were relevant for position formation. If so, they mattered at the political level of the Commission and it was a Commissioner who pursued a partisan position influenced by her political orientation in line with her prior political profession at the national level (cf. Chapter 4). In line with the finding that the large bulk of proposals were decisively formed at administrative level (see Chapter 10.3), the cases in which a Commissioner's party-political ideology made a significant difference were rather exceptional. However, they could explain some DGs' most extreme positions. One prominent case is the proposal for the services directive that clearly carried the footprint of liberal Internal Market Commissioner Bolkestein (see Chapter 5.4.2).

Likewise, the criticism social-democratic Commissioner Wallström voiced against DG SANCO's cross-border healthcare proposal, even after Sweden had seen a return to a conservative government, suggests that the Commissioner was driven by personal ideology rather than by her government's interests (Chapter 5.4.4). Thus, although the partisan coloring of the Commissioners has recently been debated in the context of Commissioner nominations and the parliamentary investigation procedure (Döring 2007; Wonka 2007; Crombez and Hix 2011), it did not systematically matter for actual policy content in our sample of legislative proposals between 1999 and 2008. This leads to the more general question of how much individuals' influence mattered for internal position formation.

11.1.4 Optional Resources in the EU Multi-level System

In an ideal bureaucracy of the Weberian type, individuals should not make a difference (Weber 1925/1978: Chapter XI), but we know from previous research that Commission officials bring various beliefs shaped by past experiences or socialization in the Commission to the drafting table (Hooghe 2001, 2012; Trondal 2010). Our case studies indeed show that individual actors within the Commission sometimes have a decisive impact on the policy position pursued. Following our counterfactual approach, our material revealed that in at least 18 of our 48 cases an act carries the thumbprint of a desk official or a member of the DG's political leadership. In these cases, provisions would have looked otherwise if a particular individual with his or her own agenda or convictions and beliefs had not contributed to drafting.

Often this concerned the Commission's political level and largely the same cases for which we traced the influence of partisan ideology above. Commissioner Diamantopoulou—a Socialist who had actively participated in the Women's Movement in the past—was, for instance, crucial in driving the General Framework for Equal Treatment towards its interventionist approach (Chapter 5.2.4). However, officials also relied on individual agendas at the administrative level. One example is the eContent Plus programme, where the responsible director insisted on a shift in the programme's main beneficiaries from the private to the public sector, where he had spent large parts of his former career (Chapter 6.2.3). And the overall interventionist thrust of the food information proposal cannot be explained without reference to a vigorously battling Director-General who was personally strongly committed to promoting healthy lifestyles (Chapter 7.4.4).

The influence of individuals was not only ideologically inspired or value-driven, but sometimes also aimed at maximizing personal standing or a DG's competences. In line with the concept of "bureau-shaping," bureaucrats at the top of the Commission, in particular, did engage in strategies that increase "status, prestige, patronage and influence" (Dunleavy 1991: 200). The approach of the programme on the conservation of genetic resources in agriculture was strongly influenced by the Deputy Director-General's aim of increasing the efficiency of program management, saving personnel costs, and, thus, boosting the policy-making capacity of his own DG (Chapter 6.4.1). The cross-border healthcare proposal, in turn, was strongly influenced by Commissioner Kyprianoú's wish to become visible with a directive in an area where DG SANCO had so far developed little binding legislation (see Chapter 5.4.4). A further example is the European Institute of Innovation and Technology, which was clearly a political project of Commission President Barroso designed so that he would leave a footprint of his Presidency (Chapter 6.4.2). Although individuals were not as relevant as has been argued in earlier treatises of the Commission (Ross 1994), in overall terms, our sample still does not portray the Commission as an ideal type of technocratic organization free of individual biases. Rather, it indicates that internal position formation may also be used to pursue individual ideological goals or to maximize internal influence.

A much more prevalent, albeit optional, resource from the EU's multi-level system are *organized interests*. In fact, in only six cases were we not able to trace an observed DG's position back to specific demands from organized external stakeholders. In support of the EU interest-group literature (for an overview, see Eising 2008), our results clearly show that organized interests are an essential ingredient of position formation inside the Commission.

Sometimes, organized stakeholder interests conveyed factual information that was willingly taken over by a DG seeking knowledge resources. One example is given in the public procurement case, where DG MARKT needed information from organized interests in drawing up statistical indicators that were not biased by national interests (Chapter 5.3.2). In other instances, external stakeholders were granted influence in exchange for legitimacy. In these cases, interest-group involvement underscores the rightfulness of the drafting DG's powers by indicating the support of those governed—thus improving the negotiation position of actors versus their internal Commission or external Council counterparts. One example is the Competitiveness and Innovation Framework Programme (CIP, Chapter 6.3.3), where the idea to draft only an umbrella program rather than a more radical revision was heavily supported by the stakeholder groups affected. These and other case studies highlight the variation in why and which stakeholder demands DGs took on board. Apart from the characteristics of the interest groups themselves (Eising 2007), their influence depends heavily on varying political contexts (Klüver 2011) and also to a significant degree on Commission agency (Bouwen 2009). Organized interests do offer valuable resources for actors within the Commission, but which of these resources are translated into influence is often subject to the particular policy goals of those Commission actors holding the drafting pen.

This conclusion also holds for another highly prevalent resource used by Commission actors—*experts*. This factor comprises internal and external expertise understood as specialized knowledge on particular policy issues (Hartlapp and Metz 2013). Such expertise was relevant for the DGs' policy positions through various channels. Relevant knowledge was fed into the process by contracting out scientific studies (e.g. Unfair Commercial Practices, Chapter 7.2.5), by conducting implementation reports or mid-term evaluations of existing legislation (e.g. MEDIA programmes, Chapter 6.3.1), or by "hiring expertise" through seconded national experts (e.g. financial conglomerates and reinsurance, Chapters 5.3.4 and 5.3.5). Such contact channels were influential in about 30 percent of our cases, but the bulk of relevant expertise was garnered through formalized expert groups. Chapter 8 pointed out that the strong prevalence of experts in position formation does not necessarily qualify the Commission as a knowledge-driven actor operating only in accordance with a technocratic rationale. Externally generated knowledge sometimes found an unbiased way into the final Commission proposal by offering efficient solutions to a given problem. However, our case studies also document instances in which experts were used to create political consensus or where expertise was strategically and selectively used to justify pre-defined policy agendas.

A similar conclusion holds for another factor of position formation—*international policy transfer.* We conceived the transfer of policies from other levels of government—the international level or third countries—in searching for best practices as a typically technocratic logic of Commission agency. In our sample, adopting such international templates into the position of a drafting DG occurred in roughly half of our cases across all policy areas. In the area of research and innovation, DG officials often looked to the US as a reference point when drawing up new strategies and mimicked institutions following the dominant paradigm of a "technology gap" between Europe and the United States (Dosi et al. 2006). For example, the European Institute of Technology copied the Massachusetts Institute of Technology in the US (Chapter 6.4.2) and the European Research Council was built on the role model of the American National Science Foundation (Chapter 6.2.2). Working through a different mechanism, Commission officials at the intersection of social and common market policy and in consumer policy used regulatory templates from the international level quite often to ensure that their proposed law conformed to international practices and agreements, pertaining to international organizations such as the Basel Committee on Banking Supervision (financial conglomerates, Chapter 7.3.4), OECD recommendations (reinsurance, Chapter 5.4.5), a UN agreement on explosives (pyrotech case, Chapter 7.3.2) and the WTO *Codex Alimentarius* (food fortification and health and nutrition claims, Chapters 7.4.1 and 7.4.3). These moves to avoid inconsistencies with existing international rules show that EU position formation, much like national policy-making, is today embedded in processes at higher governance levels.

But as for the reliance on extant *acquis* discussed above, the transfer of policy instruments from other government levels can also occur in a much more selective manner that supports the pre-defined goals of Commission actors. For example, in the first drafting processes on equal treatment, DG EMPL drew willingly on anti-discrimination laws in Anglo-Saxon countries such as the US, Canada, Australia, and South Africa to develop far-reaching EU rules, particularly because these countries had the most progressive minority-protection laws in the world (Chapter 5.2.1). International policy transfer as a factor of internal position formation often followed technocratic considerations, but it was also used as a strategic resource in drafting processes that explicitly pursue more political aims.

11.1.5 Factors of DG Positions in Comparative Perspective

To summarize our comparative overview on position formation in EU Commission DGs, Figure 11.1 plots the prevalence of all respective factors derived in Chapter 2 across our overall sample and the three policy fields. From this aggregate view on the factors that decisively influenced the DGs' policy positions, we can conclude that the patterns of position formation are multifarious. Many

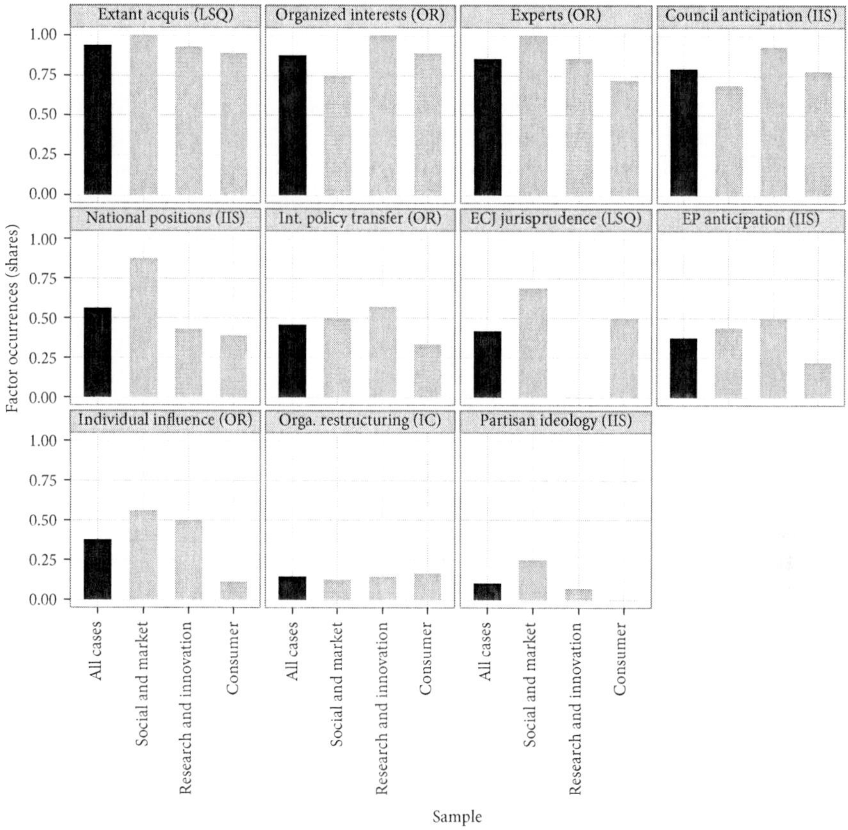

Fig. 11.1. Prevalence of position-formation factors across cases. Shares of cases in which the factor in question was needed to explain a particular DG position. Abbreviations in brackets refer to the four factor sets: legal status quo (LSQ), EU inter-institutional system (IIS), internal coordination (IC), and optional resources (OR)

different factors and external actors can potentially influence the Commission's proposals—and indeed they do so.

The comparative overview prompts two conclusions. First, and with respect to the institutional contexts derived in the analytical framework, factors from all of these four sets—legal status quo, internal coordination, inter-institutional system, and the wider EU multi-level context—yield strong explanations. In frequency terms, the extant *acquis*, organized interests, experts, and the anticipation of Council preferences are the most prevalent factors in internal position formation. We can safely conclude that these four factors are, on average, the most important sources and constraints for the policy positions of individual DGs. Particular national positions, the transfer of international policy templates, ECJ jurisprudence, and the anticipation of EP majorities bear some explanatory power and were relevant in roughly half of the cases we examined. By contrast, the influence of specific individuals, organizational restructuring, and partisan ideology are not irrelevant but seem to be much more exceptional factors regarding position formation inside the Commission.

Second, this comparative perspective on relevant factors does not characterize Commission agency in a clear-cut manner. At least for the cases we analyzed during the Prodi and Barroso I Commissions, neither the view of position formation as a technocratic and insulated process nor that of a process driven by actors' interests to maximize organizational or political utility holds across the board. Resources that at first sight clearly seemed to sustain a technocratic view of the Commission, such as the extant *acquis* or the reliance on experts, do indeed have a decisive impact on DGs' positions in general. But DGs used these factors in many different ways, depending on the particular goals they were pursuing. Moreover, classical political factors, such as organized interests and the anticipation of member-state positions, are almost as important in explaining Commission positions. Besides considering legal consistency and relying on expertise, internal Commission actors have their antennae very much oriented outwardly and skillfully resort to constraints and resources offered by the Commission's institutional context and the EU's wider multi-level governance system. These patterns suggest that there is not one type of Commission agency, but rather that it varies across drafting processes or even across DGs within one process. In this light, the naïve view of a unitary Commission with neutral aggregation of diverging positions can hardly be upheld. In the following section, we take a closer look at our second research question on the assertiveness of particular positions and DGs when it comes to internal conflict.

11.2 FACTOR PREVALENCE IN INTERNAL CONFLICT: FORMAL RULES, EXISTING COMPETENCES BUT LITTLE IMPORTANCE OF THE OUTSIDE WORLD

The six preceding empirical chapters have made clear that conflicting positions across DG boundaries are fairly ubiquitous during legislative drafting within the Commission. The bird's-eye perspective confirms this view. In fact, 38 of our 48 cases (almost 80 percent of our sample) involved disagreements on substantial points between two or more DGs. This share does not vary significantly across the three policy areas, so that we can safely conclude that internal interaction has to be taken into account systematically when explaining the policies proposed for Europe. Accordingly, this section analyses the patterns of DG interaction in the 38 conflictual cases and focuses on the prevalence of factors that explain a DG's assertiveness in such disputes.[6]

Turning to the question of which DGs were in disagreement in our sample, Figure 11.2 maps the empirical patterns of internal conflict we have observed in our case studies. For our three policy areas, it lists all the DGs that tried to influence the contents of the final Commission proposals and maps how often they were holding the drafting pen (y-axis) or were challenging the positions of the responsible department (x-axis). The higher a DG is situated on these maps,

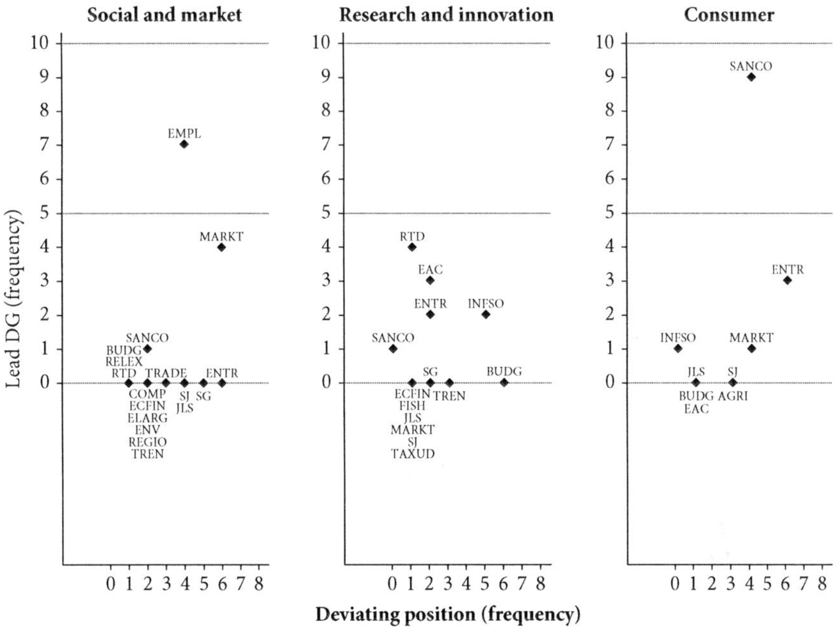

Fig. 11.2. Interaction maps of the three policy areas. Figure shows which DGs interacted on the conflictive proposals across the three covered policy fields (N = 12, 12, 14 for social and market, research and innovation, and consumer policy, respectively)

the more often it acted as the lead department. The more it tends to the right, the more often its positions deviated from those of the lead DG.

The most immediate finding from this perspective is that the field of consumer policy seems less crowded than the other two policy areas. At the intersection of social and market policy, 18 different DGs had some stakes in at least one of the cases covered. In research and innovation policy, 14 different internal actors tried to influence proposal contents. In consumer policy, only nine different players saw their interests touched upon and raised their voices accordingly. Due caution is warranted when generalizing this particular finding, but the former two policy areas seem to be characterized by a higher likelihood that one DG may be stepping into the responsibility area of other DGs. At the intersection of social and market policy, this diversification of interested actors is probably due to the cross-cutting nature of the single-market approach and the fact that reference to the four freedoms has historically been a successful strategy in advancing legislation in various, only loosely related, issue areas (Jabko 2006). Consequently, regulation in this area has a high likelihood of touching upon existing legislation managed by different DGs in the Commission. In research and innovation policy, in turn, sectoral research agendas as well as budget competition might explain why so many different internal actors hold a stake. In contrast, consumer policy is a rather young and purely regulatory policy field that may thus affect the interests of fewer internal actors.

Despite such policy-related variation, these maps show that internal interaction involves quite a diverse set of internal players. Some of them—populating the lower-left corners in Figure 11.2—hold rather specific interests and challenge the lead's position in only one or two proposals. Others are found much more often in the role of challenger—located in the two quadrants on the right-hand side. As we have shown elsewhere (Hartlapp et al. 2013), DGs with a more cross-cutting policy mandate have a higher chance of influencing a greater number of Commission proposals. DGs ENTR and MARKT, especially, challenge the contents of specific policy proposals more often than others. DG ENTR held a deviating position in 15, and DG MARKT in 11 cases, followed only by the horizontal services (DG BUDG [8], the Legal Service [8], and the Secretariat-General [7]). An interviewee underlined this succinctly by stating that "clearly, everybody will come knocking at their [DG MARKT's] door" (COM34:225), a fact that holds in a more historical perspective as well:

> The problem may actually be inherent in the horizontal nature of DG XV's [MARKT's] coordinating role (e.g. for the Single Market Action Plan), which sometimes requires it to set tight deadlines or take positions rapidly on single market principles, even where other DGs may feel that they also have competences and a right to be consulted. Similarly other services look to DG XV to provide a single market input to other policies (such as environment and the fight against crime). DG XV's argument would be that its central responsibility obliges it to take decisions and at times gives it a role of arbiter (Inspection Générale des Services 1999: 11).

However, our case studies at the intersection of social and market policy (Chapter 5) and in consumer policy (Chapter 7) also show that DG MARKT's prerogatives are often challenged by other DGs and can lead to heated ideological and turf battles within the Commission. Similarly, DG ENTR is quite often pitted against the more interventionist portfolios at EU level (DGs SANCO and EMPL). Typically, efforts to avoid red tape for enterprises and especially small- and medium-sized enterprises in more interventionist policy proposals were at stake.

In research and innovation policy, the roles of drafting DG and challenger appear more equally distributed, illustrating a stress field among DGs RTD, EAC, INFSO, and ENTR. In addition, DG BUDG appears as a horizontal service that often challenged the lead DG's position. While the policy DGs strive to increase their funding, DG BUDG keeps an eye on the proportionality of Community intervention (Chapter 6).

In the following sub-sections, we focus in on the factors that were relevant in explaining which internal actors proved to be assertive in the 38 conflictual drafting processes. In line with the analytical framework in Chapter 2 and as for the policy positions above, we first differentiate between factors flowing from the legal status quo, internal coordination, the EU inter-institutional system, and the wider EU multi-level context before providing a comparative summary.

11.2.1 Factors Grounded in the Legal Status Quo

To start with, *supranational competences* were strikingly important for DGs in defending their position against contending services. In 27 of our 38 conflictual cases, a DG successfully relied on the treaty base, the quantity of legislation, or the legal substance it controlled to assert a preferred position. The ability to draw on such supranational competences was relevant in almost all cases at the intersection of social and internal market policies and also mattered for at least half of the cases in the two other policy areas. Supranational competences served as a relevant power factor across all DGs—including those with a powerful treaty base, such as DG MARKT and those with less powerful ones, such as DG EMPL. One prominent example is the services directive, where DG MARKT constantly argued that a horizontal country-of-origin principle amounted to simply inserting existing primary and case law on the four freedoms into secondary legislation (see Chapter 5.4.2). However, treaty asymmetries favoring DGs that could frame their point as a market-enhancing policy were only one, and far from the most important, of the references to supranational competences that were used. On the contrary, in the area of anti-discrimination policy, DG EMPL purposefully and successfully exploited the then new Treaty Article 13 (TEU) on anti-discrimination to push through its market-intervening position against opposing DGs. Here, actually using competences that were only recently transferred to the supranational level was of common interest to several DGs in demonstrating the capacity of the Commission as a whole. And this made it difficult for portfolios to oppose the substance of the act in question or to block position formation entirely (Chapter 5.2.1). In addition to exploiting treaty bases that served their interests, DGs also gained weight for their positions through the legacy and quantity of legislation in their respective portfolios. This was related in part to greater experience and a broader knowledge base in the policy area that DGs could draw on. It appeared to be an advantage for DGs managing consecutive funding programs in the area of research and innovation policy. Here, internal actors could refer to the success of previous programs in order to make a strong case for continuation or for budget extensions (Chapters 6.2 and 6.3). Another example is the directive on the recognition of professional qualifications, where the drafting unit in DG MARKT argued that consolidation of existing sectoral approaches required a balance between automatic recognition and harmonization, thus producing a regulatory model in line with its preferences (Chapter 5.4.1). Summing up, a DG could draw on its supranational competences in different ways: at times political arguments about unbreakable treaty competences counted, and at times it was a DG's experience and the proof of facts related to the extant *acquis* that was the decisive asset.

11.2.2 Factors Grounded in Internal Coordination

Turning to the factors derived from internal coordination requirements, Chapter 10 showed that acting as the *lead department* as well as the support—or the lack thereof—from *horizontal services* are highly relevant factors in explaining the outcomes in the conflictual cases in our sample. Being the lead DG was the most common explanatory factor behind internal success. DGs frequently exploited being the lead DG by using either the strategic and gatekeeping advantages or the informational advances associated with this role. While the first, more strategic mechanism played out in just over half of our cases, the latter, more technocratic mechanism was applied in just under half. Likewise, Chapter 10 underlined that a DG's assertiveness against other departments can be explained almost as often by support from horizontal services—most notably, the SG, the SJ, and DG BUDG. Backed by their formal role under the current structure of internal coordination, they resolved conflicts either by appearing as preservers of technocratic quality or by acting as strategic veto players.

Alliances with other (policy) DGs also appeared as an asset, although only in about one-fourth of all cases. Though direct evidence is rare, one can suspect that the shadow of the majority requirement in College or the consensus primacy advocated by Barroso indirectly rendered more powerful those DGs that could demonstrate that their position was supported by others (Bailer 2004; Alesina et al. 2005). One example is DG ENTR's alliance-building with DGs SANCO and JLS when objecting to DG MARKT's ambition to include a mutual-recognition clause in the consumer rights directive (see Chapter 7.2.6). Other examples stem from the intersection of social and market policies where an alliance of DGs EMPL, RTD, and ENV in favor of intervention figured as a source of power in College when facing more market liberal positions jointly advanced by DGs ENTR and MARKT (sometimes supported by DGs ECFIN and COMP).[7] This worked to the benefit of the former, for instance in the employment equality framework and the race equality directives (see Chapter 5.2.1) because it was difficult for those holding the other position to ignore demands from a whole group of Commissioners. In drafting processes adhering to a political rather than a technocratic rationale, DG alliances became an internal power resource.

We also expected *workload*—that is, the personnel resources a DG can devote to the drafting of an internally conflictual case—to be a factor impacting on assertiveness. According to a technocratic understanding of the Commission, more personnel and thus also more in-house expertise should benefit DGs when elaborating proposals or fighting against provisions they oppose. However, this factor was relevant in only five of the 38 conflictual cases. One example is DG SANCO's proposal for a directive on the standards of quality and safety of human organs intended for transplantation, where the lead DG suffered from insufficient personnel devoted to this highly relevant dossier (Chapter 6.4.4).

However, equally infrequently, an *initiative's origin* was sometimes relevant for internal assertiveness. We had expected a proposal to benefit from the knowledge of the responsible desk officers when originating from the administrative level under a technocratic type of Commission agency. Alternatively, a proposal may benefit from the accompanying political force when it originated from the political apex under a more political kind of Commission agency. In fact, in the few cases in which this factor played out as a power resource, it was support from the political level that made a DG position win out in internal interactions. Prime examples are the European Institute for Innovation and Technology initiated by Commission President Barroso (EIT, Chapter 6.4.2) and the European Globalisation Adjustment Fund initiated by Social Affairs Commissioner Spidla and President Barroso (Chapter 5.2.5). Both were political top-down initiatives that met with considerable resistance from the Commission's administration. In both cases, the lead DG only managed to navigate its initiative through internal coordination thanks to explicit political interest in the proposal.

Further, we theorized that references to shared norms would grant legitimacy to the policy positions of individual DGs in line with a "logic of appropriateness" (March and Olsen 1996). With regard to *bureaucratic legitimacy*, a DG may refer to the norm that each DG serves a specific mandate, delineated by the Commission's formal internal organizational structure, which renders it the appropriate and authoritative actor on a specified set of issues. In roughly one-fourth of our cases, we could observe that claims based on this norm enabled a DG to push through its position. One example is the conflict over the responsible lending principle in the consumer credit proposal (cf. Chapter 7.2.3):

> At some stage there is an agreement that the consumer credit directive is put forth under the responsibility of the Consumer Affairs Commissioner. If this Commissioner goes into the College and says "I am convinced about this thing. I have had considerable, long, difficult, interesting, challenging discussions with my colleague in charge of the single market but I still maintain that this compromise is the most coherent and the best we could propose", then the College will eventually say "ok, let's have it your way" (COM89:118).

Public legitimacy, in turn, might bolster a DG's position in internal conflicts if this actor can credibly refer to the common understanding that the Commission should serve the citizen or the general public interest. Public legitimacy therefore stems from a backing by public sentiment or from reference to contemporaneous public debates. In 14 of our 38 conflictual cases (37 percent), such claims were successfully invoked. Examples are the equal treatment acts, where the lead DG EMPL benefited from favorable public opinion. Interestingly, DG EMPL actually enhanced the perceived legitimacy of its positions through public newspaper appearances, thus proactively pushing for policy visibility (Chapter 5.2.1). Likewise, DG SANCO's consumer-friendly approach often benefited from claims to public legitimacy. For example, in the light of an ongoing public debate on obesity in Europe, DG SANCO was able to assert mandatory nutrition declarations against the initial opposition of DG ENTR, which backed down to avoid going against public opinion (Chapter 7.4.4). References to a democratic norm mattered much less in the more technical area of research and innovation policy. The connection between public legitimacy as a factor of internal assertiveness and the public visibility of a regulatory issue seems to be more systematic. Public legitimacy claims mattered significantly more often in salient proposals than in non-salient ones (Chapter 9). Taken together, our discussion of legitimacy claims indicates that both more technocratic and more political norms are relevant in conflicts inside the Commission.

11.2.3 Factors Grounded in the EU's Inter-institutional System

Turning to the effects that the EU's inter-institutional system might have on power within the Commission, the *proximity of a DG's position to the Council's or the EP's majority* was of importance in some instances. However, whereas the shadow of the inter-institutional process strongly influenced DGs' positions across the board (Section 11.1.3), it was less systematically relevant in explaining internal DG power. A greater proximity to Council and EP majorities allowed a contested position to be asserted in 15 and 10 cases, respectively. Thus, as for internal position formation, the Council seems to be more relevant than the EP when it comes to internal conflicts.

Proximity to the Council's anticipated position was most prevalent in the area of social and internal-market policies—it was a decisive source of power in three-fourths of the conflictual cases in this policy field. Although most decisions are taken with a qualified majority, member states often hold strong positions in this policy field that can be used internally as a bargaining resource for or against a proposed provision. Proximity to the Council also decisively helped DG SANCO in disputes with other DGs: regarding the consumer rights proposal, for example, DG SANCO defeated DG MARKT's demand for a country-of-origin principle on these grounds (Chapter 7.2.6). DG SANCO successfully claimed that its position reflected the interest of the inter-institutional players and thus that harmonization would provide an optimal solution to the given policy problem of varying consumer protection. EP proximity also mattered most often for internal conflicts in the area of research and innovation policy, where the Parliament, due to its powers where the budget was concerned, was valued by DGs as an important prospective "ally." This applied, for instance, to DG INFSO, whose close contacts with the EP paid off in its battle with DG BUDG over the amount of funding for the eContent programs (Chapter 6.3.2).

A further potential source of power is the *size of a member state* backing an internally contested DG position. The low prevalence (four out of 38 conflicting cases) is striking, however, given that the size of a Commissioner's member state may matter under a political type of Commission agency following classical realist reasoning (Morgenthau 1963) and under a technocratic logic where a more sizeable member state allows a DG or its Commissioner to draw on larger national expert networks and, thus, on more information (Joana and Smith 2006: 39). The few cases in which the support of a large member state helped a DG to assert its position internally show that realist reasoning was more important here. The continuous opposition of the German government to equal-treatment principles in insurance regulation or areas pertaining to the private sphere allowed Commissioner Verheugen to secure his position on specific key provisions (Chapters 5.2.2 and 5.2.4). Similarly, French demand for the exclusion of the gambling sector from the scope of the liberalization of services directive can be explained fully only if we take into account that this demand was raised by a powerful member state (Chapter 5.4.2). Comparing the prevalence of member-state size (four out of 38 cases) and proximity to a Council majority (15 out of 38 cases) leads to a conclusion similar to that we drew above with regard to internal position formation: particular national positions matter less than the aggregate preferences of all member states in the Council.

11.2.4 Optional Resources in the EU Multi-level System

From the more optional resources DGs could draw on when asserting their positions, support from external *organized interests* was the most prevalent. In 13 of the 38 conflictual cases (34 percent), stakeholders played a decisive role in lending a DG power against opposing services, and were thus strikingly less relevant than they were for position formation. One mechanism resides in the diversification of stakeholder demands that supported a DG's position because it signaled the breadth of expertise and information that a DG put into internal coordination. This more technocratic mechanism occurred mainly in the area of social and internal market policy. Another mechanism rests on the strategic information from organized stakeholders that DGs could exploit internally in order to assert their preferred positions. In the regulation of food additives, for example, DG ENTR was able to credibly predict industry opposition that the comparatively young DG SANCO wanted to avoid at that time (Chapter 7.4.2). Overall, outside interests that supported internal DG assertiveness were most often strategically chosen in line with the DG's pre-defined goals. This finding, spanning both of our research questions on policy positions and internal assertion, is particularly interesting in the light of the literature. In contrast to characterizations of the EU as a pluralist system that is particularly open to organized interests or (negatively) influenced and captured by lobbyists, organized interests often mattered only where they fitted a position a Commission actor already held anyway. One example is the cross-border healthcare directive, where DG SANCO had consciously built up informational channels through a range of stakeholders. When it came to conflictual interactions, this helped, for example, to support the endeavor to include a health-specific treaty base the DG had favored (see Chapter 5.4.4). We observed straightforward political bargaining between DGs that strengthened their positions by referring to the backing of powerful external stakeholder groups.

Individual *entrepreneurship* helped to push a position through in 13 cases. Similar to the influence of individuals on a DG's policy position (see Section 11.1.4), here the decisive resource for assertiveness is located at the individual level where "advocates who are willing to invest their resources—time, energy, reputation, money— . . . promote a position in return for anticipated future gain in the form of material, purposive, or solidary benefits" (Kingdon 1984: 188). Other than in DG position formation, however, individuals who were relevant for internal assertiveness were not only situated in the political, but equally often in the administrative echelons. Prime examples are the public procurement cases, where DG ENV was able to successfully introduce environmental criteria into the regulation. In its battle with DG MARKT, this DG decisively benefited from an ambitious desk officer and Commissioner, both vehement defenders of environmental concerns (Chapter 5.3.1). Overall, individual actors seem to play a much more pronounced role in internal coordination than a perception of a monolithic bureaucracy operating along Weberian lines would suggest.

Finally, in about one-fourth of our conflictual cases, the "nesting" of a DG position in a parallel external *meta game* was decisive. In these cases, a DG was powerful internally when its preferred position supported the Commission's joint interest at other levels of EU governance. This happened when DG MARKT pushed back DG ENTR's demand for more favorable SME treatment with reference to the Commission's stance in WTO negotiations. Meta games as a factor of internal assertiveness most often proved relevant in the area of research and innovation policy, mainly with regard to broader budget negotiations going on in parallel. One example are the struggles between DGs RTD and BUDG around the Community expenses for the International Thermonuclear Experimental Reactor (ITER) project via the 6th Euratom Research Framework Programme. Here, DG BUDG, which argued for more restrictive book-keeping than the lead DG RTD, benefited from the pending shaky negotiations on the project at international level, making it a risky investment for the EU (Chapter 6.2.3). This exemplifies how Commission actors have strategically exploited the ability to link their own case to processes taking place at other levels of governance in the EU multi-level system.

11.2.5 Factors of DG Assertiveness in Comparative Perspective

Figure 11.3 illustrates how the various factors of internal DG assertiveness fare in comparative perspective. The aggregate view shows that factors of assertiveness are far less concentrated than our findings reported in this chapter on factors impacting on a DG's position. When it comes to internal quarrels, DGs draw on the different resources much more selectively. We also find more variation across policy areas, even among the most prevalent factors of internal power. As a first comparative conclusion, therefore, the process of internal coordination across

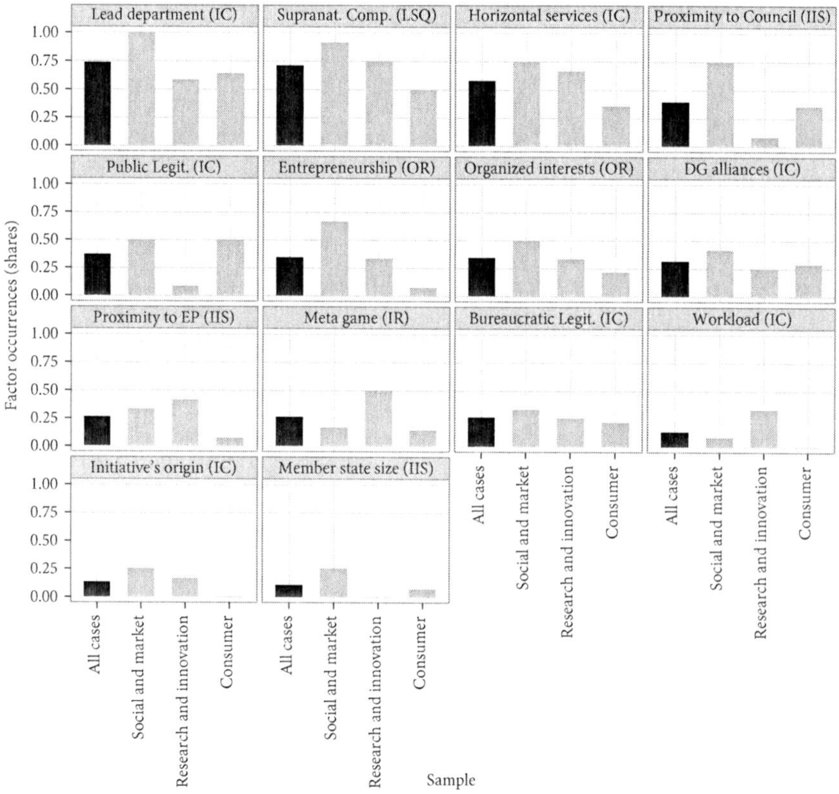

Fig. 11.3. Prevalence of interaction factors across cases. Shares of the 38 conflictive cases in the sample in which the factor in question was needed to explain the internal assertiveness of a DG position. Abbreviations in brackets refer to the four factor sets legal status-quo (LSQ), EU inter-institutional system (IIS), internal coordination (IC), and optional resources (OR)

DGs follows far less stable and predictable patterns than the process of DG position formation. With a view to our initial puzzle, the reasons for inconsistencies in the Commission's overall policy output often rest in the more volatile logics of internal coordination.

Factors deriving from the formal coordination structures are among the most stable sources of internal power—very much in line with the findings of Chapter 10. Support from a horizontal service, but especially acting as the lead department, accounts most often for explaining the assertiveness of internally contested DG positions.[8]

The only other factor that comes close to the relevance of being lead DG is being grounded in the legal status quo. The prevalence of supranational competences as a decisive power resource suggests that those DGs controlling a large *acquis* or being linked to a favorable treaty basis are among the more powerful players when it comes to conflicts with other DGs. Together with the strong influence that the extant *acquis* exerted on DG positions in the first place, this indicates that internal position formation tends to reproduce existing regulatory patterns which, however, may lead to internal conflict and controversial proposals where these differ across sectors or if they are intended to tackle policy problems that have not been on the European agenda before.

By contrast, constraints emerging from the EU's inter-institutional context or optional resources from the wider multi-level system matter much less for internal interaction than they did for the positions DGs held in the first place. While internal Commission actors often looked to the Council or to organized interests when adopting a position, this only rarely turned into a bargaining chip when it came to internal conflicts. Internal interaction is much more inwardly oriented than position formation, which can also explain why internally negotiated Commission proposals sometimes stir up sharp controversy among the external stakeholders.

11.3 CONCLUSION: BIRD'S-EYE VIEW ON POSITION FORMATION WITHIN AND ACROSS COMMISSION DGS

The comparative overview in this chapter emphasizes that position formation within and across Commission DGs is diverse and highly interactive. From the four sets of factors we derived from the Commission's institutional context in Chapter 2, only the legal status quo displays systematic explanatory power in both stages of internal legislative drafting. The extant *acquis* is a powerful explanatory factor for the positions of individual DGs, while the strength and the amount of supranational competence they already control is often turned into an advantage when different policy positions clash internally. By contrast, factors flowing from internal coordination were mainly relevant in situations of conflict, but rarely reflected back on the policy positions of individual DGs. The inter-institutional system, in turn, is relevant for these policy positions but much more rarely accounts for power in internal conflicts. And if the inter-institutional system casts a shadow on internal position formation, it most often does so in line with the aggregated member-state interests in the Council rather than along EP majorities, partisan ideologies, or specific national positions. Finally, optional resources from the EU's multi-level context—most notably input from organized interests and experts—are highly important for explaining the positions of individual DGs but do not as often matter for assertiveness in internal quarrels.

In addition, we found two broader differences across both analytical stages of policy formulation. First, the set of relevant factors is more stable across cases and policy areas in explaining the policy positions of individual DGs than it is in explaining internal assertiveness. The policy positions of individual DGs are, on average, more easily predictable than the outcomes of internal conflicts. Second, internal Commission actors seem to draw much more on external resources and constraints when forming their positions, while resorting more to internal resources when trying to assert these positions in conflicts with their counterparts. While many of the external factors and constraints have been the subject of existing EU policy-making analyses, conflict and interaction dynamics inside the Commission have been given little systematic attention to date. Our findings suggest that this second analytical stage needs to feature more prominently in explanatory accounts of the policies proposed for Europe. Only by combining external factors and constraints with the logics of internal interaction can we explain why the Commission sometimes proposes inconsistent or highly controversial policies.

However, for two reasons this comparative overview holds limited potential to answer the broader question on the type of Commission agency. On the one hand, in neither stage of policy formulation is there a clear predominance of *factors* that point to a consistently technocratic, competence-seeking or policy-seeking rationale. In position formation, for example, reliance on experts, uncovering leeway within member-state preferences, and serving organized interests are all equally important. In internal interaction, similarly, the strong prevalence of factors flowing from the formal internal rules and the legal status quo are essentially consistent with both the technocratic and the competence-seeking rationales of Commission agency. Moreover, factors pointing to a policy-seeking type of agency—such as partisan interests in position formation or ideology-driven alliances in internal interaction—occur seldom but cannot be refuted completely.

On the other hand, our discussion of individual factors highlights the fact that even those factors that seem to pertain to a specific type of Commission agency turn into a DG position or internal assertiveness through various *mechanisms* that sometimes indicate one type of agency or another. While "hard" realist resources, such as national positions, may very well also work by providing efficient policy templates, knowledge-related factors, such as expertise, may also be used strategically by Commission DGs. And while advantages flowing from formal coordination structures or the legal status quo could be used as tactical tools, they sometimes turned into internal assertiveness only because they generated superior information and improved the technical quality of a DG's demands. Thus, the individual case studies and the comparative overview have revealed that we need to look into the position formation processes to detect *how* certain factors play out or are used by actors. In order to adequately capture the type of Commission agency we need to consider both the factors and the mechanisms that link them to the policies proposed for Europe.

Having done so, our discussion so far shows that different types of Commission agency coexist when Europe's agenda-setter forms its position. At times, position formation in the Commission indeed conforms to traditional accounts of technocratic policy-making, where functional arguments count most. However, Commission actors also appear to be ideologically driven. And particularly when it comes to internally negotiating a common Commission position, vested turf considerations and competence-seeking behavior are often brought to bear. Thus, rather than looking only at factors, explaining *how* the Commission forms its positions requires a consistent structuring of different types of position formation processes, which we will provide in the following chapter.

NOTES

1. Whenever we note statistically significant differences between groups of cases in this chapter, we resort to simple two-sample t-tests for a difference in means across these groups. In this particular instance, drafting in research and innovation policy lasted 15.5 months with a standard deviation of 4.5, versus 34.8 months in consumer policy with a standard deviation of 13.4.
2. The duration of inter-institutional negotiations in our sample of cases was drawn from the PreLex database. The relationship between internal and inter-institutional duration in our 48 cases is estimated by OLS and is given by Inter-Inst Duration=18.62*** + 0.25** Internal Duration (Adj R2=0.04). The toy safety case—with an extraordinarily long internal drafting process (70 months) and a very short inter-institutional negotiation (17 months)—has a strong leverage on this result, however. Excluding it results in a relationship given by Inter-Inst Duration=15.87*** + 0.38** Internal Duration (Adj R^2=0.09).
3. This resonates well with Susanne Schmidt's (2000) "lesser evil strategy." The case of food supplements (Chapter 7.4.1) is a particularly good example of how this strategy can be successfully employed by the Commission.
4. Our sample showed no ECJ relevance for drafting in research and innovation policy, not least for lack of a broad treaty base to refer to (Pilniok 2011: 380). This may change in the future with the introduction of Article 182, para. 5 AEUV in the Lisbon Treaty, where the EU has been given regulatory competence to establish a European Research Area (see Chapter 6).
5. Note, furthermore, that EP anticipation is not systematically linked to partisan positions in our sample. In only two cases, were these two factors relevant for internal position formation at the same time, which indicates that EP anticipation is not systematically driven by partisan considerations.
6. The cases that did not involve any substantial conflicts between DGs are distributed fairly equally across policy areas and over time. Here, typically no other positions were identified due to a lack of information on interaction or the fact that discussions evolved around technical issues rather than substantial key provisions (see Chapter 3.4.1).
7. Interestingly, the intervention alliance clung together on the basis of a close partisan ideological stance by Social-Democratic Commissioners (cf. Chapter 4).
8. When we consider our assessment of the most powerful DG per drafting process (cf. Chapter 3.4.3), it was most often the lead DG that successfully pushed its position through (32 of 38 conflictual cases, 84%). Thus, the decision as to which DG is assigned to this role for a given policy issue is a strong predictor for the contents of the final Commission proposal.

12

Shaping Policies for Europe

Internal Position Formation between Problem-solving, Competence Expansion, and Political Ideology

The preceding chapters have shed much light on our initial puzzle as to why the policies for Europe proposed by the European Commission are sometimes astonishingly successful and far-reaching, at other times highly controversial and contested, and at other times again both contradictory and inconsistent. The aggregate picture still remains variegated, however. Our 48 case studies and their systematic comparison show that position formation inside the European Commission is, in fact, multifaceted. On the one hand, the factors and constraints we derived from the Commission's various institutional contexts in Chapter 2 do hold explanatory power for internal position formation. On the other, Chapter 11 has shown that only some of these factors and constraints matter in a consistent and stable manner across legislative initiatives and policy areas.

So what do these findings tell us about the kind of animal the Commission is? What do they reveal about the type of agency driving Europe's central agenda-setter? As spelled out in Chapter 2, the existing literature has most often resorted to one of three possible views. Such accounts have characterized the Commission as a technocratic, a competence-maximizing, or a policy-seeking organization, thereby assuming—often implicitly—that functional problem-solving, regulatory competence expansion, or political ideology account for the regulatory output produced by the Commission. As a result of our empirical foray into the logics of internal position formation, our perspective differs strongly from these static views. Rather than imposing only one of these models on the Commission's overall agenda-setting activity and thereby conceptualizing the Commission as an agent that is constantly motivated by the same goals, we posit that these three types of agency actually *co-exist* within the Commission. Their relative importance varies from one drafting process to another and sometimes also from one process stage to the next. Our findings also suggest that the relative importance of technocratic, competence-maximization, or policy-seeking rationales cannot be discerned by the differing prevalence of various institutional factors and constraints alone. As the extensive discussion of individual factors in Chapter 11 has shown, their inter-play, on the one hand, and the mechanisms translating them into policy positions or assertiveness, on the other, reveal the underlying type of Commission agency.

This conclusion has important implications for an emerging research field on power and conflict inside the European Commission. The significant advances, controversies, and inconsistencies in the policy agenda proposed by the Commission cannot be explained by merely asking which type of actor the Commission is. Future research should instead ask what type of process internal position formation follows and under which conditions technocratic, competence-maximization, and policy seeking rationales are more or less likely. This chapter advances such a research agenda in three distinct ways. First, and most importantly, it proposes a process typology by combining the deductively derived institutional factors with our inductively generated insights on the mechanisms that link the factors to the policy positions of DGs and their assertiveness in internal interactions. Second, it provides an initial view on the relative frequencies of each process type we observed in our sample. And, finally, it provides insights on the conditions that strengthen the relative importance of each process type.

12.1 THREE TYPES OF FACTORIAL AND MECHANISTIC CHARACTERISTICS

In an approach combining deductive reasoning and inductive insights, we discerned three ideal-typical patterns of position formation in the EU Commission. This built on our expectations regarding the external factors and constraints that should matter for internal actors, which we deduced in Chapter 2. In addition, through process-tracing, we generated inductive knowledge on how and why specific factors translated into the policy position or the internal assertiveness of particular DGs. By focusing on the commonalities of how and why particular factors affected the final Commission proposal in the 48 case studies, a threefold typology of stylized, contrasting process models of position formation in the EU Commission emerged. This allows us to capture some of the essential features of Commission position formation at a more general level.

The resulting types characterize ideal-typical processes of position formation in the form of non-exhaustive but analytically mutually exclusive categories. It is the specific agency of the Commission that discriminates between the three types, as visible in the respective combination of explanatory factors and mechanisms of position formation. More explicitly, it is the basic motivation with which the decisive internal actors enter the process that determines the kind of process we are in. In the following, we describe each of the three ideal types and enrich them with observed examples of factor–mechanism combinations. We abstract here as far as possible in order to derive more general models of position formation that are applicable over time and across policy areas.

To start with, position-formation processes that we characterize as *technocratic* are dominated by a focus on the anticipated efficiency of the policy proposal. As described in Chapter 2, this perspective ties in easily with functionalist explanations in the literature on European integration that emerged from the seminal works of Mitrany (1971) and Haas (1958/1968b). Policies emerge or existing positions are adjusted in reaction to new challenges and problems, performance crises, or the perception of welfare inefficiencies. Given these challenges, internal Commission actors enter position formation without pre-defined goals except for finding the optimal policy solution to an externally defined problem. While actors are seeking to find the best possible, that is the most efficient and effective solution to a given problem, they may, however, be constrained by their bureaucratic mandate, which is most often defined by sectoral policy portfolios in the Commission.

For a technocratic problem-solver, a broad variety of factors may be relevant when it comes to the position-formation process in the EU Commission. However, reflecting Max Weber's (1925/1978) idea of expertise as the bureaucrat's most relevant source of influence in policy-making, the dominant mechanism linking the explanatory factors to positions and assertiveness in the Commission is the provision of factual, unbiased knowledge and information. For example, the extant *acquis* and ECJ jurisprudence matter in these processes because they are a source of legal consistency, because they can be taken as a proof of facts and because they orient views towards policy models for emerging problems that have successfully worked in the past. In this process model, Commission actors operate as honest brokers who openly listen to the knowledge provided by inter-institutional actors. Moreover, in the quest for viable solutions to emerging problems, individual national positions are welcomed above the aggregate Council position if they offer efficient solutions or templates. Commission officials further consult societal actors from the wider political system of the EU in order to find the best possible response to a given problem. Responsiveness to these actors is not driven by strategic considerations or pressure politics, but by the degree to which they offer neutral internal and external expertise leading to a broadened information pool. Thus, factual information conveyed by a plurality of many different stakeholders is listened to in an unbiased manner—"to avoid extreme positions and to strike a balance" (COM115:93). This is nicely illustrated by the following quote: "If you want to monitor CO_2 emissions, the member states have the data—Germany, France, Italy, Spain—they have the data on the emissions. But you also have to double check and verify with the car manufacturers" (COM123:71). Likewise, the existence of regulatory templates from the national, supranational, or international levels bears much weight in explaining positions that were developed along functional lines. The exact interest or person behind the desired expert knowledge plays a subordinate role for a technocrat. Rather than the characteristics of the information providers, the attributes of the information itself are decisive for the involvement of expertise and the corresponding actors. The knowledge required has to concern the affected sector and has to be sound, timely, and on target.

Conflicting positions also arise in this technocratic world. Differing positions are explained on the basis of sectorally specific definitions of what constitutes the best solution to a perceived problem—depending on the socio-economic sector for which the DG is responsible (Bouwen 2003). Dividing lines between groups of actors that share preferences and ideas can be found in the Commission's sectoral organization and they play out via knowledge specific to the policy field, extant EU legislation, ECJ jurisprudence, or specific stakeholder sets. Where conflicting views meet, a functionalist approach is compatible with an understanding of competing advocacy coalitions, whose fundamentally differing problem perceptions and approaches may lead to disagreements (Sabatier 1998). However, DG interaction following technocratic considerations amounts to a coordination game where all DGs expect common spoils and adjust their positions on the basis of argumentative processes and factual expertise providing alternative policy solutions (Radaelli 1995: 179). In interactions, actors seek to realize gains for all concerned stakeholders pursuing the perceived "common weal" (Mitrany 1971). In such a coordination game, the legacy and quantity of legislation in a portfolio explains a substantial share of knowledge-based leverage. Organized interests are important for supporting a DG's position under this reasoning when they can be shown to be providers of relevant and, ideally, diversified factual information—the functionalist's most important resource for drafting efficient proposals and asserting them in internal contestations. Structural factors are relevant only where they determine access to information or the use that can be made thereof, such as having been appointed lead department. Finally, internal power also derives from bureaucratic legitimacy where a formally mandated DG is perceived as the appropriate and authoritative actor on a specific policy challenge.

Rather than striving for pareto-optimal solutions as in the preceding model, position-formation processes of the *competence-seeking* type are characterized by internal Commission actors who enter position formation with the goal of retaining or expanding their competences. Grounded in rational-choice approaches of organizational theory (Downs 1966/1967; Niskanen 1974; Dunleavy 1991) and existing EU studies that have identified "most Commissioners wanting to be responsible for as much as possible" (Nugent 2000b: 9), this type of process occurs where a DG is seeking for growth in competences and/or budget. Typically in the multi-level system, competence expansion is sought vis-à-vis the national level, but it is also complicated by turf considerations between DGs. For the Commission's internal actors, a growing bureau can better attract capable personnel, provide its leaders with increased power, income, and prestige, and simply generate more leeway from member states in policy-making and implementation. In this model, the internal actors are open to adjusting the substantive policy contents of a legislative proposal in an attempt to increase their competences or budget. As one Commission official described Commission actors' rationale in such a process: "Basically they do not really care about the policy substance. They are only concerned about how to pull all the strings that are floating around somehow together, in order to achieve some outcome" (COM110:38, authors' translation). Thus, in this model, various factors may become relevant for the Commission's position, but only do so if they help retain or increase competences and resources for internal actors or for the Commission as a whole since this is the dominant mechanism linking external factors to policy positions and internal assertiveness.

This mechanism implies that DGs draw rather selectively on the extant *acquis* and ECJ jurisprudence to defend or to extend their bureaucratic area of responsibility. Positions are often best explained by the anticipation of future decision-making in view of aggregate national interests, since political feasibility is a decisive criterion that ensures competence extension. Internal actors also accommodate other stakeholders when a DG assumes that it cannot reach its goals of extending competences in the EU multi-level system without paying tribute to these views in its position. Thus, external interests are granted influence where they deliver political support as well as acceptance and help to build alliances supporting the supranational involvement in the issue area. They may be consulted openly in this process model, but their influence ultimately depends on whether their demands matter for the competence goals of the Commission actors holding the drafting pen. Organizational restructuring may also impact on positions where these result from future anticipated or from past competence allocations between DGs. Individuals can make a difference where their action aims at maximizing personal standing.

As in the technocratic model, sectoral views differ, however, this time not because of diverging bureaucratic mandates, but in view of the distribution of benefits sought for internal and external stakeholders. Consequently, when it comes to interaction between DGs, conflicts do not resemble a coordination game, but a zero-sum game. As one DG official put it: "Part of the ethos of the Commission is that it's a win–lose situation: one DG beats another and wins the argument" (COM93:228). DGs try to win their way in a strategic manner, for example, by actively exploiting their advantages granted by the formal coordination structure that empowers the lead department as gatekeeper. And they strategically build on existing legislation and ECJ case law, claiming that selected elements of law constitute unbreakable treaty provisions or legal precedents if this fits their goal of competence-maximization against opposing internal interests. Along similar lines, organized interests may become a resource for internal assertiveness when they provide strategic information that enhances the likelihood of extending or retaining regulatory competences. Remaining conflicts may be settled by support from the political level or by competence-based concessions and recompenses (such as clear-cut scope delineations or the involvement of other DGs in implementation). In addition, DG positions in alignment with the overall growth of the Commission's supranational policy-making competences may trump the demands of individual DGs in this process model. For example, the public legitimacy of a particular DG position—sometimes actively forged by specific internal actors—can be an internal power resource because it ensures broader acceptability of Commission interventions and thereby bolsters the future retention and extension of overall Commission competences.

Finally, position-formation processes can be characterized as being of the *policy-seeking* type when actors enter the process with pre-defined ideological or normative beliefs. Accordingly, they have a clear conviction on how the solution to a given problem ought to look given particular ideological preferences or norms (Axelrod 1970; De Swaan 1973). From this third perspective, DGs are motivated by considerations regarding the social justice or normative rightfulness of the policy choices they are trying to include in the final Commission proposal. Much as in the competence-seeking model, they deviate from the null hypothesis of unbiased, technocratic decision-making and actively act in a much more political and strategic manner. Accordingly, some factors and mechanisms characterizing the resulting processes of position formation resonate with both models. However, in contrast to the competence-seeking model, particular legislative solutions are sought after as a means in themselves and not in order to accomplish other utility-maximizing goals. For the EU political system, it has been argued that rather than a primarily partisan motivation, what matters are national-cultural models and deeply rooted beliefs along a continuum of conservative and progressive conceptions of society (Hooghe 2013;

also Hooghe and Marks 2009). External factors and constraints inform policy positions and internal assertiveness where they display a normative fit between actor ideologies and the contents of the legislative proposal. In a historical source, a Commission official explained, "the main thing is to have an important idea, and then find a specialist in the area" (cited in Middlemas 1995: 247)—thus, ultimately, Commission actors' *ex ante* agenda determines the influence of factors.

Relative to the other two agency models, the Commission is perceived less as being made up of bureaucratic actors than of individuals with political predispositions and socializations (cf. Chapter 4). Accordingly, factors grounded in internal coordination or the outside world carry less explanatory power compared to factors that are directly related to the individuals working on a particular proposal. It is their value-driven agendas and beliefs that most influence the collective actors' positions. A DG's policy position carries the ideological footprint of responsible Commissioners (and sometimes that of responsible administrators). External factors matter for a DG's position only where internal actors have some control over the topic and substance of expert studies, for example. In this model, stakeholder access follows a neo-pluralist pattern under which mainly external stakeholders who are pre-committed to the DG's policy goal gain exclusive or preferential access. Following the same logic, a DG may care less about the inter-institutional decision-making context at large than about those member states with a policy that has a high normative fit. Likewise, existing regulatory templates are typically considered if they showed success in reaching the policy goals that follow the normatively preferred views. In consequence, processes of the policy-seeking type result in DG positions that differ regarding how they assess the distributive consequences of different legislative options.

Hence, with regard to conflict, internal actors disagree about norms. Conflict is typically overcome by building external and internal alliances held together by the beliefs and views expressed by the allies, for example along close party-political stances among Commissioners in College. Here, support from like-minded horizontal services or from other internal allies serves as a power resource. Likewise, the involvement of a DG's political leadership is also a resource. And individual entrepreneurship, that is, the personal commitment and the active exploitation of like-minded networks, often explains the outcomes in processes belonging to the policy-seeking type. Where the current political climate is supportive, internal assertiveness also benefits from the public legitimacy of specific ideological stances.

Once more, the illustration of the three types of position-formation processes in the EU Commission shows how the very same factors can be decisive across the different types of position formation processes. For example, national positions can be an influential factor under either a technocratic, a competence-maximizing, or a policy-seeking type of process. What discriminates instead between the three types of Commission agency is the *ex ante* agenda of internal actors and, consequently, the actual mechanism through which such factors are translated into the content of the final legislative proposal. Staying with this example, we have observed that national positions may be relevant either because they generate information for technocratic actors, because they signal political feasibility for competence-maximizers, or because they exhibit a high normative fit with the

Table 12.1. Ideal-type position-formation processes

Process type	Actor motivation	Dominant mechanism	Main logic of DG positions	Main logic of DG interaction
Technocratic	Efficient problem-solving	Provision of information and expertise	Learning about/ balancing external stakeholder interests	Coordination of sector-specific views
Competence-seeking	Maximization of regulatory/ budgetary resources	Extension or retention of competences	Pleasing most powerful external stakeholders	Zero-sum negotiations on relative internal gains
Policy-seeking	Realization of ideological ideals	Pursuit of normative fit	Creating distributional consequences for external stakeholders	Alliances according to ideological convictions and beliefs

goals of policy-seekers. In this light, it makes little sense to define the three types along dominant explanatory factors and constraints from the institutional context. What varies and what in turn may account for innovations, rifts, or inconsistencies in the policy proposed for Europe is the dominant mechanism that selects relevant factors and translates them into a specific policy choice that makes it to the European agenda: the provision of information and expertise, the extension and retention of competences, or the pursuit of normative fit. Before turning to their empirical relevance, Table 12.1 summarizes the three inductively generated process models.

12.2 FROM IDEAL TYPES TO REAL CASES: EXAMPLES AND FREQUENCY PATTERNS

These three ideal types only rarely occur in their pure form. For a particular case most closely resembling the ideal type of a technocratic process, the interested reader may refer to the sub-chapter on pyrotechnic articles (Chapter 7.3.2). Here, the lead DG ENTR initiated the process only in order to fulfill an existing legal obligation, gratefully absorbed any information it could get from experts, interest groups, and member states, and used the internal interaction mainly to optimize the legal set-up of the envisaged act. For a drafting process closely following the competence-seeking type, one may refer to the process on the European Institute of Technology (EIT, Chapter 6.4.2). In this case, the Commission, mainly driven by President Barroso, tried to increase its competences in the area of higher education, research, and innovation by founding a European university, which, however, met with strong resistance from the policy community and powerful member states. Nonetheless, the lead DG EAC did not drop the idea but only scaled it down so as to get at least some increase in bureaucratic responsibility accepted. Internal negotiations, in addition, were difficult and boiled down to zero-sum negotiations on the regulatory and budgetary competences of DGs ENTR and RTD. For rather well-fitting examples illustrating the policy-seeking type of drafting process, the histories of the various anti-discrimination proposals are cases in point (Chapters 5.2.1–5.2.4). Building on the strong normative beliefs of DG EMPL officials and (for the earlier acts) especially of the responsible Commissioner Diamantopoulou, the drafting processes were pro-actively geared towards distributing rights to potentially disadvantaged individuals, and internal rifts were more than once overcome by political alliances between Commissioners of similar ideological orientation.

Although apt examples can be found in the Commission's day-to-day policy-making, we should still bear in mind that the three models presented are ideal types. Not least the fact that internal actors may enter a particular process with diverging underlying motivations indicates that the three models may, in practice, co-exist at any one time. Thus, while one DG may have formed its position on an act following a technocratic rationale, another DG's priorities may be driven by ideological concerns. What is more, the dominant mechanism may change once we shift the analytical focus from position formation in DGs to interaction across DGs: the specific model of the position-formation process does not necessarily determine which ideal type best describes the interaction process. To nevertheless achieve a glimpse at their relative importance, our 48 cases entailed one final step of aggregation. For each process, we assessed which of the three dominant mechanisms explains most of the respective DG policy positions and the outcome of their interaction.[1]

According to these results, technocratic Commission agency characterized most of our cases under the first research question. We found that the internal positions of DGs were best explained along technocratic lines in more than 50 percent of our cases. The competence-seeking model dominated in roughly one-third of our cases, while policy-seeking was the relatively most important type in less than 15 percent of our cases. This pattern varies slightly over the policy areas covered in this book. Position formation most often followed a competence-seeking logic in research and innovation policy, while the share of cases most closely resembling the policy-seeking model was significantly larger at the intersection of social and market policies.

This picture changes when we turn to our second research question and focus on the dominant mechanism in internal interactions between DGs. Here, competence-seeking is the most typical agency logic and best explains the outcome in 55 percent of 38 conflictual cases. Interaction processes following the technocratic type are in second place (24 percent), closely followed by cases driven by a policy-seeking logic (21 percent). The predominance of the competence-seeking model in interaction patterns holds across all three policy areas, while a policy-seeking logic of interaction is again slightly more frequent for the policies at the intersection of social and market policies.

The first important result from these frequency patterns is thus the comparatively low prevalence of the policy-seeking model. The realization of ideological goals is not a central motivator when it comes to power and conflict inside the European Commission. However, its dominance in 15 percent of our position-formation and in 21 percent of our interaction cases is far too high to reject it as a relevant driver of Europe's central agenda-setter. Importantly, it characterizes the position-formation processes of some of the most extreme cases in terms of policy choice. This applies to both the formation of strongly liberalizing positions, such as in the proposal on the services directive (Chapter 5.4.2), and the more interventionist stances, for example that on consumer credit (Chapter 7.2.3) and the anti-discrimination regulation (Chapters 5.2.1–5.2.4). The rare occurrence of processes following the policy-seeking type of Commission agency corresponds to the low prevalence of individual-level factors revealed in Chapter 11. In comparison to the relevance of the more stable sectoral or organizational factors—and related mechanisms associated with the technocratic and the competence-seeking model—policy-seeking will only occur where particular individuals from the Commission's rather large workforce bring strong normative beliefs to the drafting table and work to win over ideological allies in internal interaction. But it is particularly this rare occurrence that makes the policy-seeking model so important for understanding rifts and inconsistencies in the Commission's overall policy output.

Second, we find that the central mechanism changes rather often between position formation in individual DGs and interaction across those DGs. In a substantial 17 of our 38 conflictual cases, we observed a switch from a technocratic logic explaining policy positions to one of the two more political power logics of internal interaction. While technocratic problem-solving is the dominant agency perspective for individual DGs, this changes when actors notice that there is no one best way of regulating policy challenges. In the next step, and related to their sectoral views and their major stakeholders, DGs do not engage in open-ended arguing but instead seek to strategically push their preferred positions through in a quest to retain or expand their competences (29 percent of our conflictual cases). As one Commission official described the situation: "The reasons are: they have stakeholders.... DG ENTR has a very different set of stakeholders, obviously, on the other side of the fence, to DG EMPL's stakeholders. They have to look out for what their stakeholders want" (COM86:63). Though much more rare, sometimes the emerging bargaining situations also bring ideological alliances to the fore (5 percent of our conflictual cases). Thus, although the ideal type of technocratic position formation seems to be the backdrop within DGs, turf and sometimes ideological conflicts emerge and dominate as soon as internal actors are forced to find common solutions across portfolios. By contrast, where internal actors formed their individual positions as competence- or policy-seekers in the first place, these logics most often also characterized the ensuing internal conflicts. Put more generally, while a technocratic logic will prevail where all actors share this orientation, once at least one DG seeks to extend the department's competences or pursues ideological goals, this is likely to tip the entire process towards the more political models of position formation.

The general pattern we observe, therefore, supports the idea of the EU Commission as a bureaucratic actor whose departmental structure decisively influences the policies it proposes (Cram 1994). In line with our conclusions from Chapter 11, then, the reason behind innovative, controversial, or inconsistent policy output by the European Commission is often to be found in the logics of internal conflict rather than in the DGs' exchanges with the external institutional context: when diverging sectoral views clash within the Commission, it is often other concerns than that of finding an efficient policy solution that dominate the process.

12.3 UNCERTAINTY AND SALIENCE AS MEDIATING FACTORS

The preceding sections highlight that the three ideal types are essentially driven by the basic motivations with which internal actors enter the position-formation process. However, they also clarify that actor motivations may overlap or vary across DGs in a given process. What, then, mediates which of the three models becomes dominant? In Chapter 2.3, we argued in this regard that policy-specific uncertainty and salience should affect position formation inside the Commission.

We expected that uncertainty about the effects of possible policy choices would tend to benefit the administrative level and the technocratic search for adequate, factual information. The provision of information and expertise should then be the dominant mechanism linking external factors and constraints to the policy positions chosen by Commission actors. The legal status quo or regard for the inter-institutional process and the EU multi-level system, for example, should be used to clarify the cause and effect relationship of policies or to assess "the expected outcomes of different courses of action" (George 1980, in Haas 1992: 14). By contrast, where internal actors hold a clear perception of what their interests are and how they causally relate to the different policy options on the table, we expected that the more political models, in particular competence-seeking, would be more likely.

An aggregate perspective on our sample suggests that competence-seeking behaviour in internal interactions is indeed less likely in drafting processes characterized by high policy uncertainty. One example is the drafting process on the quality and safety of human organs intended for transplantation (Chapter 6.4.4). Confronted with high uncertainty about the effects of the proposed regulatory measures, the lead DG SANCO strongly relied on related regulatory acts at EU and national level and on experts' advice. This uncertainty cast a shadow on the interaction process in which other DGs had to be convinced by the lead DG's expert authority in the area. However, we also found that interaction processes following the policy-seeking model occurred significantly more often in a context of high uncertainty. This relationship is exemplified by the case on race discrimination (Chapter 5.2.1), where large regulatory leaps into an area hitherto not covered by EU equal-treatment policies took place under substantial uncertainty about the possible effects. In such contexts, actors often joined forces on the basis of pre-existing ideological beliefs. In line with seminal policy studies, ideological orientation seems to serve as a sort of intellectual short-cut: especially under simultaneously high complexity and salience, actors resort to "basic" values when other cues are unavailable (Gormley 1986). Besides these two particular findings for internal interaction, however, the aggregate perspective on our sample yields only inconclusive results with regard to the effects of uncertainty on position formation in individual DGs, leaving it to future research to develop alternative operationalizations and to specify why we only observe loose causality.

By contrast, we can observe that salience has more robust effects. We expected that increased salience, understood as contemporaneous public attention for a proposal or the issues in question (Mahoney 2008; Epstein and Segal 2000), would push position formation towards the more political process models. Growing public attention should pull political leaders into the process and constrain the often time-consuming, open-ended search for efficient solutions. By contrast, where an issue barely mobilizes the public, the literature expects more integrative negotiations to allow some leeway for knowledge-driven interaction that helps to illuminate hitherto unknown aspects (Radaelli 1999b).

In our sample, policy choices in and interaction across DGs were more likely to follow the technocratic ideal type in cases of low public salience. Typical examples are the three proposals on financial services regulation (Chapters 5.3.3–5.3.5). In each case, the process went unnoticed by the public. In this situation, the internal actors focused on sectoral consultations and expert consultations rather than on paying attention to the wider political processes. Conversely, the two more political ideal types of position formation were more likely in high-salience cases, whereas the aggregate perspective remains inconclusive as to whether competence-seeking or policy-seeking is more likely under this condition. As the various examples in Chapter 9 demonstrate, public sentiments can be skillfully exploited by both policy- and competence-seeking actors.

Further, our comparison shows that the two more political ideal types of position formation are significantly more likely in cases characterized as top-down processes. This might well be an indirect effect of salience since the political leader of an organization will typically dedicate more time to issues garnering greater public attention. On salient issues, Commissioners often initiated or substantially influenced the position-formation process directly at the service level. The cases on consumer credit (Chapter 7.2.3) and toy safety (Chapter 7.3.4) represent vivid examples in this regard.

In sum, salience and to a lesser extent also uncertainty are policy-specific context factors that mediate the type of agency that drives position formation in the EU Commission. However, our results also show that they do not conclusively determine whether a process follows the logics of efficient problem-solving, the maximization of competences or the pursuit of ideological goals. Identifying other factors mediating between the three process models is thus a promising avenue for further research.

12.4 CONCLUSIONS: A COMBINED MODEL OF INTERNAL POSITION FORMATION

This chapter proposes a threefold typology of position formation processes in the European Commission, which constitutes the concluding conceptual contribution of this book. We argue that the legislative agenda the Commission proposes for Europe cannot be explained by one type of agency alone. While the existing literature has characterized the Commission as an agent that is constantly motivated by the same goals, we posit that different types of agency co-exist inside the Commission.

Starting from the analytical framework outlined at the beginning of the book, additional inductive insights from the empirical investigation and a comparison of 48 individual drafting processes reveal that position-formation processes inside the Commission can be grouped into three distinct process types: a technocratic, a competence-seeking, and a policy-seeking model. The type of process varies according to the internal actors' diverging motivations, which are driven either by the search for efficient problem solutions, by the maximization of regulatory and budgetary resources, or by the pursuit of normative ideals. These models cannot be distinguished in terms of particular sets of external factors and constraints alone. Importantly, they vary in line with the mechanism that links such external resources to the final policy output of the internal process.

In terms of frequency, we find that individual Commission DGs most often draw up their policy positions in accordance with the technocratic model and much more rarely follow competence- or policy-seeking considerations. However, this picture changes when DGs have to find common solutions across portfolio boundaries. In our sample, the competence-seeking model most adequately described the majority of interaction processes, whereas the technocratic exchange of arguments or alliances along ideological lines can be observed much more rarely. Overall, a technocratic logic of position formation seems to be the backdrop. However, highly innovative, controversial or inconsistent policy proposals often emerge from turf conflicts and ideological rifts within Europe's central agenda-setter. While further research is needed in this regard, we found that the dominant logic of a particular drafting process is mediated by the issue-specific policy context. High uncertainty about policy consequences restrains competence-seeking behaviour in the Commission. The public salience of the regulated issues makes both turf and ideological considerations more relevant for internal position formation. Given that public attention regarding European decisions seems to be growing over time (cf. Chapter 9) and that the Commission is increasingly led by experienced politicians socialized in partisan contexts (cf. Chapter 4), we thus expect that the conflict potential within the organization will increase over time.

In sum, we are convinced that our three ideal-type models can be applied to position formation in the Commission beyond our 48 cases. While they partly capture institutional factors and mechanisms that have been analysed in the existing literature, so far no approach has systematically and explicitly combined them. The relative importance of each model may indeed vary over time, policy acts, and policy fields. However, only by accepting that technocratic, competence-maximization, and policy-seeking rationales co-exist can we adequately understand which policies the Commission proposes for Europe.

NOTE

1. As for all the results presented in this book, this final analytical step for each case study underwent inter-subjective review by the whole team of authors.

13

Conclusion

Why We Should Care about Power and Conflict Inside the European Commission

The European Commission is at the core of the EU's political system. It has a powerful formal agenda-setting role that gives it significant leverage over the policies that govern Europe. And yet little has been known to date about the internal dynamics under way as the Commission prepares its policies. At the beginning of this book, we observed that public and academic debates feature highly inconsistent portrayals of the Commission, not least relating to the fact that the policy proposals of Europe's central agenda-setter sometimes give rise to formidable opposition from the member states and other stakeholders, introduce strikingly high or strikingly low standards, or even contradict each other in substance.

Proceeding from this point of departure, we asked whether the existing, often static, perceptions of Commission agency can adequately capture such variation in the body's policy output. The existing literature primarily takes one of the three following perspectives. The first characterizes the Commission as a *technocratic* body that adopts those policy positions it deems to be efficient and coherent solutions to new factual challenges and problems. The second conceptualizes the Commission as an inherently political bureaucracy constantly seeking to increase its *competences* particularly vis-à-vis the national level. Under the third perspective, the Commission is treated as a *policy-seeking* body in which ideologically motivated actors use their offices to accomplish what they perceive as being normatively right.

Our approach builds on the various valuable insights such literature has produced. However, we depart from the unitary-actor assumption explicitly or implicitly relied on by much of the existing research. When we look at the basic nature of policy-formation processes inside the Commission, it becomes clear that Europe's central agenda-setter cannot be treated as a "black box" that translates external stimuli into policy output along stable lines. Taking into account the tensions that exist between hierarchical levels and sectoral divisions in the Commission's organization, we argued that the individual Directorates-General (DGs) are the most relevant actors in the internal preparation of policy proposals. From this starting point, we decomposed the overarching question as to which policy is proposed for Europe into two analytically separate research questions. First: *How is the policy position of a DG formed with regard to a specific legislative proposal and how can we explain a DG's policy choices?* And second: *How are deviating DG positions coordinated and how can we explain the assertiveness of a DG in influencing the final Commission proposal's substance?*

The existing literature argues that the Commission and its individual DGs operate in institutional contexts that narrow or broaden the room for maneuver in supranational policy-making. Especially the legislative status quo ante, internal coordination requirements, the inter-institutional system, and the EU's wider multi-level character are theorized as being relevant in this regard. Combining these perspectives in a pluri-theoretical approach, we derived a bundle of factors that were expected to impact on internal policy positions and assertiveness. These sets of factors make up the analytical framework that structures the empirical parts of the book. However, since we did not have a dominant theoretical expectation regarding Commission agency and were seeking to understand complex processes about which little is yet known, we enriched our deductive approach with inductive insights emerging from the empirical analyses of 48 systematically selected policy proposals. The chosen proposals are situated at the intersection of social and common-market policies and in the areas of research and innovation as well as consumer policy and cover the terms of the Prodi and Barroso I Commissions (1999–2009). For each legislative act, we reconstructed the entire position-formation process inside the Commission using newly created data from 153 structured interviews with Commission officials and other actors who were involved, internal CIS-Net documentation, and an original database of personal and structural Commission features since its founding days. We also made systematic cross-case comparisons to find out what is typical for position formation. Beyond the detailed findings presented in the preceding chapters, here we highlight the main patterns of internal position formation. We return to the main themes elaborated in the introduction, indicate avenues for future research and dwell on the wider implications for supranational politics in the European Union.

13.1 RELEVANCE FOR EUROPE: HOW DIFFERENT INTERESTS EMERGE AND AGGREGATE IN THE EARLY PHASE OF EU POLICY-MAKING

Viewed from the outside, the Commission usually presents its policy choices as the result of a consensual decision, and, indeed, majority voting in the College of Commissioners is rare. Viewed from the inside, however, our findings tell a different story. In the first place, far-reaching policy choices are often taken at the Commission's administrative level. More importantly, here as well as at the political level, (intense) interactions and substantial internal policy conflict are the norm rather than the exception.

Importantly, position formation inside the Commission is a time-consuming process. In our sample, its average duration from the very first idea to the final adoption exceeds two years, with outliers lasting up to 70 months. This process covers formal coordination, including Impact Assessments, CIS-Net consultation, and formalized debates at the political level, as well as informal interaction, as we observed in the majority of our cases. Such long-term processes are anything but shielded from multiple internal and external interests and from political games related to inter-institutional decision-making in the EU. This finding is supported by two additional insights. First, for our 48 cases we find a robust positive relationship between the duration of position formation inside the EU Commission and the time the respective inter-institutional negotiations require. Second, particular provisions that proved to be controversial inside the Commission were also often debated in the ensuing inter-institutional process. In sum, the position-formation process inside the Commission already reflects the complexity of supranational policy-making in Europe.

In more than three-fourths of our cases, we found substantially deviating positions regarding which policy should be used to tackle a given issue. What is more, the drafting DG often faced deviating demands from several DGs at the same time and we were able to observe recurring lines of conflict between specific DGs across our cases. Beyond the deviations in the preferred policy choices, the interviewed officials also often perceived these interactions as having been conflictual. While our cases were explicitly selected to lie at the intersection of portfolio competences, the revealed complexity of coordination structures and processes as well as often voluminous CIS-net correspondence between DGs show that conflictual interaction within the Commission seems to be the norm rather than the exception well beyond our cases.

Thus, core political-science notions of power and conflict are indispensable for understanding whether one or another policy is proposed for Europe. Although the agenda-setting literature has been very successful at explaining which issues actually appear on the European agenda (see, especially, Princen 2009), only the internal position formation process can explain the aggregation of contending interests leading to the position ultimately proposed by the Commission. The final positions feeding into the inter-institutional system depend on which DGs and/or Commissioners were actually involved in the legislative drafting of the proposal and which of these actors proved to be most powerful.

Turning to explanations, among the deductively derived factors that may impact on these processes, only the legal status quo mattered systematically in both stages of internal legislative drafting. The extant *acquis* powerfully explains the positions of individual DGs, while the latter's strength and the amount of supranational competences they already control is an advantageous power resource when different policy positions clash. In these internal conflicts, factors flowing from internal coordination also help to explain the aggregation of interests. By contrast, while the inter-institutional system matters for the policy positions of individual DGs, it much more rarely accounts for power in internal conflicts. And where the inter-institutional system influences internal position formation, it most often does so in terms of anticipation of aggregated member-state interests in the Council, whereas EP majorities, partisan ideologies, or the power of specific national positions rarely explain DG positions or assertiveness. Finally, optional resources from the EU's multi-level context—most notably input from organized interests and experts—are highly important for the positions of individual DGs, but are less often turned into a bargaining chip in internal quarrels.

This leads to two broader conclusions. First, the set of relevant factors is more stable across cases and policy areas in explaining the policy positions of individual DGs than it is in explaining internal assertiveness. The policy positions of individual DGs are, on average, more easily predictable than the outcomes of internal conflicts. Particularly where these factors are of a structural or systemic nature, such as the anticipation of Council majorities or factors related to internal coordination structures, we expect them to also be relevant for other cases and policy fields. Second, internal Commission actors draw much more on external resources and constraints when forming their positions, whereas they resort more to internal resources when trying to assert these positions in conflicts with their counterparts. Although many of the external factors have been extensively studied in existing EU policy-making analyses and in opposition to "bureaucratic politics" arguments (Allison 1969) and those focusing on rifts between portfolios at the national level (Mayntz and Scharpf 1975; Müller-Rommel and Blondel 1993; Gallagher et al. 2005), conflict and interaction dynamics inside the Commission have been given little systematic attention to date. We believe that this second analytical stage needs to feature much more prominently in explanations of the policies proposed for Europe.

13.2 BEYOND THE STATE OF THE ART: HOW THE INSIDE VIEW CHALLENGES COMMON PERCEPTIONS OF EUROPE'S CENTRAL AGENDA-SETTER

13.2.1 A Unitary Actor? Differing Views and Strategic Behavior Inside the Commission

Given the incentives created by the inter-institutional system of the EU, the unitary-actor assumption comes as no surprise at first sight. It is clearly beneficial for the Commission to speak with a single voice once legislative proposals are submitted to the Council and the Parliament (Scharpf 1997a). However, one of our core findings is the substantial extent to which internal policy positions differ. As soon as one abstains from the null hypothesis viewing the Commission as a neutral clearing house, the sources of internally deviating views and strategic interactions move into the limelight.

Since the infancy of European integration, the Commission has gained competence in various societal sectors. Functional differentiation—and with it the likelihood that different perspectives clash in individual position-formation processes—has grown in parallel. In the Commission's organizational structure, this differentiation coincides with partisan cleavages and national focal points on specific issue areas. And we also observe an increasing politicization of the College of Commissioners. Thus, functional differentiation and variation in the corresponding personal characteristics of the Commission's administrative and political leadership—such as their socialization, prior employment, or partisan alignment—are part of the answer to our initial puzzle as to why the Commission produces sometimes innovative, sometimes controversial, and sometimes inconsistent policies.

The internal organization of Europe's powerhouse has responded to these pressures. Sophisticated institutional procedures exist for aggregating differing views (e.g. Cecot et al. 2008; Schout and Jordan 2008; Radaelli and Meuwese 2010; Kassim et al. 2013). Nonetheless, our findings indicate that these procedures do not rule out strategic behavior on the part of internal actors seeking to assert their specific preferences. Coordination structures first and foremost allow the lead department, but also the Secretariat-General (SG), to influence the number and constellation of other DGs involved, and also to steer the amount, sequence, and timing of administrative exchange or political debate before proposal adoption. Similarly, the Legal Service (SJ) and DG BUDG are important actors who use their internal veto powers in coordination when brokering policy choices that ultimately form the Commission's overall position. Thus, rather than being only a source of technocratic inefficiencies, internal coordination structures matter in political terms because they are often used strategically to push through positions against which internal opposition was already voiced or anticipated.

Both the personal characteristics of the Commission's leadership and their relationship to organizational structures and internal coordination complement research looking at the internal dynamics of other EU institutions (e.g. on the Council, Naurin and Wallace 2008; Tallberg and Johansson 2008; on the ECJ, Höpner 2010; Solanke 2011; Vauchez 2012). This view might fruitfully be developed into systematic thinking on how position heterogeneity in one institution may influence preference formation in the other. Such a disaggregated view on supranational decision-making promises new perspectives on the output the EU's political system produces as a whole.

13.2.2 An Efficiency-focused Technocrat? The Politics of Expertise and Legal Consistency

Our findings also depart from views portraying the Commission as a purely technocratic actor that helps to impartially coordinate member state interests by maximizing factual knowledge and legal consistency (Haas 1958/1968; Moravcsik 1993; Radaelli 1999b). Our results on expert-group involvement underline this most clearly. As we would expect from this view, the Commission most often used expert groups to improve its drafts by eliciting knowledge it did not control itself. In two-thirds of our cases, expert groups were involved in the drafting process, and in half of our cases we could trace expert group influence on DG positions. But the quantitative overview and the consideration of our cases both suggest that the involvement of experts may also occur more strategically, such as serving to substantiate pre-defined political choices or helping to garner consensus among the various external stakeholders of the Commission.

In a similar vein, the strong impact of the legal status quo on internal positions and assertiveness ought not to be confused with a focus on legal consistency. Rather, we often observed a strategic pick-and-choose approach to existing European law or ECJ decisions that served to substantiate the position an internal Commission actor preferred anyway. Our case studies highlight similar mechanisms for the transfer of national or international templates. While internal actors sometimes adopted such templates to ensure consistency in the system of multi-level governance, we also present several examples in which such transfers followed strategic considerations.

Expertise and consistency unquestionably remain important drivers of Commission position formation, but in our cases they also often mask political ambitions inside Europe's central agenda-setter. More broadly, future research on the European Commission should not only focus on the question as to which factors serve as input for position formation, but should also take into account how such factors are actually used by internal actors.

13.2.3 An Insulated Non-majoritarian Institution? Internal Position Formation in a Politicized Context

In contrast to the portrayal of the Commission as a non-majoritarian institution which is insulated from short-term public pressures (e.g. Haas 1958/1968), we find the societal politicization of European integration and its relevance for the future transfer of competences to matter. Depending on the baseline salience of the three policy fields, as well as on the actual public salience of individual initiatives, the Commission did care about the public acceptability of its policies. Internal actors either postponed unpopular choices, proactively tried to garner public support during position formation or even amended their original positions by choosing the policy options that spread regulatory benefits more widely across the European public. And in a number of cases, the greater public legitimacy attached to a DG position translated into internal assertiveness, too. What is more, a politicized context of European integration enhances the strategic repertoire of internal actors during the position formation process. We observed several examples in which internal actors used early public commitments or strategic interaction with the press as a means to internally push through their preferred policy choices.

On the one hand, this can be regarded as good news because—in contrast to insulated decision-making, which renders only direct access to decision-makers a successful lobbying strategy—the politicized context means that less resourceful public-interest groups can also use their voice to influence policy. On the other hand, hopes for increased democracy in Europe are constrained by the complexity of the internal position-formation processes, in which responsiveness to public concerns is just one of several factors and at times results in a stalemate. In any case, future research is well advised to take the Commission's interactions with the wider European public into account when explaining policy choices for Europe.

13.3 MULTI-ORGANIZATION REVISITED: DIFFERENT TYPES OF AGENCY CO-EXIST INSIDE THE COMMISSION

A more general insight emerging from the preceding chapters is that beyond the varying prevalence of different factors, one and the same factor can impinge on internal processes in different ways. The mechanisms whereby external resources and constraints translate into Commission policy positions differ in line with the basic motivations with which internal actors enter a particular process. Our findings confirm that the Commission and its internal actors are motivated by technocratic problem-solving, by maximizing their own organizational competences or by ideologically driven policy-seeking. In some cases, proposals are geared to efficiency and are mainly influenced by internal and external expertise. In other cases, Commission actors enter position formation with the goal of retaining and expanding their competences, considering national interests in this regard and engaging in vested turf disputes. In yet another group of cases, positions are the result of pre-defined normative beliefs regarding the best solutions to problems, which are then asserted in line with ideological alliances across DGs.

These perspectives are not new, but our findings contrast with existing accounts that qualify Commission agency as being dominated by only one of these types (e.g. Pollack 1997b; Nugent 2000a; or, Haas 1958/1968). We posit that the legislative agenda the Commission proposes for Europe cannot be explained by resorting to one type of agency alone. This book shows that different types of agency actually co-exist inside Europe's central agenda-setter. Thus, the main analytical contribution of this book is an abstract typology of process modes which is transportable across time and policy areas.

Empirically, our sample suggests that individual Commission DGs most often draw up their policy positions in accordance with the technocratic model, in which knowledge generation is the dominant mechanism linking external factors to internal policy positions. Position formation in individual DGs much more rarely follows competence- or policy-seeking logics. However, this picture changes drastically when DGs have to agree on a common position. At the interaction stage, the competence-seeking model fitted the majority of analyzed processes best, whereas knowledge-driven exchange of arguments or assertiveness along ideological lines were only infrequently observed. Two conclusions ensue. First, the dominant type of agency often changes between position formation within, and interaction across DGs. While technocracy seems to be the backdrop within DGs, internal interest aggregation often leads the final proposals away from technically efficient solutions. Again, this finding underscores the need to take internal interaction into account. Second, and related to the first, competence- and policy-seeking behavior is infrequent, but still accounted for the most innovative, most controversial, and most challenging policy proposals in our sample. Our case selection with a focus on initiatives with a broad scope might emphasize the political logics to the detriment of (more sectorally constrained) problem-solving. However, this does not challenge our core finding that the co-existence of different agency logics within the European Commission explains politically meaningful frictions in the legislative agenda proposed for Europe.

In consequence, it is an important task for future research to consolidate the explanations as to why one of the three logics dominates a particular process. So far, our results imply that the policy-specific context mediates the type of agency. High uncertainty about policy consequences suppresses internal competence-seeking but does not necessarily lead to more technocratic decision-making. On the contrary, uncertainty sometimes made internal actors rely on normative heuristics, thus resulting in policy-seeking processes. A high public salience of the regulated issues pulled the administrative and political leadership of DGs into the drafting processes and made both turf and ideological considerations more relevant. Given rising public attention on European decisions and increasingly experienced politicians at the Commission's helm, we thus expect an increasing potential for internal conflict over time.

These arguments are in line with other recent large-scale projects analyzing the European Commission which have fruitfully engaged with within-Commission diversity to generate insights (Ellinas and Suleiman 2012; Ban 2013). On the one hand, different logics of internal position formation are consistent with the finding that the individual attitudes of Commission officials vary strongly along several political, sectoral, and procedural dimensions (Kassim et al. 2013). On the other hand, our finding that the technocratic model of position formation is frequently challenged by competence- and policy-seeking behavior conforms to long-term analyses of the Commission's transition from a civil service to a "normal" political executive (Wille 2013). However, we go beyond this strand of literature by highlighting that the cross-sectional and cross-temporal variation it identifies indeed affects the day-to-day policy choices of the Commission. In a combined view, picturing Europe's central agenda-setter as a "multi-organization" (Cram 1994) is even more warranted in the twenty-first century. It is not only that different interests clash inside the Commission, but that the varying logics along which they are aggregated are highly relevant for the policies that govern Europe.

13.4 WHICH POLICY FOR EUROPE AND HOW COULD IT BE CHANGED?

The process models do not imply particular political decisions per se and must be filled with policy substance to make predictions. However, when we know what type of agency drives an internal position-formation process, we also know the leverage points for influencing policy substance both for regulatory and distributive proposals. To exemplify this, we return to the question that inspired much of this project: whether internal position formation contributes to explaining the predominance of market-liberal positions over more interventionist approaches in European legislation.

With regard to this dimension, the substantial positions we observed inside the Commission are highly diverse. Given that the creation of the internal market has driven European integration for a long time, it is hardly surprising that the proposals we cover in this book most often contain provisions displaying a strong free-market orientation. In these cases, the final Commission position does not address specific societal outcomes, and rather delegates their creation to market forces. In contrast, only a limited number of the analyzed provisions can be classified as clearly interventionist where the EU Commission proposes directly prescribing the desired societal outcome, often by means of distribution. Given the limited Community budget and selective competence allocation to the supranational level in favor of market-creating policies, this picture is likely to hold for other policy areas, too. However, between these two extremes, there is a highly interesting and socially relevant intermediate category (also see Hartlapp and Rauh 2013): most frequently, the legal content of the Commission proposal reveals positions that focus on changing the quality of markets. Interestingly, we particularly found such market-steering approaches where previous European legislation had liberalized the specific sector. Such re-regulations in our sample responded to perceived market failures and sometimes addressed market outcomes that were considered unsustainable or morally unjust.

While we thus see a sequential development of issue trajectories in European regulation, this does not necessarily mean that the policy output of the Commission will automatically tend towards more interventionist positions over time. On the one hand, proposals in this middle category hardly violate the Single Market paradigm and only accompany other proposals that apply the principle of negative integration to societal segments hitherto unregulated at the supranational level. On the other hand, and more importantly, the precise Commission position on the continuum between liberal and interventionist policies depends substantially on the type of Commission agency that dominates the position-formation process in question. Thus, turning our focus to concrete policy recommendations and on how to change the policies proposed for Europe, it emerges that identifying the relevant types of position-formation process in the Commission is particularly relevant.

Under the technocratic model, liberal Commission proposals can typically be explained on the basis of legal consistency with existing European law and the focus on efficient and effective solutions for problems emerging in the common market. More interventionist policy proposals can be expected particularly where internal and external expertise conducive to this end are present during the position-formation process. Accordingly, when aiming for policy change under this model, ensuring balanced access to the Commission's expert groups and creating legal precedents are key levers.

Under the competence-seeking model, Commission positions on the market-interventionism dimension are based on the extent of competence transfers they generate for internal actors and the Commission as a whole. Regarding the latter, the literature on political economy has shown that preference heterogeneity among the member states is conducive to negative integration and consequently often favors liberal Commission positions (Scharpf 1999; Höpner and Schäfer 2012). Our findings underline that the internal distribution of responsibilities also offers highly relevant levers for affecting the particular position the Commission proposes. In this sense, our cases show that organizational restructuring can stimulate departure from the extant *acquis*. Likewise, under this model we find various external interests to be granted biased access. This has been shown to influence the liberalizing extent of policy choices, for instance in the case of the industrialist tables pushing for the creation of the common market (Cowles 1995) or, more recently, in knowledge-intensive areas such as the regulation of financial markets (Willis 2009). Moreover, limiting strategic use of the internal coordination rules, thereby reducing the power resources of the lead DG, could ensure more balanced EU policies under the competence-seeking model.

Under the policy-seeking model, finally, those aiming at more balanced (in the sense of less liberal) market regulation should mainly focus on the selection of the

Commission's leading personnel and its ideological orientation. This holds for individual Commissioners, but particularly also for the Commission President. Commissioners hold substantial control over the lead DG, which has been shown to enjoy significant internal advantages. Via the SG, the Commission President in turn controls the balancing of coordination processes and the assignment of lead DGs to given European policy challenges. Combined with our insight that a policy-seeking Commission is indeed responsive to the public, open political competition for the leading positions in the Commission could thus be a key lever under the policy-seeking model.

In conclusion, this book shows that power and conflict inside the European Commission have substantial implications for the functioning of the EU political system and the governance of European societies. In addition, it also enhances our knowledge on this very process of position formation and offers several new leverage points for adjusting the policies that the European Commission proposes for Europe.

APPENDIX

Appendix A1: Interview Guidelines for Commission Officials

Background: Each of the 137 interviewees inside the European Commission had been provided with a rough sketch of our research interests beforehand while being informed about which particular legislative initiatives we wanted to discuss. The subsequent interview guideline structured these face-to-face conversations. To learn as much about each case as possible, we mainly raised open questions. Specific requests were added—for example to cross-validate findings from preliminary research—only after the interviewee had provided an initial answer. Interviewees were asked to allow recording of the conversation while being assured anonymity when referencing interviewees in our publications.

In situations where time was restricted, questions printed in italics were given preference. The guideline was largely identical for officials at the administrative and political levels of the Commission, though the latter group was asked for the positions of Commissioners or Cabinets rather than of DGs.

Introduction

Overview of Interview

The EU Commission is often treated as a unitary actor. In our research we study internal dynamics of position formation in legislative decision making—that is before a Commission proposal is introduced in the inter-institutional process.

The questions I will ask you revolve around five issue areas:

1. general information about the interviewee
2. DG position on the proposal
3. internal decision-making for this act
4. internal process of decision-making in general
5. final remarks

In case you have time constraints I would like to focus on 2 and 3.

Information about the interviewee

1. For how long have you been in your present position?
2. What is your professional background?
3. Could you briefly describe your activities in the current position?
4. For how long have you been in your (present) position as the person dealing with [ADD LEGISLATIVE ACT]? Who has been responsible for it before you?
5. Who else was concerned with the preparation of the proposal in your DG?

DG position on the proposal

6. *What was the position of your DG on the proposal? [1) OPEN QUESTION, 2) CHECK POTENTIAL CONFLICT LINES UNCOVERD IN PRELIMINARY RESEARCH SEPARATELY]*

7. *If you needed to explain to a colleague why this position was taken, what would you say? [1) OPEN QUESTION, 2) CHECK EACH SLASH SEPARATELY]*
   - answer to a (newly) emerging problem
   - legal demand
   - proactively shaping policy (vis-à-vis member states or vis-à-vis other DGs)
   - beneficial in budgetary terms
   - interest of Commissioner (why?)
   - interest of Director-General (why?)
   - (a) member state's interest (why?)
   - public appeal
   - interaction with interest groups/organized interests
   - interaction with expert groups
   - take up of other (also international) policy developments
8. Did other DGs take a substantially different position on the proposal? If yes, what would be your explanation for this?
9. Some people argue that partisan politics is quite important in the civil service; others consider the Commission as above partisan politics. Which side was closer to reality in this case?

Internal decision making process for this legislative act

10. Could you briefly describe the policy formulation process from the very first idea to officially proposing the instrument in [ADD DATE] [*1) OPEN QUESTION, 2) CHECK EACH SLASH SEPARATELY*]?
    - Who drafted the first proposal? When?
    - Initiated by the Commissioner/Cabinet?
    - When did interservice consultation start?
    - Was an inter-service group set up? If not, did an existing group address the act?
11. Were there open points left when the legislative act reached the Chef de Cabinet meeting/the College?
12. *Which aspects of the legislative act were subject to interaction within the Commission? What were the main arguments exchanged?* [*1) OPEN QUESTION, 2) CHECK EACH SLASH SEPARATELY*]
    - Was the process consensual or was it characterized by conflicts?
    - If conflicts occurred: between whom and over which issues?
    - Which DG finally succeeded in putting its position through?
13. *If the final proposal did (not) reflect the position of your DG/Commissioner, what was decisive in this respect?*
14. Did coordination within the DG work smoothly (units/Director-General/Commissioner)?
15. Did coordination among DGs work smoothly (DGs/horizontal services)?
16. Did the decision rules applied in the Council play a role?
17. Was the fact that the policy field is well established or rather new at EU level important?
18. How many people worked on the issue in your DG? To what extent would more personnel/resources have been an advantage?
19. Did your DG deal with other major policy initiatives at the time?
20. Did any specific person play an extraordinary role in the internal process?
21. Were you part of a group of DGs with similar interests? Who? If not, did you find yourself isolated among the other DGs?

22. Did you meet with officials from other DGs? If not, your colleagues? [*1) OPEN QUESTION, 2) CHECK EACH SLASH SEPARATELY*]
    - Who? (DG and rank?)
    - How frequently?
    - At what stage (during the initial drafting or later)?
    - Were these meetings required by formal rules? If not, who took the first step? Why?
23. Did the view you/your DG had on [SPECIFY ISSUES UNCOVERED IN PRELIMINARY RESEARCH] at the beginning change during the internal process?
24. Are you aware of compromises across issues or even across proposals in order to accommodate your or another DG?
25. Did you prepare reports or assessments on the issue in your DG? On what aspects? Were these published?
26. What groups and organizations have you been talking to/have you been in contact with on [ADD LEGISLATIVE ACT/SPECIFIC ISSUES]? In which form? Whose views did you value?
27. *More specifically on advisory expert groups: To what extent were existing or newly created groups like [ADD MOST IMPORTANT EXPERT GROUP] involved in drafting?*

    To what extent did the group(s) help your DG? [1) OPEN QUESTION, 2) CHECK SEPARATELY EACH SLASH]
    - Provision of information on the positions of other relevant actors (e.g. member states, other interests, etc.)
    - Provision of factual expertise/quantitative data
    - Building consensus among the affected parties/member states
    - Giving general support to your position
28. *Were you aware of any other DG significantly involving expert groups? Which? When?*
29. *Have there been any external social/political/economic events that affected the content of the proposal and/or the position of involved DGs?*

    If yes: Which events? How was the substance of the proposal affected? [1) OPEN QUESTION, 2) THEN CHECK SEPARATELY EACH SLASH]
    - preceding/upcoming EP elections
    - referenda
    - European Council summits
30. *Has the public appeal of [ADD PROPOSAL/ADD ISSUE] been a concern during the internal drafting process?*

    If yes: Whose concern was it? Is this concern typical?
31. Are the positions of other political actors—the Council or individual member states, the EP, or the ECJ—already anticipated in legislative drafting and interservice co-ordination?
32. *If you could start the process again, what should you/your DG do differently in order to see your position better reflected in the final Commission proposal?*
33. *Can you give me an assessment of whether the process we talked about was typical? If not, to what extent?*
34. Can you give me an example of internal decision-making of an act that was
    - typical
    - especially interesting for our research (why?)

Internal decision-making process in general

35. Could you walk me through a typical policy-formation process from the very first idea to officially proposing the instrument?
36. What is the role of other actors? *[1) OPEN QUESTION, 2) CHECK EACH SLASH SEPARATELY]*
    - other units in the DG
    - Commissioner
    - other DGs with an interest in the issue
    - SG
    - other horizontal services
    - interaction with national actors (who?)
    - interaction with EU level interest groups
    - expert groups
    - interaction with EP/Council
37. Is the internal decision-making process determined by formal rules?
38. What happens in case of conflict between DGs? [*1) OPEN QUESTION, 2) CHECK EACH SLASH SEPARATELY*]
    - coordination structures
    - veto power
39. *Some people claim that divisions between DGs often weaken the Commission in its dealings with other institutions, others argue that the Commission usually presents a united front vis-à-vis other interests. Which side is closer to reality?*
40. *As in national administrations, DGs have quite different reputations. Which would be the three most powerful DGs in 2008, you think? Which are the three weakest in your opinion? Is your current rank order different from, say five years ago? Is there a particular "rising star"?*
41. *Some people claim that the Commission's DGs reveal different self-conceptions as visible in the way policy issues are approached and in the way they communicate and consult with other DGs. How would you describe your DG in both respects?*
42. Thinking about your role as senior civil servant in DG [ADD NAME] what would you say are [were] the two or three most important duties and responsibilities involved?

Final points

43. Could you refer me to other persons who would be interesting to talk to given my research interest (within DG, other DGs, outside COM)
44. Any documentation? [CIS-NET?]

Is there anything I should know that I forgot to ask about but that I should know in order to understand the internal formation process of this legislative act? [TAPE OFF AND PUT OBVIOUSLY ON TABLE]

Appendix A2: Construction of the Power and Democratic Credentials Indices

Table A.1 provides a list of former professions attributed to Commission personnel with assigned values for power and democratic credentials indices. In equivocal cases, where the person under consideration had occupied more than one of the listed position groups, he or she was assigned the category for the hierarchically highest post.

Table A.1. List of former professions attributed to Commission personnel with assigned values for power and democratic credentials indices

Position	Power index score	Democratic credentials index score
Prime Minister[a]	2.27	1
Minister for Finance[a]	1.62	1
Minister for Foreign Affairs[a]	1.41	1
Minister for the Interior[a]	1.29	1
Minister for Economy, Budget[a]	1.22	1
Minister for Justice[a]	1.1	1
Minister for Labour and Social Affairs[a]	1.1	1
Minister for Industry and Trade[a]	1.01	1
Minister for Education, Science and Technology[a]	0.99	1
Minister for Defence[a]	0.98	1
Minister for Health[a]	0.96	1
Minister for Agriculture, Fishery, Forestry[a]	0.92	1
Minister for Transport and Communication[a]	0.91	1
Minister for European Integration[a]	0.87	1
Minister for Regional Development, Construction and Housing[a]	0.77	1
Minister for the Environment[a]	0.73	1
Minister for Culture[a]	0.72	1
Junior Minister[b]	0.5	1
Secretary of State[b]	0.5	0
Regional Government[c]	0.45	1
Party Leader[c]	0.4	0
Parliamentarian[b]	0.33	1
Diplomat[c]	0.3	0
Bureaucrat[c]	0.28	0
Union Leader[c]	0.27	0
Business[c]	0.26	0
Academic[c]	0.24	0
Activist[c]	0.22	0
Other[c]	0.2	0

[a] Position and average power index score resulting from surveys by Druckman and Warwick (2005) and Druckman and Roberts (2008). Positions considered by Druckman and Warwick (2005) and Druckman and Roberts (2008) that did not appear in the empirical backtracking of former positions have not been included.
[b] Position and power index score according to Döring (2007, 2013).
[c] Position and power index score newly added.

More information on the underlying data sources is provided in the codebook of the PEU database available at: <http://www.wzb.eu/sites/default/files/downloads/peu-database_manual.pdf> (last accessed: December 4, 2013).

References

Aberbach, Joel D. and Bert A. Rockman (2002) 'Conducting and coding elite interviews', *Political Science & Politics* 35(4): 673–6.

Aberbach, Joel D., Robert D. Putnam, and Bert A. Rockman (1981) *Bureaucrats and Politicians in Western Democracies.* Cambridge: Harvard University Press.

Aberbach, Joel D., Hans-Ulrich Derlien, Renate Mayntz, and Bert A. Rockman (1990) 'American and German federal executives—technocratic and political attitudes', *International Social Science Journal* 42(1): 3–18.

AE (1997) 'EU/Insurance: BEUC and BIPAR call for European directive liberalising activities of insurance intermediaries', *Agence Europe*, April 1, 1997.

AE (1998) '(EU) EU/Social: Gender Equality not only an Obligation, but also a Precondition for Europe's economic Prosperity, Notes on the "Equality is the Future" Congress', *Agence Europe*, September 23, 1998.

AE (1999) 'Next Programme of Aid to the Audiovisual Sector to be more Devoted to the Promotion and Distribution of European Films and New Forms of Creation', *Agence Europe*, November 20, 1999.

AE (2002) 'EU/Insurance: Council adopts insurance broker directive', *Agence Europe*, September 30, 2002.

AE (2003a) '(EU) EU/Social: Anna Diamantopoulou expects lengthy Discussion before a Directive is adopted to ban gender Discrimination', *Agence Europe*, June 30, 2003.

AE (2003b) '(EU) EU/Social: College examines Draft Directive on implementing Equal Treatment for Men and Women, notably in Insurance', *Agence Europe*, November 4, 2003.

AE (2008) '(EU) EP/Equality: EP demands that European Commission show "More political Courage" by proposing a "General" Anti-Discrimination Directive and "Results"', *Agence Europe*, May 20, 2008.

Aldrich, John, John Sullivan, and Eugene Borgida (1989) 'Foreign affairs and issue voting: Do presidential candidates "waltz before a blind audience"?', *The American Political Science Review* 83(1): 123–41.

Alemanno, Alberto (2006) 'Food Safety and the Single European Market'. In: C. Ansell and D. Vogel (eds), *What's the Beef?: The Contested Governance of European Food Safety.* Boston, MA: MIT Press.

Alesina, Alberto, Ignazio Angeloni, and Ludger Schuknecht (2005) 'What does the European Union do?', *Public Choice* 123: 275–319.

Alexandrova, Petya, Marcello Carammia, and Arco Timmermans (2012) 'Policy punctuations and issue diversity on the European Council Agenda', *Policy Studies Journal* 40(1).

Allison, Graham T. (1969) 'Conceptual models and the Cuban Missile Crisis', *The American Political Science Review* 63(3): 689–718.

ALTER-EU (2009) A captive Commission—the role of the financial industry in shaping EU regulation. Brussels: Alliance for Lobbying Transparency and Ethics Regulation in the European Union.

Alter, Karen J. and J. Vargas (2000) 'Explaining Variation in the Use of European litigation startegies: European Community law and British equality policy', *Comparative Political Studies* 33.

Andeweg, Rudy B. (1988) 'Centrifugal forces and collective decision-making: The case of the Dutch cabinet', *European Journal of Political Research* 16: 125–51.

Andeweg, Rudy B. (2000) 'Ministers as double agents? The delegation process between cabinet and ministers', *European Journal of Political Research* 37(3): 377–95.

André, Michel (2009) 'Architects of European research', *research*eu*, No. 59, March 2009, [cited November 26, 2012]. Available from <http://ec.europa.eu/research/research-eu/pdf/research_eu_59_en.pdf>.

Andrée, Dan (2008) 'A rough guide to the FP7 Work Programmes', *External Publications*. Stockholm.

Andrée, Dan (2009) 'Priority-setting in the European Research Framework Programmes', *Vinnova Analysis* Stockholm, July 2009.

ANEC (2006) ANEC Position paper on the Revision of the New Approach. In *Commission Working Document—Certif 2005-16 Rev. 2: Elements for a horizontal legislative approach to technical harmonisation*, edited by European Association for the Co-ordination of Consumer Representation in Standardisation. Brussels.

Ansell, Christopher and David Vogel (eds) (2006) *What's the Beef?: The Contested Governance of European Food Safety*. Boston, MA: MIT Press.

A.U.R.A. (1972a) Rapport à la Commission sur le fonctionnement interne de ses Services. In *Association Universitaire de Recherche en Administration, Universite de Louvain*: Archive Historique des Communautés Européennes. Florence: AHCE.

A.U.R.A. (1972b) Synthèse du rapport à la Commission sur le fonctionnement interne de ses Services. In *Association Universitaire de Recherche en Administration, Universite de Louvain* Archive Historique des Communautés Européennes. Florence: AHCE.

Axelrod, Robert (1970) *Conflict of Interest*. Chicago: Markham.

Azzi, Giuseppe Ciavarini (2009) 'What does the European Commission do?'. In: R. Dehousse, F. Deloche-Gaudez and S. Jacquot (eds), *What is Europe up to?* Paris: Presses de Sciences Po.

Bachrach, P. and M. Baratz (1962) 'The two faces of power', *The American Political Science Review* 56: 947–52.

Bailer, Stefanie (2004) 'Bargaining success in the European Union: The impact of exogenous and endogenous power resources', *European Union Politics* 5(1): 99–123.

Balint, Tim, Michael W. Bauer, and Christoph Knill (2008) 'Bureaucratic change in the European administrative space: The case of the European Commission', *West European Politics* 31(4): 677–700.

Ban, Carolyn (2013) *Management and Culture in an Enlarged European Commission. From Diversity to Unity?* Basingstoke: Palgrave Macmillan.

Banchoff, Thomas (2002) 'Institutions, inertia and European Union research policy', *JCMS: Journal of Common Market Studies* 40(1): 1–21.

Barroso, José Manuel. *John Peterson interviews the European Commission President. 17 July 2007* EU-CONSENT, Constructing Europe Network [cited August 4, 2008]. Available from <http://www.eu-consent.net/library/BARROSO-transcript.pdf>.

Barry, Brian (1980) 'Is it better to be powerful or lucky?: Part I', *Political Studies* 28(2): 183.

Bartolini, Stefano (2006) 'Should the Union be "politicised"? prospects and risks', *Notre Europe*, Policy Paper 19.

Bauer, Michael W. (2008) 'Diffuse anxieties, deprived entrepreneurs: Commission reform and middle management', *Journal of European Public Policy* 15(5): 691–707.

Bauer, Michael W. and Jörn Ege (2012) 'Politicisation within the European Commission's Bureaucracy', *International Review of Administrative Sciences* 78(3): 403–24.

Bauer, Michael W., Christoph Knill, Tim Balint, and Stefan Benzing (2008) Decentralisation following the Reform of the European Commission: Evaluation and Perception. Study on behalf of the European Parliament. Konstanz: University of Konstanz.

Baumgartner, Frank R. and Bryan D. Jones (1993) *Agendas and instability in American politics*. Chicago: University of Chicago Press.

Baumgartner, Frank R., Sylvain Brouard, Christoffer Green-Pedersen, Bryan D. Jones, and Stefaan Walgrave (2011) 'The dynamics of policy change in comparative perspective', *Comparative Political Studies (Special Issue)* 44(8).

Bell, Mark (2002) 'Beyond European Labour Law? Reflections on the EU Racial Equality Directive', *European Law Journal* 8(3): 384–99.

Bergman, Torbjörn, Wolfgang C. Müller, and Kaare Strom (2000) 'Introduction: Parliamentary democracy and the chain of delegation', *European Journal of Political Research* 37(3): 255–60.

Berry, Jeffrey M. (2002) 'Validity and reliability issues in elite interviewing', *Political Science & Politics* 35(4): 679–82.

BEUC (2000a) BEUC comments on the proposal for a directive of the European Parliament and of the Council on universal service and users' rights relating to electronic communication networks and services, edited by Bureau Européen des Unions de Consommateurs. Brussels.

BEUC (2000b) BEUC's position on the Revision of the General Product Safety Directive Com(2000)139—final/2, edited by Bureau Européen des Unions de Consommateurs. Brussels.

BEUC (2000c) Final BEUC Position on the use of health related claims for foodstuffs, edited by Bureau Européen des Unions de Consommateurs. Brussels.

BEUC (2002a) BEUC comments on the proposed Regulation on denied boarding and of cancellation or long delay of flights, edited by Bureau Européen des Unions de Consommateurs. Brussels: BEUC.

BEUC (2002b) Credit for consumers—BEUC position. In *Proposal for a Directive of the European Parliament and of the Council on the harmonisation of laws, regulations and administrative provisions of the Member States concerning credit for consumers. COM (2002) 443.*, edited by Bureau Européen des Unions de Consommateurs. Brussels.

BEUC (2002c) Position on the proposed regulation on Sales Promotions edited by Bureau Européen des Unions de Consommateurs. Brussels: BEUC.

BEUC (2003a) BEUC Position Paper—Comments on the proposal for a Regulation of the European Parliament and the Council on nutrition and health claims—COM(2003)424 (01), edited by Bureau Européen des Unions de Consommateurs. Brussels.

BEUC (2003b) General thoughts on fortification of food: BEUC's consideration for the stakeholder meeting on 24 February, edited by Bureau Européen des Unions de Consommateurs. Brussels.

BEUC (2004a) Addition of vitamins and minerals and of certain other substances to Foods: BEUC Comments, edited by Bureau Européen des Unions de Consommateurs. Brussels: Beate Kettlitz.

BEUC (2004b) Unfair Commercial Practices—BEUC Comments, edited by Bureau Européen des Unions de Consommateurs. Brussels: Bureau Européen des Unions de Consommateurs.

BEUC (2006) BEUC position paper on the Commission proposals for a regulation on food additives, food enzymes and food flavourings, edited by Bureau Européen des Unions de Consommateurs. Brussels.

BEUC (2008) Food information to consumers—Summary of the BEUC position on the Commission proposal, edited by Bureau Européen des Unions de Consommateurs. Brussels: BEUC.

BEUC (2009) The future of European Consumers' rights: BEUC's reaction to the fundamental issues raised by the Proposal for a directive of the European Parliament and of the Council on consumers rights, edited by Bureau Européen des Unions de Consommateurs. Brussels.

BEUC and ANEC (2008) Revision of the Toy Safety Directive: How can we make toys safer?, edited by Bureau Européen des Unions de Consommateurs and European Association for the Co-ordination of Consumer Representation in Standardisation. Brussels.

Beyers, Jan (2004) 'Voice and access: Political practices of European Interest Associations', *European Union Politics* 5(2): 211–40.

Beyers, Jan and Bart Kerremans (2004) 'Bureaucrats, politicians, and societal interests: How is European policy making politicized?', *Comparative Political Studies* 37(10): 1150.

Boomgaarden, Hajo, Rens Vliegenthart, Claes De Vreese, and Andreas Schuck (2010) 'News on the move: Exogenous events and news coverage of the European Union', *Journal of European Public Policy* 17(4): 506–26.

Borrás, Susana (2003) *The Innovation Policy of the European Union. From Government to Governance*. Cheltenham: Edward Elgar.

Börzel, Tanja A. (1997) 'What's so special about policy networks?—An exploration of the concept and its usefulness in studying European governance', *European Integration online Papers (EIoP)* 1(16).

Boswell, Christina (2008) 'The political functions of expert knowledge: Knowledge and legitimation in European Union immigration policy', *Journal of European Public Policy* 15(4): 471–88.

Boswell, Christina (2009) *The Political Uses of Expert Knowlegde: Immigration Policy and Social Research*. Cambridge: Cambridge University Press.

Bounds, Andrew, Nikki Tait, and Jenny Wiggins (2008) 'EU proposes food label rules', *The Financial Times*, January 31, 2008: 4.

Bouwen, Pieter (2002) 'Corporate lobbying in the European Union: The logic of access', *Journal of European Public Policy* 9(3): 365–90.

Bouwen, Pieter (2003) 'The democratic legitimacy of business interest representation in the European Union: Normative implications of the logic of access', *Preprints of the Max Planck Institute for Research on Collective Goods* 2003 (8).

Bouwen, Pieter (2009) 'The European Commission'. In: D. Coen and J. Richardson (eds), *Lobbying the European Union: Institutions, Actors, and Issues*. Oxford: Oxford University Press.

Braun, Dietmar, Fabrizio Gilardi, Katharina Füglister, Stéphane Luyet, and Covadonga Meseguer (2007) 'Ex pluribus unum: Integrating the different strands of policy diffusion theory', *Politische Vierteljahresschrift* 38: 39–55.

Braun, Jan Frederik (2009) 'Multiple sources of pressure for change: The Barroso Commission and energy policy for an enlarged EU', *Journal of Contemporary European Research* 5(3): 428–51.

Brent, Richard (1995) 'The binding of Leviathan—the changing role of the European Commission in competition cases', *International and Comparative Law Quarterly* 44(2): 255–79.

Brochhagen, Lena (2010) Seeking advice in a multi-level governance system—a sectoral analysis of the composition of expert groups to the European Commission. In *Magisterarbeit an der Philosophischen Fakultät der Universität zu Köln*. Köln.

Broscheid, Andreas and David Coen (2007) 'Lobbying activity and fora creation in the EU: Empirically exploring the nature of the policy good', *Journal of European Public Policy* 14(3): 346–65.

Browne, Anthony (2006) 'EU's £340m aid package for globalisation victims', *Times Online*, March 2, 2006.

Buckley, Neil (1999) 'Toymakers' softener falls foul of Brussels' hardline on safety: EU "precautionary principle" has prompted a ban on some phthalates used in PVC toys and dummies', *The Financial Times*, December 16, 1999: 6.

Budge, Ian and Hans Keman (1990) *Parties and Democracy: Coalition formation and government functioning in twenty states*. Oxford: Oxford University Press.

Bulmer, Simon J. (1993) 'The governance of the European Union: A new institutionalist approach', *Journal of Public Policy* 13(4): 351–80.

Burt, Tim and George Parker (2003) 'Media dismay at EU sex bias bill', *Financial Times*, June 25, 2003.

Caporaso, James A. and Joseph Jupille (2001) 'The Europeanization of gender equality policy and domestic structural change'. In: M. G. Cowles, J. A. Caporaso and T. Risse (eds), *Transforming Europe: Europeanization and Domestic Change*. Ithaca, NY: Cornell University Press.

Caporaso, James A. and Sidney Tarrow (2009) 'Polanyi in Brussels: Supranational institutions and the transnational embedding of markets', *International Organization* 63(4): 593–620.

Cecot, Caroline, Robert Hahn, Andrea Renda, and Lorna Schrefler (2008) 'An evaluation of the quality of impact assessment in the European Union with lessons for the US and the EU', *Regulation & Governance* 2(4): 405–24.

CEEA (1959) Note sur les Reglements Interieurs des Trois Executifs. Brussels: Communauté Européenne de l'Energie Atomique.

Centre de Droit de la Consommation (2000) *The Practical Application of Council Directive 92/59/EEC on General Product Safety*, February 2000, Louvain-la-Neuve [cited February 3, 2010]. Available from <http://ec.europa.eu/dgs/health_consumer/library/surveys/sur13_en.html>.

CEPS (2006) 'Impact of selected topics of the proposed directive on pyrotechnic articles: Briefing note'. *IPOL/A/IMCO/2006-11*. Brussels: August 2006.

Chopin, Isabelle (1999) 'The Starting Line Group: A harmonised approach to fight racism and to promote equal treatment', *European Journal of Migration and Law* 1(1): 111–29.

Christiansen, Thomas (1996) 'A maturing bureaucracy? The role of the Commission in the policy process'. In: J. J. Richardson (ed.), *European Union. Power and Policy-Making*. London: Routledge: 77–95.

Christiansen, Thomas (1997) 'Tensions of European governance: Politicized bureaucracy and multiple accountability in the European Commission', *Journal of European Public Policy* 4(1): 73–90.

Christiansen, Thomas (2001) 'Intra-institutional politics and inter-institutional relations in the EU: Towards coherent governance?', *Journal of European Public Policy* 8(5): 747–69.

Christiansen, Thomas and Emil Kirchner (eds) (2000) *Committee Governance in the European Union*. Manchester: Manchester University Press.

CIAA (2003) Positions—Nutrition and Health claims: Proposal for a regulation of EP and of the Council on Nutrition and Health Claims made on Foods, edited by Confédération des Industries Agro-Alimentaires de l'UE. Brussels.

CIAA (2006) CIAA Recommendation for a Common Nutrition Labelling Scheme, edited by Confédération des Industries Agro-Alimentaires de l'UE. Brussels: Confederation of the food and drink industries of the EU.

CIAA (2008) CIAA Statement on the European Commission Proposal on the provisions of food information to consumers, edited by Confédération des Industries Agro-Alimentaires de l'UE. Brussels.

CIAA (2011) *Data & Trends of the European Food and Drink Industry 2010*. Brussels: Confédération des Industries Agro-Alimentaires de l'UE.

Cini, Michelle (1996) *The European Commission: Leadership, organization and culture in the EU administration*. Manchester: Manchester University Press.

Cini, Michelle (2000) 'Administrative culture in the European Commission. The case of competition and environment'. In: N. Nugent (ed.), *At the Heart of the Union. Studies of the European Commission*. Second edition. Houndmills: Macmillan.

Cini, Michelle (2007) *From Integration to Integrity: Administrative Ethics and Reforms in the European Commission*. Manchester: Manchester University Press.

Clergeau, Christophe (2005) 'European food safety policies: Between a single market and a political crisis'. In: M. Steffen (ed.), *Health Governance in Europe: Issues, Challenges, and Theories*. London: Routledge.

Coen, David (1997) 'The evolution of the large firm as a political actor in the European Union', *Journal of European Public Policy* 4: 91–108.

Coen, David (1998) 'The European business interest and the nation state: Large-firm lobbying in the European Union and member states', *Journal of Public Policy* 18(1): 75–100.

Coen, David, and Alexander Katsaitis (2013) 'Chameleon pluralism in the EU: An empirical study of the European Commission interest group density and diversity across policy domains', *Journal of European Public Policy* 20(8): 1104–19.

Comité des Trois (1979) *Rapport sur les Institutions Européennes*. Présenté au Conseil européen par le Comité des Trois. Florence: Archive Historique des Communautés Européennes (AHCE).

Commission of the European Communities (2002a) 'Commission welcomes a big step ahead in Air passengers rights: huge increase of compensations for denied boarding and cancellation'. *IP/02/1812*. Brussels: December 5, 2002.

Commission of the European Communities (2002b) 'Improving the knowledge base for better policies', Communication from the Commission on the collection and use of expertise by the Commission: Principles and guidelines. *COM(2002) 713 final* Brussels.

Commission of the European Communities (2003) 'Commission staff working paper: Extended impact assessment on the Directive of the European Parliament and of the Council concerning unfair business-to-consumer commercial practices in the Internal Market and amending directives 84/450/EEC, 97/7/EC and 98/27/EC'. *SEC(2003)724*. Brussels: June 18, 2003.

Commission of the European Communities (2004) 'Communication from the Commission to the Council and the European Parliament: Building our common future policy challenges and budgetary means of the enlarged Union 2007–2013'. *COM(2004) 101 final*. Brussels: February 26, 2004.

Commission of the European Communities (2005a) 'Commission Decision of 15 November 2005 amending its Rules of Procedure'. *(2005/960/EC, Euratom) Official Journal*. Brussels: November 15, 2005.

Commission of the European Communities (2005b) 'Communication to the Spring European Council—"Working together for growth and jobs. A new start for the Lisbon strategy"'. *COM(2005) 24 final*. Brussels, February 2, 2005.

Commission of the European Communities (2006) 'Proposal for a Regulation of the European Parliament and the Council establishing the European Institute of Technology'. *COM (2006) 604*. Brussels, October 18, 2006.

Commission of the European Communities (2008a) 'Executive Summary of the Impact Assessment—Commission Staff Working Document Accompanying the Proposal for a directive on consumer rights'. Brussels: July 30, 2008.

Commission of the European Communities (2008b) 'Guide de la procédure à suivre pour le traitement des consultations interservices'. Internal working document. Brussels.

Commission of the European Communities (2008c) 'Proposal for a Council Regulation on the Community legal framework for a European Research Infrastructure (ERI)'. *COM (2008)467*. Brussels, July 25, 2008.

Commission of the European Communities (2008d) 'Safety first: Commission proposes new strict rules for toys'. *IP/08/91*. Luxembourg: January 25, 2008.

Consumers in Europe Group (1997) 'Response to the Commission Green Paper: Financial services: Meeting consumers' expectations', *Journal of Consumer Policy* 20: 379–94.

Coombes, David (1968) *Towards a European Civil Service*. London: Chatham House Publishers.

Coombes, David (1970) *Politics and Bureaucracy in the European Community. A Portrait of the Commission of the EEC*. London: Allen & Unwin.

Cowles, Maria Green (1995) 'Setting the agenda for a new Europe: The ERT and EC 1992', *Journal of Common Market Studies* 33(4): 501–26.

Craft, Jonathan, and Michael Howlett (2013) 'The dual dynamics of policy advisory systems: The impact of externalization and politicization on policy advice', *Policy and Society* 32(3): 187–97.

Cram, Laura (1994) 'The European commission as a multi-organization: Social policy and IT policy in the EU', *Journal of European Public Policy* 1(2): 195–217.

Cram, Laura (1997) *Policy-making in the EU—conceptual lenses and the integration process*. London: Routledge.

Crombez, Christophe (1997) 'The Codecision Procedure in the European Union', *Legislative Studies Quarterly* 22: 97–119.

Crombez, Christophe (2000) 'Institutional reform and co-decision in the European Union', *Constitutional Political Economy* 11(1): 41–57.

Crombez, Christophe, and Simon Hix (2011) 'Treaty reform and the Commission's appointment and policy-making role in the European Union', *European Union Politics* 12(3): 291–314.

Cseres, Katalin (2005) *Competition Law and Consumer Protection*. The Hague: Kluwer Law International.

D'Acunto, Salvatore (2004) 'La proposition de directive sur les services dans le marché intérieur', *Revue du Droit de l'Union européenne* (2): 201–48.

Dahl, Robert (1971) *Polyarchy: Participation and Opposition*. New Haven, CN: Yale University Press.

Daviter, Falk (2009) 'Schattschneider in Brussels: How policy conflict reshaped the biotechnology agenda in the European Union', *West European Politics* 32(6): 1118–39.

De Swaan, Abram (1973) *Coalition Theories and Cabinet Formations*. Amsterdam: Elsevier.

De Vreese, Claes, Susan Banducci, Holli Semetko, and Hajo Boomgaarden (2006) 'The news coverage of the 2004 European Parliamentary Election Campaign in 25 Countries', *European Union Politics* 7(4): 477–504.

De Wilde, Pieter (2011) 'No polity for old politics? A framework for analyzing the politicization of European integration', *Journal of European Integration* 33(5): 559–75.

De Witte, Bruno (2007) Setting the Scene: How did Services get to Bolkestein and Why? Mitchell Working Paper Series No. 3/2007. Edinburgh: Europa Institute, School of Law Edinburgh.

Dehousse, Renaud and Nicolas Monceau (2009) 'Are EU Policies meeting europeans' expectations?'. In: R. Dehousse, F. Deloche-Gaudez, and S. Jacquot (eds), *What is Europe up to?* Paris: Presses de Sciences Po.

Deutsche Bundesbank (2005) 'Die Aufsicht über Finanzkonglomerate in Deutschland'. In: *Monatsbericht April 2005*. Frankfurt a.M.

Dexter, Lewis Anthony (2006 [1970]) *Elite and Specialized Interviewing*, Colchester: ECPR Press.

DG Health and Consumer Protection (2001) 'Discussion paper on nutrition claims and functional claims'. *SANCO/1341/2001*. Brussels: July 2001.

DG Health and Consumer Protection (2002) 'Draft Proposal for a Regulation of the European Parliament and of the Council on nutrition, functional and health claims made on foods—Working document'. *SANCO/1832/2002*. Brussels.

DG Health and Consumer Protection (2007) 'Preparatory work for the Impact Assessment on the Review of the Consumer Acquis: Analytical report on the Green Paper on the Review of the Consumer Acquis submitted by the Consumer Policy Evaluation Consortium'. Brussels: November 6, 2007.

DG III of the European Commission (1997) 'Addition of vitamins and minerals to foods and food supplements. A discussion paper'. *DGIII/5934/97*. Brussels.

Dickie, Mure (2007) 'Beijing promises to address EU fears about dangerous products ', *The Financial Times*, July 25, 2007: 6.

Directorate-General Health and Consumer Protection (2005) 'Draft Working Paper—Regulation of the European Parliament and of the Council on food additives'. *WGA/004/03 rev10*. Brussels: February 2, 2005.

Directorate-General for Health and Consumer Protection (2006) 'Labelling: competitiveness, consumer information and better regulation for the EU—A DG SANCO Consultative Document'. Brussels: February 2006.

Directorate-General for Health and Consumer Protection (2006) 'Summary of results for the consultation document on: "Labelling: competitiveness, consumer information and better regulation for the EU"'. Brussels: December 2006.

Döring, Holger (2007) 'The Composition of the College of Commissioners: Patterns of delegation', *European Union Politics* 8: 207–28.

Döring, Holger (2013) 'The Collective Action of Data Collection: A data infrastructure on parties, elections and cabinets', *European Union Politics* 14: 161–78.

Dosi, Giovanni, Patrick Llerena, and Mauro Sylos Labini (2006) 'The relationships between science, technologies and their industrial exploitation: An illustration through the myths and realities of the so-called "European Paradox"', *Research Policy* 35(10): 1450–64.

Down, Ian and Carole Wilson (2008) 'From permissive consensus to constraining dissensus: A polarizing union?', *Acta Politica* 43(1): 26–49.

Downs, Anthony (1957) *An Economic Theory of Democracy*. New York: Harper & Row.

Downs, Anthony (1966/1967) *Inside Bureaucracy*. Boston: Little, Brown and Company.

Druckman, James N. and Andrew Roberts (2008) 'Measuring portfolio salience in Eastern European parliamentary democracies', *European Journal of Political Research* 47(1): 101–34.

Druckman, James N. and Paul V. Warwick (2005) 'The missing piece: Measuring portfolio salience in Western European parliamentary democracies', *European Journal of Political Research* 44(1): 17–42.

Dunleavy, Patrick (1991) *Democracy, Bureaucracy and Public Choice: Economic Explanations in Political Science*. New York: Harvester Wheatsheaf.

Dunleavy, Patrick (1997) 'Explaining the centralization of the European Union: A public choice analysis', *Aussenwirtschaft* 52(1–2): 183–212.

Düro, Michael (2009) *Crosswalking EUR-Lex: A proposal for a metadata mapping to improve access to EU documents*. Luxembourg: Office for Official Publications of the European Communities.

Eberhardie, Christine (2007) 'Nutritional supplements and the EU: is anyone happy?', *Proceedings of the Nutrition Society* 66(04): 508–11.

Eckstein, Harry (1975) 'Case study and theory in political science'. In: F. I. Greenstein and N. W. Polsby (eds), *Handbook of Political Science*. Reading, MA: Addison-Wesley.

ECTAA (2009) European travel industry agrees on EU passenger rights rules, edited by European Travel Agents' and Tour Operators' Associations. Brussels.

Egan, Michelle (forthcoming) *Single Markets. Economic Integration in Europe and the United States*. Oxford: Oxford University Press.

Egeberg, Morten (1994) 'Bridging the gap between theory and practice: The case of administrative policy', *Governance* 7(1): 83–98.

Egeberg, Morten (1996) 'Organization and nationality in the European Commission services', *Public Administration* 74(4): 721–35.

Egeberg, Morten (2006a) 'Executive politics as usual: Role behaviour and conflict dimensions in the College of European Commissioners', *Journal of European Public Policy* 13(1): 1–15.

Egeberg, Morten (ed.) (2006b) *Multilevel Union Administration: The Transformation of Executive Politics in Europe*. Edited by M. Egan, N. Nugent, and W. Paterson. Houndmills: Palgrave.

Eising, Rainer (2007) 'Institutional context, organizational resources and strategic choices—Explaining interest group access in the European Union', *European Union Politics* 8(3): 329–62.

Eising, Rainer (2008) 'Interest groups in EU policy-making', *Living Reviews in European Governance* 3(4).

Elgström, Ole and Christer Jönsson (2000) 'Negotiation in the European Union: Bargaining or problem-solving?', *Journal of European Public Policy* 7: 684–704.

Elgström, Ole and Magdalena Frennhoff Larsén (2008) 'The Role of Commission and Council (Dis-)Unity in International Trade Negotiations: A Case Study of the EPA Negotiations'. In: *Fourth Pan-European Conference on EU Politics (ECPR)*. Riga.

Ellinas, Antonis A. and Ezra N. Suleiman (2012) *The European Commission and Bureaucratic Autonomy. Europe's Custodians*. Cambridge: Cambridge University Press.

Enterprise and Industry Directorate-General (2005) 'The role and significance of the CE marking'. *Draft Certif Doc 2005–11*. Brussels: March 30, 2005.

Epstein, Lee and Jeffrey Segal (2000) 'Measuring Issue Salience', *American Journal of Political Science* 44(1): 66–83.

EPTO (2009) EPTO—The EU Commission Proposal for a Regulation on the rights of passengers in international bus and coach transport: Overview & Comments, edited by European Passenger Transport Operators. Brussels.

Erridge, Andrew, Ruth Fee, and John McIlroy (1998) 'European Union public procurement policy and electronic commerce: problems and opportunities', *European Business Review* 98(5): 252–9.

ESBG (2003) On the Commission's Proposal for a Directive of the European Parliament and of the Council on the harmonisation of laws, regulations and administrative provisions of the Member States concerning credit for consumers—COM (2002) 443 Final, edited by European Savings Banks Group. Brussels.

ETUC (1998) 'Public procurement in the European Union. Resolution adopted by the ETUC Executive Committee'. December 15–16, 1998.

ETUC (2005) ETUC welcomes the setting up of the European Globalisation Adjustment Fund but would like to see a reinforcement of the social partners' role in the process of reintegration into employment.

EurActiv (2008) 'Patient mobility', *EurActiv*, June 8, 2008.

EURO COOP (2003) EURO COOP Comments to the Proposal for a Directive of the European Parliament and of the Council Concerning unfair business-to-consumer commercial practices in the Internal Market (COM (2003) 356 final), edited by European Community of Consumer Co-operatives. Brussels.

EuroCommerce (2003) Position Paper: Proposal for a Regulation of the European Parliament and of the Council on Nutrition and Health Claims made on Foods, COM(2003) 424, edited by EuroCommerce a.i.b.s. Brussels.

EuroCommerce (2007) Initiative of the Commission in favour of the free movement of goods—Position Paper, edited by EuroCommerce a.i.b.s. Brussels.

EuroCommerce (2008) Commission Proposal for a Regulation on Food Information to Consumers—Position Paper, edited by EuroCommerce a.i.b.s. Brussels.

Europe Information Service (1992) 'Pharmaceuticals: AESGP criticises EEC Commission's paper on food supplements', *European Report*, March 18, 1992.

Europe Information Service (1997a) 'Food supplements: Commission opens debate on harmonisation', *European Report*, June 20, 1997.

Europe Information Service (1997b) 'New food supplement industry group set up', *European Report*, May 30, 1998.

Europe Information Service (1999) 'Agri-Foods: Infringement procedures against France, Germany and Greece for barriers to trade', *European Report*, July 14, 1999.

Europe Information Service (2000) 'Single Market: Commission pursues action against seven member states', *European Report*, January 15, 2000.

European Commission (2001a) 'Analytical report: Sales promotions in the Internal Market'. Internal working paper—DG MARKT. Brussels.

European Commission (2001b) 'Discussion paper for the amendment of Directive 87/102/EEC concerning consumer credit'. Brussels.

European Commission (2005a) 'Commission Staff Working Paper: Rights of passengers in international bus and coach transport. A Consultation Document by the Services of the Directorate General for Energy and Transport'. Brussels: July 14, 2005.

European Commission (2005b) 'Communication from the Commission to the Council and the European Parliament: Outcome of the screening of legislative proposals pending before the Legislator'. *COM(2005)462.* Brussels: September 27, 2005.

European Commission (2005c) 'Impact Assessment Guidelines'. SEC(2005) 791. June 15, 2005.

European Commission (2005d) 'Proposal for a Directive of the European Parliament and of the Council on the placing on the market of pyrotechnic articles: Impact assessment'. Brussels: October 11, 2005.

European Commission (2006a) 'Summary of contributions received by the Commission in response to the Commission Staff Working Paper "Rights of passengers in international bus and coach transport"'. Brussels: January 30, 2006.

European Commission (2006b) 'Summary of contributions received by the Commission in response to the Commission Staff Working Paper "Strengthening the protection of the rights of passengers travelling by sea or inland waterway in the European Union"'. Brussels: January 30, 2006.

European Commission (2008) 'Public Procurement: EU proposes protection from discrimination beyond the workplace', *Press Release* IP/08/1071, July 2, 2008.

European Commission (2010a) 'Communication from the President to the Commission: Framework for the Commission expert groups: horizontal rules and public register'. C(2010) 7649 final. Brussels, November 10, 2010.

European Commission (2010b) 'The Working Methods of the Commission 2010–2014. Communication from the President'. C(2010)1100. February 10, 2010.

The European Evaluation Consortium (2003) 'Evaluation of the food labelling legislation—Final Report'. *Framework Contract No. BUDG-02-01 L2; Request for Services by DG SANCO.* Tickenham, UK: October 18, 2003.

European Parliament (2001) 'Report on the Commission communication to the European Parliament and the Council on the protection of air passengers in the European Union'. A5-0249/2001. Brussels: June 29, 2001.

Europolitics (2007) 'Health Care: Wallström raises objections to Kyprianou's Directive', *European Report* 18 (December 2007).

External Advisory Group—Fission (2001) 'Research and Training Programme (Euratom) in the Field of Nuclear Energy (1998 to 2002)': Advice on the Implementation of European Support to Nuclear Fission Related Research in the Framework of the European Research Area (ERA). In EAG-FISSION-02/2-9 Final, April 27, 2001.

Falkner, Gerda (1998) *EU Social Policy in the 1990s: Towards a Corporatist Policy Community.* London/New York: Routledge.

Falkner, Gerda (2000) 'Policy networks in a multi-level system: Convergence towards Moderate Diversity?', *West European Politics* 23(4): 94–121.

Falkner, Gerda, Treib Oliver, Hartlapp Miriam, and Leiber Simone (2005) *Complying with Europe. EU Minimum Harmonisation and Soft Law in the Member States.* Cambridge: Cambridge University Press.

Farrell, Henry and Adrienne Héritier (2007) 'Introduction: Contested competences in the European Union', *West European Politics* 30(2): 227–43.

Feldman, Martha S. and James G. March (1981) 'Information in Organizations as Signal and Symbol', *Administrative Science Quarterly* 26(2): 171–86.

Fiorina, Morris P. and Kenneth A. Shepsle (1989) 'Formal theories of leadership'. In: B. D. Jones (ed.), *Leadership and Politics: New Perspectives in Political Science*. Lawrence: University of Kansas Press.

Follesdal, Andreas and Simon Hix (2006) 'Why there is a democratic deficit in the EU: A response to Majone and Moravcsik', *Journal of Common Market Studies* 44(3): 533–62.

Franchino, Fabio (2000) 'Control of the Commission's executive functions: Uncertainty, conflict and decision rules', *European Union Politics* 1(1): 63–92.

Franchino, Fabio (2009) 'Experience and the distribution of portfolio payoffs in the European Commission', *European Journal of Political Research* 48(1): 1–30.

Franklin, Mark and Christopher Wlezien (1997) 'The responsive public: Issue salience, policy change, and preferences for European unification', *Journal of Theoretical Politics* 9(3): 347–63.

FT (2003) 'Women drivers: They are safer, so should pay less for insurance', *Financial Times*, May 31, 2003.

Gallagher, Michael, Michael Laver, and Peter Mair (eds) (2005) *Representative Government in Modern Europe. Institutions, parties, and governments.* Boston: McGraw Hill.

Ganghof, Steffen (2005) 'Kausale Perspektiven in der Politikwissenschaft: X-Zentrierte und Y-Zentrierte Fortschungsdesigns'. In: S. Kropp and M. Minkenberg (eds), *Vergleichen in der Politikwissenschaft*: VS Verlag.

Garrett, Geoffrey (1992) 'International cooperation and institutional choice: The European Community's internal market', *International Organization* 46(2): 533–60.

Garrett, Geoffrey and George Tsebelis (1996) 'An institutionalist critique of intergovernmentalism', *International Organization* 50(2): 269–99.

Gelderman, Kees, Paul Ghijsen, and Jordie Schoonen (2010) 'Explaining non-compliance with European Union procurement directives: A multidisciplinary perspective', *Journal of Common Market Studies* 48(2): 243–64.

George, Alexander L. (1979) 'Case studies and theory development: The method of structured, focused comparison'. In: P. G. Lauren (ed.), *Diplomacy. New approaches in history, theory, and policy.* London: Collier Macmillan.

George, Alexander L. and Andrew Bennett (2005) *Case Studies and Theory Development in the Social Sciences.* Cambridge, MA: MIT Press.

Gerring, John (2008) 'The mechanismic worldview: Thinking inside the box', *British Journal of Political Science* 38(01): 161–79.

Goldstein, Kenneth (2002) 'Getting in the door: Sampling and completing elite interviews', *PS: Political Science and Politics* 35(4): 669–72.

Golub, Jonathan (2007) 'Survival analysis and European Union decision-making', *European Union Politics* 8(2): 155–79.

Gormley, William T. (1986) 'Regulatory issue networks in a federal system', *Polity* 18(4): 595–620.

Gornitzka, Åse and Ulf Sverdrup (2008) 'Who consults? The configuration of expert groups in the European Union', *West European Politics* 31(4): 725–50.

Grande, Edgar and Jürgen Häusler (1994) *Industrieforschung und Forschungspolitik—Staatliche Steuerungspotentiale in der Informationstechnik.* Frankfurt/New York: Campus.

Gronbaek, David J. v H. (2003) 'A European Research Council: An idea whose time has come?', *Science and Public Policy* 30: 391–404.

Grossman, Emiliano and Cornelia Woll (2011) 'The French debate over the Bolkestein directive', *Comparative European Politics* 9: 344–66.

Groupe de Personnalités Indépendantes (1979a) Compte-rendu sommaire de la réunion tenue à Bruxelles le 2 février 1979. Florence: Archive Historique des Communautés Européennes (AHCE).

Groupe de Personnalités Indépendantes (1979b) La Commission et ses Services. (Projet révisé par le Secrétaire conformément aux instructions données par le Groupe lors de sa réunion des 26 et 27 avril). Florence: Archive Historique des Communautés Européennes (AHCE).

Guigner, Sébastien (2004) 'Institutionalizing public health in the European Commission: The thrills and spills of politicization'. In: A. Smith (ed.), *Politics and the European Commission. Actors, interdependence legitimacy.* London: Routledge.

Guzzetti, Luca (1995) *A Brief History of European Union Research Policy.* Brussels: European Commission.

Haas, Ernst B. (1958/1968) *The Uniting of Europe: Political, Social, and Economic Forces 1950–1957.* Stanford, CA: Stanford University Press.

Haas, Peter M. (1992) 'Introduction: Epistemic communities and international policy coordination', *International Organization* 46(1): 1–35.

Häge, Frank M. and Dimiter Toshkov (2011) 'Anticipating resistance: The effect of member state preferences on the European Commission's agenda-setting activity', *Limerick Papers in Politics and Public Administration* 2011 (1).

Hagelüken, Alexander (2006) 'Der Kommissar ist nur ein Hausbesetzer', *Süddeutsche Zeitung*, October 5, 2006.

Hagenmeyer, Moritz (2006) 'The food additives revival', *European Food and Feed Law Review* (5): 295–301.

Hall, Peter A. (2008) 'Systematic process analysis: When and how to use it', *European Political Science* 7(3): 304–17.

Hall, Ronald (2005) 'The future of European regional policy: Issues surrounding "An Agenda for a Growing Europe"', *Regional Studies* 39(7): 966–71.

Haller, Max (2009) *Die Europäische Integration als Elitenprozess. Das Ende eines Traums?* Wiesbaden: VS Verlag für Sozialwissenschaften.

Hammond, Thomas H. (1986) 'Agenda control, organizational structure, and bureaucratic politics', *American Journal of Political Science* 30(2): 379–420.

Harcourt, Alison J. (1998) 'EU Media Ownership Regulation: Conflict over the definition of alternatives', *Journal of Common Market Studies* 36(3): 369–89.

Hargreaves, Deborah (2001) 'Business group opposes Commission's plan', *The Financial Times*, April 1, 2001: 6.

Hartlapp, Miriam (2007) 'Intra-Kommissionsdynamik im Policy-Making: EU-Politiken angesichts des demographischen Wandels', *Politische Vierteljahresschrift* 40(PVS-Sonderheft 2007/2): 139–60.

Hartlapp, Miriam (2011) 'Organising exits from the Joint-Decision Trap? Cross-sectoral (non-)coordination in the European Union'. In: G. Falkner (ed.) *The EU's Decision Traps. Comparing Policies* Oxford: Oxford University Press.

Hartlapp, Miriam (2012) 'Deconstructing EU old age policy: Assessing the potential of soft OMCs and hard EU law', *European Integration Online Papers. Mini special issue* 16(3).

Hartlapp, Miriam and Julia Metz (2013) 'Expertise in transnationalen Verwaltungen: das Beispiel der Europäischen Union'. In: S. Kuhlmann and S. Kropp (eds), *Wissen und Expertise in Politik und Verwaltung. DMS Sonderheft 1/2013*: 183–202. Leverkusen-Opladen: Barbara Budrich.

Hartlapp, Miriam and Christian Rauh (2013) 'The Commission's internal conditions for social re-regulation: Market efficiency and wider social goals in setting the rules for financial services in Europe', *European Journal of Government and Economics* 2(1): 25–40.

Hartlapp, Miriam, Julia Metz, and Christian Rauh (2010a) 'The agenda set by the EU Commission: The result of balanced or biased aggregation of positions?', *LEQS Paper No. 21*, April 2010, London School of Economics.

Hartlapp, Miriam, Julia Metz, and Christian Rauh (2010b) 'How external interests enter the European Commission: Mechanisms at play in legislative position formation', *WZB Discussion Paper* SP IV 2010–501.

Hartlapp, Miriam, Julia Metz and Christian Rauh (2013) 'Linking agenda setting to coordination structures: Bureaucratic politics inside the European Commission', *Journal of European Integration* 53(4): 425–41.

Hatzopoulos, Vassilis and Thien Uyen Do (2006) 'The case law of the ECJ concerning the free provision of services: 2000–2005', *Common Market Law Review* 43: 923–91.

Hauer, Christian (2006) 'The regulation on nutrition and health claims', *European Food and Feed Law Review* 2006(6): 355–61.

Heclo, Hugh (1974) *Modern Social Politics in Britain and Sweden. From Relief to Maintenance.* New Haven, CT: Yale University Press.

Héritier, Adrienne (1999) *Policy-Making and Diversity in Europe: Escape from Deadlock.* Cambridge: Cambridge University Press.

Hervey, Tamara and Louise Trubek (2007) 'Freedom to provide health care services in the EU: an opportunity for "hybrid government"', *The Columbia Journal of European Law* 13: 623–47.

Hervey, Tamara and Bart Vanhercke (2010) 'Enabeling patient mobility in the EU: Between free movement and coordination'. In: E. Mossialos, G. Permanand, R. Baeten, and T. K. Hervey (eds), *Health Systems Governance in Europe. The Role of EU Law and Policy.* Cambridge: Cambridge University Press.

Hix, Simon (2006) 'Why the EU needs (left–right) politics: Policy reform and accountability are impossible without it', *Notre Europe Policy Paper No. 19.*

Hix, Simon and Christopher Lord (1997) *Political Parties in the European Union.* Houndmills: Palgrave Macmillan.

Hix, Simon and Abdul Noury (2009) 'After enlargement: Voting patterns in the Sixth European Parliament', *Legislative Studies Quarterly* 34(2): 159–74.

Hix, Simon, Abdul Noury, and Gérard Roland (2005) 'Power to the parties: Cohesion and competition in the European Parliament, 1979–2001', *British Journal of Political Science* 35(2): 209–34.

Hoffmann, Stanley (1966) 'Obstinate or obsolete? The fate of the nation-state and the case of Western Europe', *Daedalus* 95(3): 862–915.

Hooghe, Liesbet (2000) 'Euro-Socialists or Euro-Marketeers? EU top officials on capitalism', *The Journal of Politics* 62(2): 430–54.

Hooghe, Liesbet (2001) *The European Commission and the Integration of Europe. Images of governance.* Cambridge: Cambridge University Press.

Hooghe, Liesbet (2003) 'Europe divided?: Elites vs. public opinion on European integration', *European Union Politics* 4(3): 281–304.

Hooghe, Liesbet (2005) 'Several Roads Lead To International Norms, But Few Via International Socialization: A Case Study of European Commission', *International Organization* 59(4): 861–98.

Hooghe, Liesbet (2012) 'Images of Europe: How Commission officials conceive their institution's role', *JCMS: Journal of Common Market Studies* 50(1): 87–111.

Hooghe, Liesbet (2013) 'What Officials Believe'. In: H. Kassim, J. Peterson, L. Hooghe, M. W. Bauer, S. Connolly, R. Dehousse, and A. Thompson (eds), *The European Commission in Question.* Oxford: Oxford University Press.

Hooghe, Liesbet and Garry Marks (2009) 'A Postfunctionalist theory of European integration: From permissive consensus to constraining dissensus', *British Journal of Political Science* 39(1): 1–23.

Hooghe, Liesbet, Gary Marks, and Carole Wilson (2002) 'Does left/right structure party positions on European integration?', *Comparative Political Studies* 35(8): 965–89.

Höpner, Martin (2005) 'Parteien oder Nationen? Die zwei Konfliktlinien der europäischen Finanzmarktintegration', *Zeitschrift für Internationale Beziehungen* 12(2): 251–73.

Höpner, Martin (2010) 'Warum betreibt der EuGH Rechtsfortbildung? Die Politisierungshypothese', *Sozialer Fortschritt* 59(5): 141–51.

Höpner, Martin and Bojan Jurczyk (2012) 'Kritik des Eurobarometers. Über die Verwischung der Grenze zwischen seriöser Demoskopie und interessengeleiteter Propaganda', *Leviathan* 40(3): 326–49.

Höpner, Martin and Armin Schäfer (2012) 'Embeddedness and regional integration. Waiting for Polanyi in a Hayekian setting', *International Organization* 66(3): 429–55.

Hoyland, Bjorn (2006) 'Allocation of codecision reports in the Fifth European Parliament', *European Union Politics* 7(1): 30–50.

Hug, Simon (2003) 'Endogenous preferences and delegation in the European Union', *Comparative Political Studies* 36: 41–74.

Hymans, Jacques E. C. (1999) 'Do too many chefs really spoil the broth? The European Commission, Bureaucratic Politics and European Integration', Harvard University, Government Department, Program for the Study of Germany and Europe Working Paper 9(2).

Imig, Doug and Sidney Tarrow (2001) *Contentious Europeans: Protest and Politics in an Integrating Europe*. Lanham: Rowman & Littlefield Publishers, Inc.

Inspection Générale des Services (1999) Dessiner la Commission de demain—Designing Tomorrow's Commission. Report of team No. 10 on Group 'Internal Market, Financial Services, Taxation and Customs'. Florence: Archive Historique des Communautés Européennes (AHCE).

Jabko, Nicolas (2006) *Playing the Market. A political strategy for uniting Europe, 1985–2005*. Ithaca, NY: Cornell University Press.

Joana, Jean and Andy Smith (2006) 'The politics of collegiality. The non-portfolio dimension'. In: A. Smith (ed.), *Politics and the European Commission. Actors, Interdependence, Legitimacy*. London: Routledge.

Joerges, Christian and Jürgen Neyer (1997a) 'From integrovernmental bargaining to deliberative political processes: The constitutionalisation of comitology', *European Law Journal* 3(3): 273–99.

Joerges, Christian and Jürgen Neyer (1997b) 'Transforming strategic interaction into deliberative problem-solving: European comitology in the foodstuffs sector', *Journal of European Public Policy* 4(4): 609–25.

Joerges, Christian and Ellen Vos (1999) *EU Committees: Social Regulation, Law and Politics*. Oxford: Hart.

Jordan, Andrew and Adriaan Schout (2006) *The Coordination of the European Union: Exploring the Capacities of Networked Governance*. Oxford: Oxford University Press.

Kassim, Hussein (2004) 'The Secretariat General of the European Commission, 1958–2003: A singular institution'. In: A. Smith (ed.), *Politics and the European Commission. Actors, Interdependence, Legitimacy*. London: Routledge.

Kassim, Hussein (2006) 'The Secretariat general of the European Commission'. In: D. Spence and G. Edwards (eds), *The European Commission*. London: John Harper.

Kassim, Hussein (2008) '"Mission impossible", but mission accomplished: the Kinnock reforms and the European Commission', *Journal of European Public Policy* 15(5): 648–68.

Kassim, Hussein (2010) A silent transformation: Leadership and Coordination in the European Commission. Oslo: ARENA—Center for European Studies, University of Oslo.

Kassim, Hussein, John Peterson, Michael W. Bauer, Sara Connolly, Renaud Dehousse, Liesbet Hooghe, and Andrew Thompson (2013) *The European Commission of the Twenty-First Century*. Oxford: Oxford University Press.

Kiewiet, D. Roderick and Mathew D. McCubbins (1991) *The Logic of delegation: Congressional parties and the appropriations process*. Chicago: University of Chicago Press.

King, Nigel (1995) 'The qualitative research interview'. In: C. Cassell and G. Symon (eds), *Qualitative Methods in Organizational Research. A practical guide*. London: Sage.

Kingdon, John W. (1984) *Agendas, Alternatives, and Public Policies*. Boston/Toronto: Little, Brown and Company.

Klüver, Heike (2011) 'The contextual nature of lobbying: Explaining lobbying success in the European Union', *European Union Politics* 12(4): 483–506.

Knill, Christoph (2005) 'Introduction: Cross-national policy convergence: concepts, approaches and explanatory factors', *Journal of European Public Policy* 12(5): 764–74.

Knill, Christoph and Jale Tosun (2010) *Politikgestaltung in der Europäischen Union. Die Entstehung und Umsetzung der Dienstleistungsrichtlinie*. Baden-Baden: Nomos.

Koepke, Jason and Nils Ringe (2006) 'The second-order election model in an enlarged Europe', *European Union Politics* 7(3): 321–46.

Kohler-Koch, Beate (1999) 'The evolution and transformation of European governance'. In: B. Kohler-Koch and R. Eising (eds), *The Transformation of Governance in the European Union*. London: Routledge.

König, Thomas, Brooke Luetgert, and Tanja Dannwolf (2006) 'Forum section: Quantifying European legislative research. Using CELEX and PreLex in EU legislative studies', *European Union Politics* 7(4): 553–74.

Koopmans, Ruud (2007) 'Who inhabits the European public sphere? Winners and losers, supporters and opponents in Europeanised political debates', *European Journal of Political Research* 46(2): 183–210.

Koopmans, Ruud and Jessica Erbe (2004) 'Towards a European public sphere?', *Innovation: The European Journal of Social Sciences* 17(2): 97–118.

Kreppel, Amie (2010) 'Looking "Up", "Down" and "Sideways": Understanding EU Institutions in Context', *West European Politics* 34(1): 167–79.

Kriesi, Hanspeter (2007) 'The role of European integration in national election campaigns', *European Union Politics* 8(1): 83–108.

Kriesi, Hanspeter, Edgar Grande, Romain Lachat, Martin Dolezal, Simon Bornschier, and Timotheos Frey (2008) *West European Politics in the Age of Globalization*. Cambridge: Cambridge University Press.

Kröger, Sandra (2008) 'Nothing but consultation: The place of organised civil society in EU policy-making across policies', *European Governance Papers (EUROGOV)* No. C-08-03.

Kurpas, Sebastian, Caroline Gron, and Piotr Kaczynski (2008) 'The European Commission after Enlargement: Does more add up to less?', Centre for European Policy Studies Brussels: Special Report February 2008.

Leech, Beth L. (2002) 'Asking questions: Techniques for semistructured interviews', *PS: Political Science and Politics* 35(04): 665–8.

Leibfried, Stephan (2010) 'Social policy. Left to the judges and the markets?'. In: H. Wallace, M. Pollack, and A. R. Young (eds), *Policy-Making in the European Union*. Oxford: Oxford University Press.

Leibfried, Stephan and Paul Pierson (1995) 'Semisovereign welfare states: Social policy in a multitiered Europe'. In: S. Leibfried and P. Pierson (eds), *European Social Policy: Between Fragmentation and Integration*. Washington, DC: The Brookings Institution.

Lequesne, Christian (2000) 'The European Commission: A balancing act between autonomy and dependence'. In: K. Neunreither and A. Wiener (eds) *European Integration after Amsterdam: Institutional Dynamics and Prospects for Democracy*. Oxford: Oxford University Press.

Levy, Roger (2006) 'European Commission Overload and the pathology of management reform: Garbage cans, rationality and risk aversion', *Public Administration* 84(2): 423–39.

Lindberg, Leon and Stuart Scheingold (1970) *Europe's Would-be Polity*. Englewood Cliffs, NJ: Prentice-Hall.

Littig, Barbara (2008) 'Interviews mit Eliten—Interviews mit ExpertInnen: Gibt es Unterschiede?', *Forum: Qualitative Research (FQS)* 9(3).

Lorenzen, Hannes and Antje Kölling (2008) 'Demystifying Slowness', *die tageszeitung*.

Lubbers, Marcel (2008) 'Regarding the Dutch "Nee" to the European Constitution: A test of the identity, utilitarian and political approaches to voting "No"', *European Union Politics* 9(1): 59–86.

Ludlow, Peter (1991) 'The European Commission'. In: R. O. Keohane and S. Hoffmann (eds), *The New European Community. Decisionmaking and Institutional Change*. Boulder, CO: Westview.

McDonald, Maryon (2000) 'Identities in the European Commission'. In: N. Nugent (ed.), *At the Heart of the Union—Studies of the European Commission*. Houndmills: Palgrave Macmillan.

McElroy, Gail (2006) 'Committee representation in the European Parliament', *European Union Politics* 7(1): 5–29.

MacMaoláin, Caoimhín (2007) *EU Food Law: Protecting Consumers and Health in a Common Market*. Oxford: Hart Publishing.

Mahoney, Christine (2004) 'The power of institutions: State and interest group activity in the European Union', *European Union Politics* 5(4): 441–66.

Mahoney, Christine (2007) 'Lobbying success in the United States and the European Union', *Journal of Public Policy* 27(01): 35–56.

Mahoney, Christine (2008) *Brussels vs. the Beltway: Advocacy in the United States and the European Union*. Washington, DC: Georgetown University Press.

Mair, Peter (2005) 'Popular democracy and the European Union polity', *European Governance Papers* No. C-05-03.

Majone, Giandomenico (1996) *Regulating Europe*. London: Routledge.

Majone, Giandomenico (2002) 'The European Commission: The limits of centralization and the perils of parliamentarization', *Governance* 15(3): 375–92.

Majone, Giandomenico (2005) *Dilemmas of European Integration: The Ambiguities and Pitfalls of Integration by Stealth*. Oxford: Oxford University Press.

Manow, Philip, Armin Schäfer, and Hendrik Zorn (2007) 'Europe's party-political center of gravity, 1957–2003', *Journal of European Public Policy* 15(1): 20–39.

March, James G. and Johan P. Olsen (1989) *Rediscovering Institutions: The Organizational Basis of Politics*. New York: The Free Press, Macmillan.

March, James G. and Johan P. Olsen (1995) *Democratic Governance*. New York: Free Press.

March, James and Johan Olsen (1996) 'Institutional perspectives on political institutions', *Governance* 9(3): 247–64.

March, James G. and Johan P. Olsen (1998) 'The institutional dynamics of international political orders', *International Organization* 52(4): 943–69.

March, James G. and Herbert A. Simon (1993) *Organizations*. Cambridge: Blackwell.

Martin, S. and K. Hartley (1997) 'Public procurement and the European Union: Issues and policies', *Public Procurement Law Review* 6(2): 92–113.

Martinsen, Dorte Sindbjerg (2009) 'Conflict and conflict management in the cross-border provision of healthcare services', *West European Politics* 32(4): 792–809.

Mason, John and George Parker (2005) 'Brussels warns on junk food: Industry given year to stop targeting children', *The Financial Times*, January 20, 2005: 1.

Mattila, Mikko and Jan-Erik Lane (2001) 'Why unanimity in the Council?: A roll call analysis of Council voting', *European Union Politics* 2(1): 31–52.

Mattli, Walter and Ngaire Woods (2009) 'In whose benefit? Explaining regulatory change in global politics'. In: W. Mattli and N. Woods (eds), *The Politics of Global Regulation.* Princeton, NJ: Princeton University Press.

Mayntz, Renate and Fritz Scharpf (1975) *Policy-Making in the German Federal Bureaucracy.* Amsterdam: Elsevier.

Mayntz, Renate and Fritz W. Scharpf (1995) 'Der Ansatz des akteurzentrierten Institutionalismus'. In: R. Mayntz and F. W. Scharpf (eds), *Gesellschaftliche Selbstregelung und politische Steuerung.* Frankfurt/New York: Campus.

Mazey, Sonia (1995) 'The development of EU equality policies: Bureaucratic expansion on behalf of women?', *Public Administration* 73(4): 591–609.

Mazey, Sonia and Jeremy Richardson (eds) (1993) *Lobbying in the European Community.* Oxford: Oxford University Press.

Menz, Georg (2010) 'Are you being served? Europeanizing and re-regulating the single market in services', *Journal of European Public Policy* 17(7): 971–87.

Metz, Julia (Forthcoming.) *The European Commission, Expert Groups and the Policy Process: Demystifying Technocratic Governance.* Houndmills: Palgrave Macmillan.

Michelmann, Hans J. (1978a) 'Multinational staffing und organizational functioning in the Commission of the European Communities', *International Organization* 32(2): 477–96.

Michelmann, Hans J. (1978b) *Organisational Effectiveness in a Multinational Bureaucracy.* Farnborough: Saxon House.

Micklitz, Hans W. and Stephen Weatherill (1993) 'Consumer policy in the European Community: Before and after Maastricht', *Journal of Consumer Policy* 16(3): 285–321.

Micklitz, Hans, Norbert Reich, and Stephen Weatherill (2004) 'EU Treaty revision and consumer protection', *Journal of Consumer Policy* 27(4): 367–99.

Middlemas, Keith (1995) *Orchestrating Europe: The Informal Politics of the European Union, 1943–95.* London: Fontana Press.

Minder, Raphael (2003) 'Gender banned from use in setting premiums', *Financial Times,* November 6, 2003.

Mitrany, David (1941/1975) 'A War-time submission—terretorial, ideological, or functional international organisation?'. In: D. Mitrany (ed.), *The Functional Theory of Politics.* New York: St. Martin's Press.

Mitrany, David (1971) 'The functional approach in historical perspective', *International Affairs* 47(3): 532–43.

Moodie, John and Cathrine Holst (2013) 'For the sake of democracy? The European Commission's justifications for democratizing expertise'. In *EPISTO kick-off conference.* Oslo, April 4–5, 2013.

Moravcsik, Andrew (1991) 'Negotiating the Single European Act: National interests and conventional statecraft in the European Community', *International Organization* 45(1): 9–56.

Moravcsik, Andrew (1993) 'Preferences and power in the European Community: A liberal intergovernmentalist approach', *Journal of Common Market Studies* 31(4): 473–524.

Moravcsik, Andrew (1998) *The Choice for Europe: Social Purpose and State Power from Messina to Maastricht.* Ithaca, NY: Cornell University Press.

Moravcsik, Andrew (2002) 'In defence of the "Democratic Deficit": Reassessing legitimacy in the European Union', *Journal of Common Market Studies* 40(4): 603–24.

Morgenthau, Hans J. (1963) *Macht und Frieden.* Gütersloh: Bertelsmann.

Mörth, Ulrika and Malena Britz (2004) 'European integration as organizing: The case of armaments', *Journal of Common Market Studies* 42(5): 957–73.

Mügge, Daniel (2010) *Widen the Market, Narrow the Competition. Banker interests and the making of a European capital market.* Colchester: ECPR Press.

Müller-Rommel, Ferdinand and Jean Blondel (1993) *Governing Together. The extent and limits of joint decision-making in Western European national cabinets.* London: Macmillan.

Naurin, Daniel and Helen Wallace (eds) (2008) *Unveiling the Council of the European Union. Games Governments Play in Brussels.* Edited by M. Egan, N. Nugent, and W. Peterson. Houndmills: Palgrave Macmillan.

Nicolaidis, Kalypso and Susanne K. Schmidt (2007) 'Mutual recognition "on trial": The long road to services liberalization', *Journal of European Public Policy* 14(5): 717–34.

Niskanen, William A. (1974) *Bureaucracy and Representative Government.* Chicago: Aldine.

Noël, Emile (1979) Note à l'attention de Monsieur Stuart. Florence: Archive Historique des Communautés Européennes (AHCE).

Noël, Emile (1991) Interview 30—Round table 'Origins of the EC administration'. In *European Union Institute. European Oral History.* Florence: Historical Archives of the European Union.

Nugent, Neill (ed.) (2000a) *At the Heart of the Union. Studies of the European Commission.* Second edition. Houndmills: Macmillan.

Nugent, Neill (2000b) 'Introduction: At the Heart of the Union'. In: N. Nugent (ed.), *At the Heart of the Union—Studies of the European Commission.* Houndmills: Palgrave Macmillan.

Nugent, Neill and Sabine Saurugger (2002) 'Organizational structuring: The case of the European Commission and its external policy responsibilities', *Journal of European Public Policy* 9: 345–64.

Olsen, Johan P. (2006) 'Maybe it is time to rediscover bureaucracy', *Journal of Public Administration Research and Theory* 16(1): 1–24.

Olsen, Johan P. (2010) *Governing through Institution Building: Institutional Theory and Recent European Experiments in Democratic Organization.* Oxford: Oxford University Press.

Oppermann, Kai and Henrike Viehrig (eds) (2011) *Issue Salience in International Politics.* London: Routledge.

Page, Edward C. (1985) *Political Authority and Bureaucratic Power: A Comparative Analysis.* Brighton: Wheatsheaf Books.

Page, Edward C. (1987) 'Comparing bureaucracies'. In: J.-E. Lane (ed.), *Bureaucracy and Public Choice.* London: Sage.

Page, Edward C. and Linda Wouters (1994) 'Bureaucratic politics and political leadership in Brussels', *Public Administration* 72(3): 445–59.

Panke, Diana (2012) 'Lobbying institutional key players: How states seek to influence the European Commission, the Council Presidency and the European Parliament', *Journal of Common Market Studies* 50(1): 129–50.

Parker, George (2003) 'EU targets sex bias in media and insurance: Ambitious move to enshrine "respect for human dignity" could force up premiums', *Financial Times*, June 24, 2003.

Pearson plc (1998) *Annual Report 1998.* London: Pearson plc.

Pelkmans, Jacques (1987) 'The new approach to technical harmonization and standardization', *JCMS: Journal of Common Market Studies* 25(3): 249–69.

Peters, B. Guy (1992) 'Bureaucratic politics and the institutions of the European Community'. In: A. M. Sbragia (ed.), *Europolitics: Institutions and Policy-Making in the "New" European Community.* Washington, DC: Brookings.

Peters, B. Guy (1994) 'Agenda-setting in the European community', *Journal of European Public Policy* 1(1): 9–26.

Peters, B. Guy and Jon Pierre (2004) *The Politicization of the Civil Service in Comparative Perspective: A Quest for Control.* Routledge.

Peterson, J. (1995) 'Playing the transparency game: Consultation and policy-making in the European Commission', *Public Administration* 73(3): 473–92.

Peterson, John (2008) 'Enlargement, reform and the European Commission. Weathering a perfect storm?', *Journal of European Public Policy* 15(5): 761–80.

Pfeffer, Jeffrey and Gerald R. Salancik ([1978] 2003) *The External Control of Organizations: A resource dependence perspective*. Stanford, CA: Stanford University Press.

Pierson, Paul (1996) 'The path to European integration—a histrorical institutionalist analysis', *Comparative Political Studies* 29(2): 123–63.

Pierson, Paul (2000) 'Increasing returns, path dependence, and the study of politics', *The American Political Science Review* 94(2): 251–67.

Pilniok, Arne (2011) *Governance im europäischen Forschungsförderverbund: Eine rechtswissenschaftliche Analyse der Forschungsförderung und Forschungspolitik im Mehrebenensystem*. Tübingen: Mohr Siebeck.

Pollack, Mark A. (1994) 'Creeping competence: The expanding agenda of the European Community', *Journal of Public Policy* 14(2): 95–145.

Pollack, Mark A. (1997a) 'The Commission as an agent'. In: N. Nugent (ed.), *Studies of the European Commission*. Houndmills: Macmillan.

Pollack, Mark A. (1997b) 'Delegation, agency and agenda setting in the European Community', *International Organization* 51(1): 99–134.

Pollack, Mark A. (1997c) 'Representing diffuse interests in EC policy-making', *Journal of European Public Policy* 4: 572–90.

Ponzano, Paolo, Daniela Corona, and Costanza Hermanin (2012) 'The Power of Initiative of the European Commission: A Progressive Erosion?', *Notre Europe*, Studies & Research No. 89.

Princen, Sebastiaan (2009) *Agenda-Setting in the European Union*. Houndmills: Palgrave.

Princen, Sebastiaan (2012) 'The DEU approach to EU decision-making: A critical assessment', *Journal of European Public Policy* 19(4): 623–34.

Putnam, Robert D. (1988) 'Diplomacy and domestic politics: The logic of two-level games', *International Organization* 42(2): 427–60.

Quaglia, Lucia (2010a) 'Completing the single market in financial services: the politics of competing advocacy coalitions', *Journal of European Public Policy* 17(7): 1007–23.

Quaglia, Lucia (2010b) *Governing Financial Services in the European Union: Banking, Securities and Post-trading*. Abingdon: Routledge.

Radaelli, Claudio M. (1995) 'The role of knowledge in the policy process', *Journal of European Public Policy* 2(2): 159–83.

Radaelli, Claudio M. (1999a) *Technocracy in the European Union: Political Dynamics of the European Union*. London: Longman.

Radaelli, Claudio M. (1999b) 'The public policy of the European Union: Whither politics of expertise?', *Journal of European Public Policy* 6: 757–74.

Radaelli, Claudio M. and Anne C. M. Meuwese (2010) 'Hard questions, hard solutions: Proceduralisation through Impact Assessment in the EU', *West European Politics* 33(1): 136–53.

Rauh, Christian (2012) *Politicisation, issue salience, and consumer policies of the European Commission: Does public awareness and contestation of supranational matters increase the responsiveness of Europe's central agenda-setter?* PhD Thesis, Department of Political and Social Sciences, Freie Universität, Berlin.

Rhodes, Martin (1995) 'A Regulatory conundrum: industrial relations and the social dimension'. In: S. Leibfried and P. Pierson (eds), *European Social Policy. Between Fragmentation and Integration*. Washington, DC: The Brookings Institution.

Ringe, Nils (2005) 'Policy preference formation in legislative politics: Structures, actors, and focal points', *American Journal of Political Science* 49(4): 731–45.

Rischkowsky, Franziska (2007) *Europäische Verbraucherpolitik: Theoretische Grundlagen und neue Probleme am Beispiel des Internet*. Marburg: Metropolis.

Risse, Thomas (2003) '"Let's Argue!": Communicative action in world politics', *International Organization* 54(1): 1–39.

Rittberger, Berthold (2003) 'The creation and empowerment of the European Parliament', *JCMS: Journal of Common Market Studies* 41(2): 203–25.

Robert, Cécile (2012) 'Expert groups in the building of European public policy', *Globalisation, Societies and Education* 10(4): 425–38.

Rometsch, Dietrich (1999) *Die Rolle und Funktionsweise der Europäischen Kommission in der Ära Delors*. Frankfurt/M.: Peter Lang.

Rose, Richard (1991) 'What is lesson drawing?', *Journal of Public Policy* 11(1): 3–30.

Ross, George (1994) 'Inside the Delors Cabinet', *Journal of Common Market Studies* 32(4): 499–523.

Ross, George (1995) *Jacques Delors and European Integration*. Cambridge: Polity Press.

Rossi, Federica (2005) 'Innovation policy in the European Union: instruments and objectives', *MPRA Paper* (No. 2009, posted November 7, 2007).

Sabatier, Paul A. (1978) 'The acquisition and utilization of technical information by administrative agencies', *Administrative Science Quarterly* 23(3): 396–417.

Sabatier, Paul A. (1998) 'The advocacy coalition framework: Revisions and relevance for Europe', *Journal of European Public Policy* 5(1): 98–130.

Sandholtz, Wayne and John Zysman (1989) '1992: Recasting the European Bargain', *World Politics* 42(1): 95–128.

Schäfer, Jérôme (2012) European Commission Officials' Policy Attitudes. Paper presented at the *19th International Conference of Europeanists* Boston, MA.

Scharpf, Fritz W. (1988) 'The joint-decision trap: Lessons From German Federalism and European integration', *Public Administration* 66(3): 239–78.

Scharpf, Fritz W. (1997) *Games Real Actors Play: Actor-centered Institutionalism in Policy Research (Theoretical Lenses on Public Policy)*. Boulder, CO: Westview Press.

Scharpf, Fritz W. (1999) *Governing in Europe: Effective and democratic?* Oxford: Oxford University Press.

Scharpf, Fritz W. (2006) 'The joint-decision trap revisited', *Journal of Common Market Studies* 44(4): 845–64.

Scharpf, Fritz W. (2010) 'The asymmetry of European integration, or why the EU cannot be a "social market economy"', *Socio-Economic Review* 8(2): 211–50.

Schmedes, Hans-Jörg (2007) *Wirtschafts- und Verbraucherschutzverbände im Mehrebenensystem: Lobbyingaktivitäten britischer, deutscher und europäischer Verbände*. Wiesbaden: VS Verlag.

Schmidt, Susanne K. (1998) *Liberalisierung in Europa: die Rolle der Europäischen Kommission*. Frankfurt/New York: Campus.

Schmidt, Susanne K. (2000) 'Only an agenda setter? The European Commission's power over the Council of Ministers', *European Union Politics* 1(1): 37–61.

Schmidt, Susanne K. (2009) 'When efficiency results in redistribution: The conflict over the Single Services Market', *West European Politics* 32(4): 847–65.

Schmidt, Susanne K. (2012) 'Who cares about nationality? The path-dependent case law of the ECJ from goods to citizens', *Journal of European Public Policy* 19(1): 8–24.

Schmitter, Philippe (1969) 'Three neo-functional hypotheses about international integration', *International Organization* 23(1): 161–6.

Schnapp, Kai-Uwe (2004) *Ministerialbürokratien in westlichen Demokratien—Eine vergleichende Analyse*. Opladen: Leske + Budrich.

Schön-Quinlivan, Emmanuelle (2006) Administrative reform in the European Commission: From rhetoric to re-legitimisation. In *EU-CONSENT Workshop 'The Commission and the European Civil Service'*. Paris: Sciences Po.

Schout, Adriaan and Andrew Jordan (2008) 'The European Union's governance ambitions and its administrative capacities', *Journal of European Public Policy* 15(7): 957–74.

Schulze, Reiner and Hans Schulte-Nölke (2003) *Analysis of National Fairness Laws Aimed at Protecting Consumers in Relation to Commercial Practices*, report commissioned by the Directorate-General Health and Consumer Protection of the European Commission, June 2003 [cited August 29, 2011]. Available from <http://ec.europa.eu/consumers/cons_int/safe_shop/fair_bus_pract/green_pap_comm/studies/unfair_practices_en.pdf>.

Seawright, Jason and John Gerring (2008) 'Case Selection Techniques In Case Study Research: A Menu Of Qualitative And Quantitative Options', *Political Research Quarterly* 61(2): 294–308.

Secrétariat Général (2003) Minutes of the 1633rd meeting of the Commission held in Brussels (Breydel) on Wednesday 5 November 2003 (morning), PV(2003)1633 final, edited by European Commission. Brussels.

Shepsle, Kenneth and Mark S. Bonchek (1997) *Analyzing Politics*. New York: W.W.Norton.

Siefken, Sven T. (2007) *Expertenkommissionen im politischen Prozess: eine Bilanz zur rot-grünen Bundesregierung 1998–2005*. Wiesbaden: VS Verlag für Sozialwissenschaften.

Sifft, Stefanie, Michael Brüggeman, Katharina Kleinen-von Königslow, Bernhard Peters, and Andreas Wimmel (2007) 'Segmented Europeanization: Exploring the legitimacy of the European Union from a public discourse perspective', *JCMS: Journal of Common Market Studies* 45(1): 127–55.

Simon, Herbert Alexander (1970) *Administrative Behaviour*. Second edition. New York: Macmillan.

Siotis, Jean (1964) 'Some problems of European secretariats', *Journal of Common Market Studies* 2(3): 222–50.

Smith, Mike (1999) 'Brussels seeks tougher rules on discrimination', *Financial Times*, November 3, 1999.

Smyrl, Marc E. (1998) 'When (and how) do the Commission's preferences matter?', *Journal of Common Market Studies* 36(1): 79–99.

Solanke, Iyiola (2011) '"Stop the ECJ"?: An empirical analysis of activism at the Court', *European Law Journal* 17(6): 764–84.

Somek, Alexander (2011) 'The social question in a transnational context', LEQS Paper No. 39, June 2011, London School of Economics.

Soroka, Stuart (2003) 'Media, public opinion, and foreign policy', *The International Journal of Press/Politics* 8(1): 27–48.

Spence, David (2006a) 'The Directorates General and the services. Structures, functions and procedures'. In: D. Spence and G. Edwards (eds), *The European Commission*, 25–74. London: John Harper.

Spence, David (2006b) 'The President, the College and the cabinets'. In: D. Spence and G. Edwards (eds), *The European Commission*, 128–55. London: John Harper.

Spence, David and Anne Stevens (2006) 'Staff and personnel policy in the Commission'. In: D. Spence and G. Edwards (eds), *The European Commission*. London: John Harper.

Spierenburg, Dirk (1979) Proposals for reform of the Commission of the European Communities and its services. Report made at the request of the Commission by an Independent Review Body under the chairmanship of Mr. Dirk Spierenburg. Brussels: European Communities.

Stokes, Donald (1963) 'Spatial models of party competition', *The American Political Science Review* 57(2): 368–77.

Stone Sweet, Alec and Wayne Sandholtz (1997) 'European integration and supranational governance', *Journal of European Public Policy* 4(3): 297–317.

Streeck, Wolfgang and Philippe C. Schmitter (1991) 'From national corporatism to transnational pluralism: Organized interests in the Single European Market', *Politics and Society* 19(2): 133–64.

Strøm, Kaare, Wolfgang C. Müller, and Torbjörn Bergman (eds) (2003) *Delegation and Accountability in Parliamentary Democracies*. Oxford: Oxford University Press.

Suvarierol, Semin (2007) *Beyond the Myth of Nationality: A study on the networks of European Commission Officials*. Delft, NL: Eburon Academic Publishers.

Taggart, Paul and Aleks Szczerbiak (2002) 'The party politics of Euroscepticism in EU member and candidate states', *SEI Working Paper* 51.

Tallberg, Jonas (2008) 'Bargaining power in the European Council', *Journal of Common Market Studies* 46(3): 685–708.

Tallberg, Jonas (2002) 'Delegation to supranational institutions: Why, how, and with what consequences?', *West European Politics* 25(1): 23–46.

Tallberg, Jonas and Karl Johansson (2008) 'Party politics in the European Council', *Journal of European Public Policy* 15(8): 1222–42.

Tansey, Oisín (2007) 'Process tracing and elite interviewing: A case for non-probability sampling', *Political Science & Politics* 40(04): 765–72.

Tholoniat, Luc (2009) 'The temporal constitution of the European Commission: A timely investigation', *Journal of European Public Policy* 16(2): 221–38.

Thomson, Robert (2008) 'National actors in international organizations: The case of the European Commission', *Comparative Political Studies* 41(2): 169–92.

Thomson, Robert (2011) *Resolving Controversy in the European Union. Legislative decision-making before and after enlargement*. Cambridge: Cambridge University Press.

Thomson, Robert, Frans Stokman, Christopher Achen, and Thomas König (eds) (2006) *The European Union Decides. The empirical relevance of policy making models*. Cambridge: Cambridge University Press.

Tömmel, Ingeborg (1998) 'Transformation of governance: The European Commission's strategy for creating a "Europe of the Regions"', *Regional and Federal Studies* 8(2): 52–80.

Toshkov, Dimiter (2011) 'Public opinion and policy output in the European Union: A lost relationship', *European Union Politics* 12(2): 169–91.

Toshkov, Dimiter and Anne Rasmussen (2012) 'Time to decide: The effect of early agreements on legislative duration in the EU', *European Integration Online Papers* 16(11), Article 11.

Trenz, Hans-Jörg (2005) 'The European public sphere: Contradictory findings in a diverse research field', *European Political Science* 4.

Trondal, Jarle (2010) *An Emergent European Executive Order*. Oxford: Oxford University Press.

Tsakatika, Myrto (2005) 'Claims to legitimacy: The European Commission between continuity and change', *JCMS: Journal of Common Market Studies* 43(1): 193–220.

Tsebelis, George and Geoffrey Garrett (2001) 'The institutional foundations of intergovernmentalism and supranationalism in the European Union', *International Organization* 55(02): 357–90.

Tsebelis, George and Geoffrey Garrett (2000) 'Legislative politics in the European Union', *European Union Politics* 1(1): 9–36.

Tyson, Adam (2001) 'The negotiation of the European Community Directive on racial discrimination', *European Journal of Migration and Law* 3: 199–229.

Uba, Katrin and Fredrik Uggla (2011) 'Protest actions against the European Union, 1992–2007', *West European Politics* 34(2): 384–93.

UEAPME (2000) Position paper on the Draft Directive replacing Council Directive 92/59/| EEC of 29 June 1992 on General Product Safety, edited by Union Européenne de l'Artisanat et des Petites et Moyennes Entreprises. Brussels.

UEAPME (2006) UEAPME Position on European Globalisation Adjustment Fund. April 4, 2006.

UEAPME (2008) Updated UEAPME position on the Proposal for a 'Regulation of the European Parliament and of the Council on the provision of food information to consumers' COM(2008) 40 final, edited by Union Européenne de l'Artisanat et des Petites et Moyennes Entreprises (Working group on foodstuffs). Brussels.

UITP (2005) European Commission staff working paper on 'Passenger Rights in International Coach and Bus Services'—Position of the UITP European Union Committee, edited by Union Internationale de Transportes Public. Brussels.

UITP (2006) European Commission Staff Working Paper on 'Strengthening the protection of the rights of passengers travelling by sea or inland waterway in the European Union'—UITP Draft Response, edited by Union Internationale de Transportes Public. Brussels.

UK Healthcare Commission (2007) The European Commission's Public Consultation on Cross-border Healthcare: response by the Healthcare Commission.

UNICE (2003) Position paper—Proposal for a directive concerning unfair business-to-consumer commercial practices in the Internal Market (COM (2003) 356 final), edited by Union of Industrial and Employers' Confederations of Europe. Brussels.

UNICE (2004) UNICE Position Paper 'Commission's proposal for a recast directive on the implementation of the principle of equal opportunities and equal treatment of men and women in matters of employment and occupation'. October 26, 2004.

Vaqué, Luis González and Sebastián Melchor Romero (2008) 'Wine labelling: Future perspectives', *European Food and Feed Law Review* 2008 (1).

Vauchez, Antoine (2012) 'Keeping the dream alive: the European Court of Justice and the transnational fabric of integrationist jurisprudence', *European Political Science Review* 4(1): 51–71.

Vos, Ellen (1999a) 'EU Committees: the evolution of unforeseen institutional actors in European product regulation'. In: C. Joerges and E. Vos (eds), *EU Committees: Social Regulation, Law and Politics*. Oxford/Portland: Hart Publishing.

Vos, Ellen (1999b) *Institutional Frameworks of Community Health and Safety Regulations: Health and Safety Regulation Committees, Agencies and Private Bodies*. Oxford: Hart Publishing.

Vos, Ellen (2000) 'EU Food Safety Regulation in the aftermath of the BSE Crisis', *Journal of Consumer Policy* 23(3): 227–55.

Weatherill, Stephen (2005) *EU Consumer Law and Policy*. Cheltenham: Edward Elgar.

Weber, Max (1925/1978) *Economy and Society. An Outline of Interpretative Sociology*. 2 vols. Vol. 1. Berkeley: University of California.

Weiss, Carol H. (1979) 'The many meanings of research utilization', *Public Administration Review* 39(5): 426–31.

Wellenstein, Edmund (1991) Interview 33—Round table 'Origins of the EC administration'. In *Euroepan Union History. European Oral History*. Florence: Historical Archives of the European Union.

Wille, Anchrit (2013) *The Normalization of the European Commission: Politics and Bureaucracy in the EU Executive*. Oxford: Oxford University Press.

Willis, Andrew (2009) 'Commission finance experts same bankers that caused crisis, says report.' *EUobserver*, November 5, 09.

Wilson, James Q. (1980) 'The politics of regulation'. In: J. Q. Wilson (ed.), *The Politics of Regulation*. New York: Basic Books, Inc.

Windholz, Eric and Graeme A. Hodge (2013) 'Conceptualising social and economic regulation: Implications for modern regulators and regulatory activity', *Jerusalem Papers in Regulation & Governance*. Working Paper No. 49 (Feburary 2013).

Wonka, Arndt (2007) 'Technocratic and independent? The appointment of European Commissioners and its policy implications', *Journal of European Public Policy* 14(2): 169–89.

Wonka, Arndt (2008) *Die Europäische Kommission. Supranationale Bürokratie oder Agent der Mitgliedstaaten?* Baden-Baden: Nomos.

Young, Alasdair R. (1997a) 'Consumption without representation? Consumers in the Single Market'. In: H. Wallace and A. R. Young (eds), *Participation and Policy-Making in the European Union.* Oxford: Clarendon Press.

Young, Alasdair R. (1997b) 'European consumer groups. Multiple levels of governance and multiple logics of collective action'. In: J. Greenwood and M. Aspinwall (eds), *Collective Action in the European Union: Interests and the New Politics of Associability.* London: Routledge.

Young, Alisdair R. (2010) 'The Single Market. Deregulation, reregulation, and integration'. In: H. Wallace, M. Pollack, and A. R. Young (eds), *Policy-Making in the European Union.* Oxford: Oxford University Press.

Zegart, Amy B. (2004) 'Blue ribbons, black boxes: Toward a better understanding of Presidential Commissions', *Presidential Studies Quarterly* 34(2): 366–93.

Zürn, Michael (2006) 'Zur Politisierung der Europäischen Union', *Politische Vierteljahresschrift* 47(2): 242–51.

Index